The Sublett (Soblet) Family
of Manakintown, King William Parish, Virginia

by Cameron H. Allen, JD, FASG
edited by James N. Jackson
with additional notes by Donald J. Sublette
Originally published in 1982, 1985, and 1994 by
The Detroit Society for Genealogical Research, Inc.
c/o Burton Historical Collection
Detroit Public Library
5201 Woodward Avenue
Detroit, MI 48202
(www.DSGR.org)
Based on a series of articles that appeared in 1963 in the
Magazine of the Detroit Society for Genealogical Research
Volume 27: pages 3-10, 49-54, 97-103,141-148;
Volume 28: pages 3-8, 49-57, 103-110, 151-159;
Volume 29: pages 14-22, 61-70, 105-114, 151-161;
Volume 38: pages 1-2;   Volume 41: pages 1-3.

Huguenot Migrations

by Cameron Harrison Allen, FASG
edited by Kenn Stryker-Rodda, FASG.
Originally published in
Genealogical Research, Volume 2 (1971)
Part 2, Chapter II, pages 256-290
The American Society of Genealogists
(www.FASG.org)
Reprinted with permission.

The Soblets of the European Refuge

and

Ancestral Table of Susanne Brian, Wife of Abraham Soblet

by Cameron H. Allen, FASG
edited by David L. Greene, FASG
Originally published in *The American Genealogist*
Volume 75, No. 2 (April 2000): pages 99-108;
Volume 78, No. 4 (October 2003): pages 245-252.
The American Genealogist
P.O. Box 398
Demorest, GA 30535-0398
(www.AmericanGenealogist.com)
$40.00 a year (four issues)
Reprinted with permission.

The Sublett (Soblet) Family of Manakintown, King William Parish, Virginia
Original articles © 1963-1994 by The Detroit Society for Genealogical Research, Inc.
Reprinted with permission.

Huguenot Migrations
From *Genealogical Research, Volume 2*
© 1971 by The American Society of Genealogists
Reprinted with permission.

The Soblets of the European Refuge
Original article © 2000 by David L. Greene, *The American Genealogist*
Reprinted with permission.

Ancestral Table of Susanne Brian, Wife of Abraham Soblet
Original article © 2003 by David L. Greene, *The American Genealogist*
Reprinted with permission.

This 50th Anniversary edition
compiled and edited by Phillip L. Sublett
Copyright © 2013 by
Sublett Family Association
P.O. Box 160603
Sacramento, CA 95816-0603
(www.Sublett.org)

ISBN: 978-1495489518

Printed in the United States of America

TABLE OF CONTENTS

PREFACE

The Soblet/Sublett family became of interest to me only obliquely, as so frequently happens in genealogy. I was working on the Allen family when I encountered Susanna Allen's marriage into the Sublett family, and I became interested in learning of the man she had married, his origin and their immediate progeny. By the time I had accomplished this objective, I had gathered so much material that I thought it would be a shame to throw it away. Thus, I extended the research in the standard way, plowing through deeds, wills and estates, court records, census returns, anything I could locate that gave flesh to the early generations of an entire family. Finally, as you may perceive, I am not in any degree a Soblet descendant, much as I would wish to be!

But having ventured into a Virginia Huguenot Manakin Town family, I became very intrigued by the history of King William Parish (Manakin Town) and its fascinating group of families. My curiosity extended into how this group of families came together for their trans-Atlantic migration. Was it mostly fortuitous, or was it by design? From what European places of refuge had they come? Was there a possibility of establishing a precise place of origin for each immigrant in France? As I got into the study of other Manakin Town families, I came to realize how slip-shod had been much of the published, fragmentary work on other Manakin Town families, melding together *some* valid material of record with the most improbable borrowings from people of similar name, to whom no geographical nor genealogical link could be established, and treating all these matters as entitled to equal credibility. I have, since venturing into Manakin genealogy on the Soblets/Subletts, written studies of the following families:

Chastain	(in *The American Genealogist*)
Chaudoin	(in *The Virginia Genealogist*)
Depp	(in *The Genealogist*)
Gevaudan	(in *The Virginia Magazine of History and Biography*)
Jouany	(in *The Virginia Genealogist*)
LaForce	(in *The Genealogist*)
LeFevre	(in *The Virginia Magazine of History and Biography*)
LeSueur	(in *The American Genealogist* and in *The Virginia Genealogist*)
LeVillain	(in *The American Genealogist*)
Perrault/Perrow	(in *The Virginia Genealogist*)
Sasin/Sasseen	(in *The Virginia Genealogist*)

The Chastain family, as a direct result of my articles, organized a family association, which has issued a multi-volume family history with my articles as the initiating focus, but expanding information down to the present. I believe that the LaSueur family is thinking along similar lines. Now the Sublett Family Association is undertaking the republication of my articles in this single volume. I trust that this will lead to the successful compilation and publication of genealogical material, bringing the entire family into the Twenty-first Century. My kindest wishes in the accomplishment of this worthwhile objective.

In closing, let me emphasize what intellectual pleasure the study of these Manakin Town families has brought to my life, from none of whom I descend. Thank you, Subletts all, for the serendipity that Susanna Allen's marriage led me into the study of Manakin Town families.

Cameron Allen

Cameron Allen
May 2006

INTRODUCTION (1994)

It has been over 30 years since Cameron Allen prepared the authoritative Sublett Genealogy and Family History; the first article of a series of 12 appearing in the Magazine of the Detroit Society for Genealogical Research, Inc., in 1963, Volume 27 No. 1. Dr. Allen had worked for some ten years on the Soblet-Sublett study as a parallel to that of his own family -- the Allens, one of the Allens having intermarried with a Sublett.

Before we proceed further, it should be noted that all the Subletts in the U.S. and Canada are probably descended from Abraham Soblet and Susanne Brian, the original French Huguenot immigrants. The original spelling clearly shown in the records of the French Reformed Church is Soblet. A possible variant may be Soublet but Sobler and Sobley are transcription errors. In Virginia by 1750, the Anglicization Sublett had been generally adopted. Other variants found in the records are: Sublet, Soublet, Soublett, Subblet. The spelling Sublette was probably first used by the St. Louis Wm. Lewis Sublette and his brothers. This latter spelling has been widely adopted but is no indication of descent or relationship.

It was hoped at the time of the original publication of Allen's Sublett articles, by the many Sublett descendants who had cooperated with Dr. Allen in collecting the genealogical and other data, that the publication of this series of articles would lead to the publication in book form a still more comprehensive genealogy of the Sublett Family. To date this hope is still far from realization.

The late Nancy Louise Sublette did publish a book in 1974: "Generations Remembered -- Sublette Family 1700-1850." But, this is largely a re-hash of the Allen articles. The late Hester Geraldine Lester Searl in her "Hester Genealogy" (1972) also "lifted," without credit to Dr. Allen, her data on the Subletts.

One extension of the Allen work and inspired by it was the publication in 1981 of "James Sublett & Sally Ford: Genealogy and Family History." Indebtedness to Cameron Allen is fully acknowledged. In addition to amplifying and correcting the data on James and his siblings and bringing down to 1981 the enumeration and data on James' descendants, the early history of the Soblets in France and England with the original research by the author, Donald Jackson Sublette, in these counties and their records is extended.

A series of articles by Dr. Doyce B. Nunis Jr., a history professor at the University of Southern California and one time professor at the University of California at Los Angeles, concerned the exploits of William Lewis Sublette, "Mountain Man," and his brothers. Dr. John E. Sunder, professor at the University of Texas, has written the definitive biography of Wm. L. Sublette (1959). In their historical aspects both Nunis and Sunder provide some interesting incidents — but their genealogy is far from being either adequate or accurate.

The demand for the original Cameron Allen articles has continued to the present time. The appropriate issues of the DSGR Magazine are no longer available and the Nancy Louise Sublette book is "out of print." The officers of the Detroit Society for Genealogical Research, Inc., have from time to time attempted to supply urgent requests for the Allen articles by personally photocopying the appropriate sections from file copies of the Magazine. This has been expensive and a far from satisfactory procedure to meet the demands.

This "reprint" or "publication" is an attempt to supply a few copies at a reasonable price to sincere students of Sublett Genealogy. The articles are being "mass produced" by photocopying in their original form with the original pagination — without changes, additions or corrections. However, to increase the usefulness of the original articles, there is being added: this explanatory introduction, a table of contents listing with page number the principal descendants — families and sub-families, an every name index mostly extracted by the cut-and-paste method from the published general index to volumes 26-30 of the *DSGR Magazine*. (The Subletts are to be found only in volumes 27, 28 and 29.) For completeness, there are also being added three other DSGR articles on the Soblet-Subletts, by Mrs. Searl and Sublette. This is strictly a "limited edition" and is being prepared mostly for the convenience of family genealogists.

As to Dr. Allen and his background, the following is copied verbatim from the program of the Genealogical Conference sponsored jointly by the National Genealogical Society and the Indiana Historical Society held in Indianapolis in May 1982.

> *CAMERON ALLEN. Fellow, American Society of Genealogists. Born, Springfield, Clark County, OH; resident, Newark, NJ. B.A., Otterbein College, Westerville, OH; M.A., U of Wisconsin, Madison; M.S.L.S., U of Illinois, Champaign; J.D., Duke U, Durham, NC. Professor of Law and Law Library, Rutgers U, School of Law, Newark, NJ, since 1965. Corps of Engineers, U. S. Army. Secretary, American Association of Law Libraries, 1977-80; member, Huguenot Society of London. Interested in Virginia, North Carolina; overseas origins of British, Dutch and French/Huguenot families.*

This introduction would be more meaningful if there had been secured a statement as to Dr. Allen's qualifications, the events leading to his genealogical work on the Subletts and his procedures and experiences in assembling data and writing articles. Volume 2 (1971) of "Genealogical Research" contains the following very brief statement: "Cameron Allen, B.A., M.A., J.D., F.A.S.G., 351 Broad St., Newark, N.J. 07104. Law Librarian Rutgers University, Contributing Editor — TAG." The American Society of Genealogists is the publisher of "Genealogical Research"; F.A.S.G. means a Fellow of that Society and is a recognition of professional competence as a genealogist. TAG presumably stands for "The American Genealogist," a genealogical publication.

Dr. Allen is in demand as a lecturer at genealogical conferences, particularly on Huguenot genealogy. Dr. Allen also was the author of a series of three articles on "The Chastain Families of Manakintown, Virginia and their Origin Abroad." These articles were published in the American Genealogist in 1963-64. Ann Soblet Chastain is an important part of early American Chastain genealogy and unquestionably should be included with the male Soblets in a complete "Sublett Genealogy and Family History." Unlike Allen's articles on the male Subletts and their descendants, the Chastain Genealogy has been updated (1980) in "Chastain Kith & Kin, 1700-1980" by Mary Avilla Abel Hall Farnsworth-Milligan. The Chastain descendants have formed a permanent and well financed association, "The Pierre Chastain Family Association," and publish a Quarterly devoted to printing research results and updating.

It is hoped that this reproduction of the Cameron Allen articles will prove useful to those interested in Soblet-Sublett genealogy.

Donald J. Sublette
November 1982

Some extracts from a note to D.J.S. by Dr. Cameron Allen, dated 1 Feb. 1984, written in Columbus, OH. (As regards the reprint of the D.S.G.R. articles by Dr. Allen on the Soblet-Sublett Family):

> *"... It is indeed good to have it in this format, especially with your two articles on the Sedan-Jametz-St. Menges origins included. As you know from seeing my reference in Genealogical Research v. 2, I had secured further information on the origins, but never could find time to write this up ... I have often wondered whether Jean Soblet, father of Abraham, was a brother to Philibert Soblet. Their families were born over a similar period of time. Philibert was the known son of Eli & Susanne Renaudin. If Philibert & Jean were brothers, this would make Eli the grandfather to Abraham. ... Like yourself, I hope that further work by interested descendants will result in a full history of the Sublett Family. The Chastains (Anne Soblet) seem headed in this direction..."*

Note to Second Printing:

The last page of this introduction has been slightly modified. In this reprint a few corrections have been made, and a slight amount of additional data added, particularly where it will clarify the original data, or lack thereof.

Donald J. Sublette
July 1985

Note to 4th, 5th, and 6th Printing:

Handwritten changes — D.J.S.

The previous notes from Donald J. Sublette were reproduced with his permission. Mr. Sublette approached the board of the Detroit Society for Genealogical Research, Inc., for permission to reproduce this series through his own labor and provide the Society with copies of his manuscript, complete with his own index. Over the years, many additions and corrections have been added by hand to the original manuscript, which resulted in a somewhat confusing publication.

The Detroit Society for Genealogical Research, Inc., has re-organized the original material and incorporated Donald J. Sublette's hand-written notes into the text, with proper source identification in the footnotes. The pagination has been simplified and an entirely new index has been prepared.

This Society is extremely grateful to Donald J. Sublette for his many years of painstaking research on this family, and his contributions of corrections and additions to this manuscript. In addition, he solicited the Sublette data of all those who purchased this book, and carried on correspondence with many of the contributors. He assumed the responsibility of having reprints of the book made whenever the supply ran low. The popularity of this publication is in the fact that under Mr. Sublette's supervision, there were six printings, before this current revision.

Donald Jackson Sublette died 28 March 1994 in Royal Oak, Oakland County, Michigan.

James N. Jackson
June 1994

PUBLISHED GENEALOGIES

Sublett(e) & Allied Lines

Allen, Cameron, JD — "The Sublett Family of Manakintown, VA" Volumes 27-29 (1963-66) *Magazine of the Detroit Society for Genealogical Research, Inc.*

Allen, Cameron, JD — "The Chastain Families of Manakintown" — published serially in *The American Genealogist* — 1963-64.

Clark, Edith Maxey — "The Maxeys of Virginia" — Baltimore, MD — 1980.

Farnsworth-Milligan, Mary A.A.H. — "Chastain Kith & Kin" — Newton, KS — 1980.

Oates, Chas. E., MD — "Oates-Sublett Family" — N. Little Rock, AR — 1953.

Searl, Hester G. L. — "Genealogy of John Hester" — Patterson, CA — 1972.

Sublette, Donald J. — "Sublett & Ford" — Birmingham, MI — 1981

Sublette, Nancy Louise — "Generations Remembered" — 1974.

Sublett, Sam'l. S. — "History Huguenot Soblets" — Richmond, VA — 1896.

Sunder, John E. — "Bill Sublette, Mountain Man" — Norman: University of OK Press — 1959

Yates & Trabue — "Trabue Family in America" — Baltimore, MD — 1983.

Note: Titles of the above are abbreviated.

The Sublett (Soblet) Family
of Manakintown, King William Parish, Virginia

Compiled by Cameron Allen
of East Orange, New Jersey

The comparatively recent publication of the Register of the Church of La Patente de Soho, 1689-1782, London, has made possible the location of the first item of information (other than legendary) on the European origin of the Soblet family, and has also made necessary the revision of the slight amount of published material which has appeared on the family, so that the following outline of the early generations of the family would appear to be timely.

The Church of La Patente de Soho was one of several churches established in London to minister to the spiritual needs of the swarm of Huguenot refugees who fled France in terror for their lives and souls following the Revocation of the Edict of Toleration (Nantes) in 1685. Certain of the Huguenot churches in London conformed to the doctrine of the Church of England, but La Patente de Soho was a nonconformist chapel, its name deriving from the fact that its foundation rested upon Letters Patent issued by the Romanist king, James II, in 1688.[1] The single Soblet item in the aforementioned register follows:

> [entry #] *225. SOBLET. 1698, 1 Mai. Robert, f. d'Abraham, de Sedan, en France, et de Susanne Brian; bap. par Mr. Malide, l'un des Pasts. de cette ég. P. Robert de Camp.*[2] *M. Dlle. Judith de Longne. Tous dem. dans cette ville de Londres où cet enfant est né 20 Av. Tém. Judith Delogne.*[3]

So for the first time it is known that Abraham Soblet came from Sedan: presumably his wife Susanne (Brian) was a native of the same town, for it seems to have been customary in this Register to list the place of nativity of each parent, if they came from different localities. It is not without significance to note that the Soblets were not the only Manakintown settlers to come from Sedan: by his will Abraham Michaux identifies himself as a native of the same place,[4] and it is said that Bartholomew Dupuy's wife also came from Sedan.[5]

This baptismal entry for the infant Robert Soblet also makes clear for the first time the identity of Abraham's wife Susanne. She seems inescapably to have been a Brian, but she has been identified heretofore (without benefit of any known primary source material) varyingly as both a Dupuy and a Chastain.[6] The persons responsible for such misidentification seemed moved by the

---

1   Huguenot Society of London. *Publications*, v. 45, p. xiii. London, 1956. (Registers of the Churches of La Patente de Soho, Wheeler Street, Swansfields and Hoxton; also, the Répertoire Général; ed. by Susan Minet).

2   Accent marks not included in original text. Added to all French words.

3   *Ibid.*, v. 45, p. 19.

4   Henrico County, Virginia, Miscellaneous Court Records [Deeds, Wills, Etc.], 1650-1807, vol. 1 [1650-1717], p. 354.

5   Charles W. Beard, *History of the Huguenot Emigration to America*, New York, Dodd, Mead, 1885, v. 2, pp. 109-111.

6   B. H. Dupuy, *The Huguenot Bartholomew Dupuy and His Descendants*, Louisville, Courier-Journal, 1908, p. 263, identifies her as a Dupuy. So also does Mrs. H. D. Pittman, *Americans of Gentle Birth*, St. Louis, 1903, v. 1, p. 181. Both these accounts were based on the Sublett MS. of Dr. John Sublett Logan, a copy of which is to be found at the Kentucky Historical Society, Frankfort, Kentucky. James Garvin Chastain, *A Brief History of the Huguenots and Three Family Trees: Chastain-Lochridge-Stockton*, 1933, pp. 263-264, identifies her as a Chastain. This same Chastain identification is given

desire to tie the Soblets in with other early Manakin Town settlers; yet with her new identity as now revealed, this desire is apparently fulfilled, for there were early Huguenot Brians at Manakin Town. Thomas Brian is listed for the first time as a tithable in 1710,[7] and Jacques Brian in 1725.[8] That a connection between these very Brians and the Soblets existed may be inferred from repeated evidences of intimate friendship: for example, "Louy Soblet, Jr." served as godfather to Jacques Brian's daughter Marie in 1746.[9] And quite conceivably the presence of the name Jacques in both the Soblet and Brian families is more than coincidence. Presumably, then, these Brians of Manakin also came from Sedan. This belief is strengthened by the fact that there were Huguenot Brians from Sedan in London prior to the time that Abraham Soblet resided there. On 27 August 1679 "Daniel Brian *et sa fem.*" produced their *témoignage* (certificate of communicant status) from the Huguenot Church of Sedan in the process of affiliating with the Huguenot Threadneedle Street Church in London.[10]

There was at least one other Soblet in London contemporary with Abraham. This was Peter Soblet who on 24 Sept. 1690, being "of St Clem^ts Danes, Midd., Taylor, Bach^r, abt 45" applied for a license to marry Charity Hunt, "of the same, Wid., ab^t 33," the event to occur at St. Clements Danes.[11] From the fact that Abraham named a son Pierre Louis, this Peter appears to be a near relative, presumably a brother, to Abraham. Peter or another Soblet sired progeny who remained in England, for on 25 May 1766 Marie Anne Soblet became a member of the Huguenot Threadneedle Street Church in London; and on 7 June 1746 Sara Soblet stood godmother to one George Hartman at "La Chapelle Royale de Saint James."[12]

The registers of the Huguenot Church of Sedan are still in existence, being in the custody of the Société de l'Histoire du Protestantisme Français, 54, Rue des Saints-Pères, Paris. M. Philippe de Félice of the Société very kindly searched the registers of Sedan for the period 1654-1665 in

---

also in the Huguenot Society: Founders of Manakin in the Colony of Virginia, *Yearbook*, No. 1, 1924, p. 11; and in The Huguenot Society: Founders of Manakin in the Colony of Virginia, *Publication*, No. 7, 1933-1935, pp. 278-281. These last two cited works also set forth a description of a Sublett arms, ignoring the fact that the Soblet arms were granted to a Soblet in another part of France at just about the time that Abraham and his family were being harried out of the country. The Dupuy history gives a background sketch on the family, unhappily incorrect in virtually every detail which can be checked against primary sources. For example, it credits the first Abraham with a son Littleberry, "born at Littleberry, England." Actually the first Littlebury to whom extant sources refer is a Sublett of two generations later (#41) and his name was a family name which, while originating as a given name in Virginia with the Eppes family, had spread in popularity far beyond the demonstrable blood lines of that family, and was in widespread use in that later generation in Virginia. This same account is contained in Pittman, *op. cit.*, and, again, both it and the Dupuy history's reference to the Sublett background originate in the Sublett MS. of Dr. John Sublett Logan. This highly fanciful account has again quite recently found its way into print in Doyce B. Nunis, Jr., "The Sublettes: A Study of a Refugee Family in the Eighteenth Century," *Virginia Magazine*, 69:42-66 (1961). Incidentally, this Nunis account straddles the issue as to whether Susanne was a Dupuy or a Chastain; and finally does not say whether Susanne was a Dupuy, but attempts to demonstrate that Susanne could not have been a Chastain, although the method used results in what is genealogically an absolute *non sequitur*.

7   *Virginia Magazine of History and Biography*, 11:302 (King William Vestry Book transcription).

8   *Ibid.*, 12:256.

9   R. A. Brock, "Documents, Chiefly Unpublished, Relating to the Huguenot Emigration to Virginia and to the Settlement at Manakin-Town," *Virginia Historical Collections*, new series, v. 5, p. 107, Richmond, Virginia Historical Society, 1886.

10   Huguenot Society of London. *Publications*. Vol. 21, "Tesmoignages de l'Eglise de Threadneedle Street, 1669-1789." London, 1909.

11   Harleian Society *Publications*, v. 31, p. 155. "Allegations for Marriage Licenses Issued by the Vicar-General of the Archbishop of Canterbury, July 1687 to June 1694," ed. by George J. Armytage. London, 1890.

12   Huguenot Society of London. *Publications*. v. 21, p. 247. (cited above); v. 28, p. 6.

which decade he considered most likely the birth of Abraham to have occurred. His search did not yield an entry for Abraham, but considering the fact that Peter of London was born about 1645, it seems probable that Abraham also was born earlier than 1654. M. de Félice did encounter two Soblet men procreating in the decade he searched:

Philbert Soblet had by his wife Anne (Godin):[13]

1.	Jean Soblet	b.	19 Oct. 1654, d. in childhood
2.	Jeanne Soblet	b.	17 Jan. 1656
3.	Jacques Soblet	b.	4 Mar. 1657
4.	Elisabeth Soblet	b.	28 July 1658, d. in childhood
5.	Judith Soblet	b.	25 Aug. 1660
6.	Rachel Soblet	b.	8 Jan. 1662
7.	Jean Soblet	b.	30 Aug. 1664
8.	Elisabeth Soblet	b.	10 Dec. 1665

Jean Soblet had by his wife Judith (Lombart):

1.	Judith Soblet	b.	7 May 1656
2.	Marie Soblet	b.	26 Oct. 1663

M. de Félice could not spare the time from his official duties to search further, and reported that he could recommend no one to continue the search through the registers of Sedan.

The fact that Philbert Soblet's wife Anne was born a Godin is of interest, because studies of the Michaux family of Manakintown show that the immigrant Abraham Michaux (1672-1717) was descended from the Godin family of Sedan. His father Jacob Michaux was the son of Abraham and Marie (Godin) Michaux.[14] Thus, it would appear that Abraham Soblet and Abraham Michaux of Manakintown were, if not relatives, at least family connections of sorts. Doubtless, further study of the Sedan registers will uncover some other interesting relationships among the Manakintown settlers.

There is evidence that there were Soblets from Sedan who became fugitives for conscience sake other than Abraham and Peter: Among the men who served the French Reformed congregation at Emmerich on the Rhine as combination school master and "*lecteur-chantre*" ("reader-chanter") in the services were Jacques Soblet (*de Sedan*) (died 1705); and Guillaume Soblet (died 1752) "*sans doute son fils*." (Société de l'Histoire du Protestantisme Français. *Bulletin*. 32:38.) It seems more than probable that Abraham Soblet initially sought refuge at Emmerich himself with his relative Jacques. One of the ancient traditions of the Sublett family was that he had come to England via Germany and The Netherlands. If so, a study of the Church records of the Emmerich congregation (which extend from 1690-1820) would probably disclose the baptism of one or more of his children in that locality.

Not long after the birth of his son Robert in London in 1698, Abraham Soblet joined the group

---

13   Sedan, Reformed Church, *Les Registres des Baptême*, as abstracted in letter of 24 May 1960 from M. Philippe de Félice to the contributor.

14   Joseph D. Eggleston, "Michaux Family," *Virginia Magazine of History and Biography*, v. 44, pp. 365-374 (1936); also in Archibald Bennett, *Advanced Genealogical Research*, Salt Lake City, Bookcraft, 1959, pp. 87-94.

of French refugees who determined to cast their fortunes in Virginia. Abraham, the husband and father, went on ahead of his wife to Virginia, with their oldest sons, embarking 19 April 1700 in the *Mary and Ann*. Governor Francis Nicholson on 12 August 1700 wrote to England of the arrival of the first shipload of Manakin-bound Huguenots: "They were on board the ship *Mary and Ann*, of London, George Haws, Commander, who had about thirteen weeks passage, and the 23d of the last month [July] arrived at the mouth of this River" [the James]. To his letter Gov. Nicholson appended a "List of ye Refugees," among whom appear "Abraham Sablet et des deux enfants."[15] Abraham was joined in Virginia in the fall of the year 1700 by "Susanne Soblet and 3 Enfans" according to the "List of All ye Passengers from London to James River, in Virginia, Being ffrench Refugees Imbarqued in the Ship Ye *Peter and Anthony*, Galley of London, Daniel Perreau, Commander, James Towne, in Virginia, ye 20th of Sept'r. 1700."[16] In "Xbre 1700," "Susanne Soblet, et trois enfans" are likewise catalogued in the "Liste des personnes du second convoy qui serent toute l'annee a Manicantown."[17] Early the next year "Soblet, his wife and five children" appear in "A list of the refugees who are to receive of ye miller of Falling Creek Mill one bushel a head of Indian meale monthly as settled at or about King Williams Town to begin in ffeb 1700 [1701]."[18] By 10 Nov. 1701 an infant mortality had occurred in the family, for William Byrd's "List of ye French Refugees That are Settled Att ye Mannachin Town" of that date accounts for "Sublet, his wife and four children."[19]

Abraham Soblet early assumed a fairly prominent position among the Manakintown settlers. When the colony's beloved elder pastor, M. Benjamin Dejoux, died early in the history of the settlement, Abraham Soblet joined the other pastor, M. Claude Philippe de Richebourg, in appraising his estate. Soblet's own signature may be found signed to the original "Inventaire des effets mounez dans la maison de Residence ou Mr Dejoux est mort le mercredi 3- mart a deux heurs du matin," which was recorded 1 August 1703.[20] Abraham Soblet also witnessed on 1 Nov. 1709 a deed for a "tract in the Monocantown" from "Anthony Promiseall and Mary his wife widow & Relict of Abraham Minet deceased to John Jones" (*i.e.*, Jean Jouany).[21]

According to the deposition of Abraham Salle on 2 Sept. 1707 "Not long after the erecting of Monocantown into a Parish, the Parishioners were assembled to elect a Vestry, and the Plurality of voices fell upon the following persons ... Abra. Soblet."[22] In such a position of responsibility, it was inevitable that he would become embroiled in the controversy which shook Manakintown asunder and sent many of the settlers, led by M. Philippe de Richebourg, on their journey to the Carolinas. It was an early case in this country of vestry versus rector. On 27 March 1707 the vestry assembled at Manakintown, "Abra. Sobler" being one of those present. "It was decreed that in view of the indirect methods and the unusual and irregular conduct displayed at the session by Mr. Philipe, the minister, that Mr. Amonnet, vestryman, signify and protest in the presence of the congregation to the said S^r. Philipe that the arrangement and agreement which he has made with several parishioners is entirely disapproved by the vestry, being contrary to the laws and

---

15   Virginia Historical Society, *Collections*, *n.s.*, v. 6, pp. 64-66.

16   Brock, *op. cit.*, p. 14.

17   *Ibid.*, p. 24.

18   *Ibid.*, p. 27.

19   *Ibid.*, p. 46.

20   Henrico County, Virginia, Miscellaneous Court Records [Deeds, Wills, Etc.] 1650-1807, vol. 1, [1650-1717], p. 147.

21   Henrico County, Virginia, Records [Deeds and Wills], 1706-1709, p. 189.

22   Brock, *op. cit.*, p. 70; *Calendar of Virginia State Papers*, vol. 1, pp. 114-115. This must have occurred about Dec. 1700 when Manakin was set apart as a separate parish. See James L. Bugg, Jr., "The French Huguenot Frontier Settlement of Manakin Town," *Virginia Magazine*, 61:382 (1953).

customs established in Virginia and without the participation of the vestry, that therefore the vestry will make no order nor lay no tax for its payment."[23] When on Sunday, 30 March, "after the divine service," Jacob Amonnet attempted to read the vestry's declaration protesting the conduct of Mr. Philipe, "he was interrupted by the said Sr Philipe, who addressed himself to Sʳ Reynaud, clerk of the church and of the said vestry, warning him with much heat that if he would not give over to him the book of christenings he would exclude him from the communion, as well as all of those generally who did not go to him to get their tickets or order-number. He declared publicly that he did not recognize any vestry and that the people ought not to recognize it."[24] Thereupon there were heated exchanges between supporters of either faction in this very un-Anglican congregational meeting after Morning Prayer, Abraham Salle alone seeming to remember that this was "neither the place nor the occasion" for such conduct. Suffice it to say that when M. Philippe and his disgruntled company departed for the Carolinas several years later, Soblet stayed on in King William Parish.

Shortly after this gallic outburst of public emotion, Soblet by 20 Dec. 1707 had moved on up the ladder, from merely one of the vestry to Church Warden of King William Parish, along with Louis Dutartre.[25] On 25 May 1708 "The Srs. Abraham Soblet and Louis Dutartre, church wardens, having tendered their resignations to the vestry, their year having expired, it was enacted that the said resignations be accepted."[26] They were replaced by Anthoine Trabue and Gideon Chambon. Soblet dropped from the vestry, and when on 3 October 1710 he was selected again for a position on the vestry, he declined, "Abraham Soblet having declared that he did not wish to take the said oath [of qualification], not having the intention of qualifying himself for the said office."[27] Presumably from this wording, Soblet had no scruples as to the particular oath required, but simply a disinclination to resume the responsibilities of the office and their presently attendant unpleasantness, what with M. Philippe still in the neighborhood. Whether being at outs with M. Philippe had anything to do with it, Abraham Soblet did not pay his levy for 1709.[28] On 30 June 1711 he was listed as a tithable to pay for the services so far that year of M. Philippe.[29]

Abraham Soblet, called either "père" or "l'ainé" to distinguish him from his son of the same name, on the verge of manhood (called "fils" or "le jeune"), appears as a tithable in King William Parish in each year down at least through 1715. On 30 Dec. 1715 a "List of Tithables for the Present Year 1715" includes both "Abra. Soblet, l'ainé" and "Abra. Soblet, jeune."[30] By July 1717 one of the Abraham Soblets had apparently died, for in the "List of Tithables Returned in July 1717" only one Abra. Soblet appears.[31] Which one of the Abraham Soblets was the survivor, it seems impossible to say. The survivor appears for the last time on a "List of Tithables of King William Parish for the present year, 1719, taxed at 1½ bu. of wheat each."[32] By the time the list of tithables for 1720 was taken, he too had gone to a better world.

In attempting to establish the outline of his family, one of the most useful documents is an

---

23   *Virginia Magazine*, 11:427.

24   *Ibid.*, 11:428.

25   *Ibid.*, 11:296.

26   *Ibid.*, 11:297.

27   *Ibid.*, 11:299.

28   *Ibid.*, 11:301.

29   *Virginia Magazine*, 11:304.

30   *Ibid.*, 12:22.

31   *Ibid.*, 12:26.

32   *Ibid.*, 12:241.

undated one, but one which has been estimated to date from about 1714. This "Liste Générale de Tous les Francois Protestants Refugies, Establys Dans la Paroisse du Roy Guillaume, Comte d'Henrico en Virginia, y Compris les Femmes, Enfans, Veuses, et orphelins." gives the following:[33]

| | | Enfans | | |
Nom des Hommes	Femmes	Garçons	Filles	Total
Jacques Sobler	1	1	1	4
Louis Sobler	1	1	--	3
Abra. Sobler, lesne [*i.e.*, l'aîné]	--	--	--	1
Abra. Sobler, le jeune	1	--	--	2

From this it may be seen that Susanne (Brian) Soblet had died before the year 1714 or thereabouts.

Issue of Abraham Soblet, père, and Susanne (Brian):

- 1   i   Pierre-Louis Soblet, b. say 1686, d. 1754/5, Cumberland County, Virginia; m. (2nd)? Marthe Martain (Martin).

- 2   ii   Jacques Soblet, b. say 1689, d. 1741/2, Goochland County, Virginia; m Marthe ---.

- 3   iii   Anne Soblet, b. say 1684; m. Pierre Chastain. This identity is subject to a bit of debate. The sole reference to her is: "3 April, 1723, died Anne Soblet the -- ------sieur Pierre Chastain, aged about -- years; was buried the fourth of the month."[34] To achieve the identity suggested above, it is necessary to supply in the blanks "the wife of." Unaided by other references, it would be just as possible to supply alternatively "the daughter of" and thus make her wife of one of the young Soblets. However, the death register also gives this reference: "The 12th of January, 1722 [1723], died Janne Chastain, daughter of ---ieur Chastain and of Anne Chastain, her father and mother, aged about 6 years; was buried the 13th of the month, on Sunday, at three o'clock in the afternoon."[35] This presumably refers to the same Anne and makes her wife to Pierre Chastain, hence, born a Soblet.

- 4   iv   Abraham Soblet, fils, b. say 1694; d. by 1720.

- 5   v   Robert Soblet, b. 20 April 1698, London; bp. 1 May 1698 at the Church of La Patente de Soho. Died in childhood. He may have been one of the five children of Abraham listed at Manakintown in Feb. 1701, deceased by 10 Nov. 1701. If so, then Abraham had no other children who survived, because the c. 1714 "Liste Générale" shows no children living with Abraham père; the 1701 "Census" shows him with five children [demonstrably (1) Pierre-Louis, (2) Jacques, (3) Abraham fils, since they are not listed separately as heads of family there, plus probably (4) Anne, unless she was already married by 1701, which is quite unlikely; plus, perhaps, (5) Robert or another. If another, it was likely a second daughter older than Robert.] Abraham père in all probability had no children born subsequent to 1701 who survived, for none are listed with him in 1714, (assuming, of course, that none are counted as "Enfans" residing

33   Brock, *op. cit.*, p. 74, reprinted from William Stevens Perry, *Papers Relating to the Church in Virginia*, pp. 193-195.
34   *Ibid.*, p. 110.
35   Brock, *op. cit.*, p. 110.

with either elder brother, Pierre-Louis or Jacques.)

1. Pierre-Louis Soblet, b. say 1686, is referred to in the records of his parish and county varyingly as "Pierre Louis," "Louis Pierre," in the anglicized form "Peter Lewis"; "Louis P[re]," and alternately simply either as Louis or Pierre. Louis seems to have been his preferred name. He is listed as a tithable as Louis Soblet in the year 1710,[36] and in the list of parish expenses for the year 1710 he was allowed 6 shillings 7 pence "for three days work of himself and one day of his horse."[37] He appears as Louis in 1711, 1712, 1713, 1714, and 1715, but in 1717 as Peter.[38] On 26 Dec. 1718 Louis Soblet was elected to the vestry along with his brother Jacques[39] and on 26 March 1719 "The S[rs] Jacques Soblet and Louis P[re] Soblet, heretofore named as vestrymen, took to-day the oaths of the vestry and signed the test."[40] The 1719 List of Tithables calls him P[re] Louis Soblet.[41] On 20 April 1720, "The S[rs] Estienne Chastaine and Louis Soblet were elected by the vestry present as church wardens of the said parish, and the oaths were taken."[42] On the very same day, the parish being without a full-time resident clergyman, "It was decreed that the Sr. Louis Soblet have the use of the glebe for the term of two years, commencing Christmas of the year 1721, in consideration of which the said Louis Soblet binds himself to make repairs to the house which is built on the glebe; viz., he binds himself to roof the house, to fit on the two chimneys and in case there are any holes about the house, he is to close them with clap-boards, all at hls own cost and expense. In addition he binds himself to make a thousand rails for the corn-field of the said glebe." He signed this agreement with the parish vestry as Pierre Louis Soblet.[43] Apparently, however, this arrangement proved unsatisfactory, for on 29 July 1721, before the lease was to take effect, it was agreed by the vestry that "Daniel Guerrant the elder [is] to have the use of the glebe for one year, commencing the first of the year 1722 ...; in case it happens that we have a minister, he shall vacate the house in order to provide him a lodging ..."[44]

On 28 March 1722 "The Sieur Etiene Chastain and Louy Soblet churchwardens, offered their resignations, and the vestry assembled granted their discharge."[45] They were replaced by "the Sieur Anthoine Rapine and the Sieur Abraham Sallee." Louis continued however to serve on the vestry through the period 1722-1726; by 23 July 1726 "Mr. Pierre Louys Soblet" was again serving as church warden along with "Mr. Pierre Chastain."[46] On 2 September 1727 the latter two churchwardens were succeeded by "the Sieur Daniel Guerent and the Sieur Jean du Pree."[47] Again Soblet continued on the vestry, from 1727 until 18 August 1733 when "Pierre Louis Soblet tendered his resignation" from the vestry, which was accepted.[48] During this term on the vestry he took an active part on the building committee for the new parish church, for on 19 Sept. 1730 the vestry appointed "the Srs. Anthoine Rapine, Louis Soblet, Isac Salle to make a contract for a

---

36   *Virginia Magazine*, 11:302. (King William Vestry Book).

37   *Ibid.*, 11:300.

38   *Ibid.*, 12:26.

39   *Ibid.*, 12:31.

40   *Ibid.*, 12:31.

41   *Ibid.*, 12:241.

42   *Ibid.*, 12:243.

43   *Virginia Magazine*, 12:243-244.

44   *Ibid.*, 12:248.

45   *Ibid.*, 12:248.

46   *Ibid.*, 12:370.

47   *Ibid.*, 12:373.

48   *Ibid.*, 12:73.

church."[49] On 24 Oct. 1730 "It was agreed with Francoi Jams that he build a church for the sum of twenty-one thousand six hundred pounds of tobacco, to be paid in three years, he to furnish the hogshead and the press, the same here at Manakintown. The Churchwardens and Louy Soblet and Estienne Chastain were appointed to make a contract with the carpenter next Saturday."[50] On 29 March 1735 the parish once again confronted the problem of a clergyless glebe, and it was "rented by the church wardens, David Lesueur and Pierre Guerant. Louys Soblet rented it until next Christmas for three bushels of wheat, payable to the church wardens."[51] The final appearance of Soblet in the parish vestrybook occurs on 20 Aug. 1739 when "The vestry appointed ... Pr. Louys Soblet and Thomas Porter [to procession the land] from the creek below to the creek above, the old line of the ten thousand acres" [which had been patented to the refugees].[52]

On 20 July 1738 there was patented to "Peter Lewis Soblet ... 133 acres in the County of Goochland on the south side of James River beginning at a small corner locust parting Matthew Oage [*i.e.*, Agee] and the said Soblet ... the same being part of the last five thousand acres of land surveyed for the french Refugees."[53] On 5 June 1746 Peter Louis Soblet patented a 385 acre tract in the county of Henrico beginning at a white oak in Micheaux line."[54]

The will of Peter Lewis Soblet "of Cumberland County and King William Parish," made 5 Nov. 1754, was probated 27 January 1755. By it he left to "my son William Soblett one certain tract or parcel of Land whereon I now dwell [*i.e.*, the 133 acre tract patented in 1738] ...; to my son Abraham Soblett, my negro man Prymus ...; to my son Lewis Soblett, a negro woman Candis and one certain tract or parcel of Land containing 385 acres lying in Chesterfield County on the branches of the Lower Manakin Creek; to my son Benjamin my horse, bridel and saddell and all my waring cloaths, and more I doe appoint and order my executors to pay all the debts that my son Benjamin owes at this day, to paid out of my movebel estat; to my son Lewis Soblett one negro gall named Juday Provisor he pay William Soblett and Abraham Soblett five pounds. All movebel of mine be equally divided between my four sons, William, Abraham, Lewis and Benjamin." Executors named were the two sons William and Lewis. The will was witnessed by Jos. Bingley, Ginkins (x) Selfe, and Abram (x) Selfe.[55]

It seems to this observer quite probable that Pierre Louis Soblet was married twice. His son Peter seems to have been substantially older than his five other sons, for as will be shown, Peter, Jr., had patented land in 1715, was listed as a tithable from 1729 on, and under the terms of Pierre Louis' will received considerably less than the younger sons, presumably because he had received his fair share much earlier. (Conceivably the patent of 1715 represents such a share. And it will be noted that when Pierre Louis came to divide the residue of his estate, the moveables, he provided for their division among "my four sons," Peter being conspicuous by his absence. The identity of such posited first wife is unknown; it was presumably she who was listed as his wife on the "Liste Générale" of c. 1714, along with one son (Peter, Jr.). This first wife probably died soon after 1714, and he married (2d) about 1722 Marte [Martha] ---. No extant documents conclusively establish her maiden name, but all writers agree that she was Marthe (Martin). Such

49   *Ibid.*, 12:380.
50   *Ibid.*, 12:380.
51   *Ibid.*, 12:79.
52   *Ibid.*, 12:182.
53   *Virginia Patent Bk. 18*, p. 62.
54   *Ibid.*, Bk. 25, p. 76.
55   *Cumberland County, Virginia, Will Bk. 1*, p. 88.

identity seems quite reasonable, especially considering how the Martains recurringly stood at the font as godparents for her children. Marte is known to have mothered the youngest three children, and is believed to have been the mother of William and Abraham also. (Abraham named his eldest daughter Martha; William did likewise.) But if Marte was a Martin and a Huguenot, she must have been a daughter of Jean Martin, the immigrant, who does not name her in his will. He names wife Margaret, sons James, John and Peter, and daughters Judith Chateen (*i.e.*, Chastain) and Jane Martin, as well as some grandchildren. One of the witnesses to his will was James Soblet. (Goochland County, Virginia, Deeds, &c., Bk. 3, p. 210; will dated 12 March 1736; probated 15 May 1739.) James, John and Jane Martin served as godparents to Marte's children.

Issue of Pierre Louis Soblet, the youngest five presumably by a second wife, Marte (Martain):

- 6   i   Peter Sublett, Jr.; b. say 1712; d. 1783 Powhatan County, Virginia; m. Elizabeth ---.
- 7   ii   William Sublett, b. say 1723; d. 1780, Charlotte County, Virginia; m. by 1751 Susanna (Allen).
- 8   iii   Abraham Sublett, b. say 1726; d. 1782, Charlotte County, Virginia; m. by 1751 Elizabeth ---.
- 9   iv   Louis (Lewis) Sublett, b. 1728; d. 1802, Chesterfield County, Va,; m. Frances Hill. "The 9th April 1728 was born Louis Soblet, son of Pierre Louis Soblet and of Marte, his wife, was baptised by Mr. Na[irn?] minister of Varaine [Varina?]. He had for godfather Jean Martain and Jacob Trabue; for godmother, Marie Martain. The father has declared that the child was born the day and year above."[56]
- 10 v   Jacques Soblet, b. 1730/1; d. in childhood. "The 14th March 1730 [1731], Jaque Soblet, son of Pierre Louis Soblet and of Marie [*i.e.*, Marte], his wife, was baptized by Mr. Marye; he had for godfather Jaque Soblet and Jaque Martain; for godmother, Janne Martain. The parties have declared that he was born the 3d of the month of January, 1730 [1731]."[57]
- 11 vi   Benjamin Soblet, b. 1733; d. 1816, Warren County, Kentucky; m. 1762 Elizabeth Jordon. "The 23d April, 1733, was born Bainjamain Soblet, son of Pierre Lours and of Marte, his wife; had for godfather, Gedeon Chanbon, and Wollter Stot; for godmother, Anne David. The parties have declared that he was born the day and year above named."[58]

2. Jacques Soblet, b. say 1689, is mentioned as a tithable under his own name for the 1710,[59] and again for the year 1711.[60] In 1712 he is conjoined with his father and brother Abraham, as if resident in one household:[61]

> Ab. Soblet, pere   )
> Jacque Soblet, fils   ) 3 [tithables]
> Ab. Soblet, fils   )

---

56   Brock, *op. cit.*, p. 80.
57   *Ibid.*, p. 84-85.
58   *Ibid.*, p. 88.
59   *Virginia Magazine*, 11:302.
60   *Ibid.*, 11:304.
61   *Ibid.*, 11:435.

Thereafter, he annually goes his separate way, as if in his own separate household.[62] In the c. 1714 "Liste Générale" he appears as "Jacques Sobler" with a wife, one son and one daughter.[63] With this size family, he must have been married about 1711, despite his appearance in the same household with his father in 1712. It is important to note here that his son in the "Liste Générale" cannot have been the James Soblet [Jr.], sole heir to James at his death in 1741, for James, Jr., was a minor as late as 1750.

On 21 Nov. 1711 the vestry of King William Parish allowed Jacques Soblet 5 shillings 9 pence for two days' labor of himself and of his horse for the parish.[64] By 26 Dec. 1718 Jacques was sufficiently advanced in years to command enough respect that he was selected for the vestry along with his brother Louis and Jean Calvet.[65] On 26 March 1719 "The S[rs] Jacques Soblet and Louis P[re] Soblet, heretofore named as vestrymen, took to-day the oaths of vestry and signed the test."[66] On 29 July 1721 "It was decreed by the vestry present that Jaques Soblet be granted the sum of five pounds per year, commencing July 29th of the current year, 1721, for filling the office of clerk or secretary of this vestry and for reading the word of God in the Church of the parish of King William, the said five pounds to be paid him according as the harvests shall fall; viz., in wheat at three shillings per bushel, or maize at eighteen pence per bushel or tobacco as shall be agreed on for the levies which the vestry shall judge proper to make."[67] It has been said of his vestry clerkship: "Jacques Soblet's clerkship lasted until 1726, the last entry in his hand being on July 21 of that year. In the matter of clerkly neatness he is not to be compared with Reynaud nor Justice Salle, and the character of his French shows many marks of degeneration; as regards the spelling of proper names, particularly of English names, he out-trumps all the other clerks in irregularity and carelessness."[68] On 30 Sept. 1723 "Jaque Soblet having tendered his resignation as vestryman, it was accepted by the vestry assembled."[69] On 23 Sept. 1727, "Jean Chastain was elected clerk of this church in the place of Mr. Jaques Soblet."[70] Jacques Soblet appears virtually annually as a tithable in King William Parish through the year 1738.

On 1 Nov. 1737 "James Soblet of Goochland County, Planter" sold to Benjamin Harris of the same county, carpenter, an 88 acre tract "lying in Manacan Town," which tract was by "Patent bearing date" 23 March 1715.[71] The description in the 1737 deed is precisely the same as that of the 88 acres "in Henrico County on the south side of James River" patented 23 March 1715 to Abraham Soblet jun[r].[72] Though the 1737 deed does not state how this tract passed from Abraham Soblet jun[r]. to James and there are no extant records of a will or an estate for Abraham; presumably James inherited it from his apparently childless brother Abraham. But not: Without a will made by Abraham, this tract, the only property known to have been owned by Abraham, should have been inherited jointly by his two brothers, Jacques and Pierre Louis. This puzzling fact raises the possibility that the grantor James of 1737 was a son to Abraham, Jr., and not a

---

62   *Ibid.*, 11:439; 12:19, 23, 26.

63   Brock, *op. cit.*, p. 74.

64   *Virginia Magazine*, 11:430.

65   *Ibid.*, 12:31.

66   *Ibid.*, 12:31.

67   *Virginia Magazine*, 12:247-248.

68   *Ibid.*, 12:247.

69   *Ibid.*, 12:250.

70   *Ibid.*, 12:374.

71   *Goochland County, Virginia, Deeds, Wills, Inventories, v. 3*, p. 99.

72   *Virginia Patent Bk. 10*, p. 267.

brother. Abraham, Jr. is shown by the "Liste Générale" of c. 1714 to have had a wife and though he did not long survive, it lies within the range of possibility that he procreated a single son. However, the tithe lists of King William Parish show a single James without a significant break and absolutely no indication of the contemporaneous existence of two Jameses. For this reason, it is assumed that the grantor James of 1737, the testator James of 1741/2, Jacques the clerk of the vestry, and Jacques the son of Abraham Sr. and brother of Abraham Jr. are one and the same.

Jacques Soblet last appears as a tithable in King William Parish in 1738. On 15 May 1739 "Benjamin Harris of the Parish of Saint James'es and County of Goochland" sold to "James Sublett late of the Parish of King William and County aforesaid" 200 acres in St. James Parish on Dithsays Branch, witnesses being John Dupuy, Joseph Scott and Jean Pierre Bilbau.[73]

The will of James Soblet of the County of Goochland and Parish of King William dated 18 May 1741, probated 16 March 1741 [*i.e.*, 1741/42], was witnessed by John Gordon, James (x) Martin, and Jean (x) Martin. He devised "to my dear and loving Son, James Soblet, my Plantation, Land and Negro, when he comes to age, only my dear and loving wife Martha Soblet, to have her upon the aforesaid Plantation and Land (sic), and if my child, James Soblet, should depart this life before he comes of age, my will is that my dear and loving wife should fully, clearly, and absolutely posses negro, land and all my whole and sole estate. My will is my child have learning, and that when he is fit that he be bound to a trade. My will is also, that my son shall chuse his trade." The wife Martha was named executrix.[74] The "Inventorie of the Estate of James Soblet Deceased," appraised 13 July 1742, included a "parcel of ffrench books" valued at 20 shillings and "one wigg."[75]

Issue of Jacques Soblet (the third at least probably by wife Martha ---):

12	i	A son, name unknown, b. say 1712, d. in childhood.[76]
13	ii	A daughter, name unknown, b. say 1714, d. in childhood.[77]
• 14	iii	James Sublett, b. 1729 or later, but before 1736.
		Referred to as a child to be educated in his father's will of 1741/2.

3. Anne Soblet, b. say 1684, married perhaps as early as 1701 to the widower Pierre Chastain. Pierre, "sa femme et cinq enfants" were fellow passengers with Abraham Soblet on the *Mary and Ann* during its transatlantic voyage, April-July 1700.[78] In the Falling Creek Miller's list of February 1700/01, only "Chalaine & 5 children" are listed.[79] Inferentially, then, his first wife had succumbed during their first half year in Virginia. But Byrd's list of 10 Nov. 1701 accounts for "Mr. Peter Chalin, his wife & 3 chil'n."[80] If these three lists are accurate, then Pierre had remarried by the latter date. This would, incidentally, account for the decline in the size of Abraham Soblet's family from 5 children to four over the same period of time, without supposing

73   *Goochland County, Virginia, Deeds, Wills, Inventories, v. 3*, p. 208.

74   *Goochland County, Virginia, Deeds, Wills, Inventories, v. 3*, p. 533-534.

75   *Ibid.*, v. 4, p. 107.

76   Step-Children issue of Elizabeth, relict of Pierre Sabatie, *The Huguenot* #29, p. 137. Addition by Donald J. Sublette, hereafter cited as [DJS].

77   *Ibid.*

78   Virginia Historical Society. *Collections*, new series, v. 6, pp. 65-67.

79   *Ibid.*, n.s., v. 5, p. 27.

80   *Ibid.*, n.s., v. 5, p. 45.

an infant mortality's occurrence. Anne (Soblet) Chastain died 3 April 1723 in King William Parish, survived by Pierre, who married Mrs. Magdelaine (Flournoy) Trabue, daughter of Jacob Flournoy and widow of Antoine Trabue, sometime between 30 Jan. 1723/4 when Trabue was buried[81] and 3 Oct. 1726 when "Magdalene Chastain" returned inventory of Trabue's estate.[82] Pierre Chastain died in the Parish of King William, by then in Goochland County, sometime between 3 Oct. 1728 and 20 Nov. 1728, the dates of the making and probate of his will.[83]

Issue of Pierre Chastain, père, and Anne (Soblet): (Jean the oldest son of Pierre was by his first wife; the eldest daughter Judith may have been the daughter of either the first wife or of Anne.)

i   Susanna Chastain, b. say 1705, named for her maternal grandmother; m. by 1730 to James Robinson, who died in King William Parish sometime in 1748/49.

ii   Pierre Chastain, fils, b. c. 1707; settled in Buckingham County, Virginia.

iii   Mary Chastain, b. say 1709, d. without issue between Nov. 1728 and June 1731.

iv   Elizabeth Chastain, b. say 1711, probably m. c. 1732 to David LeSueur of King William Parish (1704/5-1771/2), son of David and Catherine (Fell) LeSueur of London, England.

v   René Chastain, b. c. 1713, d. 1786 Edgefield District, South Carolina; m. c. 1732/3 Mrs. Judith (Martin) Gevodan, daughter of Jean Martin and widow of Thomas Gevodan.

vi   Janne Chastain, b. c. 1716, d. 12 January 1722/3 in King William Parish.

vii   [Marie] Magdelaine Chastain, b. c. 1720, m. c. 1740 as his second wife Guillaume Salle (c. 1705-c. 1789), son of Abraham and Olive (Perrault) Salle; settled in Buckingham County, Virginia.

4. Abraham Soblet, fils, "le jeune," or "Jun[r]," born say 1694, does not appear with his brothers and father as a separately identified tithable in the list for 1710 for King William Parish, but is presumably accounted for with his father Abraham as one of the latter's two tithables in that year.[84] In the list of tithables for 1711, the two Abrahams are separately listed, but bracketed together with Jacques.[85] The 1712 listing continues that same triple bracketing: Ab. Soblet, père; Jacque Soblet, fils; Ab. Soblet, fils.[86] Completely separate listing of the three occurs in the years succeeding; in 1714 and 1715, "Abra. Soblet, le jeune," is listed, as distinguished from "Abra. Soblet, l'aine."[87] In the "List of Tithables Returned in July 1717," only one Abra. Soblet is listed.[88] Uncertainty exists as to whether the survivor was "père" or "fils," but as pointed out earlier, both were dead before the List for the year 1720 was composed.[89] In the "Liste Générale" of c. 1714 "Abra. Sobler, le jeune" is credited with a wife.[90] On 23 March 1715 [1715/16]

81   *Ibid.*, n.s., v. 5, p. 111.
82   *Henrico County, Virginia, Deeds and Wills, 1725-1737*, p. 59.
83   *Goochland County, Virginia, Deeds, Wills, etc., Bk. 1*, p. 43.
84   Virginia Magazine 11:302.
85   *Ibid.*, 11:431.
86   *Ibid.*, 11:435.
87   *Ibid.*, 12:19, 22.
88   *Ibid.*, 12:26.
89   *Ibid.*, 12:244.
90   Brock, *op. cit.*, p. 74.

Abraham Soblet jun[r] patented "88 acres lying and being in Henrico County on the south side of James River beginning at a stump standing on the river parting Peter David and the said Soblet ... it being part of the first five thousand acres of land surveyed for the french Refugees."[91] This tract was conveyed on 1 Nov. 1737 by "James Soblet of Goochland" to Benjamin Harris, the 1715 patent being referred to. While as pointed out previously, the outside possibility exists that this James was a sole son of Abraham born between the c. 1714 "Liste Générale" (no child of Abraham le jeune is listed there) and the demise of Abraham fils (sometime between 1716 and 1720) (as a grantor in 1737, James would necessarily have been born in 1716 or earlier), it seems much more reasonable to suppose that the grantor James of 1737 was Jacques the brother of Abraham fils, and that Abraham fils died *sine prole*.

6. Peter Sublett, born say 1712, is listed as a son in the "Liste Générale" of c. 1714 of King William Parish. On 23 March 1715 (1715/16) there was patented to "Peter Soblet jun[r] ... a tract containing ninety acres lying and being on the south side of James River in the County of Henrico ... beginning at a corner hickory standing on the river ... It being part of the first five thousand acres surveyed for the french Refugees."[92] It is believed that he was thus provided for by his father, his mother dying early, in advance of his father's second marriage. He is not listed as a tithable until the year 1729, when his father Pierre Louis Soblet is listed with two tithables, the second one not being named.[93] In the List of Tithables of the Parish of King William for the year 1730, he is bracketed with his father, Pierre Soblet and Pierre Soblet, s.[94] A similar bracketing treatment is accorded to him in 1731, 1732, and 1733, Pierre Louy Soblet and Pierre Soblet.[95] In 1735 the two first appear separately, as Louys Soblet and Piter Soblet.[96] They are similarly treated of in 1736, 1737 and 1738, as Pierre Louis Soblet and Pierre Soblet.[97]

On 21 Feb. 1744 Peter Soblet Jun[r] of the County of Goochland sold to Benjamin Harris "one certain tract containing ninety acres ... beginning adjacent to the south side of James River between the two Manakan Creeks being granted to the said Peter Soblet jun[r]. by patent bearing date [23 March 1715].[98] On 24 July 1745 Benjamin Harris of the County of Goochland sold to Peter Soblet of the same county 95 acres on the south side of James River adjacent to the said River Between the Lands of Peter Lewis Soblett and the Lands of Peter fford."[99] On 9 Dec. 1748 Dan[l]. Ford of the Parish of King William and County of Goochland sold to Peter Soblet of the same Parish and County a plantation of 107 acres in the Parish of King William "lying between the lines of the said Peter Soblet and the Lands of Dan[l]. Perro, adjacent to James River."[100] This seems to have ended the acreage acquisitions of Peter in this old Manakin Town area in what ultimately became Powhatan County. He was the only son of Pierre Louis to stay in this old area.

For a while he was the owner of land down in Charlotte County, Virginia, where three of his younger brothers moved, although there is no particular reason to believe that he ever resided

91	*Virginia Patent Bk. 10*, p. 283.
92	*Ibid.*, Bk. 10, p. 283.
93	*Virginia Magazine*, 12:378.
94	*Virginia Magazine*, 12:382.
95	*Ibid.*, 13:67, 70, 75.
96	*Ibid.*, 13:80.
97	*Ibid.*, 13:177, 179-180, 181-182.
98	*Goochland County, Virginia, Deeds, Wills, Inventories, v. 4*, p. 537.
99	*Ibid.*, Deed Bk. 5, p. 113.
100	*Ibid.*, Deed Bk. 5, p. 552.

there. On 5 Nov. 1770 David George of Charlotte County sold 450 acres on Louse Creek in Charlotte to Peter Sublett of Cumberland County, bounded by land of William Sublett.[101] On 16 July 1781 "Peter Sublet Sen[r] of Powhatan County" sold this tract "beginning on William Sublets corner hickory" to Wilson Maddox.[102]

In July 1783 Peter Sublett of Powhatan County attempted to make his last will. "Being Sick and Weak, in his own Dwelling House ..., he did request his friend Anthony Martin to write his the said Peter's Last Will ... with which (the said paper hereto annexed being read to him) he the said Peter Sublett Dec[d] declared himself well satisfyed but departed this life without duly Publishing the same."[103] To carry out his testamentary intention and to "prevent Disputes and Controversies," his heirs on 1 Dec. 1783 entered into Articles of Agreement under which the will was given legal effect, as if validly published. By his theoretically abortive will he gave "to my beloved son Peter Sublett after the death of my wife the Land I live upon containing by estimation 333 acres and three negroes..." Eighteen other negroes he apportioned rather evenly among "my beloved son[s] William Sublett ... John ... Benjamin ... and my beloved Daughter Mary Merraman." "Item, I give unto my grandson Peter Dutoy Sublett one Boy Bob. My will and desire is that my Beloved Wife Elizabeth Sublett should have during her life the use of these negroes, Tom, Isham, Jude, Will and Biddy, and all the land that I hold." Executors were to be the four sons, Peter, William, John and Benjamin.[104]

Issue of Peter and Elizabeth (---) Sublett:

- 15   i   Peter Sublett, b. 1747, d. 1812, Powhatan County, Virginia; m. Martha Smith.
- 16   ii   William Sublett, b. say 1750, d. c. 1794-1796, Powhatan County, Virginia; m. 1788 Betsy Hughes.
- 17   iii   John Sublett, b. say 1755, d. 1815, Warren County, Ohio; m. --- Porter.[105]
- 18   iv   Benjamin Sublett, b. say 1759, d. 1825, Powhatan County, Virginia; m. 1785 Betty Ann Street.
-   19 v   Mary Sublett, m. Francis Merriman.[106]

7. William Sublett, born say 1723, first appeared in the public records when his father Peter Lewis Soblet on 5 Nov. 1754 willed him "one certain tract or parcel of Land whereon I now dwell," and named him an executor of the will.[107] Shortly after the probate of the will on 27 Jan. 1755, "William Soblet of Albemarle County" on 22 September 1755 sold this 133 acres located in the old Parish of King William (at this date in the new county of Cumberland) to his brother Peter, reciting that it was the tract "which was granted unto the said William Soblets father Peter Lewis Soblet by a patent bearing date the 13th day of July 1738 and given to his said son William by his last will."[108] William's young wife Susannah relinquished her right of dower. It is probable that William had been for several years a resident of Albemarle County, presumably in that portion which ultimately became Buckingham County, for he had married Susanna Allen of that

101   *Charlotte County, Virginia, Deed Bk. 2*, p. 352.

102   *Ibid.*, Deed Bk. 5, p. 62.

103   *Powhatan County, Virginia, Deed Bk. 1*, p. 236-237.

104   *Powhatan County, Virginia, Deed Bk. 1*, p. 237-238.

105   John Sublett m. Phoebe Porter [DJS].

106   Mary Sublett m. as his 1st wife Francis Merriman, 17 Jun 1782, Powhatan County [DJS].

107   *Cumberland County, Virginia, Will Bk. 1*, p. 88.

108   *Ibid.*, Deed Bk. 2, p. 245.

county sometime prior to 7 Nov. 1751, when Susanna's father William Allen made his will and mentioned his daughter "Susanna Soblet."[109] William Sublett appears to have continued his residence in Albemarle County into the period when this portion had become Buckingham County (1761) and as a consequence [thanks to the destruction of the Buckingham records] there is no record of any land sale by him in the area. On 4 May 1765 Mattox Mayes of the County of Halifax sold to "William Soblett of the County of Charlotte" 220 acres on the north side of "Turnup Creek" in the newly-formed County of Charlotte.[110] But the order books of Charlotte show that even previously, on 1 April 1765, William Sublet was appointed Surveyor of the Roads in his precinct.[111] He was joined in Charlotte in 1767 by his brother Abraham and by 1780 by his brother Benjamin. In 1770 he sold his tract "on the north side of Stanton River and on the east side of Turnip Creek" to Joseph Fuqua.[112]

"William Subblett" made his will 13 March 1780 and was dead by 7 August 1780 when it was admitted to probate in Charlotte County. His will is disappointingly brief: "I lend and Bequeath to my beloved Wife Susanner Subblett all the living that I now am possessed of during her Life after her decease I order that Lands negroes with whatsoever may Remain be immediately sold and the money equally divided amogst the children." The "children," alas, were not named. Executors were to be John White, Samuel White, and wife "Susanner." Witnesses were John Weatherford, John Holland, and Phillip Sowel. Samuel and John White renounced their executorships and Susanna assumed the task alone, Charles McKenny and John Wheeler being her securities.[113]

The failure to name his children is less disastrous than it might have been, for both his brothers who resided in Charlotte left wills apparently naming their issue exhaustively; the marriage bonds are of some aid; and Susanna, bless her, almost completely dominated the selection of the names of the children of the union, naming them for her parents, brothers and sisters. For this reason, an excursus into her area of the Allen family is not only in order, but absolutely required to reconstruct her issue.

Susanna Allen was born 8 February 1732[114] presumably in Goochland County, Virginia, daughter of William Allen, originally of St. Peter's Parish, New Kent County, Virginia, by his second wife, Mrs. Mary (Hunt) Minge (1695-1763), daughter of William and Tabitha Hunt of Charles City County, Virginia, and widow of Robert Minge, son of Valentine Minge. (After William Allen's death in 1752, his widow Mary (Hunt) married, 3rd, the widower Field Jefferson (1702-1765), after drawing up a prenuptial agreement on 1 Nov. 1753.[115] Field Jefferson was the uncle of President Thomas Jefferson.) Susanna's full brothers and sisters were: Ann Allen (b. 1721); William Hunt Allen (b. 1724), John Hunt Allen (1726-1754), Valentine Allen (1730-1799), George Hunt Allen (1734-1778), Mary Allen (b. 1738), and Philip Allen (1740-1763). (In addition, Susanna had brothers and sisters of the half-blood on both the Allen and Hunt-Minge sides, though none on the Hunt-Jefferson side.)

Issue of William and Susanna (Allen) Sublett:

---

109   *Albemarle County, Virginia, Wills and Deeds No. 1, 1748-1752*, pp. 33-36.

110   *Charlotte County, Virginia, Deed Bk. 1*, p. 56.

111   *Ibid.*, Order Bk. 1, p. 8.

112   *Ibid.*, Deed Bk. 2, p. 284.

113   *Charlotte County, Virginia, Will Bk. 1*, p. 224.

114   Allen Family Bible, *William and Mary College Quarterly*, 1:22:194-196 (1914). This Bible was owned in 1914 by William Archer Chambers of Richmond Virginia. Does anyone know its present whereabouts?

115   *Tyler's Quarterly Magazine*, 10:174-176; Tyler's, 7:119-124; Tyler's, 2:113-114.

- 20   i   Martha Sublett, b. say 1752, d. post Nov. 1829, Pittsylvania County, Virginia; m. the Rev. John Weatherford; named for her paternal grandmother.
- 21   ii   Valentine Sublett, b. say 1754, d. 1808, Green County, Kentucky; m. 1782 Mrs. Margaret (Caldwell) Brent; named for his uncle Valentine Allen.
- 22   iii   Mary Hunt Sublett, b. say 1756, d. post 1810; to Lincoln County, Kentucky; m. 1782 John Dudgeon; named for her maternal grandmother.
- 23   iv   Ursula Sublett, b. say 1758, via Lincoln County and Green County, Kentucky, to Illinois; m. 1778 Edward Day.
- 24   v   Celia Sublett, b. c. 1760; m. 1782 her first cousin Abraham Sublett, Jr. (#36; see him for issue); migrated to Lincoln County, Kentucky.
- 25   vi   George Allen Sublett, b. say 1762; m. 1791 Isabella Akin; to Lincoln County, Kentucky; named for his uncle George Hunt Allen.
- 26   vii   William Allen Sublett, b. say 1764; m. 1787 Sally Akin; d. 1839 Rutherford County, Tennessee; named for his uncle William Hunt Allen; for his maternal grandfather William Allen, and, of course, for his own father.
- 27   viii   Susanna Sublett, b. say 1766; m. 1781 Jesse Lowe; to Lincoln County, Kentucky; named for her mother, and her mother's aunt, Susanna (Allen) Burton.
- 28   ix   Nancy Sublett, b. 1768; m. 1785 Bartlee Greenwood; to Lincoln County, Kentucky; named for her aunt Nancy Ann (Arnold) Allen.
- 29   x   Abraham Sublett, b. say 1770; m. 1790 Polly Smith; to Green County, Kentucky; named for his uncle Abraham Sublett.
- 30   xi   Philip Allen Sublett, b. say 1774, d. 1820; via Lincoln County and Pulaski County, Kentucky, to St. Charles County, Missouri; m. 1797 Isabella Whitley; named for his uncle Philip Allen.
- 31   xii   Field Sublett, b. say 1776; to Green County, Kentucky; named for his Grandmother Allen's third husband, Field Jefferson.

Following William Sublett's death in 1780, his widow Susanna (Allen) married a widower, Perrin Allday (Alday), presumably a descendant of the Perrins and Alldays of Henrico County, Virginia.[116] They were certainly married by 6 Oct. 1784 when "Perrin Allday and Susanna his wife Executors of William Sublet decd," brought a suit against George Pattillo for nonperformance of a contract with "Plaintifs Testator."[117] Chances are they were married somewhat earlier, by 6 May 1782 when Perrin Allday served as security for the executors of Abraham Sublet.[118] Susanna (Allen) (Sublett) Allday died sometime between 17 Oct. 1803 (when "Perrin Alday and Susannah his wife" conveyed 86 acres to John White)[119] and 24 July 1805 when Perrin Allday and Anne B. Tankersley (widow) were bonded to marry.[120] Anne Johnston, widow, had previously married John Tankersley (date of bond) 7 July 1783.[121] Perrin Allday's will, dated 10 Oct. 1813, was probated 6 Dec. 1813 in Charlotte County.[122]

---

116   The will of Anne Perrin, dated 6 Jan. 1711/12 probated 3 March 1711/12, Henrico County, Virginia, Miscellaneous Court Records [Deeds, Wills, Etc.], 1650-1807, vol. 1 [1650-1717], p. 205, mentions daughter "Elesebeth Allday."

117   *Charlotte County, Virginia, Order Bk. 5*, p. 221.

118   *Ibid.*, Will Bk. 1, pp. 236-237.

119   *Ibid.*, Deed Bk. 10, p. 57.

120   *Ibid.*, Marriage Bonds, 1765-1863 (typescript), Genealogical Society of Utah, 1937.

121   *Ibid.*

122   *Charlotte County, Virginia, Will Bk. 3*, p. 243.

8. Abraham Sublett was born say 1726 and is first mentioned in the will of his father, Peter Lewis Soblet, dated 5 Nov. 1754, probated 27 Jan. 1755, by which he was given "a negro man Prymus."[123] He must have been married by about 1751 to Elizabeth ---, surname unknown. He appears to have followed the lead of his brother William into old Albemarle County (the portion subsequently Buckingham) and again to have followed William shortly after the latter relocated in Charlotte County, Virginia, for on 5 Jan. 1767 Robert Weakly of Halifax County, Virginia, sold 190 acres on Cubb Creek in Charlotte to Abraham Sublet of Buckingham County.[124] On 6 May 1776 Abraham Sublet was appointed surveyor of the roads in his precinct.[125]

"Abraham Sublet S[r] of the County of Charlotte and Parish of Cornwall" by his will dated 13 June 1781, probated 6 May 1782, left to his wife Elizabeth "during her Natural life the Land whereon I now live, all my slaves, stock of every kind, household furniture and plantation tools. Item — I desire that at the marriage of my children that my wife may assist them in housekeeping to such necessaries as she may think proper or can best spare ... Item. I desire at the death of my above mentioned wife that all my Estate personal and real with the lands whereon Edward Ayres and William Sublet now live may be appraised and equally divided amongst my children, to wit, Martha, William, Abram, Sarah, Elizabeth, Jean and Nancy." Executors were to be his widow, trusty friend Edward Ayres, William Soblet and Abram Soblet Jun[r]. Witnesses were Joseph Holt and William Kersey.[126] The inventory of his estate made 2 Sept. 1782 included seven negroes.[127] Abraham Sublet was last listed for taxes in Charlotte in 1782 as the owner of seven slaves, four horses and eighteen cattle.[128] The following year his widow Elizabeth Sublet is listed with seven slaves (including Primus, presumably the same slave Abraham had inherited from his father Peter Lewis Soblet), two horses and fourteen cattle.[129] On 2 April 1792 Elizabeth Sublett appeared before the county court and successfully requested that her negroes Primus and Lucy be exempt from payment of levies and taxes in future "for reasons appearing to the Court."[130] (The connection of the negro slave Prymus with this family can be traced from his birth: "On the 15 Xber 1732 was born a black to Pierre Louis Soblet, his name is Prymus."[131] He was willed by P. L. Soblet to his son Abraham in 1754/5; and by Abraham to his widow Elizabeth, in 1781-1782.) Elizabeth Sublet is listed for taxes in every year from 1783 through the year 1805. Her death apparently occurred during the course of the year 1805, for on 7 Dec. 1805 the heirs of Abraham Sublett decd. disposed of his real estate in accordance with the terms of his will, which provided same should be held intact until the death of his widow.[132]

Issue of Abraham and Elizabeth (---) Sublett:

34   i   Martha Sublett, born say 1752; d. without issue between 1781 and 1805.
•   35   ii   William Sublett, born say 1754, m. Susannah ---;[133] died in 1811 or 1812;

123   *Cumberland County, Virginia, Will Bk. 1*, p. 88.
124   *Charlotte County, Virginia, Deed Bk. 1*, p. 230.
125   *Ibid.*, Order Bk. 4, p. 80.
126   *Charlotte County, Virginia, Will Bk. 1*, pp. 236-237.
127   *Ibid.*, Will Bk. 1, pp. 304-306.
128   *Ibid.*, Personal Property Tax, 1782, p. 1.
129   *Ibid.*, 1783, p. 4.
130   *Ibid.*, Order Bk.
131   Brock, *op. cit.*, p. 88.
132   *Charlotte County, Virginia, Deed Bk. 10*, pp. 184-185.
133   William Sublett m. Susannah Keirsey [DJS].

                    remained in Charlotte County, Virginia.

- 36   iii   Abraham Sublett, Jr., born c. 1756; m. 1782 his first cousin Celia (Selah) Sublett (#24); settled in Lincoln County, Kentucky; d. there in 1844.

    37   iv   Sarah Sublett, b. say 1758; m. --- Pugh; d. between 1781 and 1805 in Charlotte County, Virginia, leaving an only son:
   1. Abraham S. Pugh, m. 21 Dec. 1803 in Charlotte County, Virginia, to Anna Tottey, his uncle Caldwell Wood being surety.[134]

- 38   v   Elizabeth Sublett, b. c. 1760, m. 1781 Campbell Daniel. d. 1841 Nelson County, Virginia.

- 39   vi   Jane (Jean) Sublett, b. say 1764, m. 1782 Edward Eanes; settled in Pittsylvania County, Virginia.

- 40   vii   Nancy Sublett, b. c. 1770, m. 1785,[135] Caldwell Wood; settled in Lincoln County, Kentucky.

9. Lewis Sublett, born 9 April 1728, was baptized that date as "Louis Soblet," godparents being Jean Martain, Jacob Trabue and Marie Martain.[136] He served himself as godfather (he is denominated "Louy Soblet Jr.") to the infant Marie Brian, born 15 May 1746, daughter of Jacques Brian.[137] Lewis Sublett was willed 385 acres on Lower Manakin Creek in Chesterfield by his father Pierre Louis Soblet by his will of 5 Nov. 1754, proved 27 Jan. 1755.[138] Part of this tract (124 acres) he sold on 7 April 1758 to his wife's relative Edward Hill;[139] 84 acres he sold the same day to John Bransford;[140] and 103 acres the same day to James Harris.[141] All three deeds refer to the patent of 5 June 1746 to Peter Lewis Soblet. In the meantime, he had bought 200 acres in the Parish of Dale and County of Chesterfield from Edward Hill, 4 March 1758.[142]

    While most of the printed works have referred to Lewis Sublett's wife as Frances McGruder, it is quite certain that she was Frances Hill.[143] The error seems to have arisen from the fact that Lewis Sublett, Jr., (#42) named a daughter Frances McGruder, and someone, jumping to conclusions, assumed she was named for Lewis, Jr's mother. She was named rather for Lewis Jr's sister, Mrs. Frances (Sublett) McGruder (#47). While the published version of *The Douglas Register* refers to Lewis Sublett's wife as Frances <u>Hillason</u> [the sole entry: Lewis Sublet & Frances Hillason a son named Abraham born 28 May 1763, bp. Jul:24, 1763][144] an examination of the photostat of the original *Douglas Register* in the Virginia State Library shows that the transcriber ran "a son" into her maiden name Hill as one word and then repeated the "a son" to show relationship.[145] Frances (Hill) Sublett's son Littlebury Sublett named a son Hill Sublett, which serves to confirm the maiden name identification of *The Douglas Register*.

---

134   Nancy Sublett m. 1788 [DJS].

135   Nancy Sublett m. 1788 [DJS].

136   Brock, *op. cit.*, p. 80. (Manakin Town Register).

137   *Ibid.*, p. 107.

138   *Cumberland County, Virginia, Will Bk. 1*, p. 88.

139   *Ibid.*, Deed Bk. 3, p. 238.

140   *Ibid.*, Deed Bk. 3, p. 245.

141   *Ibid.*, Deed Bk. 3, p. 247.

142   *Chesterfield County, Virginia, Deed Bk. 3*, p. 240.

143   For example, the McGruder error appears in Dupuy, *op. cit.*, p. 263; Railey, *op. cit.*, p. 45; Nunis, *op. cit.*, 57:21; and Erma Jett Darnell, *Forks of Elkhorn Church*, Frankfort, Kentucky, 1946, p. 289.

144   W. Mac Jones, *The Douglas Register*.

145   *The Douglas Register*, p. 65 (photostatic copy of the original, Virginia State Library).

Presumably it was the "grey" [horse] of this "Lewis Sublet" and not of his son Lewis which was pressed into service by "Henry Morriss by order Genl. Muhlenberg" in April 1781, for which he was allowed £45.[146]

Lewis Sublett lived out his life in Chesterfield County, and made his will there 18 Jan. 1802. He was dead before 20 Dec. 1802 when sales were made by the estate.[147] His will refers to his unnamed wife; "I confirm to the Heirs of my son Littleberry Sublett deceased a negroe boy named Primus which he had in his possession in his lifetime; I give to my son Lewis Sublett of the State of Kentucky and his Heirs all the Lands to which I am entitled in that state ..." There were further bequests and devises "to my son Abraham Sublett; to my son Arthur Sublett; to my daughter Frances McGruder; and to my son William Sublett." Executors were to be his sons Abram, Arthur and William Sublett and Isaac Salle.[148]

Issue of Lewis and Frances (Hill) Sublett:

- 41   i   Littlebury Sublett, b. say 1757, d. 1800, Green County, Kentucky; m. Sarah Burton.
- 42   ii   Lewis Sublett, b. 1759, d. 1830, Woodford County, Kentucky; m. (1st) 1779 Mary Trabue; m. (2nd) c. 1794 Sarah Samuel.
- 43   iii James Sublett, b. c. 1761, d. 1781 as a prisoner of the British in the Revolution.
- 44   iv   Abraham Sublett, b. 1763, d. 1820 Chesterfield County, Virginia; m. Edith Burton.
- 45   v   Arthur Sublett, b. say 1766, d. 1834 Powhatan County, Virginia; m. 1797 Mrs. Betsy (Hughes) Sublett.
- 46   vi   William Sublett, b. say 1768, d. 1839, Chesterfield County, Virginia; m. 1800 Mrs. Mary (Forsee) Sublett.
- 47   vii Frances Sublett, b. say 1771, m. 1792 Zepheniah McGruder, Chesterfield County, Virginia.

11.   Benjamin Sublett was born 23 April 1733 and was baptized as "Bainjamain Soblet" with godfathers being "Gedeon Chanbon and Wollter Stot" and godmother being Anne David.[149] To his youngest son, Pierre Louis Soblet by his will dated 5 Nov. 1754, probated 27 Jan. 1755, gave "my horse, bridel and saddell and all my waring cloaths, and more I doe appoint and order my executors to pay all the debts that my son Benjamin owes at this day, to paid (sic) out of my movebel estate."[150]

Benjamin Sublet was married to Elizabeth Jordan 24 June 1762 by Parson Douglas.[151] Elizabeth was the daughter of Charles and Hellenah (---) Jordan. He stayed on for some years in old King William Parish where most of his chidren were born. The last family baptism recorded there was of his son Samuel who was baptized 31 Mar. 1777.[152] Some time thereafter and before

---

146   Chesterfield County, Virginia, Public Service Claims: Court Booklet, p. 54, Virginia State Library.
147   *Chesterfield County, Virginia, Will Bk. 6*, pp. 250-252.
148   *Ibid.*, pp. 1-3.
149   Brock, *op. cit.*, p. 88.
150   *Cumberland County, Virginia, Will Bk. 1*, p. 88.
151   W. Mac Jones, *op. cit.*, p. 45.
152   *Ibid.*, p. 300.

another child could be baptized apparently (unless the prevailing Virginia disaffection with the Anglican Church was already materializing in this portion of the Sublett family), he had moved to join his brothers William and Abraham in Charlotte County, Virginia, where on 1 March 1780 his brother-in-law Charles Jordan sold him 150 acres on the Middle Fork of Cub Creek; both men are described as "of Charlotte County"[153] This same tract he sold on 13 March 1806 to John Bibb,[154] preparatory to his migration with his family to Kentucky. If this is the Benjamin of Revolutionary service, it would seem that his Revolutionary service was performed from his old home in King William Parish, and after discharge from the Continental Army on 8 Dec. 1779, he followed the typical veteran's pattern of moving on shortly to greener pastures; it will be noted that his first purchase recorded in Charlotte was made on 1 March 1780.

He and his sons Benjamin Branch and Samuel are all last listed for taxes in Charlotte County, Virginia, in 1806;[155] by 1807 they had left Virginia. Benjamin's eldest son Charles Jordan Sublett had preceded them; he is last listed for taxes in Charlotte County in 1803. As early as 15 July 1799 Charles J. Sublett had received a land grant of 200 acres on the Barren River in Warren County, Kentucky,[156] but seems to have delayed his removal thence. The only son of Benjamin who failed to join in this migration was his youngest, Matthew, relatively a newly-wed at this time. On 30 May 1814 Benjamin Sublett, Sr., of Warren County, Kentucky, deeded to his son Mathew Sublet of Charlotte County, Virginia, a negro "now at John Fares of Campbell County, Virginia."[157] Charles J. Sublet served as a witness. On 19 May 1815 Benjamin Sublett, Sr., of Warren conveyed to his son Benjamin B. Sublett "for natural love ... 183 acres ... where I now live, he to pay the balance due Michael Finley on the land."[158] William E. Sublett witnessed the deed. By his will dated 19 Sept. 1809, probated Feb. 1816, Benjamin Sublett gave one negro each to his children, Charlye J., Benjamin, Samuel, Usley Porter, Marthew, Martha Garland, Mary Sublett, and Elizabeth (no last name given for the last). "My daughter Sally Fore" was given "one dollar and no more." Executors named were sons Charlye J., Benjamin and Samuel. Witnesses were Peter Tylor, John Hines and Ezra Bostick.[159]

A Benjamin Sublett (Sublit) served as a Corporal in the 5th, 11th and 15th Virginia Regiments, Continental Line, during the Revolution.[160] Benjamin Sublett received Continental Line Warrant No. 899, Military District of Ohio, for three years' service during the Revolution as a Sergeant.[161] The D.A.R. has accepted (#11) Benjamin as the Benjamin with this Revolutionary service, and has caused his grave in Warren County, Kentucky, to be marked with a government stone proclaiming that fact, though it is clear that there was a second Benjamin Sublett in Virginia of an age well suited to military service in that conflict (#18). On the basis of the extant public documents alone, the contributor cannot see any particularly good reason for selecting one Benjamin over the other to identify with the Revolutionary soldier. Both are known to have had early realty interests in Kentucky. On 20 June 1782 Benjamin Sublett entered 1,178 and 2/3rds acres on "Stinking Creek," then in Lincoln County, Kentucky.[162] The same day, 20 June 1782,

153   *Charlotte County, Virginia, Deed Bk. 4*, p. 211.

154   *Ibid.*, Deed Bk. 11, p. 18.

155   Charlotte County, Virginia, Personal Property Tax Books, 1782-1815.

156   Willard R. Jillson, *The Kentucky Land Grants* [Filson Club Pub. No. 33] Louisville, 1925, p. 418.

157   *Warren County, Kentucky, Deed Bk. F6*, p. 294 (as abstracted in Kentucky Hist. Soc.).

158   *Ibid.*, Deed Bk. G7, p. 42 (as abstracted in typescript in the Kentucky Historical Society, Frankfort).

159   *Ibid.*, Will Bk. B, p. 92.

160   John H. Gwathmey, *Historical Register of Virginians in the Revolution*. Richmond, Dietz, 1938.

161   Gaius Marcus Brumbaugh, *Revolutionry War Records*, vol. 1; Virginia.

162   *Lincoln County Entries, Bk. 1*, p. 276, abstracted in Willard Rouse Jillson, *Old Kentucky Entries and Deeds* [Filson Club

Benjamin Sublett entered 2,000 acres on Skaggs Creek in Lincoln County.[163] This entry was amended on 26 March 1785.[164] On 20 June 1783 Benjamin Sublett received Military Warrant No. 899 for 200 acres, for "3 years as a Sgt. in the Virginia line."[165] On 6 Nov. 1797 Benjamin Sublett was granted 1,178 acres in Lincoln County on the Cumberland River.[166] On 18 March 1800 Benjamin Sublett, a <u>resident of Powhatan County, Virginia</u>, deeded away <u>1,128 and</u> $^2/_3$rds acres on the Cumberland River.[167] This last record definitely refers to Benjamin's (#11) nephew Benjamin (#18) of Powhatan County, and might conceivably tip the scales in favor of Benjamin (#18) as being the Revolutionary corporal and sergeant.

A study of a couple of the men who served in the same company as Benjamin is inconclusive, as there is no correlation between their geography and either of the two Benjamins. Capt. James Gray, the company commander, on 5 July 1777 was noted as "on furlough to Southampton County" of which he was therefore inferentially a resident.[168] The Revolutionary Pension Application of Sublett's comrade John Barker shows that he enlisted from Sussex County, Virginia, although he was married in Prince George County.[169]

However, in spite of the inconclusiveness of the public records, there is every indication from sources of family tradition that the Revolutionary soldier was Benjamin (#11). A county history remarks of this Benjamin that he "was a Revolutionary soldier."[170] Several of the branches handed it down by word of mouth that Benjamin served in the Revolution and one tradition was specific enough concerning Benjamin (#11) to say that he had served at Valley Forge.[171] Besides tradition, the greater age and maturity of Benjamin (#11) would in this era perhaps have made him a likelier man to serve as a non-commissioned officer than the considerably younger nephew of the same name. Further, as we have noted, there is a quite interesting correlation between the date of the discharge of the soldier, and Benjamin's (#11) removal from King William Parish to Charlotte County.

Accepting, therefore, Benjamin (#11) as the man with the Revolutionary service, Benjamin Sublett (Sublet, Sublit, Sublitt) is first listed as a private in June 1777 in Capt. James Gray's County, 15th Virginia Regiment of Foot commanded by Lt. Col. James Innes, although subsequent muster rolls show that he had enlisted for a term of three years on 6 Dec. 1776. By July 1777 he was a corporal. In Sept. 1777 he was noted "sick in hospital"; in October, as "absent"; in November and December as "sick — absent." The monthly Muster Rolls of March, April, May and June 1778 are dated at Valley Forge, the company then being commanded by Maj. Gustavus B. Wallace. The May 1778 Muster shows that he was sick again, though present at Valley Forge. By June 1778 the company had returned to the command of Capt. James Gray. Gray's company in a regiment subsequently commanded variously by Daniel Morgan and Col.

Publication No. 34] Louisville, 1926, p. 65.

163   *Lincoln County Entries, Bk. 1*, abstracted in Willard Rouse Jillson, *Old Kentucky Entries and Deeds* [Filson Club Publication No. 34] Louisville, 1926, p. 65.

164   *Ibid.*, Bk. 2, p. 200, abstracted in *Ibid.*, p. 65.

165   [Kentucky] Military Warrants, abstracted in *Ibid.*, p. 363.

166   Old Kentucky Grants, Bk. 10, p. 128, abstracted in Jillson, The Kentucky Land Grants, p. 241.

167   Kentucky Court of Appeals Deeds, Bk. E, p. 62, abstracted in Jillson, Old Kentucky Entries and Deeds, p. 532.

168   Revolutionary War Military Service File: James Gray, Capt. 5 and 11 Virginia Regt., National Archives, Washington, D.C.

169   John Barker, Revolutionary Pension Application W 8340, National Archives, abstracted in John Frederick Dorman, comp., *Virginia Revolutionary Pension Applications*, v. 4, Washington, D. C., 1960.

170   James Battle *et. al.*, *History of Kentucky*, 1885, p. 160.

171   Richard A. Sublett (#3247) so informed W. W. Moon, husband of Sophronia (Sublett) Moon (#389).

Abraham Buford, was at White Plains in August 1778, at Newark in Sept. 1778, at Pompton in October and November 1778, at Middlebrook from December 1778 through April 1779. In May 1779 he was transferred to Major Stephenson's Company of the 5th and 11th Virginia Regiment of Foot commanded by Col. William Russell. The company was at Smith's Clove in May-June 1779, at Ramapough in July, at Smith's Clove in August, at Ramapough in September, at Haverstraw in October, and at Camp Morristown in November, with the notation on 9 Dec. 1779 that "Sublit" had been "dischg'd."[172] The full muster roll of the company on 30 Nov. 1778 shows that James Gray was Captain, Samuel Jones Lt., and Thomas Davis, Ensign.[173] His discharge papers show that "Benjamin Sublett a soldier in the eleventh Virginia Ridgment has faithfully served the time for which he Enlisted and is hereby Discharged from any further Duty in the said Ridgment given under my hand this eighth Day of December [1779] Ja^s. Wood Col^o. Comd^r. 1 Virg^a. Brigade." Attached thereto is a certificate that "Benjamin Sublett Inlisted with me as Sargent in the Continental Army the sixth Day of December [1776] James Harris Cap. June 14, 1783."[174] On that day 14 June 1783 a certificate was issued at the auditors office of Virginia to "Benjamin Sublett Sergt. Inf." for the sum of £ 54.4.5, received by himself.[175]

His comrade Barker's pension application pens a clearer picture of the geography of his Revolutionay service. Barker declared that "he enlisted in 1776 or 1777 for three years in Capt. James Gray's Company in Sussex County, Virginia, ... They marched to Williamsburg where they rendezvoused and were stationed a short time and then to Dumfries where they were innoculated for the small pox, and remained about a month. They then marched to Baltimore and from there sailed to Philadelphia. He immediately marched to New Jersey and joined the army of Gen. Washington at Middlebrook. The regiment was attached to the brigade of Gen. Woodford. He was at the erecting of the fort or garrison on North River above New York. He marched for South Carolina through Philadelphia (where he remained a short time and, the winter being cold, drew some clothing) and Petersburg, where his term of enlistment expired and he was discharged. He was at the storming and taking of Stony Point." Presumably Sublett was in on all this activity, except the march to South Carolina, his term having expired prior to this.[176]

Issue of Benjamin and Elizabeth (Jordan) Sublett:

48	i	Sarah Sublett, b. 26 Dec. 1763; bp. 22 Jan. 1764;[177] m. 27 March 1782 John Fore.[178]
• 49	ii	Charles Jordan Sublett, named for his maternal grandfather; sometimes called Jordan and sometimes known as Charles; b. 31 July 1766; bp. 3 Sept. 1766;[179] m. 1 Jan. 1789 Polly Davis, daughter of Temple Davis;[180] resided in Butler County and Warren County, Kentucky; d. Warren County.
• 50	iii	Ursula (Ursley, Usley) Sublett; b. 24 Mar. 1769; bp. 21 May 1769;[181] m. (1st) 7

172   Revolutionary War Military Service File: Benjamin Sublett, 5 and 11 Virginia Regt., Pvt. and Cpl., National Archives.

173   W. T. R. Saffell, *Records of the Revolutionary War*, New York, Pudney and Russell, 1858, p. 266.

174   Revolutionary War Bounty Warrant File, Virginia State Library: "Sublett, Benjamin (Sgt.)."

175   Volume "War 4," p. 342, Virginia State Library, Richmond.

176   John Barker, R.P.A. W 8340, National Archives, abstracted in Dorman, *op. cit.*, v. 4, pp. 70-71.

177   Jones, *op. cit.*, p. 300, checked in the *Douglas Register*, photostats of the original in the Virginia State Library, p. 66.

178   Catherine L. Knorr, *Marriages ... of Charlotte County, Virginia*, p. 28.

179   Jones, *op. cit.*, p. 300; checked in *Douglas Reg.*, orig., p. 75.

180   Knorr, *op. cit.*, Charlotte County, Virginia, p. 80.

181   Jones, *op. cit.*, p. 300; checked in *Douglas Reg.*, orig., p. 54.

April 1788 Joel Ferguson;[182] m. (2d) 19 Aug. 1790 Samuel Porter; settled in Wythe County, Virginia.

51   iv   Elizabeth Sublett, b. 14 Oct. 1771; bp 21 Dec. 1771;[183] and apparently again bp. 28 May 1775;[184] m. 22 Dec. 1790 Warner Hewitt.[185]

• 52   v   Benjamin Branch Sublett, b. 29 Mar. 1774; bp. 1 June 1774;[186] m. (date of bond) 8 Nov. 1797 Mary Akin, daughter of Joseph Akin;[187] migated via Warren County, Kentucky, to Jackson County, Alabama.

• 53   vi   Samuel Sublett, b. 29 Aug. 1776; bp. 31 Mar. 1777;[188] m. (1st) as "Samuel Subley" (date of bond) 22 Aug. 1799 Fanny Taylor, daughter of Charles Taylor;[189] m. (2d) 8 Nov. 1810 Mary Sumpter. Resided in Warren County, Kentucky.

• 54   vii   Matthew Sublett, b. c. 1781, m. (date of bond) 18 Feb. 1803 Frances Key;[190] moved to Giles County, Virginia.

55   viii   Martha Sublett, b. say 1784, m. 5 Oct. 1805 David Garland.[191] This couple is said to have moved to Lunenburg County, Virginia, where he served as sheriff.

56   ix   Mary Scott Sublett, b. 12 Feb. 1788; d. 8 April 1862 Jackson County, Alabama. Married her cousin William Sublett (#235 *q.v.*)

14.   James Sublett, b. between 1729 and 1736, was referred to as a child to be educated in his father's will of 1741/2. "Renne Chasteen Guardian of James Soblet" on 13 Feb. 1750 filed his guardian's account in the court of Albemarle County, Virginia, as follows:

> *April the 2ᵈ day 1748 My account against James Soblet to the Doctors charge for the cure of his negro and for the child's maintenance 1750 — for the child's maintenance ... for three years schooling.[192]*

Absent any further guardian's accounts, James, Jr., presumably achieved his majority shortly after this. He certainly had become an adult by 23 May 1757 when as "James Sublett of Albemarle County" he sold to Stephen Pankey of Chesterfield County the 200 acres his father had bought from Benjamin Harris in 1738 ("being part of a tract granted by patent unto Benjamin Harris").[193] On 10 May 1759 William Salle Juʳ. of Albemarle County sold 300 acres on Joshuas Creek to James Sublet of the same county.[194] This James Sublet is certainly the James Sublet who appears as a taxpayer in old Albemrle's southern half, Buckingham County, in 1782, with two

182   Knorr, *op. cit.*, Charlotte County, Virginia, p. 27.

183   Jones, *op. cit.*, p. 300; checked in *Douglas Reg.*, orig., p. 91.

184   Jones, *op. cit.*, p. 300, checked in *Douglas Reg.*, orig., p. 98.

185   Knorr, *op. cit.*, Charlotte County, Virginia, p. 41.

186   Jones, *op. cit.*, p. 300; checked in *Douglas Reg.*, orig., p. 69.

187   William Wade Hinshaw, ed., *Encyclopedia of American Quaker Genealogy, v. 6*: Virginia, p. 857 (Campbell County, Virginia, Marriage Bonds), Ann Arbor, 1950.

188   Jones, *op. cit.*, p. 300; checked in *Douglas Reg.*, orig., p. 101.

189   Hinshaw, *op. cit.*, p. 857.

190   *Ibid.*, p. 857.

191   Knorr, *op. cit., Charlotte County, Virginia*, p. 31.

192   *Albemarle County, Virginia, Wills and Deeds, vol. 1*, p. 18.

193   *Cumberland County, Virginia, Deed Bk. 2*, p. 407.

194   *Albemarle County, Virginia, Deed Bk. 2*, p. 108.

polls and no slave.[195] The William Sublet who appears with him in Buckingham in 1782 is presumably a son. The second poll listed under James' name is in all probability his son James, Jr. By 1783 the three had disappeared from the tax rolls of Buckingham. They moved to Henry County, into that portion which in 1791 became Patrick County. There on 23 August 1793 "Arch[s]. Hughes of the County of Patrick sold to James and William Sublet of the County aforesaid" a 304 acre tract lyng on Green Creek.[196]

Issue of James Sublett, name of wife unknown:

- 61   i   William Sublett, b. say 1760 in Albemarle County, Virginia; served in the Virginia militia in 1784 or before; m. (1st) c. 1783 probably in Buckingham County, Virginia, to Ruth Ford; settled in Henry, later Patrick County, Virginia; migrated from there to Madison County and Gerrard County, Kentucky, where he m. (2d) 1806 Mrs. Nancy Harris.

  62   ii   James Sublett, Jr. (possibly), b. say 1763 in Buckingham County, Virginia; settled in Henry, later Patrick County, Virginia. On 13 May 1784 a warrant for £ 8.5.4 was issued to James Sublett for service in the militia.[197] This entry could refer either to this James or to his father. It cannot refer to James Sublett (#43) for he had died in 1781, and there is no notation of payment to an heir. A descendant of Daniel Sublett believed Daniel (#506) to be the son of "James Sublett by his wife Elizabeth Ford, from Henry County, Virginia" but other sources indicate that Daniel was the son of William (#61) by his wife Ruth Ford, so that this appears to be a case of jumbled memories.[198] Nothing further is known of this James, if indeed in fact he existed.

  63   iii   Frances (Frankey) Sublett, m. 16 March 1792 in Patrick County, Virginia, to John Ward. Their marriage bond states that she was the daughter of James Sublett; William Sublett was security.[199]

  64   iv   Martha (Patty or Patsy) Sublett, named for her paternal grandmother; m. 15 April 1797 in Patrick County, Virginia, to James Innis (Ennis).[200] The couple apparently migated to Kentucky, for on 1 June 1812 "James Innis of the State of Kentucky" sold two tracts containing 50 acres each to Thomas Dix of the County of Henry and James Calquhoun of the County of Pittsylvania.[201]

15. Peter Sublett, born in the year 1747, was married (date of bond) on 27 Nov. 1777 in Powhatan County, Virginia, to Martha Smith, his surety being his brother William.[202] Martha, the daughter of Thomas and Magdalen (Trabue) Smith, was born 10 Sept. 1759 and died in January

---

195   Augusta B. Fothergill and John Mark Naugle, *Virginia Taxpayers. 1782-1787, Other Than Those Published by the U. S. Census Bureau.* 1940.

196   Patrick County, *Virginia, Deed Bk. 1*, p. 135.

197   Virginia State Library, *Auditor's Account Bk., 1783-1784*, v. XVIII, p. 653.

198   Indiana Mounds Chapter D.A.R., Kentucky, *Wills and Bible Records*, 1948, p. 5, typescript at the National D.A.R. Library, Washington, D.C.

199   *Patrick County, Virginia, Marriage Register, 1791-1853*, p. 3, a compilation from the county marriage bonds at Virginia State Library.

200   *Ibid.*, p. 16.

201   Patrick County, Virginia, Deed Bk. 3, p. 571.

202   Catherine L. Knorr, *Marriage Bonds and Ministers' Returns of Powhatan County, Virginia, 1777-1830.* Pine Bluff, Arkansas, 1957, p. 63.

1835.[203] Probably it was this "Peter Sublit," rather than his father, who furnished the Revolutionary forces "34 ½ bu. of wheat" on 16 Feb. 1781;[204] and "4 bu. corn, 40 bu. fodder" on 7 Sept. 1781; "675 lb. grass beef" on 18 Oct. 1781, and "100 bu. wheat" on 21 Dec. 1781.[205] On 13 Dec. 1788, Peter, apparently thoroughly imbued with Jeffersonian principles and motivated doubtless by religious impulses as well, recorded an interesting deed, stating that "I believe That all men are by nature equally free and independent and therefore from a clear conviction of the injustice and criminality of depriving my Fellow Creatures of their natural and dearest Right, do hereby emancipate or set free the following Men, Women and Children." Six slaves were given their freedom that very Christmas, and the nine remaining slaves were emancipated on a staggered schedule, up to the year 1802, Christmas Day in each case being the day selected for this noblest of all human gifts.[206] Peter, it seems, while a Jeffersonian, was an early-day gradualist. He died 17 Sept. 1812 in Powhatan.[207]

Issue of Peter and Martha (Smith) Sublett, all born in Powhatan County; dates of births and deaths from the family Bible:[208]

70   i   Elizabeth S. (Betsy) Sublett, b. 6 Sept. 1778, d. 17 Sept. 1813; m. (date of bond) 25 Oct. 1799 Robert Wren.[209] Five children are listed in Sublett's *A Partial History*.

71   ii   Mary Magdalen Sublett, b. 5 Oct. 1780, d. 4 Oct. 1812; m. (date of bond) 22 Feb. 1802 Josiah Ellet;[210] six children.

72   iii   Peter Sublett, b. 16 May 1784; d. 18 Oct. 1851; m. (date of bond) 12 Oct. 1808, Anne P. Baker, dau. of Thos.[211] Eleven children.

73   iv   Thomas Smith Sublett, b. 5 May 1788; d. 4 Oct. 1844; m. Sarah Lackland, dau. of Zadoc Lackland; 5 children.

74   v   William Sublett, b. 2 Mar. 1790; d. 10 Aug. 1872; m. Mary Lackland; 4 children.

75   vi   Martha Sublett, b. 5 May 1792; d. in 1850 in Texas; m. 13 Feb. 1812 James Foresee, descendant of the Huguenot Farci family.[212]

76   vi   Judith G. Sublett, b. 24 May 1795; d. 8 April 1833; m. 6 Jan. 1820 Thomas Merriman;[213] two chlldren.

16.   William Sublett, born say 1750, was married 24 April 1788 (date of bond) in Amelia

203   Family Bible of Peter Sublett, as published in Samuel S. Sublett, *A Partial History of the French Huguenots by Name Soblets ...* Richmond, 1896, pp. 17, 29. Sublett calls Thomas Smith's wife Margaret (Trabue). The will of Thomas Smith, dated 14 June 1786, prob. 16 Nov. 1786, calls his wife Magdalen and names daughter Martha Sublett. (*Powhatan County, Virginia, Will Bk. 1*, p. 116) Also, the will of Magdalen Smith, dated 15 May 1787, prob. 16 Aug. 1787, names dau. Martha Sublett. (*Powhatan County, Virginia, Will Bk. 1*, p. 132).

204   Powhatan County, Virginia, Public Service Claims: Certificates, Virginia State Library.

205   *Powhatan County, Virginia, Public Service Claims*: Court Booklet, p. 6, Virginia State Library.

206   *Ibid.*, Virginia, Deed Bk. 1, p. 487.

207   Sublett, *A Partial History* ..., p. 17.

208   *Ibid.*, p. 17.

209   Knorr, *Marriages ... Powhatan County, Virginia*, p. 40.

210   *Ibid.*, p. 49.

211   *Chesterfield County, Virginia, Mar. Reg.* p. 93.

212   Knorr, *op. cit.* Powhatan County, Virginia, p. 24.

213   Knorr, *op. cit.* Powhatan County, Virginia, p. 42.

County, Virginia, to Betsy Hughes, John Hughes being named on the bond.[214] We may be sure that William who married in Amelia County was the son of Peter (#6), because Peter by his will left his son William negroes named Isaac, Cesar, Rachel and Sawney.[215] By his will dated 28 April 1794, probated 17 Sept. 1800, William Sublett left to his wife Betsey "the use of the following slaves, viz., Isaac, Cesar, Sawney and Rachel."[216] Despite the fact that his will was not probated until 17 Sept. 1800, it seems quite likely that William died several years in advance of this, much nearer to the making of the will than to its probate, as the "Betsey Sublett" who married (date of bond) 17 May 1797 his first cousin Arthur Sublett (#45) is believed with some reason to have been his widow, Betsey (Hughes). (See #45 for discussion.)

Issue of William and Betsy (Hughes) Sublett:

77   i   Samuel Sublett, b. c. 1789, m. (1st) 5 Aug. 1817 (date of bond) Harriet Duval, daughter of Benjamin Duval, in the city of Richmond.[217] She was buried 2 June 1827, aged 27, in Shockoe Hill Cemetery, Richmond, Virginia.[218] Samuel m. (2nd) 1832 at Lynchburg, Virginia, to Antoinette C. Carlton.[219] She died 8 March 1852, age 43, and is buried in Shockoe. He died 29 April 1856, aged 67; buried at Shockoe. Samuel Sublett served as a vestryman at historic St. John's Episcopal Church, Richmond, from 1829 to 1843. A child of his was buried there in the churchyard in 1841. Among his issue:
1. Virginia Sublett.
2. Charles Morton Sublett, b. 22 Oct. 1834, bp. at St. John's Church 26 Jan. 1838.

78   ii   Nancy Sublett, b. say 1791; m. (date of bond) 20 June 1810 in Powhatan County, Virginia, to Francis Branch.[220]

79   iii   John Sublett, b. say 1793. This was probably the John Hughes Sublett, b. 14 May 1793, d. 30 March 1862, who was married in Kentucky in 1818 to Frances A. M. L. Towles, b. 16 Aug. 1800, d. 17 Feb. 1861, daughter of Col. Thomas and Mary (Smith) Towles.[221]

17.   John Sublett, born say 1755, was married to a Miss --- Porter,[222] the daughter of John and Sarah (Watkins) Porter,[223] the granddaughter of Thomas and Elizabeth (Dutoit) Porter, and great-granddaughter of Pierre Dutoit, the Huguenot immigrant.[224] Presumably she was dead before 27 April 1784 when John Porter made his will, not mentioning her, but naming "my grandson Peter

---

214   Amelia County, Virginia, Marriage Bonds, abstracted in *William and Mary College Quarterly*, 1:17:37.

215   Will of Peter Sublett, made July 1783, *Powhatan County, Virginia, Deed Bk. 1*, pp. 237-238.

216   Will of William Sublett, *Powhatan County, Virginia, Deed Bk. 2*, p. 668.

217   Anne Waller Reddy and Andrew L. Rife, *Virginia Marriage Bonds: Richmond City*, p. 24.

218   A. Bohmer Rudd, Register of Interments, Shockoe Hill Cemetery, Richmond, Virginia, 1822-1850, p. 5.

219   *Lynchburg Marriage Register, 1*, p. 27.

220   Knorr, *Marriages ... Powhatan County, Virginia*, p. 10.

221   "The Towles Family," *Virginia Magazine*, 8:428, as to marriage and her parentage; vital dates are from their tombstones, Henderson (Kentucky) City Cemetery.

222   Phoebe Porter [DJS].

223   Sublett, *A Partial History* ..., p. 29.

224   See will of Peter Dutoit, dated 3 May 1726, prob. 3 Oct. 1726, Henrico County, Virginia, *Miscellaneous County Records* [Deeds, Wills, etc.] (1650-1807), vol. 2 (1718-1736), p. 659. Will of Isaac Dutoy, dated 9 Dec. 1750, prob. Mar. 1752, Cumberland County, Virginia, abstracted in *Virginia Magazine of History and Biography*, 32:395.

Sublett" to whom he gave "a negroe girl Jane, and in case of his decease without lawful issue to be divided equally among all my children."[225] "John Sublit" is named on a subscription list taken in Powhatan County for the purpose of "paying bounties to recruits and preventing a draught of the militia."[226]

His wife in an early grave, John Sublett left his only son behind in Virginia and accompanied his brother-in-law James Smith (1757-1800) who had married Elizabeth Porter, his wife's sister, to Ohio in 1798.[227] There, in Hamilton County, Territory Northwest of the Ohio River, on 5 Nov. 1799 James Smith of Hamilton County engaged "to make good title to Peter Sublett to 500 acres."[228] Witness was John Sublett. The records (both land and probate) of Hamilton County, Ohio (and its daughter county, Warren County, Ohio, where the land eventually lay) are devoid of references to John Sublett, although they contain references to this James Smith. It is said that John Sublett died in 1815 in Ohio (presumably in Warren County, which by that time had been carved from Hamilton County).[229]

Issue of John and --- (Porter) Sublett:

- 80   i   Peter Dutoy Sublett, b. prior to July 1783 when his paternal grandfather, Peter Sublett, made his will giving "my grandson Peter Dutoy Sublett one Boy named Bob."[230] He married Nancy Wingo, daughter of John, June 1805, Amelia County, Virginia.[231]

18.   Benjamin Sublett, born say 1759; m. (date of bond) 20 Jan. 1785 Betty Ann Street.[232] His will, dated 4 March 1824, probated 21 Apr. 1825, names the following children:[233]

Issue of Benjamin and Betty Ann (Street) Sublett:

   81   i   William Sublett. Samuel S. Sublett's *A Partial History* ..., correctly lists three sons for Benjamin: William, John and Joseph. Of these, he says: "William went west and became an inhabitant with the Indians and was very prominent."[234] It seems quite likely that he was really thinking of William L. Sublette (#206) son of Philip Allen Sublette. (#30)

   82   ii   John Sublett.

   83   iii Joseph Sublett, b. c. 1793, from the fact that on 27 March 1871, aged 78, he applied for a pension based on his service in the War of 1812 as a private in the militia company of Capt. Samuel Marshall from 4 Mar. 1813 to 14 Aug. 1813. Joseph Sublett was described on his enlistment papers as 5'10" in height, dark skin, grey eyes and black hair. He died in Powhatan County 2 Jan. 1873. He

225   *Powhatan County, Virginia, Will Bk. 1*, p. 98.

226   *Virginia Magazine of History and Biography*, 24:329.

227   Sublett, *A Partial History* ..., p. 29; *History of Warren County, Ohio*, Chicago: Beers, 1882, p. 379.

228   *Powhatan County, Virginia, Deed Bk. 3*, p. 608.

229   Sublett, *A Partial History* ..., p. 29

230   Powhatan County, Virginia, Deed Bk. 1, pp. 237-238.

231   "Amelia County, Virginia, Marriage Bonds," abstracted in *William and Mary College Quarterly*, 1:17:38.

232   Knorr, *Marriages ... Powhatan County, Virginia*, p. 63.

233   *Powhatan County, Virginia, Will Bk. 7*, p. 162.

234   Sublett, *A Partial History* ..., p. 9.

married on 6 Feb. 1840 Mrs. Ann M. ("Nancy") (Winfree) Morrisett. She was born c. 1805, the daughter of John Winfree, and married (1st) 12 Nov. 1825 in Powhatan County, John F. Morrisett. Morrisett died 12 Oct. 1835, leaving one son, Beverley F. Morrisett. Joseph and Ann (Winfree) Sublett also had one son, Benjamin T. Sublett, of Danville, Virginia.[235]

84	iv	Judith Sublett, m. 11 Dec. 1817 in Powhatan County to Littleberry Boatright.[236]
85	v	Mary (Polly) Sublett, m. 19 Feb. 1818 to William Owen.[237]
86	vi	Elizabeth (Betsy) Sublett, m. (date of bond) 21 June 1841 Elder John Wooldridge.[238]
87	vii	Nancy Sublett.
88	viii	Phebe Sublett.
89	ix	Eliza Sublett,[239] m. (date of bond) 15 Dec. 1830 to Bennett Maxey.[240] 1804-1877; 5 ch. Eliza d. 27 June 1895 in Virginia.
90	x	Mariah Sublett.

20.   Martha (Patsy) Sublett, b. say 1752, named for her paternal grandmother, married at an undetermined date presumably in Charlotte County, Virginia, John Weatherford.[241] They were married prior to 25 March 1775 when John Weatherford "of Charlotte County and the Parish of Cornwall" conveyed a tract to Michael Oharoe, in which Martha relinquished her right of dower.[242] Weatherford was born, it is said, about 1740 in Charlotte County and certainly by 1743 if the statement that he was more than ninety years of age at his death is true.[243] Weatherford was one of the earliest Baptist ministers in Virginia, so early, in fact, that he is one of the few Virginia dissenters whose descendants are entitled to membership in the Society of the Descendants of the Colonial Clergy. [The Rev. Frederick Lewis Weis, *The Colonial Clergy of Virginia, North Carolina, and South Carolina*, Boston, Mass., 1955, pp. 53-54. (Society of Descendants of the Colonial Clergy, Publication No. 7).] Though his parents were Presbyterians, he was converted to the Baptist faith "before he had reached his twentieth year" under the preaching of Elder Saumel Harriss. He almost immediately began holding prayer meetings in his neighborhood in Charlotte, despite the fact that he was "a plain man without any pretensions to learning."[244] His preaching soon carried him throughout southern Virginia, and by 1773 had gotten him into trouble with the authorities. In June 1773, in Chesterfield County, "John Tanner and John Weatherford appearing

---

235   Joseph Sublett, War of 1812 Pension File, S. O. 4741, S.C. 2987, W. O. 30077, W.C. 25553 National Archives, Washington, D.C.

236   Knorr, *op. cit.*, Powhatan County, Virginia, p. 8.

237   *Ibid.*, p. 49.

238   *Powhatan County, Virginia, Marr. Reg., 1777-1853*, p. 136.

239   Eliza Sublett d. 27 Jun 1895, Virginia, m. Bennett Maxey, 1804-1877. 5 children [DJS].

240   *Ibid.*, p. 110.

241   Martha's listing as a child of William and Susanna (Allen) Sublett is suggested only in the *Sublett Family Chart* compiled by Ann Catherine (Dement) Thompson about 1894, from family papers and first-hand knowledge. A copy of this chart is in the possession of Mrs. H. W. (Louise Walton) Barnett, Benton, Louisiana. The principal written sources upon which Mrs. Thompson based her chart were: (1) an old-fashioned "Family Tree" made in the 1850s in Rutherford County, Tennessee, by a granddaughter of William Allen Sublett (#26), which Mrs. Thompson found in the possession of the maker's daughter, Mrs. Mattie Herrigus, in 1894 of Nashville, Tennessee, and (2) a "Scrap Book" with family records compiled by Capt. Philip S. Lowe (#172) before the Civil War, in Rutherford County, Tennessee.

242   *Charlotte County, Virginia, Deed Bk. 3*, p. 510.

243   James B. Taylor, *Lives of Virginia Baptist Ministers*, 2nd ed., Richmond, Virginia, 1838, pp. 46-50.

244   *Ibid.*, p. 48.

in court, being taken up by a warrant issued by Archibald Cary, Gent., for that purpose & acknowledging themselves to be of the religious Sect called Baptists and that they had practised preaching and assembling the people together in this and other counties in this Colony without having any License for so doing" were ordered to give surety for their "good Behavior & keeping the peace for the space of one Year each in penalty of £ 50 with two sureties in penalty of £ 25 each and be committed to <u>Goal</u> til they do so."[245] It is said that Weatherford was confined for five months there and gained his liberty with the aid of Patrick Henry.[246] Returning to Charlotte County, he became pastor of Cub Creek Church in that county and of Lower Fallings Church of adjacent Campbell County. At one time he filled the pulpit of Hat Creek Church in Campbell County.[247] In 1813 he removed to Halifax County, Virginia, and in 1823 to Pittsylvania County, Virginia, where he died 23 January 1833. On 5 April 1827 John Weatherford of Pittsylvania and Patsey his wife conveyed a Charlotte tract to Josiah Mason.[248] "His temporal circumstances were far from being comfortable. With a large family, having had 15 children, 12 of whom were daughters, he often found it difficult to obtain for them the necessaries of life."[249] His will, made 5 Nov. 1829, probated 18 March 1833, fails to account for anything like the reputed 15 children. It names only eight children, plus his wife Martha, who is thus seen to be yet living in 1829.[250] She seems to have survived for a number of years, for not until 18 Dec. 1841 did Jesse Woodson, executor of John Weatherford's will, deed a tract to William Wamack (Womack) reciting that "whereas by the direction of said will the executor was required that after the death of Martha Weatherford that a certain tract of land should be sold at public auction and whereas the said Martha Weatherford having also departed this life the said executor in pursuance of said will advertised the tract of land ... to be sold on the premises on the 27th Nov. 1841 at public auction."[251]

Issue of the Rev. John and Martha (Sublett) Weatherford:

101	i	John W. Weatherford.
102	ii	Charles A. Weatherford. Among his issue:
		1. Elizabeth H. Weatherford, m. 28 Aug. 1827 William McDowell.[252]
		2. Susanna A. (Allen?) Weatherford, m. 5 Nov. 1829 Richard Jennings.[253]
		3. Ann Weatherford, m. 25 Nov. 1839 William Abbott, Jr.[254]
		4. Louisa Weatherford, m. 9 Dec. 1840 George W. Moore.[255]
		5. Sally S. Weatherford, m. 21 June 1841 Sherwood B. Dove.[256]
103	iii	Elizabeth Weatherford, m. (date of bond) 30 Dec. 1803 in Charlotte County, Joseph Mason. Surety: John W. Weatherford.[257]

245   *Virginia Magazine of History and Biography*, 11:416 (1904), abstract from the Chesterfield County, Virginia, records.

246   Tayor, *op. cit.*, p. 49.

247   Ruth Hairston Early, *Campbell Chronicles and Family Sketches: Embracing the History of Campbell County Virginia, 1782-1926*. Lynchburg, Virginia, 1927, p. 29.

248   *Charlotte County, Virginia, Deed Bk. 18*, p. 168.

249   Taylor, *op. cit.*, p. 51.

250   *Pittsylvania County, Virginia, Will Bk. 1, 1814-[1820]-1845*, pp. 227-229.

251   *Ibid.*, Deed Bk. 45, p. 304.

252   *Ibid.*, Marriage Bonds, 1767-1862, p. 89.

253   *Ibid.*, p. 94.

254   *Ibid.*, p. 119.

255   *Ibid.*, p. 123.

256   *Ibid.*, p. 125.

257   Knorr, *Marriages ... Charlotte County, Virginia*, p. 55.

104   iv   Agnes Weatherford, m. (date of bond) 12 Jan. 1804 in Halifax County,
           Virginia, Thomas Combie (Cumbey, Comba).[258] She was deceased prior to
           1829 leaving a single infant surviving her, raised by Eunice and John
           McDowell.[259]

105   v   Louisa Weatherford, m. (date of bond) 20 Dec. 1809 in Charlotte County,
           Virginia, Obadiah Mason.[260]

106   vi   Martha Weatherford, m. (date of bond) 11 March 1812 in Charlotte, Jesse
           Mason. Surety: Charles A. Weatherford.[261]

107   vii William W. Weatherford.

108   viii Eunice ("Unise") Weatherford, m. (date of bond) 27 Nov. 1820 in Pittsylvania
           County, Virginia, John McDowell.[262]

21.   Valentine Sublett, b. say 1754, married 4 Nov. 1782 in Charlotte County, Virginia, Mrs.
Margaret (Caldwell) Brent, widow of Major John Brent.[263] Brent was a member of the
Committee of Charlotte County, 1775-1776; served several years in the Revolution as a Captain
in the Continental Line; was a member of the House of Delegates in 1780; re-entered the army
and died in the service in 1781. By her first husband, Margaret had a number of children: James;
Thomas Caldwell Brent; Jane, m. James Smith; Elizabeth, m. Samuel Rogers; Catherine, m. (1st)
Nathaniel Rogers, (2nd) --- Henderson; Julia Ann Newton Brent, m. (1st) William Cobb, (2nd)
Samuel H. Thomas; Margaret, m. Liberty Green; and Sarah, m. Robert Hughes.[264]

On 3 Feb. 1794 Valentine Sublett was recommended by the County Court as an Ensign of the
militia of Charlotte County,[265] and on 5 Jan. 1795 as Lieutenant.[266] On 2 Feb. 1795 he produced
his commission as Lieutenant and took the oath of office.[267] By 4 July 1796 he had produced his
commission as Captain of the militia.[268] In January 1799 Valentine Sublett sold his remaining
land in Charlotte County, preparatory to his migration to Lincoln County, Kentucky, where
brothers and sisters had preceded him.[269] He disappears from the personal property tax lists of
Charlotte County also in that very year. In August 1800, he was listed for taxes in Lincoln
County, Kentucky.[270] After several years in Lincoln County, he moved on to Green County,
Kentucky, where his brother Abraham was then living. There on 11 Feb. 1808 he made his
will;[271] it was probated 23 May 1808.[272] After reciting that he was "at present truly sick in body
... so that I think that the Lord hath appointed shortly to lead me out of this world," he requested
"that my body be d_ea_cently buried according to the custom of the Baptist Church." He left four

---

258   *Halifax County, Virginia, Marriage Bond Register No. 1*, 1753-1889, p. 55.

259   *Will Bk. 1*, p. 229, Pittsylvania County, Virginia.

260   Knorr, *op. cit.*, Charlotte County, Virginia, p. 55.

261   *Ibid.*, p. 55.

262   *Pittsylvania County, Virginia, Marriage Bonds, 1767-1862*, p. 71.

263   Knorr, *Marriages ... Charlotte County, Virginia*, p. 80.

264   *Virginia Magazine*, 8:105.

265   *Charlotte County, Virginia, Order Bk. 9*, p. 157.

266   *Ibid.*, Order Bk. 10, p. 9.

267   *Ibid.*, Order Bk. 10, p. 13.

268   *Ibid.*, Order Bk. 10, p. 201.

269   *Ibid.*, Deed Bk. 8, p. 143.

270   Clift, *op. cit.*, p. 176.

271   *Green County, Kentucky, Will Bk. 1*, pp. 43-44.

272   *Ibid.*, Order Bk. No. 4, p. 170.

Negroes to his wife Margaret, a negro girl to his daughter Susanah Clifton, and as to the remainder, desired "that an equal devide of said Property take place between my four sons, v^z. Allen, Branch, Field, and William." Executors were his step-son-in-law Liberty Green and "Danel" Henry.

Issue of Valentine and Margaret (Caldwell) Sublett:

> 117   i   Allen Sublett, b. say 1783, m. (date of bond) 30 April 1804 in Lincoln County, Kentucky, to Agnes Simpson.[273]
> • 118   ii   Branch Sublett, b. say 1785, m. (date of bond) 7 Jan. 1808 in Lincoln County, Kentucky, to Polly Bratton, dau. of John.[274]
> • 119   iii Field Sublett, b. say 1787, m. (date of bond) 21 Sept. 1809 in Green County, Kentucky, to Eleanor Bratton (Bralden).[275]
> 120   iv   Susannah Sublett,[276] b. say 1789, m. (date of bond) 28 Jan. 1807 in Green County, Kentucky, to Burdet (Burdey, Burdette) Clifton.[277] Burdet was probably a descendant of Burdet Clifton, b. 3 Feb. 1736, Stafford County, Virginia, m. Rebecca (Kenner) and as a Revolutionary veteran moved to Kentucky. This latter Burdet was the son of Burdet and Frances (Hill) Clifton of St. Paul's Parish, Stafford County, Virginia.[278]
> 121   v   William Sublett, b. say 1791.

22.   Mary Hunt Sublett ("Mollie"), named for her maternal grandmother, b. say 1756 was married in Charlotte County, Virginia, 5 June 1782 to John Dudgeon,[279] son of William Dudgeon, Senr.[280] On 5 Dec. 1796 John Dudgeon sold his 200 acres in Charlotte County, Virginia, his wife Mary relinquishing dower in the same,[281] and joined the early-1797 migration to Lincoln County, Kentucky, with her brothers and sisters Abraham, Field, Philip, Ursula Day, and Susanna Lowe. There on 23 August 1800 "John Dudgin" was listed for taxes.[282] On 10 April 1804 John Dugean (Dungean) made his will there; it was proved 10 June 1805.[283] His widow, "Mary Dugin," is listed in the 1810 Census of Lincoln County, Kentucky, aged over 45, with one son, 26-45, two sons and one daughter, aged 16-26.[284]

Issue of John and Mary Hunt (Sublett) Dudgeon:

---

273   Lincoln County, Kentucky, Marriage Index.

274   *Ibid.*

275   Green County, Kentucky, Marriage Bk. 1, p. 76.

276   Susannah Sublett d. 30 Jun 1862, m. (1st) Burdet Clifton, m. (2nd) 3 Aug 1811, Wm. B. Bratton [DJS].

277   *Ibid.*

278   *Virginia Magazine of History and Biography*, 26:320.

279   Ann C. (Dement) Thompson, *Sublett Family Chart*, previously cited.

280   *Charlotte County, Virginia, Deed Bk. 5*, p. 116.

281   *Ibid.*, Deed Bk. 7, p. 229.

282   *Clift, "Second Census" of Kentucky*, p. 84.

283   *Lincoln County, Kentucky, Will Bk. B*, p. 274, abstracted in the *Register* of the Kentucky Hist. Soc., 39:339, and also in McAdams, *Kentucky Pioneer and Court Records*, Lexington, 1929 p. 51.

284   Annie Walker Burns, *Third Census of the U.S. (1810 Census), Lincoln County, Kentucky*, Washington, D.C., 1936, (mimeo.), p. 5.

122   i   William Dudgeon,[285] m. (it is said) a Miss Phillips.[286] m. (2d) 1830 Jane Edington in Kentucky.

123   ii   Susanna Dudgeon, named for her maternal grandmother, m. (date of bond) 6 January 18(14?) in Lincoln County, Kentucky, Armstrong Kerr (Carr).[287] Though a transcription of the marriage bonds gives the year as 1814, John Dudgeon calls Armstrong Kerr a son-in-law by his will of 1804, so 1814 is presumably wrong. Armstrong Kerr became captain of a company of Kentucky militia in the 13th Regiment of Kentucky Infantry, commanded by Lt. Col. William Dudley, in the War of 1812, and deposed in behalf of his wife's cousin, John S. Sublett (#238), who served in his company. Armstrong Kerr is listed in the Lincoln County 1810 Census as 26-45, wife 26-45, one daughter 10-16, two sons and three daughters under 10.[288]

124   iii   Nancy Dudgeon (Dugens), b. 1784 or later (1810 Census) m. 11 May 1801 in Lincoln County, Kentucky, to John Rogers, John Sally being bondsman.[289] Listed in the 1810 Census of Lincoln County as John Rogers, 26-45, wife 16-26, two sons and two daughters under 10 and one slave.[290]

125   iv   John Dudgeon, m. 20 May 1805 in Madison County, Kentucky, to Nelly Rogers.[291]

126   v   Mary (Polly) Dudgeon (Dudgins), m. (date of bond) 18 Feb. 1808 in Lincoln County, Kentucky, to Andrew Hall.[292] The Ann C. Thompson chart says Hall married her sister Margaret and that Mary m. Samuel Phillips, but this seems to be a case of cloudy memory.[293]

127   vi   Margaret (Peggy) Dudgeon.

128   vii   Martha (Patsy) Dudgeon, m. 11 Jan. 1815 in Lincoln County, Kentucky, to John Williamson, John Rogers being bondsman.[294]

129   viii   Sublett Dudgeon,[295] m. (it is said) Mary Phillips.[296]

23.   Ursula Sublett, born say 1758, was married in 1778 to Edward Day, Jr., son of Edward Day, Sr. Edward Day, born according to his own statement in Charlotte County, Virginia, in 1760, in his Revolutionary Pension Application made 7 Oct. 1832 in Sangamon County, Illinois, says, "I think in the fall of the year perhaps of '78 (note: "78" was first written, "79" written over it, and the words "or 80" were written in and then erased) I married and remained in the County of

---

285   William Dudgeon m. (1st) 22 Oct 1814, Sophia Phillips, (2nd) 1830, Kentucky, Jane Edington [DJS].

286   Thompson, *Sublett Family Chart*.

287   Annie Walker Burns, *Kentucky Vital Statistics: Record of Marriages in Lincoln County Kentucky for the Period of Years 1780 to 1851*. Frankfort, Kentucky, (mimeo.), 1931, p. 38.

288   Burns, *Third Census, Lincoln County, Kentucky*, p. 10.

289   Burns, *Kentucky Vital Statistics: ... Lincoln County*, p. 59.

290   Burns, *Third Census, Lincoln County, Kentucky*, p. 15.

291   Thompson, *Sublett Family Chart*, confirmed by "Madison County Marriage Records," 37 *Register* of the Kentucky Hist. Soc., p. 352.

292   Burns, *Kentucky Vital Statistics: ... Lincoln County*.

293   Thompson, *Sublett Family Chart*.

294   Lucy Kate McGhee, *Historical Records of Old Crab Orchard, Kentucky, v. 3*, p. 162 (Marriage Records of Lincoln County, 1780-1852.)

295   Sublett Dudgeon m. 6 Jun 1812, Mary Phillips, Green County (daughter of Wm. Phillips, Jr. [DJS].

296   Thompson, *Sublett Family Chart*.

Charlotte."[297] Unfortunately he failed to list the bride. "I first entered the service as a volunteer in the year 1776 ... under Capt[n]. Collier and Lieut[nt] Douglass Watson in Col. Margains Regiment ... against the Cherokee Indians in which service I volunteered and remained about five months. I was in a detachment under the command of Isaac Shelby who defeated a body of Indians at the long island of Holson (sic) where we killed a number of Indians." Later tours of duty were under Capt[n]. William Price; Capt. Collier a second time, at Williamsburg, Hampton, Portsmouth and Suffolk; Capt. Gideon Spencer, at Little York in 1781 "where we remained untill after the siege of York and taking of Cornwallis and his army."

On 6 Feb. 1797 "Edward Day and Ursula his wife of Charlotte" deeded a tract to John Smith, Sr.; "Usley" relinquished her dower following private examination.[298] On 7 March 1797 "Edward Day and Ursley his wife of the County of Charlotte" sold 100 acres to John Stewart of Campbell County. "Edward Day" and "Ursula Day" both signed without mark.[299] The Days and Subletts were neighbors on Turnip Creek and Cub Creek in Charlotte County. For example, when on 2 March 1783 "Edward Day Senr. of the County of Gilford in the State of North Carolina" conveyed a tract to John Clayton Jun[r]. the deed was witnessed by Edward Day (Jr.) and William Sublet.[300]

The two deeds by Edward and Ursula early in 1797 apparently heralded their removal to Kentucky, for Day is last listed for personal property taxes in Charlotte in 1796.[301] Their daughter Rebecca in her reminiscenses said: "Am from Virginia — We cultivated tobacco and sent it to Richmond. We came to Kentucky about 1798 when I was eight years of age. We came in a squad of 40 persons to Cumberland Mountains as we came to Kentucky — sold our waggons — packed our horses — Men generally walked — Women and children rode."[302] The "squad of 40 persons" referred to can be identified rather easily: it would seem to have included the following groups from Charlotte County who settled in Lincoln County, Kentucky:

(10)   1 John and Mary (Sublett) Dudgeon (#22) and 8 ch.
(13)   2 Edward and Ursula (Sublett) Day (#23) and the oldest 11 of their 14 children.
(10)   3 Jesse and Susanna (Sublett) Lowe (#27) and the oldest 8 of their 12 children.
(1)   4 Philip Allen Sublett (#30), young bachelor and also these groups who quickly moved on to Green County:
(5)   5 Abraham and Polly (Smith) Sublett (#29) and three children.
(1)   6 Field Sublett (#31), young bachelor.

Total 40 — which would seem to demonstrate that Rebecca was amazingly accurate in her "squad of 40" remark. Shortly other Subletts swelled their ranks in Lincoln County:

1799 — Valentine and Margaret (Caldwell) Sublett (#21), plus five children and step-children.
1800 — Bartley and Nancy (Sublett) Greenwood (#28) and 5 ch.
1807 — George Allen and Isabella (Akin) Sublett (#25)

---

297   Edward Day, Revolutionary Pension Application S 32200, National Archives, Washington, D.C.

298   *Charlotte County, Virginia, Deed Bk. 7*, p. 245.

299   *Ibid.*, Deed Bk. 12, p. 100.

300   *Charlotte County, Virginia, Deed Bk. 5*, p. 44.

301   *Ibid.*, Personal Property Tax Books, 1782-1815.

302   Herndon-Weik Collection of Lincolniana, Group IV, Papers of William H. Herndon, v. 16: Interview of Rebecca Day Herndon with her son William H. Herndon, Sept. 28, 1866. (Library of Congress, Manuscripts Division).

The major Sublett migration to Lincoln County occurred in 1797, for Philip was married there that year. The migration seems to have occurred early in the year 1797, for these are the final sales of realty in Charlotte County by the persons involved in the move:

>*John Dudgeon — 5 Dec. 1796*
>*Edward Day — 3 Mar. 1797*
>*Jesse Lowe — 4 Mar. 1797*

Edward Day is listed for taxes in Lincoln County in August, 1800.[303] According to his own statement, however, he continued to reside in Charlotte "untill the year 1802, when I removed to Lincoln County, Kentucky. ... I lived in various counties in that state ... until the year 1819 when I removed to Illinois, ... Matison County (sic); from thence to Sangamon County, from thence to McLean County, where I now live."[304] When Abraham Sublett (#29) was appointed constable on 14 March 1808 in Lincoln County, Edward Day was security on his bond.[305] Thereafter he was in Green County, Kentucky. Early in 1819 he moved to Madison County, Illinois, where in the Illinois State Census for 1820 he is listed with three white males above twenty-one years of age, and four "other white persons" in his household.[306] Thereafter his residence was in Sangamon, McLean and Macon counties, Illinois. His wife Ursula (Sublett) died between 1826 and 1828 in what was then Sangamon County, Illinois, and was buried in the graveyard of Lebanon Church (Cumberland Presbyterian) six miles east of Petersburg, Illinois, in what is now Athens Precinct, Menard County.[307] Edward Day died in what was then Macon County, Illinois on 11 April 1837 in that portion of the county which subsequently became DeWitt County, and is buried in the DeWitt Cemetery, DeWitt, Illinois.[308] A published record gives 1836 as the date of his death.[309]

A couple of published accounts credit Edward Day with the emancipation of his slaves.[310] Rebecca (Day) Herndon told her son William: "Am an abolitionist in sentiment ... Your grandfather Day was through the Revolution — was a true and tried Patriott — emancipated his slaves about 1789 — as I now recollect. You remember he used to tell you his Revolutionary stories — his trials — sufferings — his good old head ever undaunted — You remember how you when a little lad used to fire up and your eyes well over with tears at the recitle of American wrongs — at our hardships, &C."[311] The emancipation account was soon embroidered: "In 1781 ... Colonel Day [note that Day was an enlisted man in the Revolution] 'desiring that no man should ever again call him master', emancipated his slaves in Western Virginia, and emigrated into Kentucky. He had received his small patrimony while the law of primogeniture was still in force; and when he parted with his slaves, he was compelled to work."[312] The tax records for Charlotte County for 1794, 1795 and 1796 show that Edward Day owned no slaves.

---

303   Clift, *"Second Census" of Kentucky*, p. 76.

304   Edward Day, Revolutionary Pension Application S 32200.

305   *Lincoln County, Kentucky, Order Bk. No. 6*, 1801-1808, p. 433.

306   Illinois State Historical Library, *Collections*, v. 26: Illinois (State) Census Returns, 1820, ed. by Margaret Cross Norton. 1934. p. 152.

307   Herndon-Weik Collection, *op. cit.*; papers in the possession of Gray Herndon, Esq., Springfield, Illinois; *History of Menard and Mason Counties, Illinois*. Chicago, O. L. Baskin and County, 1879, pp. 233, 244, 336.

308   Records of the Illinois Veterans' Commission, Division of War Veterans Grave Registration, Springfield, Illinois.

309   Harriet J. Walker, *Revolutionary Soldiers Buried in Illinois*, Los Angeles, 1917, p. 27.

310   David Donald, *Lincoln's Herndon*, New York, Knopf, 1948, p. 7.

311   Herndon-Weik Collection, *loc. cit.*

312   Caroline Dall, "Pioneering," *Atlantic Monthly*, v. 19, p. 404 (1867).

Issue of Edward and Ursula (Sublett) Day; apparently arranged chronologically by sex:[313]

- 133   i   Valentine Day, b. say 1780; resided in Lincoln County, Kentucky; m. 31 July 1809 in Mercer County, Kentucky, to Elizabeth Adams.

134   ii   George Day, b. say 1783.

135   iii   Edward Day III, b. say 1785.

- 136   iv   William Day, b. 1789, d. 1875, Keokuk County, Iowa; m. 27 Sept. 1813 in Lincoln County, Kentucky, Dolly Embree.

- 137   v   Benjamin Sublett Day, b. 6 Nov. 1792; d. 24 Feb. 1845, DeWitt County, Illinois; m. 3 Sept. 1813 in Garrard County, Kentucky, to Catherine Onstott.

138   vi   Charles Day, b. say 1793.

139   vii   Philip Day, b. say 1795.

140   viii John Day,[314] b. say 1797, m. 8 Aug. 1816 in Green County, Kentucky, to Nancy Bottom.

141   ix   Abraham Day, b. say 1800.

142   x   Mary Day, b. say 1781. She is said to have married John Renfro.[315] John S. Renfro, b. 1 March 1806 in Kentucky, "taken when young to Illinois by his grandfather, by whom he was reared to manhood," is believed to have been their son. He was for a long period of time a mail carrier on the Springfield to Lewistown, Illinois, route.[316] He m. Telitha, daughter of Abraham Hollenbeck, and took part in the Black Hawk War. He moved in 1849 from Illinois to Keokuk County, Iowa.[317]

143   xi   Elizabeth Day, b. say 1786.

- 144   xii   Rebecca Day, b. 2 Feb. 1790; d. 19 Aug. 1875, Springfield, Illinois; m. (1st) 13 March 1806 in Lincoln County, Kentucky, to James Johnson; m. (2nd) 9 March 1817 in Green County, Kentucky, to Archer Gray Herndon.

145   xiii Susannah Day, b. say 1798, m. 4 Oct. 1814 in Lincoln County, Kentucky, to Jeremiah Sutton.[318]

146   xiv   , b. 1802, d. 1854, DeWitt County, Illinois; m. 1819 Hiram Chapin (1797-1871), a native of North Carolina, who died at LeRoy, McLean County, Illinois. Hiram was for a time a boatman on the Mississippi. Following his marriage, he migrated with his in-laws to Madison County, Illinois, in 1819, where he is listed in the 1820 State Census of Illinois, with a wife and one child.[319] In 1823 he moved to Sangamon County, Illinois, (that portion which

---

313   Sole authority for this listing of issue is a descendant, Mrs. Gladys D. Swearingen, Pueblo, Colorado (Letter of 3 Nov. 1959). She states that Ursula was a Sublett. Another descendant, Gray Herndon, attorney, Springfield, Illinois, is in possession (1960) of a considerable body of correspondence relating to the Day family's claims to a share in the Sublette estate in St. Louis through Ursula (Sublett) Day, and a number of newspaper clippings of fifty to seventy years ago from newspapers of St. Louis and elsewhere relative to the prolonged suits over the same. (See, #30 for particulars). The striking repetition of distinctively Sublett names as the names of the Day children is corroborative of Ursula's identification as a Sublett. The Thompson chart and the Shurtleff genealogy also so identify her.

314   John Barber Day m. Nancy Bottom, 1797-1885 [DJS].

315   Thompson, *Sublett Chart.*

316   *History of Menard and Mason Counties, Illinois,* p. 336.

317   *A Genealogical and Biographical History of Keokuk County, Iowa.* Chicago, Lewis Publishing County, 1903, pp. 54-56. This work lists his twelve children.

318   Thompson, *Sublett Chart*; McGhee, *Old Crab Orchard,* v. 3, p. 145.

319   Illinois State Historical Library *Collections,* v. 26, p. 152.

eventually became Menard County).[320] In 1828 he settled at Waynesville, DeWitt County, Illinois. Hiram and Martha (Day) Chapin were members of the Cumberland Presbyterian Church.[321] Their issue were six daughters and four sons, including:[322]

1. John D. Chapin, d. without issue.
2. Stillman A. Chapin, b. 13 August 1821.
3. George D. Chapin, d. without issue.
4. Abraham D. Chapin.
5. Martha A. Chapin.
6. Elsey A. Chapin.
7. Rebecca H. Chapin.
8. Nancy A. Chapin, d. without issue.
9. Mary A. Chapin, d. in infancy.

25.   George Allen Sublett (named for a maternal uncle) was born say 1762. It seems probable that this was the George Sublett who on 4 May 1784 received a Virginia grant of 405 acres on Mill Creek in Fayette County, Kentucky,[323] since no other George Subletts of this generation are known of, barring the slim possibility of a George Sublett among the small Buckingham County, Virginia, Sublett family. (See #2). About 1788 Allen Sublette signed "The petition of sundry inhabitants of the district of Kentucky" who protested the decision to cut Kentucky off from Virginia to form a new state.[324] However, if George Allen Sublett and George and Allen of Fayette county are one and the same, his sojourn at this time in Kentucky was brief, for he is listed for personal property taxes in Charlotte County, Virginia, from 1788 through 1806 under the varying appellations of George A. Sublett, A. George Sublett, George Allen Sublett, and just plain Allen Sublett.[325] It is worth noting that he is <u>not</u> listed in the "First Census" of Kentucky, the tax lists of 1790.[326] On 14 Nov. 1791 (date of bond) he was married in Campbell County, Virginia, to Isabella Akin, daughter of Joseph Akin.[327] The will of the latter refers to "my daughter Ibey Subbett"(sic). George A. Subbett was security for his widow-executrix Anne.[328] By 1807 he had left Charlotte County, Virginia, for Lincoln County, Kentucky, where the 1810 Census lists "George Sublett," aged over 45, with a wife 26-45, two sons aged 16-26, two sons and one daughter aged 10-16, two daughters under 10, and two slaves.[329] The 1820 Census of Lincoln County lists him as "Allen Sublett," himself and wife over 45, plus seven children and/or

320   *History of Menard and Mason Counties, Illinois*, p. 371.

321   *The Biographical Record of DeWitt County, Illinois*, Chicago, Clarke, 1901, pp. 277-278; Newton Bateman, ed., Historical *Encyclopedia of Illinois, and Hist. of McLean County*, Chicago, 1908, v. 2, pp. 966-968.

322   *History of DeWitt County, Illinois*, Philadelphia, Brink, 1882, p. 286, amplified by a notarized statement given 18 Apr. 1908 at Holder, Illinois, by Stillman Chapin to Dr. Frank Fleury, in possession, 1960, of Gray Herndon, Springfield, Illinois.

323   W. R. Jillson, *The Kentucky Land Grants*, p. 124, (abstract of *Virginia Grants, Bk. 7*, p. 367).

324   James Rood Robertson, *Petitions of the Early Inhabitants of Kentucky to the General Assembly of Virginia 1769 to 1792*. [Filson Club Publication No. 27] Louisville, 19??, Petition No. 58.

325   Charlotte County, Virginia, Personal Property Tax Lists, 1782-1815.

326   Charles B. Heinemann and Gaius M. Brumbaugh, *"First Census" of Kentucky*, 1790, Washington, D. C., 1940, p.

327   Willium Wade Hinshaw, ed., *Encyclopedia of American Quaker Genealogy, vol. 6: Virginia*. Ann Arbor, Edwards Brothers 1950, p. 857. (Campbell County, Virginia, Marriage Bonds).

328   *Campbell County, Virginia, Will Bk. 3*, p. 186, Will of Joseph Akin, dated 15 May 1809, probated 13 Sept. 1812.

329   Third Census of the U. S., 1810, Lincoln County, Kentucky, transcribed by Annie Walker Burns.

grandchildren.[330] On 12 May 1828 George A. Sublett came into Lincoln County Court to register his stock mark.[331] The 1830 Census of Lincoln County lists "Allen Sublett," aged 60-70, wife aged 50-60, one son and one daughter between 15-20, and one son aged 10-15.[332]

Partial list of the probable issue of George Allen Sublett and Isabella (Akin):

- 148   i   William C. [Caldwell][333] Sublett, b. c. 1792, m. (date of bond) 6 April 1818 in Lincoln County, Kentucky, Elizabeth Barnett.[334] Migrated to Lewis County, Missouri. This <u>may</u> be the Crawford Sublett Mrs. Thompson mentions as a son of George Allen Sublett.[335]

  149   ii   Mary (Polly) Sublett, m. 15 Nov. 1824 in Lincoln County, Kentucky, to Elijah Hubbard, George Sublett being bondsman.[336] Resided in Lewis County, Missouri.

  150   iii   Jabez A. Sublett, b. 8 July 1815, d. 17 Apr. 1906, Boone County, Missouri; m. (date of bond) 11 June 1836 in Lincoln County to Eliza Hogan[337] (Logan?), b. 9 Nov. 1820, d. 8 Feb. 1901. Both are buried in the Churchyard of the Locust Grove Missionary Baptist Church, near Riggs, Boone County, Missouri.[338] Among their issue:
       1. Samuel P. Sublett, b. 1 May 1837, d. 18 May 1914.[339]
       2. Benjamin Sublett, b. 12 March 1845, d. 28 Feb. 1913.

  151   iv   Philip C. Sublett, b. c. 1812, Lincoln County, Kentucky; settled in Lewis County, Missouri; m. Mary ---,[340] b. c. 1828 in Kentucky. Issue:[341]
       1. Belle M. Sublett, b. c. 1842 in Missouri; named for her paternal grandmother Isabella (Akin) Sublett.
       2. John A. Sublett, b. c. 1844 in Missouri.
       3. Hannah C. Sublett, b. c. 1846 in Missouri.
       4. George Sublett, b. c. 1849 in Missouri, named for his paternal grandfather.

  152   v   Valentine Sublett, settled in Lewis County, Missouri; b. c. 1798.

26.   William Allen Sublett (named for his maternal grandfather and for a maternal uncle) was born say 1764. On 20 December 1787 (date of bond) in Campbell County, Virginia, he was married to Sarah (Sally) Akin, daughter of Joseph Akin (Aiken).[342] He was first listed for personal property taxes in Charlotte County in 1791, and appears there for the last time in

330   Fourth Census of the U. S., 1820, Lincoln County, Kentucky.

331   *Lincoln County, Kentucky, Order Bk. 9*, 1824-1831, folio 168.

332   Fifth Census of the U. S., 1830, Lincoln County, Kentucky, p. 47.

333   William Caldwell Sublett [DJS].

334   Lincoln County, Kentucky, Marriage Index.

335   Ann Catherine (Dement) Thompson, *Sublett Family Chart*.

336   Annie Walker Burns, *Kentucky Vital Statistics, Marriages of Lincoln County, Kentucky*, p. 35.

337   Lincoln County, Kentucky, Marriage Index.

338   Rella Bright Evans and Mrs. J. Frank Thompson, *Tombstone Records of Boone County, Missouri*. Columbia, Missouri, 1934, mimeo., p. 66.

339   *Ibid.*, p. 66.

340   Mary Ann Stephens [DJS].

341   U. S. Census, 1850, Lewis County, Missouri, p. 355.

342   William Wade Hinshaw, ed., *Encyclopedia of American Quaker Genealogy*, vol. VI, "Virginia." Ann Arbor, Edwards Brothers, 1950, p. 857, Campbell County Marriage Bonds.

1794.[343] On 27 Dec. 1793 his father-in-law Joseph Akin of Campbell County deeded to "William Allen Sublet of the County of Charlotte 148 acres on the waters of Louse Creek in the County of Charlotte."[344] This tract of land was disposed of on 3 October 1800 by "William Allen Sublett of the County of Halifax to Thomas Cumbee."[345] The deeds of Halifax record no realty transactions involving him. By May 1805 he was a resident of Rutherford County, Tennessee.[346] When his father-in-law made his will on 15 May 1809 he left a bequest to "my daughter Sarah Subbett" [sic] and named "my wife Anne Akin and my friend Samuel Jordan Executor; and my two son in laws in the tenesee William Subbett and Charles Pucket to be gaurdeens to this my last will."[347] In the 1810 Census of Rutherford County, Tennessee, Wm. A. Sublett is listed as aged over 45, with a wife 26-45, one son aged 18-26, one son and one daughter aged 10-16, one son under 10 and two slaves.[348] In the 1820 Census for the same county, "Wm. A. Sublett" and wife, both over 45 are listed, with two sons aged 18-26, and one son and one daughter under 10.[349] On 1 March 1822 John Nash Read gave two acres of land to Daniel Nelson and William A. Sublett, Trustees for the Baptist Church, on which Enon Baptist Church, six miles north of Murfreesboro, was built.[350] William Allen Sublett appears to have married a second time. A family chart states that he married (2nd) Rebecca Brown,[351] but the marriage record in Wilson County, Tennessee, of William A. Sublett to Rebecca Puckett, on 1 January 1838, presumably refers to him.[352] It is possible that this was her name in widowhood, and that the family chart gives her maiden name. William Allen Sublett died in Rutherford County, Tennessee, in 1839, where on 26 Nov. 1839 his son Abner C. Sublett was appointed Administrator of his estate.

Issue of William Allen Sublett by his first wife Sarah (Akin):

- 161   i   George Allen Sublett, b. say 1790, m. 29 May 1821 in Rutherford County, Tennessee, Elizabeth M. Ledbetter.
  162   ii   Abner Caldwell Sublett, b. say 1795, printer, m. Louisa Lewis.[353],[354] Issue:
  1. George Allen Sublett, m. a Miss Kennedy.
  2. Sarah Sublett,[355] m. a Dr. Bilbro or Belbro. Resided at Milton, Rutherford County, Tennessee.
  3. Susan Sublett, m. George Allen Brown.[356]
  4. Horace A. Sublett, of Rutherford County; b. 27 Dec. 1841, Lascassas, Tennessee; d. 30 May 1907, near Trenton, Tennessee. Served in the C.S.A. at Shiloh, Missionary Ridge, and the Campaign to Atlanta. Imprisoned at Camp Chase, Ohio.

---

343   Charlotte County, Virginia, Personal Property Tax Lists, 1782-1815.

344   *Ibid.*, Deed Bk. 8, p. 14.

345   *Ibid.*, Deed Bk. 8, p. 263.

346   *Rutherford County, Tennessee, Record Bk. A-1*, p. 17.

347   *Campbell County, Virginia, Will Bk. 3*, p. 186. Will of Joseph Akin, dated 15 May 1809, probated 13 Sept. 1812.

348   Martha Lou Houston, *Tennessee Census Reports, No. 1, Rutherford County, 1810*. Washington, D.C., 1933, mimeo., p. 11.

349   Martha Lou Houston, *1820 Census of Rutherford County, Tennessee*, Washington, D.C., 1936.

350   *Rutherford County, Tennessee, Deed Bk. O*, pp. 224-225; abstracted in Jeanette Tillotson Acklen, Tennessee Records: Tombstone Inscriptions and Manuscipts. Nashville, 1933, p. 449.

351   Thompson, *Sublett Family Chart*.

352   *Wilson County, Tennessee, Marriages, 1802-1840*, p. 256.

353   Louisa Pryor Lewis [DJS].

354   Thompson, *Sublett Family Chart*.

355   Sarah Sublett b. 9 Feb 1834, d. 24 Mar 1911, m. Dr. B. H. Bilbro b. 8 Oct 1823, d. 4 Nov 1868 [DJS].

356   Susan Sublett m. 12 Mar 1856, Rutherford County, George Allen Brown [DJS].

163 iii Mary Ann Sublett, b. 1797, d. 1843, m. 2 Oct. 1816 in Rutherford County to Robert Lawing, b. 1788, d. 1865.[357] Issue:[358]
1. Allen Lawing.
2. Mary Lawing, m. her cousin Preston Hatchitt, of Maxwell, Franklin County, Tennessee.
3. Susan S. Lawing, m. Mr. Vaughan.
4. Frances Lawing, m. Mr. Sully.
5. James Lawing.
6. Elizabeth Lawing.
7. Robert Lawing, Jr.

• 164 iv William A. Sublett, b. c. 1800, m. 9 Feb. 1821 in Rutherford County, Tennessee, to Ann Robinson or Robertson. Settled in Tarrant and Dallas Counties, Texas.

165 v Elizabeth Sublett.

166 vi Valentine Sublett, a physician, of Maury County, Tennessee; unmarried, it is said.

167 vii Susan Sublett, m. Archie Hatchitt. Issue:[359]
1. Thomas Hatchitt.
2. William Hatchitt.
3. Susan Hatchitt, m. Granville Merritt.
4. Preston Hatchitt, m. his cousin Mary Lawing.

168 viii Preston Sublett.

169 ix Sarah Sublett, m. John Black. Among issue:
1. Mary Caldwell Black.

27. Susanna (Susan) Sublett, b. say 1766, named for her mother, was married 18 September 1781 in Charlotte County, Virginia, to Jesse Lowe (Loe).[360] In a letter written 10 October 1898 to Julia Robards, Kate (Dement) Thompson, the couple's granddaughter, said: "It was my privilege to spend two weeks reading and copying the county court records of Charlotte County, Virginia. ... I have the marriage bond given by Jesse Lowe in marriage with Susan." Interpreted literally, it would seem that Mrs. Thompson appropriated the original bond to herself. In fairness, this literal interpretation may be doing her an injustice, but at any rate the bond today is not to be found at Charlotte Court House. The moral is clear: in case your lawyer hasn't told you recently, never commit anything to writing that you might be embarrassed to have the general public reading sixty years later.

Jesse Lowe (Low) served as a private in the company commanded at various times by Capt. Thomas Patterson and Capt. Billey Haley Avery, in the 6th Virginia Regiment of Continental Forces, under the command of Lieut. Col. James Hendricks, during the Revolutionary War. He was with this company at least as early as April 1777 and a Muster Roll of the Company shows he was at Middlebrook in May, 1777. In June 1777 he was one of a number of men selected from the army at large to compose Col. Daniel Morgan's Rifle Regiment of the Continental Troops, and as a private was assigned to Capt. Samuel Jordan Cabell's Company of Detached Riflemen,

---

357 Mellcene Thurman Smith and Jessymin Thurman Lewis, comp., *History and Lineage Book, National Society of the American Colonists in Missouri.* St. Louis, 1936, p. 146.

358 Thompson, *Sublett Family Chart.*

359 *Ibid.*

360 Notes found in the papers of Major William Martin Walton.

which by December 1777 was commanded by Capt. Benjamin Taliaferro. The final record of his service occurs on the 24 Feb. 1778 Pay Roll of Capt. Taliaferro's Company, by which pay was allowed to Low and remainder of the Company from 1 Feb. 1778 "to the expiration of their service including 15 days allowed them for going to Virginia."[361]

On 4 Dec. 1796 Jesse Loe sold 100 acres in Charlotte to Parrish Green, his wife Susannah relinquishing dower.[362] On 4 March 1797 Jessee Loe sold two tracts of 100 acres and 150 acres to Gabriel Folks and Thomas Spaulding.[363] Thereupon in early 1797 the couple migrated to Crab Orchard, Lincoln County, Kentucky, with numerous of Susanna's brothers and sisters. Jesse Lowe is listed for taxes there 23 August 1800.[364] Jesse Lowe died in Lincoln County between the making, 10 February 1814, and the probate of his will, 11 April 1814, or rather before that, by 7 March 1814 when inventory was made of his estate by John Wilkerson and Joseph Sproul. His will lists all twelve of his children in order of age, and gives his five slaves to his wife Susanna for life. Executors named were Benjamin Hiatt and his wife Susanna.[365]

Issue of Jesse and Susanna (Sublett) Lowe; first eight b. in Charlotte County, Virginia; last four b. in Lincoln County, Kentucky:[366]

- 171   i   George Allen Lowe, b. 20 Sept. 1782; m. (1st) 4 April 1809 in Lincoln County to Martha (Patsy) Wilkerson, daughter of John Wilkerson.[367] Lowe m. (2nd) Tabitha Owen, and died 17 Sept. 1835 in Hot Springs County, Arkansas.
  172   ii   Philip Sublett Lowe, b. 2 Sept. 1784; m. Mary Bedford. Issue; *inter alia*:
    1. George Allen Lowe.
    2. Susan Lowe, m. her cousin Samuel Davis.
  173   iii   Martha Lowe, b. 4 May 1786; m. Joseph Davis; d. Alabama. Among their issue:
    1. Susan Davis.
    2. Mary O. Davis, m. L. Hendricks.
    3. Jane Davis, m. --- Teague.
    4. Samuel Davis, m. his cousin Susan Lowe.
  174   iv   David Lowe, b. 25 August 1788; m. Nancy Givert (?), Givens or Gilbert. Among their issue:
    1. Garret Lowe, m. Miss --- Miller.
    2. Martha Lowe, m. William Rodgers.

---

361   Revolutionary War Military Service File, Jesse Low, Pvt., Capt. Thomas Patterson's Company 6th Virginia Regt., and Revolutionary War Military Service File, Jesse Low, Pvt., Morgan's Rifle Regt., Continental Troops, National Archives, Washington, D.C. (two separate service files).

362   *Charlotte County, Virginia, Deed Bk. 7*, p. 225.

363   *Ibid.*, Deed Bk. 8, pp. 53-54.

364   Clift, *"Second Census" of Kentucky*, p. 176.

365   Lincoln County, Kentucky, Will Bk.

366   Names and birthdates are from a broadside printed by their cousins "G. A. & A. C. Sublett, Murfreesborough, T- for P. S. Lowe" entitled Births of the Sons and Daughters of Jesse Lowe and Susannah, his wife." This unusual broadside is in the possession of Mrs. H. N. Barnett, Benton, Louisiana, who kindly furnished the compiler with a photocopy of the same. In faded writing on the same document a notation is entered that "Wm. Sublett married Susan Allen. Their daughter Susannah married Jesse Lowe." Marriages are from the Thompson *Sublett chart* and also from the Family Tree compiled by Sarah (Sublett) Stewart in 1859 in Rutherford County, Tennessee, as copied by Mary (Sublett) Elliot in 1898. Grandchildren are from the same sources.

367   Burns, *Kentucky Vital Statistics: ... Lincoln County*, p. 41.

               3.   Catherine Lowe, m. John Jones.

175   v   Susannah Lowe, b. 30 April 1790; m. Samuel Sprawl[368] (Sproul). The Thompson chart gives his name as Joseph Sproul. Among their issue:

               1.   Margaret Sproul, m. James Bracken.
               2.   Willis Sproul.
               3.   Jesse Sproul, m. Miss --- Hoffman.

176   vi   Thomas Lowe, b. 20 May 1792; m. Margaret Dudgeon; lived in Mississippi.

177   vii William Sublett Lowe, b. 5 Jan 1795; m. Lucretia Phillips.

178   viii Mary Hunt Lowe, b. 19 August 1796; m. John Warren; lived in West Tennessee. Among their issue:

               1.   Caldwell Warren.
               2.   Elizabeth Warren.
               3.   Amanda Warren, m. Mr. --- Woods.
               4.   John Warren.
               5.   Mary Warren, m. M. Rushing.
               6.   Thomas Warren.

179   ix   Nancy Branch Lowe, b. 4 August 1798; m. Jesse James. Among their issue:

               1.   Mary Lowe James, m. Mr. --- Pharr.
               2.   John Lowe James.

•   180   x   John Jefferson Lowe, b. 18 July 1800; m. his cousin Elizabeth Sublett (#1802); migrated to Arkansas and Texas.

•   181   xi   Celia (Selah) Williams Lowe, b. 11 March 1802; m. John Dement; migrated to Alabama.

182   xii Willis Fields Lowe, b. 26 March 1805; m. a Miss --- Phillips. Among their issue:

               1.   Susan D. Lowe.
               2.   David Lowe.

28.   Nancy Sublett was born 13 September 1768 according to the Family Bible records filed with her husband's Revolutionary Pension application.[369] She was married 13 October 1785 in Campbell County, Virginia, according to her own statement, to Bartlee Greenwood. The bond which was issued 11 Oct. 1785 in Campbell County[370] was returned 13 October 1785 by the Rev. John Weatherford (her brother-in-law) to the Charlotte County court, her name being given thereon as "Mary."[371] Her cousin Nancy (Sublett) Wood deposed that she had witnessed the ceremony.

    Bartlee (Bartley, Bartelot) Greenwood was born 18 July 1764, son of William Greenwood.[372] He enlisted "in the year 1777 for the term of the war at Hillsborough in the State of North Carolina in the company of Capt. James Gunn, regiment commanded by Col. Anthony W. White in the line of the State of Virginia or the Virginia Continental Establishment, that he continued to serve in said corps for between 4 & 5 years when he was despatched to Petersburg in Virginia to guard some publick waggons, that he was permitted to return to his Father's in Charlotte

---

368   *Ibid.*

369   Bartlee Greewood, Revolutionary Pension Application W 3013, National Archives, Washington, D. C.; abstracted also in Lucy K. McGhee, *Historical Records of Old Crab Orchard, Lincoln County, Kentucky*, vol. 1, 1951.

370   Hinshaw, *op. cit.*, p. 821.

371   Knorr, *... Charlotte County, Virginia*, p. 33.

372   Frederick Greenwood, *Greenwood Genealogies*, New York, 1914, p. 468.

County."[373] "Bartellot Greenwood" is listed for taxes for the last time in Charlotte County in 1795.[374] His grandson, G. W. Greenwood, stated that the family spent some years in Botetourt County, Virginia, before migrating to Lincoln County, Kentucky, about 1800.[375] This is borne out by a deed in July 1790, from "Bailey Greenwood and Nancy his wife" of the County of Botetourt for land on Dunlops Creek patented in 1782 by Greenwood.[376] He is listed in Lincoln County by the 1810 Census as "Bartlet Greenwood."[377] By 1812 he was serving as a constable there.[378] He died in Lincoln County 28 September 1837.[379] In the 1830 Census he is listed as "Bartlett Greenwood" with wife and three slaves.[380]

Issue of Bartlee and Nancy (Sublett) Greenwood:[381]

183	i	Elizabeth Greenwood, b. 18 Feb. 1787.
184	ii	Abraham S. Greenwood, b. 1 May 1789.
• 185	iii	William Mc. Greenwood, called "Mac," b. 6 March 1791; m. Elizabeth Legg.[382]
• 186	iv	Susanna A. Greenwood, b. 16 Feb. 1793, m. 24 Feb. 1813 in Lincoln County, Kentucky, to Richard Flint.[383]
187	v	John Greenwood (called Jack), b. 18 July 1796.
188	vi	Sally Greenwood, b. 8 July 1799, m. 10 Oct. 1819 to William Childress, Valentine Sublett being bondsman.[384]
189	vii	Patsey Greenwood, b. 15 Nov. 1801.[385]
190	viii	Lee Greenwood (presumably a contraction of Bartlee), b. 8 May 1804; m. (date of bond) 4 March 1828 Barbara Feland; residing in Illinois in 1839.
191	ix	Lucretia Greenwood, b. 19 December 1806.
192	x	George A. Greenwood, b. 21 June 1809.

29. **Abraham Sublett** was born say 1770 and was first listed for taxes in Charlotte County, Virginia, in 1789.[386] The tax books usually designate him as "Abraham Sublett Junr." to distinguish him from his older first cousin of the same name, "Abraham Sublett Sen[r]." (#36), who married his sister Celia. (The latter Abraham started appearing on the tax books first as Abraham Jun[r]. to distinguish him from his own father Abraham Sen[r]. (#8), but as the true Abraham Sen[r].

373   R.P.A. W 3013, cited above.

374   Charlotte County, Virginia, Personal Property Tax Lists, Virginia State Library, Richmond.

375   R.P.A. W 3013, letter of 1908 from G. W. Greenwood, Topeka, Kansas.

376   *Botetourt County, Virginia, Deed Bk. 4*, pp. 196, 217.

377   *Lincoln County, Kentucky, 1810 Census*, transcribed by Annie Walker Burns, p. 7.

378   *Ibid.*, Order Bk. 1812-1815, folio 15.

379   R.P.A. W. 3013.

380   Fifth Census of the U.S., 1830, Lincoln County, Kentucky, p. 65.

381   Copy from Family Bible, among papers submitted in R.P.A. W 3013.

382   Ann Catherine (Dement) Thompson, *Sublett Family Chart*, says her name was Elizabeth Jordan, but the Family Bible and notations by her son George W. Greenwood say her name was Elizabeth Legg. (These latter materials are in the possession of his grandson, George W. Greenwood, Topeka, Kansas, 1961).

383   Lucy K. McGhee, *Historical Records of Old Crab Orchard, Lincoln County, Kentucky*, vol. 3, p. 47. (Marriage Bonds of Lincoln County)

384   *Ibid.*, v. 3, p. 24.

385   Patsey Greenwood m. Harrison Brown [DJS].

386   Charlotte County, Virginia, Personal Property Tax Lists, 1782-1815.

died in 1782, he became for some years the sole Abraham on the books, until in 1789 his younger first cousin entered the tax picture.)

That Abraham (#29) was the son of William (#7) may be deduced from this series of facts: Of his grandfather Pierre Louis's five reproductive sons, two, Peter and Lewis, stayed on in the old Powhatan-Chesterfield area. Peter's will names no son Abraham. Lewis's son Abraham demonstrably stayed on in Chesterfield County until his death without issue in 1820. Of the three sons of Pierre Louis who moved to Charlotte County, Benjamin names no son Abraham in his will, which, naming nine children, would seem to omit no son. Abraham, Sr., had a son, Abraham, Jr., who moved to Lincoln County, Kentucky. That leaves William as the only possible father to this Abraham. Further it is known that in Green County, Kentucky, this Abraham was involved with Field Sublett as a neighbor (apparently son to William) and in February 1806 "Voluntine Sublett and Abraham Sublett of Green" joined in a deed to Simon Engelman.[387] Valentine was clearly son to William. Chronology virtually overrules the possibility that Abraham could have been a great-grandson of Pierre Louis.

On 6 Sept. 1790 (date of bond) Abraham Sublett was married in Charlotte County to Polly Smith, John Smith being surety.[388] He is listed for taxes in Charlotte County through the year 1797. Thereupon he apparently moved to Green County, Kentucky, where he is listed for taxes in 1800.[389] On 28 Oct. 1801 Abraham Sublett was serving as Captain in the 16th Regiment, Green County, Kentucky, Militia.[390] On 3 September 1803 he was involved in a land transaction,[391] and on 24 May 1804 obtained 100 acres on Roberson's Creek in Green County from John Middleton.[392] In the 1810 Census he is listed, aged 26-45, with a wife in the same age range, one daughter over 16, one son and two daughters between 10-16, and two sons and three daughters under 10.[393] Abram Sublett is listed in the 1820 Census of Green County as over 45 years of age, with a wife still 26-45, a daughter over 26, two sons 18-26, two daughters 16-26, one son and two daughters 10-16, and one son under 10.[394]

When Thomas Smith on 23 August 1832, aged 70 years, applied in Green County, Kentucky, for a Revolutionary pension based on his service as a private and corporal following his enlistment in Charlotte County, Virginia, his application was supported by his brother John Smith who stated that they had served together and by Abraham Sublett who deposed in Green County that he himself had actually seen Thomas' discharge. Presumably Thomas Smith was a near relative to Abraham's wife Polly Smith, and the John Smith who was surety on Abraham's marriage bond conceivably was the veteran John Smith who deposed in Thomas' behalf.[395]

No will was located for this Abraham Sublett, but the following seem to have been among his at least ten children. Such relationship is inferred from close association with Abraham in Green County transactions, and from lack of a parent for the children, after the process of elimination had overruled other possible senior Subletts in the area.

---

387   *Green County, Kentucky, Deed Bk. 4*, p. 286.

388   Knorr, ... *Charlotte County, Virginia*, p. 80.

389   Clift, *"Second Census" of Kentucky*.

390   G. Glenn Clift, *The "Corn Stalk" Militia of Kentucky. 1792-1811*. Frankfort, Kentucky Historical Society, 1957, p. 96.

391   *Green County, Kentucky, Deed Bk. 4*, p. 103.

392   *Warren County, Kentucky, Deed Bk. B2*, p. 229.

393   Third Census of the U.S., 1810, Green County, Kentucky, transcribed by Annie Walker Burns.

394   Fourth Census of the U.S., 1820, Green County, Kentucky, p. 14.

395   Thomas Smith, Revolutionary Pension Application S 11430, National Archives, Washington, D.C.

Tentative list of issue of Abraham and Polly (Smith) Sublett:

193   i   Susanna Sublett (possibly) named for her paternal grandmother; m. B. Chisholm.[396] On 15 March 1841 Abraham's grandson Henry W. Sublett sold to Abram Sublett of Green County "all my interest in the tract of land containing about 50 acres whereon said Abraham now lives, my interest being the dowable interest of Susanna Chisholm which I purchased of said Susanna Chisholm 25 February 1841."[397] Many years earlier on 16 July 1811 Abraham Sublett of Green County had sold 300 acres on Robersons Creek to B. Chisham of Green County.[398]

194   ii   John Smith Sublett (possibly), although Abraham had a nephew John S. Sublett who settled in Green County (#238) and he may have been John Smith Sublett, although one would rather expect to find John Smith Sublett a son to Polly (Smith), named for her surety on her marriage bond, John Smith. The John Sublett, for whose War of 1812 service an attempt was made to secure a pension for his widow, may tentatively be identified with this John Sublett. (John Sublett, War of 1812 Pension File W.O. 43509, National Archives, Washington, D.C.) This John Sublett is said to have served in the company of Capt. Armstrong Kerr, 29 March — 28 Sept. 1813, as did his first cousin John S. Sublett (#238). In 1828 he was m. in Overton County, Tennessee, to Celia Huff. John Sublett resided in Tennessee until 1855 when he settled in Clinton County, Kentucky, where he died c. 1862/3. Late in her life Celia lost her sanity, and as a resident of Fentress County, Tennessee, had Alvin C. Huff appointed as her guardian in 1883. Among their issue:[399]
1. Henry Sublett, b. c. 1833 "supposed to reside in the West."
2. Permelia Sublett b. c. 1838, m. Moore Medlock (Matlock); resided in Clinton County, Kentucky.
3. John Sublett, b. c. 1841, "supposed to reside in California."

195   iii   William Sublett (possibly), m. Mrs. Nancy (Phillips) Cobb, daughter of William Phillips and widow of David Cobb. The will of William Phillips, made 5 April 1831, probated 20 June 1831, mentions "the children of David Cobb dec[d]. by my daughter (now Nancy Sublett)."[400] It is possible, however, that the William who married Nancy Phillips was William Sublett (#121).

196   iv   Sylvia Sublett, m. (date of bond) 15 Oct. 1818 in Green County to Thomas Moore.[401]

• 197   v   Mary Sublett, m. (date of bond) 22 March 1821 in Green County to Robert Smith.[402]

• 198   vi   Philip Allen Sublett, b. 22 May 1802 in Green County, Kentucky; named for his paternal uncle (#30); migrated in 1824 to Durango, Mexico; prominent early Texas patriot and close friend of Sam Houston; m. Esther J. Roberts; d. 25 Feb. 1850, San Augustine, Texas. His sister Sylvia and he are the only children of

---

396   Susanna Sublett m. 26 Jun 1818, Green County, Kentucky, John L. Chisholm [DJS].
397   *Green County, Kentucky, Deed Bk. 18*, p. 188.
398   *Ibid.*, Deed Bk.
399   Seventh Census of the U.S., 1850, Tennessee, Sublits — Alexander, 20; Celia, 45; Henry, 18 [DJS].
400   *Green County, Kentucky, Deed Bk. 14*, p. 31.
401   *Ibid.*, Marriage Bk. 2, p. 15.
402   *Ibid.*, p. 151.

		Abraham Sublett named on Mrs. Thompson's chart.[403]
199	vii	Hiram Sublett, b. c. 1804, m. (date of bond) 13 Nov. 1825 in Green County to Elizabeth Tennison.[404] Witnessed a deed 31 Dec. 1834 from Samuel F. Beal to Abraham Sublett;[405] witnessed another deed from John S. Sublet to John Scandland.[406] Listed in the 1850 Census of Taylor County, Kentucky, as a miller, aged 46, b. in Kentucky.[407],[408]
200	viii	James A. Sublett, "Sr.," b. c. 1812; listed in the Taylor County, Kentucky, Census of 1850, as aged 38.

30.   Philip Allen Sublett, named for a maternal uncle, must have been born about 1774. He first appears on the personal property tax lists in Charlotte County, Virginia, in 1796. By 1797 he had migrated with a number of brothers and sisters to the Crab Orchard, Lincoln County, Kentucky, where on 21 Nov. 1797 he married Isabella Whitley.[409] She was the daughter of the celebrated William C. Whitley (1749-1813) (the alleged slayer of Tecumseh) by his wife Esther (Fuller).[410] Philip A. Sublet was listed for taxes in Lincoln County, Kentucky, August 1800.[411] Early in 1801 he moved his young family down to Pulaski County, Kentucky, where he is listed for taxes that year.[412] By 23 Feb. 1801, Phil. A. Sublett was serving as Lieutenant in the 44th Regiment, Pulaski County, Kentucky, militia.[413] He was very speedily appointed one of the commissioners to plan the new town of Somerset and to select locations for public buildings. The same year, 1801, he served as an election clerk and was appointed deputy sheriff of Pulaski County, keeper of the county jail, and in charge of stray stock.[414] In April 1802 Philip Sublett opened an "ordinary" at his "dwelling house in the town of Somerset."[415] In 1803 he was appointed clerk of the Circuit Court of Pulaski and Wayne counties, Kentucky, and the same year took an oath as a Justice of the Peace in Pulaski County. In 1805 he served as deputy surveyor. On 1 April 1807 Sublett was appointed federal postmaster of the town of Somerset, which position he held until New Year's Day, 1810.[416] Early in 1810 Philip returned with his family to Lincoln County.[417] The 1810 Census lists him in Lincoln County with wife and six children.[418] On 16 March 1812

403	Ann Catherine (Dement) Thompson, *Sublett Family Chart.*
404	*Green County, Kentucky, Marriage Bk. 2,* p. 52.
405	*Ibid.,* Deed Bk. 16, p. 76.
406	*Ibid.,* Deed Bk. 18, p. 15.
407	Taylor County, Kentucky, Census of 1850.
408	The Census of 1860 lists Hiram, 56; Elizabeth, 53; Wm., 18; Housson, 16; Milton, 14; Mildred, 11 [DJS].
409	Lincoln County, Kentucky, Marriage Bond Index; printed also in Ednah W. McAdams, *Kentucky Pioneer and Court Records* (1929), p. 120.
410	Harry W. Mills, *Lincoln County Pioneer families* (National D.A.R. Library, Washington, D.C.) (articles originally published in the Stanford, Kentucky, *Interior Journal*); Will of William Whitley, dated 26 Aug. 1812, probated 13 Dec. 1813, mentions daughter Isabella Sublet, *Lincoln County, Kentucky, Will Bk. G,* p. 14; will of Esther Whitley, dated 8 June 1829, probated 1834, mentions "the heirs of Isabell Sublett," *Lincoln County, Kentucky, Will Bk. M,* p. 67.
411	Clift, *"Second Census" of Kentucky,* p. 285.
412	Pulaski County, Kentucky, Tax List, 1801, MS., Kentucky Historical Society, Frankfort.
413	Clift, *"Corn Stalk" Militia,* p. 140.
414	*Pulaski County, Kentucky, Order Bk. No. 1, 1799-1803,* pp. 104, 244, 276, 288, and 315; *Order Bk. No. 2, 1804-1815,* p. 184. Also see: Alma Owens Tibbals, *A History of Pulaski County, Kentucky,* Bagdad, Kentucky, 1952, pp. 13, 14, 16.
415	*Ibid.,* Order Bk. No. 1, 1799-1803, p. 298; Order Bk. No. 2, 1804-1815, p. 1.
416	*Ibid.,* Order Bk. No. 1, 1799-1803, pp. 184, 399; Order Bk. No. 2, 1804-1815, p. 131; Tibbals, *op. cit.,* p. 84.
417	*Lincoln County, Kentucky, Order Bk. No. 7, 1809-1819,* p. 40.
418	Third Census of the U. S. (1810), Lincoln County, Kentucky, transcribed by Annie Walker Burns, Washington, 1936.

"On the motion of Philip A. Sublett, ordered that Tavern license be granted him to keep a Tavern at the house now occupied by him at the Crab Orchard."[419] Sublett served in the War of 1812 as a member of "Company & Ridgment 7" of the local militia but apparently never was in active service.[420] On 4 August 1818 P. A. Sublette sold to Andrew Whitley, his brother-in-law, "all my Right, title and interest to a tract of land which was left to my wife Isabella by her father William Whitley deceased."[421] Thereupon late in 1818 he moved with his family to the valley of the Femme Osage, in St. Charles County, Missouri, 22 miles north of St. Louis.[422] There Philip Sublett was granted a license by the county court to operate a ferry at his land on the Mississippi.[423] Sublett again opened a tavern in his new Missouri home, where in March 1819 he was summoned into court on charges that he had kept "a certain common misgoverned & disorderly house ... [and suffered] certain persons of evil name & fame and of dishonest conversation ... to be & remain drinking, tippling, gambling & misbehaving themselves."[424] Nothing came of the charges and Philip became a magistrate for the township. Philip Allen Sublett died on Thursday, 28 December 1820.[425] On 4 January 1821 "whereas Phillip A. Sublette ... died intestate as is said," authority to administer his estate was granted to his widow Isabella and his son William L. Sublette.[426] His widow Isabella did not long survive him, dying either the 21st or 22nd or January 1822.[427] On 27 January 1822 "whereas Isabella Sublette died intestate as is said," her son William L. Sublette was appointed administrator of the estate.[428]

Surviving issue of Philip Allen and Isabella (Whitley) Sublette — according to the list of heirs attached to the son's bond as administrator, were: (order of birth based on order in the bond listing; dates of birth estimated from the 1810 Census; two oldest and the youngest apparently born in Lincoln County; rest born in Pulaski County, Kentucky).[429]

206   i   William Lewis Sublette, b. 21 Sept. 1798 (prob.) or 1799;[430] d. 23 July 1845, Pittsburgh, Penn.; m. 21 March 1844 Frances Hereford of Tuscumbia, Alabama. The most prominent man to bear the Sublett name; he made a fortune in the fur trade and a reputation as an Indian fighter and friend; was known to the Indians as "Cut-Face." Part of the Oregon Trail was first known as Sublette's Cut-Off and Sublette's Trace. Sublette County, Wyoming, was named for him and his brothers. In 1830 he made an overland trip to Oregon and reported thereon to Secretary of War John Eaton.[431] He died without issue.

419   *Lincoln County, Kentucky, Order Bk., 1812-1815*, folio 8; Lincoln County, Kentucky, Tavern Bonds, 1810-1817.

420   *Ibid.*, Order Bk. No. 7, 1809-1819, p. 43.

421   *Ibid.*, Deed Bk. No. I, p. 167.

422   William S. Bryan and Robert Rose, *A History of the Pioneer Families of Missouri*, St. Louis, 1876, p. 187.

423   *St. Charles County, Missouri, Record Bk. A-2, 1816-1820*, p. 236.

424   St. Charles County, Missouri, suit styled "The State of Missouri *v.* P. A. Sublette & Morgan Swope," Court Files, Nov. Term 1819 to Feb. Term 1821.

425   John E. Sunder, *Bill Sublette, Mountain Man*, Norman, Oklahoma, Univ. of Oklahoma Press, 1959, p. 29.

426   St. Charles County, Missouri, File No. 3420, Estate of Phillip A. Sublette; Bk. G, pp. 49-50.

427   *Missourian* (St. Charles, Missouri), 24 Jan. 1822.

428   St. Charles County, Missouri, File No. 3419, Estate of Isabella Sublette; Wills and Letters of Administration and Letters Testamentary, 1822-1833.

429   Certain information on these children is contained in Sunder, *op. cit.*; other information derives from Dr. John Sublett Logan's *Sublett MSS.*, Kentucky Historical Soc., Frankfort, Kentucky

430   Sunder, *op. cit.*, p. 7.

431   For fuller accounts of his life, see: Sunder, *op. cit.*, Stella M. Drumm, "William Lewis Sublette," *Dictionary of American Biography*, 18:189; Doyce B. Nunnis, Jr., "The Sublettes of Kentucky: Their Early Contribution to the Opening of the

207   ii   Milton G. Sublette, b. ca 1800; d. 5 April 1837; buried near Ft. William on the Laramie [Wyoming]. Some time earlier, suffering from osteomyelitis, he amputated his own leg in February 1835.

•   208   iii   Sophronia Fuller Sublette, b. ca 1802, d. 20 April 1843 near St. Louis, Missouri; m. Grove Cook.

209   iv   Pinckney W. Sublette, b. ca 1804, d. without issue March, 1828, on the Portneuf River, slain by the Crow Indians.

210   v   Mary L. Sublette (Polly), b. ca 1806, d. without issue before 1845.

211   vi   Andrew Whitley Sublette b. ca 1808, served in the Mexican War with the Missouri Mounted Volunteers as Captain of Company A, the "Oregon" Battalion; was mustered out 6 Nov. 1848 at Fort Leavenworth and in 1849 set out overland for California. There he worked for a while in the gold fields. In June 1850 he is referred to in a reported case as "late Sheriff or Comissario of the Court of First Instances of the District of San Francisco."[432] After a siege of ill health, he moved down south to the town of Los Angeles. The California Census of 1852 lists him in Los Angeles County, Ranchero, aged 42.[433] There he died in an encounter with a grizzly bear on a hunting trip, 19 December 1853.[434] Never married.

212   vii   Sally Sublette, b. ca 1810, d. between 1819-1823.[435]

213   viii   Solomon Perry Sublette, b. ca 1813, was married 21 May 1848 at Independence, Missouri to his brother William's widow Frances (Hereford).[436] Following a long and arduous career as an Indian trader in the Southwest, principally at Santa Fe, he was appointed in October 1847 by the War Department's Office of Indian Affairs as the Osage River Indian Agent for the United Tribe of Sacs and Fox of the Mississippi.[437] He died 31 August 1857;[438] his widow Frances died shortly, 28 Sept. 1857. Issue of Solomon Perry and Frances (Hereford) Sublette:
        1.   Solomon Perry Sublette, Jr., b. 18 Dec. 1850; died 24 April 1851.
        2.   Esther Frances Sublette, b. 13 October 1853; d. 6 May 1861.
        3.   William Hugh Sublette, b. July 1856; d. 2 Nov. 1857.

This tragedy-dogged family left two progeny, with the result that certain former Sublette-owned realty in St. Louis became the object of protracted court action in 1896, 1900, 1911, 1926, and 1928 in St. Louis. The litigation had the commendable result, usual in such cases, that it encouraged various Subletts to do research into their family connections and to record the same. However, also as usual where the lure of a fortune produces a hot-house variety of genealogy,

---

West," *The Register of the Kentucky Historical Society*, 57:20-34 (Jan. 1959); 58:143. H. M. Chittenden, *American Fur Trade of the Far West*, 2 vols., (2nd ed., 1935).

432   *Sublette v. Melhado*, 1 California. 104 (Sub. Ct., California, June, 1850).

433   *California Census of 1852, v. 3*, p. 157, of typescript by Genealogical Records Committee, D.A.R. of California, 1934, National D.A.R. Library, Washington, D.C.

434   Sister Marietta (Jennings), *The Sublette MSS.*, M.A. thesis, Columbia University, 1925 (N.Y. Public Library, typescript), p. 205; also, the Sacramento *Daily Union*, 29 Dec. 1853, quoted by Doyce B. Nunis, Jr., "The Sublettes of Kentucky and the Far West, 1830-1857," *Register of the Kentucky Historical Society*, v. 58, p. 143. Andrew is himself the subject of a biography: Doyce B. Nunis, Jr., *Andrew Sublette: Rocky Mountain Prince, 1808-1853*. Los Angeles, 1960.

435   Sunder, *op. cit.*, p. 30.

436   Sister Marietta, *op. cit.*, pp. 153-154, 166, 167.

437   *Ibid.*, pp. 136, 145.

438   Sunder, *op. cit.*, p. 234.

some of the "laughing heirs" in this situation did some pushing and straining to appear as the heirs of Philip's children, and the group who pushed their claim longest and hardest were the descendants of Philip's first cousin Littlebury Sublett (#41), who, whether by design or accident, attempted to by-pass the descendants of Philip's very numerous brothers and sisters by claiming that Philip Allen Sublett was a son of Littlebury. This is manifestly erroneous, and yet the claim has fooled many people, including the author of the recent biography of William Lewis Sublette.[439] The deeds of Green County, Kentucky, make it certain that Littlebury (#41) had only six children, none of whom was named Philip Allen Sublett, and it has been shown, *supra*, that Philip Allen was named by his mother Susanna (Allen) Sublett for her brother Philip Allen.

Some much more accurate genealogical research was undertaken by Ann Catherine (Dement) Thompson and the Attorneys Walton, descendants of Susanna (Sublett) Lowe (#27), who succeeded in tracking down through reliable family records ten brothers and sisters of Philip Allen Sublette. To these the contributor would add only one other, Field Sublett (#31). A portion of the research of Mrs. Thompson and the Attorneys Walton, accomplished in the 1890s, is in the possession of Mrs. H. H. Barnett (Louise Walton), Benton, Louisiana. There is evidence also that the descendants of Ursula (Sublett) Day (#23) were excited over the prospects of a realty windfall in St. Louis. In fact, papers preserved by Gray Herndon, attorney, Springfield, Illinois, show that Rebecca (Day) Herndon (#144) and her son-in-law Frank Fleury investigated their possible interest in the estate as early as 1867 and were satisfied they had no right thereto. As it transpired, the Sublette St. Louis realty hopes were a pipe-dream, but the compiler would be very much interested to know of some other Sublett genealogical researches that were taken with the realty as a lure.

The sudden flare-up of interest in the Sublette property in 1896 is fascinating, for its inception bears every evidence at this distance of contrivance and manipulation by a small group of descendants of Littlebury Sublett (#41). Center of this little knot of "researchers" was Mrs. Thelia Ewart. She had consulted attorneys Bente and Wilson in her town, Sedalia, Missouri, some time in 1895 concerning her possible interest in Solomon Sublette's estate and that of his daughter Esther Frances. C. I. Wilson, one of these attorneys, deposed on 23 Sept. 1896 in connection with the first court action in the matter that "on 6 Nov. 1895 he received by due course of mail a yellow envelope of large size addressed to H. K. Bente, that said envelope bore the post office stamp of St. Louis dated 5 Nov. 1895 --- that he opened the envelope and found within the said envelope what purported to be the will of Solomon P. Sublette dated April 15, 1856, an old and apparently time-stained document; that he immediately took the same to the residence of Mrs. Thena Ewart and delivered the same to her and that no other writing whatever was contained in said envelope."[440] This "will," which thus mysteriously turned up forty years after it was assertedly written, sent in to Mrs. Ewart's attorney by a party who for some reason preferred to remain anonymous, in the wake of her sudden interest in the matter, was tailor-made to the interests of only the Sublett kin of Solomon, not to the Whitley kin: by it Solomon P. Sublette on 15 April 1856 left "to my beloved wife Frances all my personal property and real estate ... and at her death, bequeath all said property to my daughter Esther Frances (Fannie) and if she dies single and unmarried and without issue, I bequeath all my said property to my brother Pinkney W. Sublette, if living, and at his death, if single and unmarried and without issue, I bequeath said property to my next of kin, on my father's side" (thus cutting out his mother's kin, the Whitleys).[441] There were at least two strange things about the will: (1) In it, Solomon did not

---

439   Sunder, *op. cit.*, p. 240.

440   Copy of deposition among papers of Gray Herndon, Esq., Springfield, Illinois.

441   Copy of will among said papers.

even mention the possibility of the imminent existence of his son William Hugh, born several weeks later; (2) he refers to his brother Pinkney as living, although the Sublette papers of his brother William show that Pinkney had been killed by the Indians in 1828, and one or more of the Sublette brothers had fled from the scene of the impending murder. The Sedalia Subletts (Mrs. Ewart et al.) then paraded a group of colorful and a bit fantastic characters into the court room to show that they had seen Pinkney alive as late as 1862. (Very convenient, because it was necessary to show that Pinkney had survived his niece, little Esther Frances, who had died in 1861.) One or two of the witnesses for the proponents of the will got rather badly tangled up in testimony. The bones of a man, said to be those of Pinkney, were disinterred in Wyoming and entered as an exhibit in the St. Louis proceedings to establish the will. These bones were destined to remain in the basement of the St. Louis County Court House for over thirty years, until the last Sublett "heir" finally threw in the sponge of his hopes. Eventually they were re-interred in a new county, Sublette County, Wyoming, named in honor of the pioneering brothers.

A great deal of interest in the whole matter is indicated by the numerous reports in the popular press of such-and-such a Sublett of oft-times fantastically remote connection who was about ready to receive several million dollars. And these childless or descendant-less brothers were suddenly endowed with occasional lineal descendants in the process. For example, "Rev. M. R. Shanks of Geary, Oklahoma, to share in real estate ... which has been in controversy since the death of <u>Simon</u> P. Sublette, <u>grandfather</u> of Rev. Shanks, in 1857."[442] Attorney Thomas B. Crews wrote one heir that "the reports in the newspapers concerning the Sublette suit are very largely incorrect ... According to the newspapers, millionaires are springing up all over the U.S., all deriving their fortune from the Sublette estate ... I will add for your information that the newspapers have always exaggerated the amount of interest involved in this estate. I do not believe that the whole value at stake can exceed from three to five hundred thousand dollars; I believe that is a large estimate."[443]

31.   Field Sublett was born say 1776. He never appears on the public records of Charlotte County, Virginia, but as a quite young man apparently followed or accompanied his older brother Abraham to Green County, Kentucky, where he virtually escapes the public records. Indeed, the main reason for positing his existence is the fact that in the 1810 Census of Green County, Kentucky, there appear two Field Subletts as heads of families, one between 26-45, and the other between 16-26. The younger of the two would seem clearly to be Valentine's son Field (#120). This leaves an older man to be accounted for. Being associated in Green County with Abraham and Valentine, sons to William and Susannah (Allen) Sublett, he would appear to be the (presumably) youngest son of Susannah (Allen) Sublett, named by her for her mother Mary (Hunt) Allen's third husband, Field Jefferson. This would explain also Valentine's naming a son Field. The elder Field Sublett is shown by the Census of 1810 to have had a wife, aged 26-46, and one daughter under 10.[444]

442   St. Louis *Globe-Democrat*, Dec. 26, 1907.

443   Letter, Thomas B. Crews to Frank Fleury, dated 5 Feb. 1908, St. Louis; copy among papers of Gray Herndon. Further contemporary newspaper accounts are contained in St. Louis *Globe-Democrat*, 30 Jan. 1908; *Missouri Republic*, 30 Jan. 1908; *Woman's National Daily* (University City, St. Louis) 14 Jan. 1908; St. Louis *Post-Despatch*, 28 Dec. 1902 and 13 Feb. 1903.

444   Third Census of the U.S., 1810, Green County, Kentucky, transcribed by Annie Walker Burns Bell, p. 3; cf., Field Sublett, p. 23.

35.   William Sublett, born say 1754, married at an undetermined date Susannah ---[445] and stayed fairly clear of public records, the only exceptions arising from his guardianship of his youngest sister Nancy. On 7 Feb. 1785 she made choice of him as her guardian.[446] He was taxed in Charlotte County, Virginia on his personal property from 1785 to his death in 1811/12. During the earlier part of this period he is usually called "William Sen" to distinguish him from his younger cousin, William Allen Sublett (#26); during the latter part of the period he is called such to distinguish him from his own son.[447] The mass exodus of the Subletts from Charlotte County which occurred during the 1790s and early 1800s left him the only Sublett accounted for in the 1810 Census of Charlotte County. There he and his wife, both over 45, are listed.[448] His will, dated 16 Dec. 1811, probated 6 January 1812,[449] names wife Susannah and three children, *viz*.:

Issue of William and Susannah (---)[450] Sublett:

228   i   Ann ("Anny") Sublett, m. 5 Dec. 1799 John Burchfield (or Birchfield) in Charlotte County.[451] (Called Amy in Knorr, but other references make it certain that she was Anny, as she was denominated in her father's will.) She made her mark as Ann to a joint deed by her father's heirs.[452]

•   229   ii   William Sublett, Jr., named executor of his father's will. First taxed on personalty in Charlotte County in 1802.[453] Married Betsy Redden, July, 1805.

230   iii   Sarah (Sally) Sublett. Married 15 Feb. 1815 in Charlotte County to James Stokes (Knorr's reading);[454] however, a subsequent deed looks more like "James Leaker."[455] This reading is confirmed by the 1850 census, where she is recorded, aged 66, residing with her brother William.[456]

36.   Abraham Sublett was born about 1756, from the fact that he gave his age as 76 years on his Revolutionary Pension Application made 29 Aug. 1832.[457] He resided at the time of his military service "in the county of Charlotte, State of Virginia, about seven miles from the court house." His service embraced two tours of duty, the first one of three months' duration, January to April 1778 in the military company of Capt. Richard Gaines. During his second tour, July to November 1781, in the militia company of Capt. Gideon Spencer, he was at "the siege of York and was at the taking of Cornwallis." On 9 May 1782 he was married in Charlotte County by the Rev. John Weatherford to his first cousin, Celia (Selah) Sublett, daughter of William and Susannah (Allen) Sublett.[458]

---

445   Susannah Keirsey, daughter of Thomas and Lucy [DJS].

446   *Charlotte County, Virginia, Order Bk. 6*, p. 13.

447   Charlotte County, Virginia, Personal Property Tax Books, 1782-1815.

448   Third Census of the U.S., 1810, Charlotte County, Virginia, p. 118.

449   *Charlotte County, Virginia, Will Bk. 3*, p. 187.

450   Susannah Keirsey, daughter of Thomas and Lucy, according to DJS.

451   Knorr, *Marriage Bonds and Ministers' Returns of Charlotte County, Virginia, 1764-1815*, 1951, p. 11.

452   *Charlotte County, Virginia, Deed Bk. 14*, p. 79.

453   *Ibid.*, Personal Property Tax Books, 1782-1815.

454   Knorr, *op. cit.*, Charlotte County, Virginia, p. 79.

455   *Charlotte County, Virginia, Deed Bk. 14*, p. 79.

456   Montgomery County, Virginia, 1850 Census.

457   Abraham Sublett, Revolutionary Pension Application S 31397, National Archives, Washington, D.C.

458   Knorr, ... *Charlotte County, Virginia*, p. 80.

He continued to reside in Charlotte until "about 1798 or 1799" when he removed with his family to Lincoln County, Kentucky.[459] His pension chronology is verified by the tax records of Charlotte County, which list him there for the last time in 1797.[460] He is listed for taxes in Lincoln County, Kentucky, in August 1800.[461] On 14 March 1808 in Lincoln County he was appointed constable to replace Peter Salle, Edward Day being security on his bond.[462] His wife Cella seems to have died prior to the 1830 Census, for he is evidently wifeless therein.[463] In April 1844 it was "Ordered that it be certified to the Secretary of the War Department that it was this day proved to the satisfaction of the court by the oaths of Abram Sublett, Jr., and Nelson Martin ... that Abraham Sublett late a pensioner of the U.S. departed this life on the 1st day of March 1844."[464] On 10 Feb. 1845 Abraham Sublett Jr. and Susan Sublett obtained Letters of Administration on his estate.[465]

Abraham and Celia (Sublett) Sublett had issue, all born presumably in Charlotte County, Virginia:[466]

234   i   Susannah Sublett, named for her maternal grandmother, b. ca. 15 Jan. 1783; d. 30 Sept. 1852, Boons County, Missouri, "aged 69 yrs., 8 mo., 15 days"; buried at Rocky Fork Primitive Baptist Church, Boone County, Missouri;[467] never married; migrated to Missouri late in life with her nephew Abraham Sublett.

· 235   ii   William Sublett, named for his maternal grandfather, b. say 1785, m. 10 January 1809 in Warren County, Kentucky, a cousin, Mary Scott Sublett (#56), daughter of Benjamin and Elizabeth (Jordan) Sublett.[468] It will be noted that William's father, mother and wife were all born Subletts. William migrated to Jackson County, Alabama, and died there in 1832, where he is buried in the Larkinsville community.

236   iii   Elizabeth Sublett, named for her paternal grandmother, b. say 1787, m. (date of bond) 29 November 1804 in Lincoln County, Kentucky, to John Salle (Sallee, Sally);[469] yet living in 1848.

· 237   iv   Abraham Sublett, named for his paternal grandfather and his father, b. say 1789, m. Temperance Brooks; migrated to Jackson County, Alabama, where he died in 1840.

· 238   v   John S. Sublett, b. say 1792, m. (date of bond) 5 Aug. 1821 in Green County, Kentucky, Mrs. Nancy (Hubbard) Walker;[470] he was an invalid pensioner of the War of 1812; d. 25 August 1844 in Lincoln County, Kentucky.[471]

---

459   R.P.A. S 31397, cited above.

460   Charlotte County, Virginia, Personal Property Tax Returns, 1782-1815.

461   Clift, *"Second Census" of Kentucky*, 1800.

462   *Lincoln County, Kentucky, Order Bk. No. 6, 1801-1808*, p. 433.

463   Fifth Census of the U.S., 1830, Lincoln County, Kentucky, p. 47.

464   *Lincoln County, Kentucky, Order Bk., 1842-1846*, p. 24.

465   *Ibid.*, p. 339.

466   Information as to the extent of the family based in large part on Lincoln County, Kentucky, Circuit Court, Equity Papers, 1850 File Box, suit styled "Abram Sublete's Heirs Against Abram Sublete's Heirs."

467   Rella Bright Evans and Mrs. J. Frank Thompson, *Tombstone Records of Boone County, Missouri*, Columbia, Missouri, 1934, mimeo., p. 112.

468   Warren County, Kentucky, Marriage.

469   *Lincoln County, Kentucky, Index to Marriages, 1784-1908*, p. 244.

470   *Green County, Kentucky, Marriage Bk. 3*, p. 24.

471   John S. Sublett, Bounty Land Warrant 29777-80-55, National Archives, Washington, D.C.

• 239   vi   Valentine Sublett, b. say 1794, m. (date of bond) 12 December 1820 to Maria O'Bannon.[472]

240   vii   George A. (Allen?) Sublett, b. say 1796, d. by 9 July 1827 when his brother Valentine Sublett obtained Letters of Administration on his estate, with Abraham Sublett and Wm. Heart his securities.[473]

38.   Elizabeth Sublett was born about 1760, from the fact that she gave her age as 79 years in her application for a Revolutionary widow's pension made 18 December 1839 in Nelson County, Virginia.[474] On 3 January 1781 she was married in Charlotte County, Virginia, to Campbell Daniel. The marriage was apparently a hurried event, spurred on by wartime exigencies, for the marriage bond states that "there is a marriage suddenly intended to be solemnized between Campbell Daniel and Betsey Sublett" and Elizabeth in her application recites "she recollects distinctly shortly after marriage he was called into service and marched to Guilford." Daniel's comrade-in-arms, Thomas Harvey, testified that Daniel was drafted as a private for a three-month tour under Capt. Thomas Williams, marched to the south and was engaged in the Battle of Camden, fought in August, 1780. Daniel's second draft tour as a sergeant was performed under Capt. John Harvey, when, straight from his marriage, he marched to North Carolina to participate in the Battle of Guilford in March 1781. Later in 1781 he was at Yorktown. Campbell Daniel died 19 February 1816 in Charlotte County, Virginia, where his estate was administered.[475] Elizabeth lived on many years in Charlotte County but a few years prior to her death went to reside with her eldest daughter Nancy (Daniel) Ligon in Nelson County, Virginia, where she died 22 June 1841.

        Issue of Campbell and Elizabeth (Sublett) Daniel:

245   i   Nancy Daniel, b. 3 February 1783, Charlotte County, Virginia; d. 31 Aug. 1873; m. 12 Nov 1812 in Charlotte County to John Ligon, b. 4 Oct. 1778 in Cumberland County, Virginia; d. 1861; son of William and Elizabeth (East) Ligon.[476]

246   ii   Elizabeth Daniel, m. Charles Jones, Fluvanna County, Virginia.

247   iii   James G. Daniel.

248   iv   Sally Daniel, m. --- Harris.

249   v   Abraham S. Daniel

        Papers in Elizabeth (Sublett) Daniel's pension file show that at her death these five children were living one each in Charlotte County, Fluvanna County, and Nelson County, Virginia, one in Kentucky and one in Tennessee.

39. Jane (or Jean) Sublett was born say 1764 and married 1 April 1782 in Charlotte County, Virginia,[477] to Edward Eanes, who was born in Chesterfield County, Virginia, 2 May 1761.[478] He

---

472   Lincoln County, Kentucky, Marriage Bond Register, unpaged.

473   *Ibid.*, Order Bk. 9, 1824-1831, folio 126.

474   Campbell Daniel, Revolutionary Pension Application W 6985, National Archives, Washington, D.C., abstracted in *Tyler's Quarterly*, 14:154.

475   *Charlotte County, Virginia, Will Bk. 5*, p. 9.

476   William D. Ligon, Jr., *The Ligon Family and Connections*, 1947, pp. 691-697, *q.v.* for descendants of this couple.

477   Knorr, *Charlotte County, Virginia*, p. 23.

478   Edward Eanes, Rev. Pens. Ap. R 3186, National Archives, Wash.

was the son of Henry Eanes.[479] Eanes deposed that he served three tours in the Revolutionary militia: (1) in Capt. Spencer's Company at the Battles of Hawfields and Guilford; (2) in Capt. Bibb's Company in eastern Virginia at the time of Cornwallis' surrender; and (3) in Capt. Lee's Company, being discharged in Dinwiddie County. Eanes' pension request was rejected because he could not state the exact periods of his service. In 1813 Eanes moved with his family to Pittsylvania County, Virginia.[480] He died there between 1 Sept. 1846 and 19 June 1848, the dates of the making and probate of his will.[481]

Issue of Edward and Jane (Sublett) Eanes, named in his will; further information from the Eanes genealogy:[482]

252	i	John Eanes, b. 1783; Ensign, Virginia militia, Charlotte County, Aug. 1813.
253	ii	William Eanes, b. 1784; m. (date of bond) 26 Sept. 1812 in Charlotte County, Virginia, to Patsey Scates (Seats).
254	iii	Henry Eanes, b. 1791; m. (date of bond) 5 May 1813 in Charlotte County, Virginia, to his first cousin Sarah Eanes, b. 1788, daughter of Arthur and Eleanor or Nellie (Murry) Eanes.
255	iv	Abraham Eanes, b. ca 1795; d. in Pittsylvania County, Virginia, between 20 June 1860 and 16 Dec. 1872; m. (1st) in Pittsylvania County 15 May 1815 to Catharine Wells; (2nd) 21 April 1828 in Pittsylvania County to Cassandra Covington. Issue by first wife:

    1. Joel S. Eanes, b. ca 1816; m. 3 Aug. 1838 in Pittsylvania County to Elizabeth L. Taylor.

256	v	Nancy Eanes, m. (date of bond) 14 April 1823 in Pittsylvania County to James Riddle.
257	vi	Edward S. Eanes, b. after 1796, m. 1 Feb. 1839 in Pittsylvania County Jane Taylor.
258	vii	Herbert Eanes. This may be the Herbert Eanes who m. (1st) 3 Nov. 1828 Nancy Bernard, and (2d) 10 Oct. 1842 Mary M. Bernard.
259	viii	George W. Eanes, b. 1802, m. (date of bond) 2 Feb. 1836 in Pittsylvania County, Louisa C. Tarpley. He died between 20 April 1875 and 18 Oct. 1875. Issue:

    1. Mary Jane Eanes, b. 1837, m. Nov. 1852 James R. Perkins.
    2. William Eanes, b. 1838.
    3. Catherine Eanes, b. 1841, m. 13 May 1860 Joseph O. Cooper.
    4. Elizabeth Eanes, m. --- White.
    5. Edward Eanes, b. 1845.
    6. Joseph Eanes, b. 1847.
    7. Louisa Eanes, b. 1850.
    8. John G. Eanes, b. 1855.
    9. Susan Eanes, b. 1858.

40. Nancy Sublett was born circa 1770 from the fact that she gave her age as eighty years of age

---

479   Dr. Richard Henry Eanes, *The Descendants of Edward Eanes of Henrico and Chesterfield Counties in Virginia*, 1940 (mimeo).

480   Charlotte County, Virginia, Personal Property Tax List, 1813.

481   *Pittsylvania County, Virginia, Will Bk. 2*, p. 45.

482   Marshall Wingfield, *Franklin County, Virginia, Marriage Bonds, 1786-1858*.

when seeking a Revolutionary widow's pension 19 June 1850.[483] She was married 24 October 1785 (though she herself gave her marriage date as 27 October 1785) in Charlotte County, Virginia, to Caldwell Wood. Her first cousin Nancy (Sublett) Greenwood deposed 3 Sept. 1850 in Lincoln County, Kentucky, that she had witnessed the ceremony. Her brother Abraham, not her deceased father Abraham, as Knorr states, was surety.[484] Thereafter, "Culwell Wood" certified on 4 Sept. 1786 that he had "received of William Sublett ... full satisfaction for all her estate in his the said William Subletts hands,"[485] her brother William having served as her guardian prior to her marriage. Caldwell Wood(s) was born about 1754, son of John Wood.[486] He served two tours of duty in the Revolution, the first beginning 9 Jan. 1778 in the company of Capt. Richard Gaines; the second under Capt. Gideon Spencer, July-November 1781, involved him in the siege of Little York when Lord Cornwallis was captured. He resided in Charlotte County "about seven miles from the Court House" until 1810 when he followed his brother-in-law Abraham Sublett to Lincoln County, Kentucky; the statement of the year of migration is confirmed by the tax records of Charlotte County.[487] There in Lincoln County, Kentucky, he died 5 Sept. 1845.[488] In the closing days of her life, Nancy (Sublett) Wood formed the intention of "moving with her sons family to Missouri."[489] Whether she lived to fulfill her intention is doubtful, for sometime between the date of her application for a widow's pension (19 June 1850) and 2 Sept. 1851 she had died.[490]

Issue of Caldwell and Nancy (Sublett) Wood(s), all apparently born in Charlotte:[491]

263   i   Abraham S. Wood, b. ca 1790; resided with his brother John's widow and family in Lincoln County, Kentucky, 1850.

264   ii   John S. Wood,[492] d. between 8 May 1849 (making) and 7 January 1850 (probate of his will), Lincoln County, Kentucky.[493] Married Mary ---,[494] b. ca 1805.[495] Issue:

1. Susan Wood, m. (date of bond) 22 Dec. 1836 in Lincoln County, Kentucky, to Paschal Saunders.
2. Nancy Jane Wood, m. (date of bond) 5 Dec. 1842 in Lincoln County, Kentucky, to James Tucker.
3. Eliza Wood, m. (date of bond) 17 July 1844 in Lincoln County, Kentucky, to Samuel Owsley.

---

483   Caldwell Wood(s), Revolutionary Pension App. W 9033, National Archives, Washington, D.C.

484   Knorr, *Charlotte County, Virginia*, p. 92.

485   *Charlotte County, Virginia, Guardians Accounts, v. 2*, p. 52.

486   *Ibid.*, Deed Bk. 6, p. 34.

487   *Ibid.*, Personal Property Tax Books, 1782-1815.

488   R.P.A. W 9033, cited above.

489   *Ibid.*.

490   Lincoln County, Kentucky, Circuit Court, Equity Papers, 1854 File Box, suit styled "Caldwell Wood's Heirs *v.* Caldwell Wood's Heirs."

491   *Ibid.*, Deed Bk. Y, p. 182, considerably amplified by the papers filed in the suit cited in the preceding footnote.

492   Correspondence 1990 from Mildred (Byassee) Shannon of Paducah, Kentucky, states that (#264) John Sublett Wood, b. 2 Feb 1789, Charlotte County, Virginia; d. 6 Dec 1849 Danville, Kentucky; m. 11 Jul 1817, Mary (Polly) Mitchell, b. 5 Nov 1797, Madison County, Kentucky; d. 25 Dec 1861, Boyle County, Kentucky. [DJS].

493   *Lincoln County, Kentucky, Will Bk. Q*, p. 68.

494   Mary (Polly) Mitchell [DJS].

495   All "circa" dates supplied from the *1850 Census of Lincoln County, Kentucky*, pp. 306-307, Households No. 419, 420 and 435.

        4.   William Caldwell Wood, b. ca 1824.

        5.   Margaret Wood, b. ca 1826, m. Joseph McInnes.

        6.   Thomas Eugene Wood, b. ca 1828.

        7.   Mary Louise Wood, b. 26 Nov 1830, Danville, Kentucky; d. 3 May 1873, Columbus, Kentucky, m. 1 Feb 1855 Reuben Thos. Samuel, b. 10 Feb 1832, Danville, Kentucky, d. 10 Aug 1912, Columbus, Kentucky.[496]

        8.   Martha Wood, b. ca 1834.

        9.   Angeline Wood, b. ca 1836.

       10. Josephine Wood, b. ca 1836.

265   iii   William S. Wood, residing in 1852 in Holt County, Missouri.[497]

266   iv   Jane Wood, b. ca 1803, n.m., d.s.p. in Missouri between Sept. 1851 and Sept. 1854.

267   v   Elizabeth Sallee Wood, m. (date of bond) 13 April 1822 in Lincoln County, Kentucky, to William Clark; resident in 1852 of Holt County, Missouri.

268   vi   Susan Wood, m. Charles Tomlinson; residing in 1854 in Pope County, Arkansas.

269   vii   Nancy B. Wood, m. (date of bond) 14 Sept. 1825 in Lincoln County, Kentucky, to William Vaughan. She was dead by Sept. 1851 when her heirs (all of Montgomery County, Missouri) were:

        1.   Abraham C. Vaughn.

        2.   Mary M. Vaughn, m. William Syler.

        3.   America J. Vaughn, m. Lewis Jones.

        4.   Mersilla Vaughn, m. Lucien B. Love.

270   viii George Allen C. Wood, b. ca 1812,[498] residing in 1852 in Holt County, Missouri; m. Maria ---. Issue:

        1.   Martha Wood.

        2.   Rebecca Wood.[499]

        3.   Nancy Wood.

        4.   Henry Wood.

41.   Littlebury (Littleberry) Sublett, was born about 1757. As Littlebury (Littleby., Little B., Berry) Sublett, he enlisted 6 Feb. 1778 for the term of one year as a private in Capt. Wm. Fowler's County, 5th Virginia Regt., commanded by Col. Josiah Parker (later by Col. William Heth). He was at White Plains in August 1778, at West Point in September, at Pomton in October and November; at Middlebrook in December 1778, and February 1779. He was discharged 28 Feb. 1779.[500]

Littlebury was married in Chesterfield County, Virginia, at an undetermined date, to Sarah Burton, security being Jn°. Burton. The bond in Chesterfield County bears no date, and the

---

496   Mary Louise Wood not in original text; correspondence 1990 from Mildred (Byassee) Shannon of Paducah, Kentucky. [DJS].

497   William S. Wood d. 15 May 1879 aged 85-11-7 [DJS].

498   George Allen C. Wood b. 15 Feb 1821, Lincoln County, Kentucky, m. Minerva J. Hill, daughter of Sam'l and Rebecca [DJS].

499   Rebecca Wood, 1844-1896 [DJS].

500   Compiled Military Service Record Revolution, Littleberry Sublett, Private, 3rd Virginia Regt National Archives, Washington, D.C. John H. Gwathmey, Historical Register of Virginians in the Revolution, indicates service by him in the 3rd, 5th, and 9th Virginia Regiments.

marriage is consequently omitted from Knorr's published bonds of that county,[501] but it must have occurred about 1783. The will of her father John Burton, 2 June 1799, mentions "Littleberry Sublett."[502]

In addition to his military service, "Littleberry Sublet" supplied clothing to the military in 1779,[503] and in January 1761 "101 Bushels of corn to the troops at Chestd. Courthouse."[504] In August 1780 he furnished "15 bu. of Oats for the Publick use."[505]

On 20 July 1790 Lewis Sublett of Chesterfield "for natural love and affection which I have and do bare unto my son Littlebury Sublett" deeded him a tract of 180 acres.[506] On 13 July 1795 Littlebury (signature: Littleberry) Sublett and Sarah his wife of Chesterfield sold this tract to John Friend and departed for the new country, Kentucky, stopping briefly in Woodford County where his brother Lewis had settled, but moving on shortly to Green County.[507] There Littleberry entered a land certificate for 200 acres on the "South side of Green River" on "Greasy Creek waters of Little Barren" and on the north side of "Jone's Military Survey."[508] In Green County, Kentucky, on 15 July 1800 appraisers were appointed to value the estate of Littleburry Sublet Dec^d. and reported back to the County Court 16 Sept. 1800.[509] The will of his father Lewis, made in Chesterfield County, Virginia, 18 Jan. 1802, alludes to "the Heirs of my son Littleberry Sublett deceased."[510] In 1800 "Salley Sublett" is listed for taxes in Green County.[511] In 1803 the widow Sarah Sublett was married to Jonathan Smith.[512] On 3 Oct. 1804 "Jonathan Smith intermarried with Sarah Burton late Sarah Sublett sister to William Burton Dec^d." appointed Joseph Burton "to take negro Nelly left undisposed of by the will of Wm. Burton decd. of Chesterfield County."[513]

Issue of Littlebury and Sarah (Burton) Sublett, presumably all born in Chesterfield County, Virginia, except the last one:

    275   i   Edith Sublett, b. say 1784, m. prior to 1 Nov. 1810[514] (when they deeded their one-sixth part of her deceased father's tract to her brother Samuel).[515] Stephen Owens; probably married a number of years earlier, for Stephen Owens on 5 Dec. 1803 witnessed the apprenticeship indentures of her brother Littleberry[516] and her brother Joseph B.[517] She is said to have died without issue.[518]

501   *Chesterfield County, Virginia, Marriage Index*, p. 497.

502   Francis Burton Harrison, *Burton Chronicles of Colonial Virginia*, 1933, p. 70.

503   Gwathmey, *op. cit.*

504   Ethel Courtney Clarke, *Chesterfield County, Virginia, Records, vol. 1*, Revolutionary War Service Claims, Richmond, Virginia, mimeo., 1937, p. 31.

505   Public Service Claims: Certificates, Chesterfield County, Virginia, at Virginia State Library, Richmond.

506   *Chesterfield County, Virginia, Deed Bk. 11*, p. 738.

507   *Ibid., Deed Bk. 13*, p. 164.

508   Green County, Kentucky, *Surveys of Green County, No. 662*, p. 215.

509   *Ibid., Will Bk. 1*, pp. 52-53; Order Bk. 3, pp. 10, 16.

510   *Chesterfield County, Virginia, Will Bk. 6*, pp. 1-3.

511   Clift, *"Second Census" of Kentucky*.

512   *Green County, Kentucky, Marriage Bks. 1 and 2*, p. 52.

513   *Ibid., Deed Bk. 4*, p. 125.

514   1 Jul 1801, Green County, Kentucky. [DJS].

515   *Green County, Kentucky, Deed Bk. 6*, p. 142.

516   *Ibid., Deed Bk. 4*, p. 91.

517   *Ibid., Deed Bk. 4*, p. 75.

- 276 ii Hill Sublett (named for his paternal grandmother's family) was probably b. about Nov., 1786; m. (date of bond) 11 Dec. 1809 in Adair County, Kentucky, to Delphy Ginnett; migrated to Montgomery County, Missouri, where he died.

- 277 iii Samuel Sublett, b. ca 1788; m. (date of bond) 27 Oct. 1813 in Adair County, Kentucky, to Mary Trabue; he d. 14 April 1865.

- 278 iv Littlebury Sublett, Jr., b. 14 July 1790; m. (date of bond) 16 Jan. 1814 in Green County, Kentucky, to Polly Crouch; migrated to Clay County, Missouri, where he died in 1863.

- 279 v Joseph Burton Sublett, b. ca 1792; m. (date of bond) 5 Dec. 1816 in Green County, Kentucky, to Edith Radford; he died in June, 1865.

- 280 vi Lineus Bowlin Sublett, b. ca 1797, prob. in Green County, Kentucky; migrated to Cape Girardeau County, Misouri, where he died in 1849.

42. Lewis Sublett,[519] born in 1759, it is said, was married on 5 February 1779 (date of bond)[520] in Chesterfield County, Virginia, to Mary Trabue,[521] daughter of John James Trabue and Olympia (Dupuy). Secondary accounts say that the date of marriage was 5 March 1779.[522] Lewis served as a youth in the Revolution. Concerning Lewis' service, his brother-in-law Daniel Trabue related a couple of episodes, first, how Lewis waked his brother James in Tarleton's surprise and narrowly escaped himself the imprisonment and death which were James' fate.[523] Second, under date of 20 June 1781 or subsequent thereto, Trabue wrote: "Several of our Militia men were caught, as they were returning from General Lafayette's Army, as their time was out. Lewis Subblett my Brother-in-law and Mr. D. Morrisit and Mr. Thermon were coming home, and as they heard there were plenty of British around they were afraid to go along the road through the Plantations. They thought if they kept to the woods they could see the Enemy, and have a chance to escape. But one Day late in the evening they concluded they would call at a house, and get something to eat, and then they could walk almost all night. So they ventured up to the house and there were five red coats in the house. They ran out and ordered the three men to surrender. Morrisit and Thurman surrendered, but Subblett jumped the fence, and ran through a field. Some of them jumped on their horses, and pursued him. Before they overtook him, he was in the woods where the brush was so thick they could not find him. The British ... all staid at this house all night, and kept the landlady cooking for them, and giving them as much brandy as they could drink."[524] The landlord hid out until the British were quite drunk, and then flushed them from the house with rifle fire and freed Morrisit and Thurman.

On 10 May 1780 a Lewis Sublett entered in old Jefferson County (Kentucky, then Virginia) 405 acres located on the South Fork of the Licking.[525] This tract was entered presumably not by

---

518   "Data on the Sublette Family, copied by Council Grove Chapter, D.A.R., Putnam City, Oklahoma, 1953-1954," a typescript in the National D.A.R. Library, Washington, D.C., based on voluminous court records in St. Louis, Missouri, involving the suit over the lands of William L. and Solomon Perry Sublette (#206 and #213).

519   Lewis d. 1830, Woodford County, Kentucky. [DJS].

520   *Chesterfield County, Virginia, Marriage Register*, p. 8.

521   Mary Trabue b. 26 Jun 1758; d. 1792 [DJS].

522   B. H. Dupuy, *op. cit.*, p. 263; Dr. John Sublett Logan, Sublett MS. in Kentucky Historical Society, Frankfort, Kentucky; William E. Railey, *History of Woodford County, Kentucky*, Frankfort, Kentucky. 1938.

523   See below, under James (#43).

524   Lillie DuPuy Van Culin Harper, *Colonial Men and Times, Containing the Journal of Col. Daniel Trabue*. Philadelphia, 1916, pp. 102-103.

525   Willard R. Jillson, *Old Kentucky Entries and Deeds* [Filson Club Publication No. 34], Louisville, 1926, p. 292.

(#42) Lewis but by his father (#9) Lewis Sublett, for the latter by his will dated 18 January 1802 gave "to my son Lewis Sublett of the State of Kentucky and His Heirs all the Lands to which I am entitled in that State."[526] The son Lewis moved to Kentucky to farm this land in what is now Woodford County shortly after the 1780 entry, about 1782 or 1783, "in the company of many relatives and friends and settled on Grier's Creek in the neighborhood of Edward and Daniel Trabue. Here he built a two-story log house that is standing today in good condition, the logs joined together with wooden pins and the shingles were tacked on with wooden pegs. Several holes around the walls of the house were sawed into the logs for rifle use in case of attack from Indians. At the mouth of Grier's Creek opposite Tyrone is where he established and maintained a ferry over the Kentucky river that was known for more than 50 years as Sublett's Ferry."[527] On 12 Sept. 1787 Lewis Sublett signed "The Petition of Sundry inhabitants of the County of Fayette and those contiguous to Steeles ferry, near the mouth of Stone Lick on the Kentucky River" requesting a tobacco inspection warehouse.[528] On 17 Sept. 1788 he signed "The petition of ... Inhabitants of Fayette County" which declared "that we conceive a Division of our County would be highly condusive to the convenience, safety and public Interest of a great Number of its Inhabitants."[529] Lewis d. 1830, Woodford County, Kentucky.

Issue of Lewis and Mary (Trabue) Sublett:[530]

284   i   William Sublett, b. 3 March 1780 in Chesterfield County, Virginia Soldier in the War of 1812; d. Bellevue, Iowa, 1840; m. 1806 Mrs. Nancy (Samuel) Saunders, who d. 1845.[531]

• 285   ii   James Sublett, b. 15 July 1785, Woodford County, Kentucky, (then Fayette County, Virginia); soldier in the War of 1812; d. 9 June 1860, Clinton, Hickman County, Kentucky; m. 3 Sept. 1807 Susan (Nancy) Edzard, b. 17 May 1789; d. the same day he did, 9 June 1860.[532] She was the daughter of William and Martha (Lightfoot) Edzard.[533]

286   iii   Lewis Sublett, b. 1787, Woodford County; m. 25 April 1808 Susan Coleman, b. 1793, d. Aug. 1834,[534] Woodford County, daughter of Thomas and Susannah (Strother) Coleman. Lewis was a soldier in Capt. Z. Singleton's County, Col. James Allen's Regt., War of 1812.[535]

287   iv   John T. Sublett, b. it is said in 1790, Woodford County, Kentucky; killed in the War of 1812 at Dudley's Defeat, sometime between 13 May 1812 and Jan. 1813, the dates of the making and the probate of his will. By his will he recognized Marium Gibbeny "an illegitimate child sworn to me by Catherine Gibbeny her mother." To her he gave "one equal part of my ferry."[536] If the birthdate of 1790 is correct it seems hardly possible that this is the man referred

---

526   Will of Lewis Sublett, Chesterfield County, Virginia, Will Bk. 6, pp. 1-3.

527   Railey, *op. cit.*, p. 45.

528   John Rood Robertson, *Petitions of the Early Inhabitants of Kentucky to the General Assembly of Virginia, 1769 to 1792.* [Filson Club Publication No. 27] Louisville, Kentucky, 1914. Petition No. 43.

529   *Ibid.*, Petition No. 52.

530   Dupuy, *op. cit.*, pp. 291-297, gives more remote descendants of Lewis by his first wife Mary (Trabue).

531   *Ibid.*, p. 289.

532   *Ibid.*, p. 289.

533   Authority: Mr. J. Frederick Dorman, Lightfoot historian.

534   Lewis Sublett d. 1827 [DJS]. Susan Coleman, first cousin of President Zachary Taylor [PLS].

535   Dupuy, *op. cit.*, p. 290; Railey, *op. cit.*, p. 331.

536   *Woodford County, Kentucky, Will Bk. D*, pp. 22-23.

to repeatedly by John G. Stuart in his "Journal: Remarks or Observations on a Voyage Down the Kentucky, Ohio and Mississippi Rivers."[537] For instance, under date of 25 Feb. 1806, Stuart recorded that "This evening there came down a boat com'd by John Sublitt for Hart & County. The crew are a specimen of what I may expect to see in my voyage drinking swearing & kicking."[538] Yet the geography agrees, and Stuart is surely referring to John's brother when he records that "Jim Sublit ... told me many notable boatmen's tales."[539] Despite his remarks about the crew, Stuart seems to have regarded the Subletts themselves quite favorably.[540]

288 v Frances McGruder Sublett, m. William Vaughan;[541] named for her aunt Frances (Sublett) McGruder (#47). The fact that she was named Frances McGruder seems to have duped later members of the family into thinking she was named Frances McGruder for her paternal grandmother, whose name was clearly Frances <u>Hill</u>.

Following his first wife Mary (Trabue's) death in 1792, Lewis Sublett m. (2nd) about 1794 in Woodford County, Kentucky, Sarah Samuel, daughter of Thomas Samuel (One account says Anthony Samuel). Lewis died in Woodford County in 1830.[542]

Issue of Lewis and Sarah (Samuel) Sublett:

- 289 vi Thomas S. Sublett, apparently named for his maternal grandfather, Thomas Samuel. Migrated to Springfield, Arkansas. Not listed by Railey; listed by Logan. Born 20 August 1795, in Woodford County.[543]
  290 vii Abraham Sublett, not married, it is said.[544]
  291 viii Samuel Sublett, b. 1800, m. Fannie Aynes, b. 6 Sept. 1806, d. 8 Sept. 1872. Eleven children listed in Logan's Sublett MS:[545]
  1. Eliza Sublett, m. (1st) 1848 Benjamin Gough; m. (2nd) 1854 William Strother Hawkins.
  2. Mary Sublett, m. (1st) Moses Hawkins; m. (2nd) Dr. James Willis.
  3. Anna Sublett, m. James Hawkins.
  4. John William Sublett, m. Kate McGinnis.
  5. Arthur Sublett, m. (1st) Ruby A. McClure; m. (2nd) Inez Young.[546]
  6. Robert Frazier Sublett.
  7. Sarah Belle Sublett, m. Strother McGinnis.
  8. Samuel Sublett.
  9. Fanny Sublett.
  10. Bettie Sublett, m. Thomas McGinnis.

---

537 *Register* of the Kentucky Historical Society, v. 50:1 (Jan., 1952).

538 *Register* of the Kentucky Historical Society, 50:5.

539 *Ibid.*, 50:8.

540 This may refer to John (#501) and James (#502) Sublett [DJS].

541 Dupuy, *op. cit.*, p. 291.

542 Railey, *op.cit.*, pp. 303-304.

543 Thomas S. Sublett m. 11 Feb 1821, Mary Moorehead [DJS].

544 Railey, *op.cit.*, p. 304.

545 Dr. John Sublett Logan, *Sublett MS.*, in the library of the Kentucky Historical Society, Frankfort, Kentucky.

546 Arthur Sublett b. 29 Mar 1840, Woodford County, Kentucky; m. (1st) 10 Aug 1888, Rubi, daughter of Abr. McClure [DJS].

         11. James Sublett, m. Martha Cotton; a Union soldier in the War between the States.

292   ix   Ann Maria Sublett, m. as his first wife William A. Cotton; three children listed by Railey:[547]

         1. Elizabeth Cotton.

         2. Susan Cotton, m. John R. Darnell.

         3. Martha Ann Cotton, m. James Sublett, her 1st cousin.[548]

293   x   Elizabeth Sublett, m. her deceased sister's widower, William A. Cotton, as his second wife. Four children listed by Railey:[549]

         1. John Lewis Cotton, m. Emma Moss.

         2. William Samuel Cotton, m. Mollie Stockton.

         3. Abraham Randolph Cotton, m. Henrietta Anderson.

         4. DunLap Cotton.

294   xi   Arthur Sublett. Not listed by Railey; listed by Logan.

43. James Sublett, born say 1761, is known to us from one source alone: the journal of Daniel Trabue, who recounts James' death in the Revolution. Under date of April 16 to June 17, 1781, Trabue records the following:

"Our Army was, at this time, 25 miles from Petersburg, and they moved back towards Petersburg 12 miles; not far from Chesterfield Courthouse, at Sutsberry's Old Field. On a rainy day the men were in their tents, and some in a barn cooking, and some out of camp ... Col. Tarleton [the Britisher] with 500 horses and infantry, so there were about 1000 of them, came up on the back side. The men broke and ran; some of the Officers hollowed to the men to parade, but all in vain. Lewis Sublett, my brother-in-law, ran in the barn and took his gun and cartridge box, and waked his Brother James; but he [*i.e.*, James] was taken prisoner. One horseman came up with him. He [*i.e.*, Lewis] defended himself with his bayonet, jumped over the fence into a swamp and made his escape very narrowly. This swamp saved an abundance of men. They took 40 odd prisoners the most of the guns, all the cannon and all the wagons with the baggage, and publick Stores. These 40 odd men were taken down the River in a Prison Ship, and were taken sick and Died, every man except 3. They were Martin Bageley, John Bowman and Gabriel Vist. All the rest died by hard usage. They were plundered of their clothes, kept in a Prison Ship, had nothing to eat, not even good water. These three men told me this."[550]

It would seem that this James who died in 1781 as a prisoner of the British left no issue, for his father Lewis, who carefully provided in his will for the orphaned children of his son Littlebury, made no provision for any orphan of James. The sole public record mentioning James is a deed from James Talor of Chesterfield to his father Lewis Sublet Senr. on 1 Oct. 1778, which was witnessed by "James Subblet."[551]

---

547   Railey, *op. cit.*, p. 304.

548   *Supra.* 291-11.

549   *Ibid.*, p. 305.

550   Harper, *op. cit.*, p. 96 (Original of the journal now among the Draper MSS. at the Wisconsin Historical Society, Madison, Wisconsin.)

551   *Chesterfield County, Virginia, Deed Bk. 8*, p. 348.

44. Abraham Sublett was born 28 May 1763 and baptized 24 July 1763 by Parson Douglas.[552] He married, date unknown, Edith Burton. Abraham and Edith Sublett are mentioned in the will of her father John Burton, 2 June 1799.[553] By his will made 5 July 1812, probated 14 February 1820, Abraham Sublett "lent" his wife Edith his estate for her life, the residue then to go to his brothers Arthur and William, whom he named executors.[554] His widow Edith by her will made 14 Aug. 1828 and proved 10 Nov. 1820 left the bulk of her property to the children of her husband's sister Frances (Sublett) McGruder.[555]

45. Arthur Sublett, born say 1766, was married 17 May 1797 (date of bond) in Powhatan County, Virginia, to Betsey Sublet, John Sublet being witness.[556] Betsey's identity seems at first a mystery, but Samuel S. Sublett wrote, "Arthur Sublett married twice, the second time to a Hughes ... He settled and died in Illinois."[557] Samuel S. Sublett was quite mistaken about the Illinois migration, for Arthur's will and intervening legal records would indicate that he lived in Powhatan County throughout his adult life, but he may well have been right as to the Hughes marriage. This Betsey Sublet conceivably was the Betsey Hughes who had married in 1788 in Amelia County, William Sublett, Arthur's first cousin. If so, the recording of William's will was delayed considerably, for though he made it 28 April 1794, it was not probated until 17 Sept. 1800. Such a delay was, of course, quite possible. Absent any other Betsey Sublett to fill the role of Arthur's wife, the contributor would favor this conclusion, especially in view of Samuel S. Sublett's statement. Arthur Sublett died in 1834, between 1 April and 6 Oct., the dates of the making and probate of his will.[558]

Issue of Arthur and Elizabeth (Hughes) Sublett:

297	i	Caroline Sublett, b. say 1798, married 26 Aug. 1820 in Powhatan County, James F. Forsee.[559] At least one daughter, Adelaide Eliza Forsee.
298	ii	Matilda Sublett, b. say 1801, married 15 Nov. 1820 in Powhatan County to John H. Haskins.[560] At least one daughter, Elizabeth Haskins

46. William Sublett, born say 1768, was married (1st) (date of bond) 15 Jan. 1800 in Powhatan County, Virginia, to Mary Sublett, Silas Bryant being surety.[561] Later records make it appear that she was a Forsee, but of which Sublett she was a widow upon her marriage to William is something of a mystery. The only possibility which seems to present itself at first blush is that she was a widow of young James (#43), William's brother, who had died in 1781 as a prisoner of the British. Biologically it would be possible for a woman widowed in 1781, presumably on the heels

---

552   W. Mac Jones, ed., *The Douglas register*, Richmond, 1928, p. 300. This work contains a misprint as to his mother's name, discussed previously.

553   Francis Burton Harrison, *Burton Chronicles of Colonial Virginia*. 1933. p. 70. Harrison incorrectly lists an Edith Sublett as child of Abraham Sublett. She was rather daughter of Littleberry Sublett (#41), though still granddaughter to John Burton.

554   Chesterfield County, Virginia, Will Bk. 9, p. 239.

555   *Ibid.*, Will Bk. 11, p. 375-377.

556   Knorr, *Powhatan County, Virginia*, p. 63.

557   Samuel S. Sublett, *A Partial History ...*, p. 9.

558   *Powhatan County, Virginia, Will Bk. 9*, p. 424.

559   Knorr, *Powhatan County, Virginia*, p. 24.

560   *Ibid.*, p. 29.

561   *Ibid.*, p. 63.

ot such first marriage, to marry a second time in 1800 and mother three children. At any rate, Caroline Matilda Forsee by her will dated 6 April 1827, probated 19 July 1827, bequeathed property to "my brother Thomas Forsee, my sister Nancy Forsee, my niece Polly Malinda Sublett, and my niece Caroline Demarious Sublett."[562] The manner of such enumeration of her relatives would seem to indicate that her sister Sublett was deceased.

Now when we seek the parentage of the sisters Caroline Matilda Forsee and Mary Forsee, the mystery of Mary's first marriage increases. The two sisters were, it may be stated definitely, the children of Stephen Forsee by his wife Frances (Bryan). But this Stephen (baptized as Estienne Farci) was born 2 November 1750, son of Estienne and Marie (Perrault) Farci.[563] Hence it can be stated categorically that he could not have had a daughter old enough to marry William's brother James and to be widowed by 1781. A further difficulty is that this Stephen Forsee when he made his will on 3 Jan. 1799 listed his children as "Nancy Forsee, Mary Forsee, Margarett Forsee, Sarah Forsee, Thomas Forsee, and Caroline Matilda Forsee."[564] This narrows the possibilities of the circumstances of the 1800 Forsee-Sublett alliance to three:

1) Stephen Forsee's daughter Mary was yet single when he made his will 3 Jan. 1799, but married a relative of William Sublett's after that date, who died very shortly; and his widow Mary m. (2d) on 15 Jan. 1800 William Sublett. Unfortunately there is not a single available Sublett male to suggest for this fleeting marital encounter, and this theory would presuppose that Mary Forsee married almost contemporaneously with her father's death, that her unknown first Sublett husband died quite swiftly, and that she remarried with almost indecent haste his relative, two deaths and two marriages taking place in her life within a period of one year.

2) Mary was a Sublett widow on 3 Jan. 1799 when Stephen Forsee or the will copiest erroneously referred to her as Mary Forsee; but if so, who was her first Sublett husband?

3) Mary was still single and actually Mary Forsee on 15 Jan. 1800 when bonded to marry William Sublett and the clerk erroneously recorded her husband-to-be Sublett's name as hers also. This seems the sanest solution of the problem!

William Sublett married (2d) (date of bond) 15 June 1818 in Chesterfield County Mrs. Nancy Cheatham, widow of Leonard Cheatham. Edward Bass being surety.[565] Nancy Shackleford had married Cheatham 30 Jan. 1798 in Chesterfield County, Edward Bass (her father) being surety.[566] While William Sublett died intestate, the "Account of Mr. William Sublett by Admr. James Elam," recorded 2 October 1840, shows a "Division of the ballance among the widow and distributees of the intestate ... to Stephen F. Sublett ... one third part of the residue, to William Forsee in Right of his Wife Caroline D. ... and to Alexander Sims, guardian of Eugenia Sims and John W. Sims, infant children of his deceased wife Polly Sims (formerly Polly Sublett) ..."[567] Bond of James Elam as Administrator had been fixed 14 Oct 1839,[568] and appraisal of the estate

---

562   *Powhatan County, Virginia, Will Bk. 7*, p. 426.

563   Virginia Historical Society, *Collections*, n.s., v. 5, p. 109.

564   *Powhatan County, Virginia, Deed Bk. 2*, pp. 590-591.

565   *Chesterfield County, Virginia, Marriage Register, 1771-1853*, p. 149.

566   *Ibid.*, Marriage Register, p. 50.

567   *Ibid.*, Will Bk. 15, p. 237-238.

568   *Ibid.*, Will Bk. 15, p. 190.

made 23 Oct. 1839.[569]

Issue of William Sublett by his first wife Mary (Forsee):

301　i　　Stephen Forsee Sublett, b. ca 1801, m. (date of bond) 9 March 1829 Virginia A. Martin, b. ca 1812, daughter of Jordan Martin.[570] One known daughter, Elizabeth Sublett.[571]

•　302　ii　　Polly Malinda Sublett, m. (date of bond) 27 Sept. 1830 Alexander Sims.[572]

303　iii　　Caroline Demarious Sublett, m. (date of bond) 21 Dec. 1832 William Forsee of Powhatan County.[573]

47. Frances Sublett born say 1771, married (date of bond) 13 November 1792 in Chesterfield County, Virginia, Zephaniah Magruder (McGruder).[574] Her father Lewis by his will sought to block any participation by Zephaniah McGruder in the legacy he left Frances.[575] Frances was apparently deceased by 16 January 1843 when Zepheniah McGruder, Sr., William McGruder, Abraham McGruder, Wade S. McGruder and Polly his wife, Creed Amonette and Frances his wife, all of Chesterfield, deeded land to Zachariah McGruder.[576] Earlier, in 1828, Edith Sublett (widow of Abraham, #44) had willed property to Sublett McGruder, Frances McGruder, Jr., (to her and her heirs), to Zachariah McGruder, Jr., Cynthia McGruder, William McGruder, and Nancy Thomas.[577]

Issue of Zepheniah and Frances (Sublett) McGruder:

307　i　　Nancy McGruder, m. (date of bond) 14 April 1813 Hezekiah Thurman. Security: Wade Sublett McGruder.[578]

308　ii　　Wade Sublett McGruder, m. 7 January 1815 Polly Stanford, daughter of David Stanford.[579]

309　iii　　William McGruder, m. (date of bond) 26 August 1819 Elizabeth Goode, daughter of Benjamin Goode and of Martha (Lewis).[580] William was soldier in War of 1812.

310　iv　　Zepheniah McGruder m. (date of bond) 5 January 1824 Louisa T. Hopkins, daughter of Lund Hopkins.[581]

311　v　　Frances McGruder, m. (date of bond) 18 July 1833 Creed Amminett.[582]

312　vi　　Abraham McGruder.

569　*Ibid.*, Will Bk. 15, p. 232.

570　*Ibid.*, Marriage Register, p. 211.

571　*Ibid.*, Census of 1850, p. 84, family #375.

572　*Ibid.*, Marriage Register, 1771-1853, p. 218.

573　*Ibid.*, p. 233.

574　*Ibid.*, Marriage Register, p. 35.

575　*Ibid.*, Will Bk. 6, pp. 1-3.

576　*Ibid.*, Deed Bk. 34, p. 442.

577　*Ibid.*, Will Bk. 11, pp. 375-377.

578　*Ibid.*, Marriage Register, p. 120.

579　*Chesterfield County, Virginia, Marriage Register*, pp. 128, 408.

580　*Ibid.*, pp. 156, 418. For her family and issue, see G. Brown Goode, *Virginia Cousins*, Richmond, 1887, p. 103.

581　*Ibid.*, p. 181.

582　*Ibid.*, p. 237.

49. Charles Jordan Sublett, b. 31 July 1766, was married 1 January 1789 in Charlotte County, Virginia, to Polly Davis, b. ca 1772 in Charlotte, daughter of Temple and Ann (Baldwin) Davis.[583] As early as 15 Jul. 1799 Charles J. Sublett was granted 200 acres on the Barren River in Warren County, Kentucky,[584] but seems to have remained in Charlotte for several years. He is last listed for personal property taxes in Charlotte in 1803, which may be fixed as the date of his migration. On 12 June 1815 C. J. Sublete was elected a trustee for the town of Morgantown, Butler County, Kentucky.[585]

Charles J. Sublette died in Warren County, Kentucky, in 1846 where his will, made 13 March 1846, probated May 1846, named only one son William.[586]

Issue of Charles Jordan Sublett and Polly (Davis):

341	i	Charles Jordan Sublett, Jr., m. 19 November 1816 in Butler County, Kentucky, to Sally Talbert (unless this was a second marriage for his father?)
342	ii	Samuel D. Sublett, m. 9 February 1819 in Warren County, Kentucky, to Margaret Haiden.
343	iii	Nancy Sublett,[587] b. say 1796, m. 1 March 1818 Foster Clayton.
344	iv	Sarah Sublett, b. 6 May 1798 in Campbell County, Virginia; d. 6 June 1883 in Warren County, Kentucky;[588] m. 30 Aug. 1819 to John S. Waddle in Warren County, Kentucky; he was b. 1 Oct. 1793; d. 9 March 1860;[589] both are buried in the Smith graveyard, about 2 miles from Hadley, Warren County, Kentucky. Issue:[590]

        1. Mary D. Waddle, not married.
        2. Elizabeth Waddle, m. James B. Taylor.
        3. William P. Waddle, m. Mary D. McGinnis.
        4. George Waddle, m. Margaret McGinnis
        5. John Waddle, m. Virginia E. Rix.
        6. Sarah D. Waddle, m. Joseph McCracken.
        7. Eliza Jane Waddle, b. 20 Oct. 1837; d. 31 May 1907; m. 23 Oct. 1861 in Warren County, Kentucky, to Virgil McGown, b. 31 March 1827; d. 29 Jan. 1911.
        8. Martha Addie Waddle, m. H. S. Tucker.

• 345	v	Elizabeth Sublett, b. 27 November 1800; d. 28 May 1871; m. 3 Dec. 1817 to Mark Hardin Kuykendall, b. 12 March 1796. 9 children.
346	vi	William Sublett, b. 17 Nov. 1801 in Campbell County, Virginia; d. 17 Oct. 1877 in Warren County, Kentucky; m. (1st) Sarah Elizabeth Perkins 24 Jan.

---

583   Knorr, *Charlotte County, Virginia*, p. 80.

584   Jillson, The Kentucky Land Grants, p. 418.

585   *Butler County, Kentucky, Order Bk. B*, p. 45, abstracted in the *Register* of the Kentucky Historical Society, vol. 42, p. 313.

586   Warren County, Kentucky, Will Bk. D, p. 217.

587   Nancy Sublett d. 11 Mar 1857 in Illinois. Foster Clayton b. 1787 in SC.; d. 1875, Franklin County, Ill., according to correspondence with descendant [DJS].

588   Tombstone inscriptions, Smith graveyard, 2 mi. from Hadley, Warren County, Kentucky.

589   List contributed by Miss Ruth McGennis, Bowling Green, Kentucky.

590   Birth and death dates taken from the Bible of William Sublett, printed N.Y., 1838, owned in 1960 by H. W. Sublett, Nashville Rd., Bowling Green, Kentucky. Typed copy at the Kentucky Historical Society, Frankfort, Kentucky.

1827 in Warren County, Kentucky. She was b. 26 Nov. 1809; d. 9 Jan. 1851, daughter of William and Frances (Bowles) Perkins. After his first wife's death, William Sublet m. (2nd) Mrs. Nancy (Burger) Forsythe 26 Oct. 1854. She died 18 Aug. 1883. Issue of William and Sarah Elizabeth (Perkins) Sublett:[591]

1. William P. Sublett, b. 15 Nov. 1827.
2. Mary Frances Sublett, b. 22 Feb. 1830; d. 7 Feb. 1897; m. (1st) --- Roberts; m. (2nd) James Taylor.[592]
3. Henrietta Sublett, b. 7 June 1832.
4. Temple J. Sublett, b. 7 April 1835; m. Katherine Edmunds.
5. John Wesley Sublett, b. 8 Nov. 1837; d. 4 Feb. 1843.
6. Andrew Eugene Sublett, b. 9 Dec. 1840; d. 29 Jan. 1841.
7. Richard Watson Sublett, b. 30 May 1843; d. 10 July 1888; m. 22 June 1871 Laura A. Daniel.
8. Samuel Benson Sublett, b. 6 July 1846; d. 13 June 1926; m. 24 Jan. 1877 Lura Dean Wiley.

347 vii Benjamin B. Sublett, m. (1st) 22 Sept. 1829 in Butler County, Kentucky, to Martha Cook; m. (2nd) --- Gildersleeve.

348 viii Temple D. Sublett, m. 4 June 1835 in Green County, Kentucky, to Sarah A. Pemberton. Owned one half interest in the press and equipment of the Kentucky Republican, which he mortgaged to William Sublett.[593] Later resided in Grayson County, Kentucky.

349 ix Martha (Patsy) Sublett, m. 24 December 1830 in Warren County, Kentucky, to Joseph Adams.

350 x Adeline Sublett, b. 12 May 1814 in Warren County, Kentucky; d. 15 May 1890; m. 17 Oct. 1833 to Benjamin Wand, b. 6 June 1813; d. 16 July 1878.

50. Ursula Sublett, b. 24 March 1769, married (1st) 7 April 1788 in Charlotte County, Virginia, to Joel Ferguson.[594] He died very shortly, apparently *sine prole* (without issue), and his widow Ursual ("widow of John Farguson") married (2nd) 19 August 1790 in Charlotte Samuel Porter "of Prince Edward County."[595] Shortly thereafter the couple moved to Ivanhoe, Wythe County, Virginia, where Samuel Porter had inherited land from an uncle in 1786. Ursula died sometime between 13 May 1823 and the taking of the 1830 census of Wythe County, where Samuel Porter appears wifeless. Samuel Porter's will, dated 8 July 1830, was submitted for probate 14 February 1831.[596]

Issue of Samuel and Ursula (Sublett) Porter as named in his will:

354 i Margaret Porter ("Peggy"), m. Allen Porter.
355 ii Rebecca Porter, m. William Welsh.
356 iii Elizabeth (Betsy) Porter, m. Daniel Porter.
357 iv Samuel Ewing Porter, b. 5 June 1799, Wythe County, Virginia; d. 29 May 1893; m. (1st) 1820 Susanna Welsh; m. (2nd) (date of bond) 26 March 1847

591 *Green County, Kentucky, Deed Bk. 15*, p. 166.

592 Mary Frances Sublett m. James Taylor, 21 Oct 1850, Warren County, Kentucky. [DJS].

593 Knorr, *Charlotte County, Virginia*, p. 27.

594 Knorr, *Charlotte County, Virginia*, p. 67.

595 *Wythe County, Virginia, Will Bk. 3*, p. 445.

596 Information on this family kindly furnished by Walter A. Porter, M.D., Hillsville, Virginia.

Nancy (Polly) Winskell, b. 6 Dec. 1820, Westmoreland county, England; d. 8 July 1906; both are buried at Red Bluff Cemetery (Porter's Cross Road) near Ivanhoe, Wythe County, Virginia.

358	v	Sally Porter, m. George Keith Porter.
359	vi	Jane Porter, m. Andrew Porter, Jr.
360	vii	Jordan ("Gurden") Porter, b. 22 December 1807; d. 11 Feb 1860; m. 5 February 1826 Catherine Flannagan.
361	viii	Ursula Porter, m. Samuel Welsh.

52.   Benjamin Branch Sublett, b. 29 March 1774, was married 8 November 1797 in Campbell County Virginia, to Mary Akin, daughter of Joseph Akin. He migrated with his father and brothers to Warren County, Kentucky, about 1806 or 1807. On 19 May 1815 Benjamin Sublett, Sr., of Warren conveyed to his son Benjamin B. Sublett "for natural love" the 183 acre tract on which the grantor-father resided.[597] Shortly, Benjamin Branch Sublett migrated to Rutherford County, Tennessee. After a few years there, he moved on with his family to Jackson County, Alabama, where on 28 Sept. 1830 as "Benjamin Sublett of Jackson County, Alabama," he filed for 80 acres in S.5 T.5. R.5.[598] On 2 Oct. 1830 Benjamin Sublette of Jackson County filed for 79 acres in S.11 T.5 R.4 East.[599] He is listed in the 1830 census of Jackson County, aged 50-60, wife 50-60, two sons 20-30, one son and one daughter 15-20, 2 sons and one daughter 10-15, and one son 5-10.[600] He appears in the 1840 census of the county, aged 60-70, wife 60-70, two sons 20-30, and one son 15-20.[601] He died before the 1850 census was taken. A local history in Kentucky pertaining to his son William places his death in 1842.[602]

The very interesting tradition is related by a descendant of Benjamin that when Lafayette was making his triumphal tour of America in 1824 with an announced stop at Versailles, Kentucky, Lewis Sublett (#) of Woodford County, Kentucky, sent out an invitation to all his Sublett kin in the Western states to rally at his house to swell the number of people of French descent who were to turn out to greet him. Benjamin Sublett and his sons and other Subletts in Rutherford County, Tennessee, and doubtless Subletts from other Tennessee and Kentucky counties as well travelled in a body by horseback to Lewis' home. It was an exclusively male party that made the trip. One can well picture this spirited journey; memories of it became so well etched in the minds of those who made the trip that it is small wonder that the tale has survived as a tradition among those who heard it related many, many decades later.[603]

Issue of Benjamin Branch Sublett and Mary (Akin) .[604]

| • | 380 | i | William B. Sublett, b. 1800, Charlotte County, Virginia; d. 1862 Logan County, Kentucky; m. Mary Tyler. |
| | 381 | ii | Mary Sublett, b. say 1802; presumably the Mary who was married 2 Aug 1821 |

597   *Warren County, Kentucky, Deed Bk. G7*, p. 42.

598   Certificate 3163, Huntsville, Alabama, Land Office; Land Records Section, National Archives, Washington, D.C.

599   Certificate 3363, Huntsville, Alabama, Land Office.

600   Jackson County, Alabama, 1830 Census, p. 16.

601   *Ibid.*, 1840 Census, p. 12.

602   James Battle, et al., *History of Kentucky, 1885*, p. 160.

603   Tradition reported by Mrs. Wm. A. Wyatt, San Marcos, Texas, who has gathered a considerable body of Sublett material over the years.

604   Listing worked out by Mrs. Wyatt in large part, and very kindly supplied to the contributor.

in Rutherford County, Tennessee, to John Beadles,[605] although family records say that she married a Sublett cousin. It is conceivable that she was twice married.

382 iii Nancy Sublett, b. say 1804, m. 2 July 1823 in Rutherford County, Tennessee, to William B. Cowan.[606] Among their issue:
1. Benjamin Cowan.
2. John Cowan.
3. Mary Cowan.

383 iv Sarah Sublett, b. say 1806, m. John Adare; migrated to Hays County, Texas, 1851. Issue:
1. Mary Adare, m. Fleming Taylor; no issue.
2. George Adare, m. Alice Obannon.
3. Samuel Jordan Adare.
4. William Adare, m. Mary O'Bannon.

384 v Lavinia Sublett, b. ca 1808, Warren County, Kentucky, m. John Toliver, b. 1808 in Tennessee; migrated to Colorado County, Texas, before the 1850 Census, where John is listed as a hotelkeeper with issue:
1. Henry Toliver, b. ca 1834 in Alabama.
2. Benjamin Toliver, b. ca 1840 in Texas.
3. James Toliver, b. ca 1844 in Texas.

• 385 vi James Jefferson Sublett, b. ca 1810, Warren County, Kentucky; m. Tabitha Wilborn; resided in Jackson County, Alabama.

• 386 vii Joseph Jordan Sublett, b. ca 1812, Warren County, Kentucky; d. 1867. Married (1st) his cousin Lucinda Sublett (#1816); (2nd) Mary Sarah Wood; (3rd) Mrs. Eliza Hauck Woodall.

387 viii Martha Sublett, m. Mr. Romines. She died on the way to Texas, 1840; b. say 1814.

388 ix Monroe Sublett b. say 1816: died in Arkansas.[607]

389 x --- Sublett, a son, name unknown, b. ca 1818.[608]

• 390 xi Sophronia Elizabeth Sublett, b. 1819; died 21 April 1846, San Marcos, Texas; m. 12 May 1834 at Bellefonte, Alabama, to William Washington Moon.

391 xii George Sublett, b. ca 1822, m. Martha ---;[609] but tradition says that he married Jane Wood. Possibly she was Martha Jane. George "died in Rock Island Prison," Rock Island, Illinois, as a prisoner of war in the War Between the States.[607] Rock Island, in the middle of the Mississippi River, became the graveyard for approximately 2,000 of the Confederates confined there.[610]

53. Samuel Sublett, b. 29 August 1776, d. 14 Jan. 1866 <u>or</u> 1867 at his residence in Warren

605 *Rutherford County, Tennessee, Marriage Records, vol. 1, 1804-1837*, p. 11. W.P.A. typescript in the National D.A.R. Library, Washington, D.C.

606 *Ibid.*, p. 36.

607 Recollections of his nephew, William M. Sublett (#3246) as published in Samuel Sublett. *A Partial History ...*, p. 6.

608 Littleberry Madison Sublett (born around 1815, Warren County, Kentucky) married Mary Deskin Stanfield; children: Lumariless Catherine (Kate) Sublett, William Hosea Sublett, Samantha L. Sublett, Mary Louise (Lou) Sublett, John Sublett, and James Madison Sublett, according to 1850 and 1860 Census, Washington County, Arkansas, and correspondence with descendants [PLS].

609 Jackson County, Alabama, 1850 Census, p. 49, v. 6

610 *The Past and Present of Rock Island, Illinois.* Chicago, 1877, p. 141.

County, Kentucky.[611] He m. (1st) (date of bond) 22 August 1799 Fanny Taylor in Campbell County, Virginia.[612] On 15 January 1813 he was granted 105 acres on the Barren River in Warren County, Kentucky, where he had settled with his father and brothers six or seven years earlier.[613] Samuel served in the War of 1812 as a private in the Company of Capt. John Williams, Kentucky Militia, enlisting 18 Sept. 1812 and being discharged 30 Oct. 1812.[614] Following the death of his first wife Fanny, Samuel m. (2nd) 8 November 1810 at the residence of William Sumpter in Warren County, Kentucky, Mary (Polly) Sumpter, b. ca 1792.[615] The latter couple are listed in the 1850 Census as being aged 75 and 57 respectively.[616] Mary was alive and residing as a widow in Warren County as late as 21 Nov. 1878.

Issue of Samuel and Fanny (Taylor) Sublett:
394	i	Polly Sublett, m. Ellis Oscar Young.
395	ii	James Sublett.
396	iii	--- (a daughter).[617]

Issue of Samuel and Mary (Sumpter) Sublett:
397	iv	Nancy Sublett.[618]
398	v	Sarah Sublett.[619]
399	vi	Louisiana Sublett.
400	vii	Missouri Sublett.
401	viii	Samuel Sublett, b. ca 1819, m. Margaret ---.[620],[621]
402	ix	Benjamin F. Sublett, b. ca 1824, m. Margaret ---.[622],[623]
403	x	Delila Sublett.
404	xi	Susan Emeline Sublett, b. ca 1835.
405	xii	Mary E. Sublett, b. ca 1839.

54.   Matthew Sublett was born ca 1781 from the fact that he is first listed as a free white male above 16 years of age in the year 1798 on the tax books of Charlotte County in the household of his father Benjamin Sublett, Sr.[624] This approximate birthdate is corroborated by the fact that in the 1860 census he gave his age as 78.[625] Named for a maternal uncle, Matthew Jordan, he was

---

611   Samuel Sublett, War of 1812 Pension File W.O. 6039, W.C. 13146.

612   Hinshaw, *op. cit.*, 6:857 (Campbell County, Virginia, Marriage Bonds).

613   Jillson, The Kentucky Land Grants, p. 418.

614   Pension File W.O. 6039, W.C. 13146, cited above.

615   *Warren County, Kentucky, Marriage Register A*, p. 37.

616   *Ibid.*, 1850 Census, p. 39, Household #527.

617   Elizabeth Sublett b. ca 1804; m. 6 Sep 1821 in Warren County, Kentucky, to Jonathan Neighbors, according to correspondence with descendant [DJS].

618   Not to be confused with Nancy Sublett (#343) [PLS].

619   Sarah Sublett m. 25 Sep 1832 to Wm. H. Maxey, according to correspondence with descendant [DJS].

620   *Ibid.*, p. 39, Household #526.

621   Samuel Sublett m. 8 Feb 1849, Margaret C. Hayden, Warren Co, Kentucky, according to correspondence with descendant [DJS].

622   *Ibid.*, p. 39, Household #527.

623   Benjamin F. Sublett m. 3 Mar 1850, Margaret Boatsa Wiley, dau. Benj. , according to correspondence with descendant [DJS].

624   Charlotte County, Virginia, Personal Property Tax Lists, 1782-1815.

625   Giles County, Virginia, 1860 Census, Household #787.

married (date of bond) 18 Feb. 1803 in Campbell County, Virginia, to Frances (Frankey) Key, daughter of Thomas Key, Jacob Key being surety.[626] When his father and brothers moved on to Kentucky, Matthew stayed behind in Virginia. He is listed in the 1810 census of Campbell County, Virginia, as between 26-45 years of age, with a wife 16-26, and three sons under 10.[627] In 1814 his father in a Warren County, Kentucky, deed refers to son Matthew as "of Charlotte County, Virginia," and gives him thereby a negro "now at John Fores of Campbell County, Virginia."[628] Matthew is listed in Campbell County, Virginia, in the 1840 census, age 50-60.[629] By 1850 he had moved to Giles County, Virginia, where he is listed, aged 70, with wife Frances, 65.[630] In the 1860 census of Giles County, Matthew 78, and Frances, 73, were residing with their youngest son Allen W. Sublett.[631] He apparently died in Giles County during the succeeding decade, though he left no will.[632]

Issue of Matthew and Frances (Key) Sublett:

- 415 i Thomas Sublett, b. say 1804, m. (date of bond) 2 Oct. 1826 to a cousin, Elizabeth Jordan, daughter of Matthew Jordan.[633] Listed in the Campbell County, Virginia, Census of 1840 as between 30-40.[634]

- 416 ii Benjamin Branch Sublett, b. say 1806, m. (date of bond) 20 Nov. 1826 Nancy Johnstone Cunningham, daughter of Richard Cunningham.[635]

417 iii William Sublett, b. say 1808, m. (1st) 1 June 1834 Frances Jennings;[636] m. (2nd) 25 July 1836 Sarah Hamersley, daughter of James B. Hamersley.[637] William is said to have m. (3rd) a Miss --- Moore. Residing in Dinwiddie County, Virginia, in 1850 with issue:[638]
1. Matthew D. Sublett, b. ca 1835.
2. James W. Sublett, b. ca 1838.
3. George B. Sublett, b. ca 1847.
4. Melinda Sublett, b. ca 1849.

418 iv Elizabeth Sublett, b. say 1810,[639] m. (date of bond) 8 December 1828 in Campbell County to Caliborn Kelley;[640] resided in Giles County, Virginia.

419 v Nancy Sublett, b. say 1812, m. (date of bond) 19 Dec. 1831 in Campbell County to John Johnson;[641] resided in Charlotte County, Virginia. Issue:
1. William Johnson, m. Melvina Jordan, niece of the wife of his uncle

---

626   Hinshaw, *op. cit.*, 6:857, Campbell County Marriage Bonds.

627   Campbell County, Virginia, 1810 Census, p. 30.

628   *Warren County, Kentucky, Deed Bk. F6, p. 294.*

629   Campbell County, Virginia, 1840 Census, p. 20.

630   Giles County, Virginia, 1850 Census, Household #669.

631   *Ibid.*, 1860 Census, Household #787.

632   The contributor is indebted for this point, the Census records and the information on the family of Mary Mildred (Sublett) King to Robert D. Nance, Radford, Virginia.

633   Hinshaw, *op. cit.*, p. 857 (Campbell County, Virginia, Marriage Bonds).

634   Campbell County, Virginia, 1840 Census, p. 4.

635   Hinshaw, *op. cit.*, 6:857 (Campbell County, Virginia, Marriage Bonds).

636   *Ibid.*, 6:857.

637   *Ibid.*, 6:857.

638   Dinwiddie County, Virginia, 1850 Census, p. 464, Household #452.

639   Elizabeth Sublett, b. 19 Jan 1808 [DJS].

640   Hinshaw, *op. cit.*, 6:831.

641   *Ibid.*, 6:829.

Thomas (#415)
2. Elizabeth Johnson, m. Maurice Hamlet.
3. Martha Johnson.
4. Molly Johnson, m. (1st) Benjamin Jordan, brother of Melvina Jordan above. He was killed in the War Between the States. Molly m. (2nd) --- Harvey; moved to Texas.
5. John Johnson.

420   vi   Jacob F. Sublett, b. ca 1813, m. (date of bond) 13 October 1835 in Campbell County to Martha Hight.[642] Listed in the 1840 census of Campbell County, Virginia, as age 30-40, with wife 20-30, and three children under 5.[643] Moved to Giles County, Virginia, prior to 1850, where he is listed with children:[644]
1. William F. Sublett, b. ca 1836.
2. Susannah Sublett, b. ca 1838.
3. John P. Sublett, b. ca 1840.
4. Mary A. Sublett, b. ca 1842.
5. Martha M. Sublett, b. ca 1844.
6. Lydia M. Sublett, b. ca 1846.
7. Matthew F. Sublett, b. ca 1848.

421   vii   Martha Sublett, b. say 1816, m. (date of bond) 2 Dec. 1833 in Campbell County to Tandy P. Cobbs;[645] resided in Giles County, Virginia.

422   viii   Matthew Sublett, b. say 1818; listed in the 1840 Census of Campbell County, Virginia.[646]

423   ix   Lucy A. Sublett, b. say 1820, m. (date of bond) 26 July 1841 in Campbell County, Virginia, to John S. Dudley;[647] resided in Giles County, Virginia.

424   x   Samuel D. Sublett, b. ca 1822, m. Petro (Peterora?) ---.

425   xi   Mary Mildred Sublett, b. 1825, d. 1887, m. 12 June 1847 in Giles County, Virginia, John Bennett King, b. 6 March 1825, Wythe County, Virginia, d. 1897, son of Bennett and Bathsheba (---) King. He served in the 45th Virginia Infantry in the War Between the States, and subsequently resided in Bland County, Virginia. Issue:
1. Frances King, b. 1 Jan. 1849, m. James Munsey.
2. Lucy Ann King, b. 1 Nov. 1850, m. Robert Graham Carr.
3. Franklin Pierce King, b. 22 Feb. 1852, m. Sarah L. Woodyard on 20 Aug. 1874.
4. Millard Fillmore King, b. 8 May 1855.
5. Mary S. King, b. 1 August 1859, d. young.
6. John Matthew King, b. 1865, m. --- Shumake (Shumate?); he d. 23 Dec. 1950.
7. Laura Augusta King, b. 1869, m. --- Barley.

426   xii   Allen W. Sublett, b. ca 1828/9, m. 10 May 1851 Pulaski County, Virginia, to Mary King, daughter of Bennett and Bathsheba (---) King; settled in Giles County, Virginia, with his father and brothers Jacob and Samuel. In 1870 he

---

642   *Ibid.*, 6:857.

643   Campbell County, Virginia, 1840 Census, p. 20.

644   Giles County, Virginia, 1850 Census, Household #674.

645   Hinshaw, *op. cit.*, 6:806.

646   Campbell County, Virginia, 1840 Census, p. 20.

647   Hinshaw, *op. cit.*, 6:813.

resided in Bland County, Virginia, with issue:[648]
1. Margaret Sublett, b. ca 1854.
2. Corder Samuel Sublett, b. ca 1858.

61. William Sublett, b. say 1760 in Albemarle County, Virginia, on 13 May 1784 was issued a warrant for £4 for service in the militia (name given as "William Subbet").[649] By this date he had settled in Henry County, Virginia. The tract he and James Sublet had acquired jointly in 1793 in Patrick County, Virginia, was disposed of by him alone, 60 acres of it on 23 Aug. 1802 by "William Sublett of the County of Patrick" to William Gray;[650] and 250 acres on the headwaters of Green Creek on 4 Dec. 1804 by "William Sublet of the County of Patrick" to Thomas Brown of Henry County.[651] Thereupon he migrated to Madison and Gerrard Counties, Kentucky. The fact that he sold these jointly granted lands by himself gives rise to the supposition that the James to whom they were jointly granted was his father, who is thus seen to have died sometime between 1793 and 1802, presumably in Patrick County, Virginia.

He m. (1st) ca 1783, probably in Buckingham County, Virginia, Ruth Ford (*i.e.*, Faure or Fore, descendant of another Huguenot family of Manakintown.) Following her death, he m. (2nd) a widow, Mrs. Nancy Harris (maiden name unknown), on 24 April 1806 in Garrard County, Kentucky.[652] His migration to Kentucky may consequently be placed sometime between Dec. 1804 (land sale in Virginia) and his 1806 marriage. He is said to have resided in Madison County, Kentucky, near Richmond.

Issue of William and Ruth (Ford) Sublett, all born in either Henry County, Virginia, or its daughter county, Patrick:[653]

501	i	John Sublett, b. 16 Oct. 1784; m. Miss Phoebe ---; he is said to have migrated to Coles County, Illinois, with his brothers, but ultimately to have returned with his family to Kentucky.
• 502	ii	James Sublett, b. 4 Feb. 1786, Henry County, Virginia; d. 6 Aug. 1844, Coles County, Illinois; m. Sally Ford.[654]
503	iii	Anna Sublett, b. 20 June 1787; m. 14 August 1809 in Garrard County, Kentucky, to Alexander Trimble (Alec Tremble)[655] of Madison County, Kentucky. They migrated to Indiana. Among their issue: 1. Alec Tremble. 2. John Tremble.
504	iv	Judith Sublett, b. 30 July 1789, Henry County, Virginia; d. 20 Oct. 1843, Coles County, Illinois; n.m.; resided with the family of her brother James.

648   Bland County, Virginia, 1870 Census, p.

649   Virginia State Library, *Auditors Account Book, 1783-1784*, v. XVIII, p. 608.

650   *Patrick County, Virginia, Deed Bk. 2*, p. 151.

651   *Ibid.*, p. 151.

652   Annie Walker Burns, *Record of Marriages, Garrard County, Kentucky, 1796-1851*, typescript, 1932.

653   Notes gathered in the 1920s by George W. Sublette, son of Peter J. Sublette (#3554), and by Miss Mary Frances Sublette, dau. of Colvit Sublette (#3556), in the possession (1962) of Mrs. W. Arthur Mitchell, Boulder, Colorado, and Mrs. Florence (Sublette) Harley, Kent, Ohio; located and made available to the compiler through the energy and kindness of Mr. Donald J. Sublette, Detroit, Michigan, grandson of Peter J. Sublette.

654   James Sublett, m. 11 Oct 1811, Garrard County, Kentucky. [DJS].

655   Anna Sublett d. 1837 Rush County, Indiana. [DJS].

- 505   v   William Sublett, b. 1 July 1791; m. 27 Oct. 1813 in Garrard County, Kentucky, to Liney Wearin (Regina Warren); migrated to Coles County, Illinois.
- 506   vi   Daniel Sublett, b. 25 April 1794; settled in 1820 in Bath County, Kentucky, where he m. Julia Oakley.
- 507   vii   Elizabeth Sublett, b. 29 Dec. 1795; m. 18 March 1818 to Benjamin F. Chastine (Chastain),[656] descendant of another Huguenot family at Manakin Town. She died in 1820 after some two years of marriage. Issue:
  1. Louisiana Chastain, b. 21 Dec. 1818.
  2. William Chastain, b. 20 Dec. 1820; died in infancy.
- 508   viii   Mary (Polly) Sublett,[657] b. 15 Nov. 1796; m. Golson Emery.[658]
- 509   ix   Jane (Jinsey) Sublett, b. 3 Oct. 1799; m. John (Pruitt) Plummer.
- 510   x   Peter Sublett, b. 13 June 1802; m. 17 Dec. 1828 in Madison County, Kentucky, to <u>Tully</u> (sic) Timberlake (Timberlick). (Can this have been a pet name for Tallulah?) They migrated to Coles County, Illinois in 1833, where he died 17 May 1875.

Issue of William Sublett, by his second wife, Mrs. Nancy (---) Harris, probably all born in Madison County, Kentucky; or Garrard County, Kentucky:

- 511   xi   David Sublett,[659] m. 13 Oct. 1831 in Garrard County, Kentucky, to Mary Ann Marshall; migrated from Kentucky to Illinois, but ultimately settled in Putnam County, Indiana.
- 512   xii   Rebecca (Becky) Sublett, m. 21 June 1832 in Garrard County, Kentucky, to William Lewis, son of Berry Lewis, bondsman being Robert Harris.[660] The couple are said to have settled in Missouri, along with her brother Pleasant Sublett and her sisters Clara and Patsy and their families.
- 513   xiii   Pleasant Sublett,[661] m. (1st) Patsy Floyd; migrated to Indiana and then to Missouri. Issue:[662]
  1. James (John?) Sublett.
  2. William Sublett.
  3. David Sublett.
  4. Jane Sublett.
- 514   xiv   Clara Sublett,[663] m. 11 Jan. 1838 in Garrard County, Kentucky, to Mitchell Eagy, Bondman being Robert Harris.[664] Settled in Missouri.
- 515   xv   Patsy Sublett, m. 13 Nov. 1845 in Garrard County, Kentucky, to James Wearren (Warren), bondsman being Robert Harris.[665] Settled in Missouri.

80.   Peter Dutoy Sublett, b. prior to 1783. In June 1805 (date of bond) in Amelia County,

---

656   Benjamin Franklin Chastine b. 6 Jul 1799, Virginia; d. 7 Jun 1863, Illinois [DJS].

657   *Supra* Mary d. 8 Jan 1879, Kentucky. [DJS].

658   Golson Emery (Embry, Embree) b. 21 Feb 1803, Kentucky; d.p. 1880 [DJS].

659   David Sublett b. ca 1807 in Kentucky. [DJS].

660   Burns, *op. cit.* (Garrard County), p. 38.

661   Pleasant Sublett m. (2nd) Susan Sales. For Sales children see *DSGR Magazine* 37:56-57 [DJS].

662   For more complete list, see *DSGR Magazine* 37:55.

663   Clara B. Sublett b. 10 Mar 1818, Garrand County, Kentucky; d. 5 Feb 1869, Missouri; m. Mitchell Agee [DJS].

664   *Ibid.*, p. 105.

665   *Ibid.*, p. 61.

Virginia, Peter Sublett was m. to Nancy Wingo, daughter of John.[666] Peter D. Sublett had purchased land in Amelia in July 1805.[667] Apparently in financial straits, Peter D. Sublett of Amelia on 24 Sept. 1825 "being desirous to make provision for the support of his wife Nancy Sublett and her children" sold to John Wingo a negro girl and "one third part of 230 acres of land laying in the State of Ohio on the Small Miamena [*i.e.*, the Little Miami River] near Seesars Creek in about three miles of Wainesville, Warren County."[668] Then on 8 June 1827 "Peter D. Sublett and Nancy his wife of the County of Amelia" sold to Jesse Drake of Warren County, Ohio, "part of a tract entered in the name of John Harriss and patented to the heirs of James Smith who was assignee of said Harriss in the Virginia Military reservation ... between the Little Miami and Sciota [*i.e.*, Scioto] Rivers."[669]

The date of Sublett's death is unknown; his wife Nancy made her will in 1855 in Bedford County, Virginia, where it was probated 28 July 1862. Among the issue of Peter D. and Nancy (Wingo) Sublett:[670]

611   i   Frances Ann Sublett.

612   ii   Nancy E. Sublett.

613   iii   Chastain (Chastine) Sublett.

614   iv   Smith E. Sublett.

615   v   Edmond Wingo Sublette, m. 8 Nov. 1848 in Bedford County, Virginia, to Susan Jane Bowles. Issue: (b. Bedford County)
1. Elmira V. Sublette, b. 21 Aug. 1850, d. 23 May 1929, m. Robert Moore.
2. Martha S. Sublette, b. 2 July 1852, d. 13 Dec. 1935, m. John Beard.
3. John I. Sublette, b. 14 Oct. 1854, d. 1 March 1928, m. Nettie Ruddell.
4. Edward Lowry Sublette, b. 16 Jan. 1857, d. 19 May 1919, m. 21 March 1888, Lorena Bell Beard, b. 11 July 1864, d. 22 March 1938, sister of John Beard above. 6 children.
5. Emma M. Sublette, b. 1 June 1860, d. 4 March 1943, m. William Horton.
6. Susan A. Sublette, b. 17 Sept. 1862, d. 9 March 1921, m. William Burnette.
7. William L. Sublette, b. 22 Feb. 1866, d. 14 July 1943, m. Katey Ruddell.
8. Daisy K. Sublette, b. 30 March 1871, d. 14 May 1935, n.m.

616   vi   John Ditaway Sublett. Notice the middle name: Ditaway is a Virginia variant of his father's middle name Dutoy (Dutoit). He m. Elizabeth Thomas Jackson, and settled in Caldwell County, North Carolina. They are buried at Grace Chapel Cemetery, near Granite Falls, N.C. Among their issue:[671]
1. John Winston Sublett, b. 12 Oct. 1848, d. 5 April 1928, m. 9 Feb. 1871 Emily Agnes Peterson, b. 4 July 1850, Catawba County, N.C.; d. 9 June 1933, Hickory, N.C.; buried at Bethlehem Lutheran Church Cemetery, Hickory, N.C.
2. Betty Sublett, m. Jones Coffey.

---

666   Amelia County, Virginia, Marriage Bonds, abstracted in *William and Mary College Quarterly*, 1:17:38.

667   *Amelia County, Virginia, Deed Bk. 22*, p. 85.

668   *Ibid.*, Deed Bk. 27, p. 384.

669   *Warren County, Ohio, Deed Record 14*, p. 328.

670   Information on the descendants of Peter D. Sublett contributed by Reyborn Roy Sublette, Roanoke, Virginia (son of Edward Lowry Sublette above), and by Miss Della Spencer, Johnson City, Tennessee.

671   Information furnished by Miss Ora Sublett, Jamestown, N.C., granddaughter of John Winston Sublett.

118. Branch Sublett, born say 1787, m. (date of bond) 7 January 1808 in Lincoln County, Kentucky, Polly Bratton, daughter of John Bratton.[672] He accompanied his father Valentine to Green County, Kentucky, and is listed there in the 1810 Census, aged 26-45, with one son under 10.[673] He died there before 28 March 1814 when "on the motion of Fields Sublett and Andrew Karr they are appointed administrators of the goods and chattles of Branch Sublett dec[d].," with John Bratton and John B. Smith their securities.[674] On 23 June 1817 Joseph Robinson, Andrew Campbell and Laurance Campbell were appointed "to state and settle the accounts of Fields Sublett and And[w]. Kerr as admrs. of Branch Sublett dec[d]."[675]

Issue of Branch and Polly (Bratton) Sublett, born in Green County, Kentucky:

881   i   Valentine Sublett, b. 26 August 1808, for on 16 Sept. 1822 it was "Ordered that the clerk bind Valentine Sublett to John Cobb until he the said Sublett arrives to the age of 21 which will be on the 26 day of Aug[t]. 1829 to learn farming."[676]

882   ii   Allen Sublett, b. 4 September 1810, for on 16 Sept. 1822 "On the motion of John Barbee, it is ordered that the clerk bind Allen Sublett, child of Branch Sublett decd. unto the said Barbee until he arrives to the age of 21 years which will be 4 Septr. 1831 to learn the art and <u>mistory</u> of farming."[677]

883   iii   Branch Sublett, b. 10 February 1813, for on 18 Nov. 1822 it was "Ordered that the Clerk of Ct. bind Branch Sublett to Beverly Marshall to learn farming until he arrives to the age of 21 which will be on the 10th day of Feb. 1834."[678]

119. Field Sublett, b. ca 1787, Charlotte County, Virginia;[679] married (date of bond) 21 Sept. 1809 in Green County, Kentucky, to Eleanor Bratten (Bralden),[680] b. ca 1794. He served as administrator for his brother Branch, 28 March 1814.[681] On 3 April 1815 "On the motion of Field Sublett license is granted him to keep a tavern in the house of Thomas Sperry in the town of Columbia," Adair County.[682] On 7 April 1818 he was keeping tavern in his own house in Columbia, John Field and Daniel Trabue being securities on his license.[683] The 1810 Census of Green County, Kentucky, lists him as aged 16-26.[684] By 1820 he had migrated down to Franklin County, Tennessee, where the census records him as "Fields Sublet," aged 26-45, with a wife in the same age range, one son and one daughter aged 10 to 16, and three sons and three daughters under 10 years of age.[685]

672   Lincoln County, Kentucky, Index to Marriages.

673   Third Census of the U.S., 1810, Green County, Kentucky, transcribed by Annie Walker Burns Bell, p.3.

674   *Green County, Kentucky, Order Bk. 5* (unpaged, sixth page from the end).

675   *Ibid.*, Order Bk. 6, p. 264.

676   *Green County, Kentucky, Order Bk. 7*, p. 153.

677   *Ibid.*, Order Bk. 7, p. 153.

678   *Ibid.*, Order Bk. 7, p. 174.

679   Seventh Census of the U.S., 1850, Franklin County, Tennessee, p. 66, Household #868.

680   *Green County, Kentucky, Marriage Bk. 1*, p. 76.

681   *Ibid.*, Order Bk. 5 (unpaged).

682   *Adair County, Kentucky, Order Bk. B*, p. 505.

683   *Ibid.*, Order Bk. D, p. 36.

684   Third Census of the U.S., 1810, Green County, Kentucky, transcribed by Annie Walker Burns Bell, P. 23.

685   Fourth Census of the U.S., 1820, Franklin County, Tennessee, transcribed by Martha Lou Houston, *Tennessee Census Reports* No. 5, Washington, D.C., mimeo.

Issue of Field and Eleanor (or "Ellen") (Bratten) Sublett:

- 885   i   Caldwell Sublett, b. ca 1810, bore his paternal grandmother's maiden name; moved to Benton County, Alabama, where he was sheriff.
  886   ii   John F. Sublett, b. ca 1820, m. 8 Jan. 1843 to Dicey Ann Temple.[686] Issue:[687]
         1.   Nancy Ann Sublett, b. ca 1846.
         2.   John G. Sublett, b. ca 1849.[688]
  887   iii   Martha Sublett, m. 30 July 1843 to William B. Fogg [Fagg] .[689]
  888   iv   Eleanor Sublett, m. 28 Aug. 1845 to James P. Griffin.[690]
  889   v   W. B. Sublett, m. 24 Aug. 1848 to Elizabeth Carter.[691]
  890   vi   Susan Sublett, m. 2 Jan. 1849 to George W. Warren.[692]
  891   vii   Thomas A. Sublett, b. ca 1830, m. 25 Aug. 1856 to Frances L. Stephens.[693]
  892   viii Elizabeth G. Sublett,[694] b. ca 1832, m. 11 March 1855 to William A. Darnaby.[695]

126. Mary (Polly) Dudgeon m. (date of bond) 18 Feb. 1808 in Lincoln County, Kentucky, to Andrew Hall.[696] They migrated to Boone County, Missouri, where some Lincoln County relatives had already settled.

Issue of Andrew and Mary (Dudgeon) Hall: (all b. in Lincoln County, Kentucky)[697]

  971   i   Sarah A. Hall, b. ca 1809, not married.
  972   ii   Mary A. Hall, b. 1809; m. 20 Nov. 1856 Boone County, Missouri, Benjamin Wiley.
  973   iii   Amanda Hall, b. ca 1813.
  974   iv   Martha (Patsy) Hall, b. ca 1814, not married.
  975   v   Elizabeth J. (Betsy) Hall, b. ca 1816, not married.
  976   vi   Joanna Hall, b. ca 1817, m. 30 July 1838 Lincoln County, Kentucky, to William Coleman, b. 1815, d. 17 June 1881, Boone County, Missouri. Joanna

---

686   *Franklin County, Tennessee, Marriages, 1838-1875*, pp. 46, 52, 72, 106, 183, 200. Kindly furnished by Mrs. Hermione D. Embry, Tennessee State Library, Nashville, Tennessee.

687   Additional children: Rufus, Beauregard, Wiley T., Walter Lee, Ida, and Martha Eliz.: correspondence with descendant [DJS].

688   Seventh Census of the U.S., 1850, Franklin County, Tennessee, p. 66, Household # 875.

689   *Franklin County, Tennessee, Marriages, 1838-1875*, pp. 46, 52, 72, 106, 183, 200. Furnished by Mrs. Hermione D. Embry, Tennessee State Library, Nashville, Tennessee. William B. Fagg, according to correspondence with descendants [PLS].

690   *Ibid.*

691   *Ibid.* William Bonaparte Sublett (b. ca 1815, Green County, Kentucky; d. ca 1880) m. (1st) Elizabeth O. Strother Carter; m. (2nd) Mary Ann Knight, according to correspondence with descendants [PLS].

692   *Ibid.*

693   *Ibid.*

694   Elizabeth G. Sublett d. 29 Jan 1922 in Johnson County, TX, according to correspondence with descendant [DJS].

695   *Ibid.*

696   Burns, *Kentucky Vital Statistics: Record of Marriages in Lincoln County, Kentucky*, --- 1780-1851.

697   Information on the descendants of Mary and Andrew thoughtfully supplied by Mrs. J. Joseph Gerhart, Little Rock, Arkansas, (Gladys Canterbury, daughter of Thomas F. Canterbury and Laura Maude [Lyon], and granddaughter of Mary Catherine [Coleman] Lyon above.) Based on the 1850 and 1880 censuses of Boone County, Missouri; the 1880 Census records # 971, 974, 975, 977, and 978, all in one household, and unmarried.

d. ca 1891. Issue:

1. John W. Coleman, b. ca 1841, Boone County, Missouri; m. Susan Meredith.
2. Mary Catherine Coleman, b. ca 1844, d. 1891/2; m. 28 June 1863 Eli Kennedy Lyon, Boone County, Missouri. 6 children.
3. Andrew Hall Coleman, b. 3 Oct 1847, d. 1909, Scotts Mills, Marion County, Oregon; m. 18 Aug 1877, Missouri, Elizabeth Ann Smith, b. 21 Apr 1852, d. 29 Mar 1935, Scotts Mills, Marion County, Oregon, daughter of Jacob and Alsie [Elsie Anna] (Self) Smith.[698] Issue:
    i   Lillian Irene Coleman, b. 10 Nov 1878, Missouri; m. Wm. Edgar Brown; b. 1880; d. 1949.
    ii Maggie Belle "Margaret" Coleman, b. 28 Mar 1884, Scotts Mills, Marion County, Oregon; m. 23 May 1903, Silverton, Oregon, Clyde Ramsby, b. 1881; d. 1963. Issue.
    iii Agnes Berniece Coleman, b. 8 Apr 1885, Scotts Mills, Marion County, Oregon; d. 19 Feb 1959, Silverton, Marion County, Oregon; m. 3 Nov 1903, Alfred I. Olson, b. 1883; d. 1958. Issue.
    iv William Price Coleman, b. 28 Mar 1886, Scotts Mills Oregon; d. 1930.
4. Vianna G. Coleman, b. ca 1849, m. Lonie Hunt.
5. Martha Price Coleman, m. Columbus Conley.
6. D. Frank Coleman, m. Ilabelle Daly.
7. Sarah Coleman, b. ca 1854, d. 1926, m. George Grant.

977 vii   William F. Hall, b. ca 1819, not married.
978 viii Andrew J. Hall, b. ca 1821, not married.
979 ix   Nathaniel G. Hall, b. 9 Dec. 1824, d. 10 Feb. 1903, m. Nancy Vanlandingham, b. 1836, d. 1922. Issue:
1. Benjamin F. Hall, b. ca 1858.
2. James E. Hall, b. ca 1859.
3. Mary E. Hall, b. ca 1862, m. --- Hartley.
4. William A. Hall, b. ca 1864.
5. Amanda E. Hall, m. --- Roberts.

980 x   Nancy A. Hall, b. ca 1826, m. Joshua Wiley, son of Benjamin Wiley above, who m. Nancy's sister Mary; Joshua being a son by Benjamin's first wife, of course.
981 xi   Margaret A. Hall, b. ca 1826, not married.
982 xii   Vianna L. Hall, b. 11 June 1828, d. 1 June 1868, Boone County, Missouri; m. Robert Coleman.
983 xiii John (Jack) Hall. Issue:
1. Betty Hall
2. Margaret Hall
3. Martha Hall
4. William Hall
5. Richard Hall

133. Valentine Day, b. say 1780, listed in the 1810 Census of Lincoln County, Kentucky, aged

---

[698]   Andrew Hall Coleman, b. ca 1846, m. Lilly --- in original text. This additional information was published in *DSGR Magazine* 28:158. Information sent by a granddaughter, Mrs. Violet Dick of Crescent City, California.

26-45, with a wife 16-26, and one son under 10.[699] He had married Elizabeth ("Betsy") Adams, 31 July 1809, in Mercer County, Kentucky.[700] In July 1813 Day was appointed surveyor and superintendent of the roads in Precinct No. 16 of Lincoln County.[701] In April 1829 he was named Captain of the patrollers in his precinct.[702] He is listed in the 1830 Census of Lincoln County as aged 40-50, with wife 30-40, one son 15-20, two sons and one daughter 10-15, two daughters 5-10, and two sons and one daughter under 5.[703] When his aunt Nancy (Sublett) Greenwood (#28) sought her Revolutionary widow's pension, Day deposed on 2 Oct. 1838 in Lincoln County that he was "well-acquainted with Bartlee Greenwood and Nancy Greenwood his wife previous to the first of January 1794," demonstrating thereby that both Day and the Greenwoods came from Charlotte County, Virginia.[704]

Issue of Valentine and Elizabeth (Adams) Day, *inter alia*:

1011	i	Clarinda A. Day, m. (date of bond) 24 June 1835 to Nudget Owsley, in Lincoln County.[705]
1012	ii	Polly Day, m. 20 June 1837, Lincoln County, Kentucky, to Benjamin Cornett, Valentine Day being bondsman.[706]
1013	iii	Eliz Day b. 14 oct 1825; m. ca 1843 in Missouri to Byram Linville.[707]
1014	iv	Ursula Sublett Day b. 15 Apr 1827; m. Henderson Linville.[708]

136. William Day, b. it is said in 1789 in Charlotte County, Virginia; when grown, he is said to have exceeded six feet in height and to have weighed 220 pounds. Because of his unusual strength, which was noted throughout his area in Kentucky, he was expected to meet the bullies of other neighborhoods in fistic encounters which customarily took place at log-rollings, country dances, or on election days, and it was said of him that these embroglios "left many minor scars from the hard blows, knife or sharp teeth of his adversary."[709] Those were rough-and-tumble days. He was married 27 Sept. 1813 in Lincoln County, Kentucky, to Dorothy (Dolly) Embree.[710] She was born 1797 in Clark County, Kentucky, and died in 1875 at Martinsburg, Iowa. William appears to have accompanied his parents to Green County, Kentucky, and then in 1819 to Madison County, Illinois, where he was listed in the 1820 Census.[711] From thence he moved to Sangamon County, Illinois, into that portion which became Indian Creek Precinct of Menard County. There he succeeded his brother Benjamin in the operation of the ferry over Salt Creek

---

699   *Third Census of the U.S., 1810, Lincoln County, Kentucky*, transcribed by Annie Walker Burns, Washington, D.C., 1936, p. 4.

700   Thompson, *Sublett Chart*, confirmed by Lucy Kate McGhee, *Mercer County, Kentucky, Marriages, 1785-1852*, p. 44.

701   *Lincoln County, Kentucky, Order Bk. 7*, unpaged.

702   *Ibid.*, Order Bk. 9, 1824-1831, folio 205.

703   Fifth Census of the U.S., Lincoln County, Kentucky, p. 29.

704   Bartlee Greenwood, Revolutionary Pension Application W 3013, National Archives, Washington, D.C.

705   Lincoln County, Kentucky, Marriage Index; McGhee, *Old Crab Orchard*, v. 3, p. 110.

706   *Ibid.*, Marriage Index; McGhee, *Old Crab Orchard*, v. 3, p. 29.

707   According to correspondence with descendant [DJS].

708   *Ibid.* [DJS].

709   MS. written by his grandson, Samuel Sublette Day (#4155), deposited in the Sons of the American Revolution Library, Los Angeles, California.

710   Lucy Kate McGhee, *Historical Records of Old Crab Orchard, Kentucky*, v. 3, p. 34.

711   Illinois State Historical Library, *Collections*, v. 26, p. 199.

where the state road from Springfield to Havana crossed.[712] Later he followed some of his children to Iowa, Keokuk and Jefferson Counties, where he died at Martinsburg in 1875 and is buried in the Rayburn Cemetery.[713]

Issue of William and Dolly (Embree) Day:[714]

- 1041   i   Franceway Day, b. 5 July 1814, Lincoln County, Kentucky; d. 10 Feb. 1896 Sullivan County, Missouri; m. Mary Ann Noble.

  1042   ii   John Day, b. ca 1816, Green County, Kentucky; m. Mary ---. Issue:
              1. Mary Day, m. Isaac Carr.

  1043   iii   Valentine Day, b. 14 Jan. 1818 Green County, Kentucky; d. 1879; m. (1st) 1840 Elizabeth Barns; m. (2d) 1862 Rachael Hillman.

  1044   iv   Ursula Day, b. 1819, Madison County, Illinois; named for her paternal grandmother; d. 3 March 1868, Mercer County, Missouri. She m. (1st) --- Tregaskis. One daughter:
              1. Mary Jane Tregaskis, b. 15 Nov. 1840, Mineral Point, Wis.; d. 7 March 1904, Mercer, County, Missouri; m. 28 May 1858 at Martinsburg, Iowa, to William Johnston, b. 15 Nov. 1859, Ft. Wayne, Indiana; d. 3 April 1925, Mercer County, Missouri.
              Ursula m. (2nd) Reuben Walker. Issue:
              2. Eugenia Walker, b. 2 Jan. 1849, d. 25 April 1867; m. Harrison Widner.
              3. Eliza Walker.
              4. William Walker.
              5. Marcellus Walker.
              6. George Walker.
              7. Suzanne Walker.

  1045   v   Elizabeth Day, b. 13 Sept. 1820, Madison County, Illinois; m. John Meeker.[715]

- 1046   vi   Philip S. Day, b. 25 Feb. 1824, Madison County, Illinois; m. 1847 Grace Taylor; resided in Keokuk County, Iowa.

- 1047   vii   Joseph Peyton Day, b. 25 Jan. 1826, Sangamon County, Illinois; d. 3 May 1896, Sullivan County, Missouri.

  1048   viii (Charles) Allen Day, b. ca 1829, m. --- McBeth. He died in service during the Civil War, and is buried at Jefferson Barracks, Missouri. Issue:
              1. Lillian Day.
              2. Alice Day.
              3. Lester Day.
              4. Dora Day.

  1049   ix   Abraham Day, b. 26 Jan. 1831, Sangamon County, Illinois (now Menard County); d. 29 Dec. 1908; d. at Pagosa Springs Colorado; m. 30 Oct. 1854 Mary Ann McMillen.

- 1050   x   Dorothy Day, b. ca 1833, m. 28 Feb. 1851, to George Washington Taylor; she died 15 July 1863.

---

712   *History of Menard and Mason Counties, Illinois*, Chicago, Baskin, 1879, p. 371.

713   Gravestones: Wm. S. d. 16 Apr 1861 ae 86-2-25; Dorothy d. 7 Jun 1871 ae 78-0-1; correspondence with descendant [DJS].

714   Information as to issue kindly supplied by Miss Jean Richardson, Trenton, Missouri, and Mr. Max McKee, Redondo Beach, California.

715   M. (1st) John Wesley Meeker, (2nd) 2 July 1871 David S. Dayton, according to correspondence with descendant [DJS].

137. Benjamin Sublett Day, b. 6 Nov. 1792, Charlotte County, Virginia; m. 3 Sept. 1813 in Garrard County, Kentucky, to Catherine Onstott, b. 22 Jan. 1797, Garrard County, Kentucky, d. 23 May 1853, DeWitt County, Illinois, daughter of Nicholas and Mary (Sherffy) Onstott.[716] Benjamin Sublett Day served in the War of 1812 as a fifer under Col. Dudley. He migrated along with his parents to Madison County, Illinois, where he was listed by the 1820 Census, aged over 21, with five other white persons in his household.[717] Benjamin shortly moved to that portion of Sangamon County, Illinois, which ultimately became Indian Creek Precinct of Menard County, and there entered the ferry on Salt Creek where the state road from Springfield to Havana crossed. After some years there, he turned the ferry over to his brother William, and in 1834 settled in what is now DeWitt County, Illinois.[718] There in 1836 he laid out the town of Marion (now the town of DeWitt). The first election in the township was held at his house and the first school was conducted in his kitchen. He died 24 Feb. 1845 in DeWitt County, Illinois.[719]

Issue of Benjamin S. and Catherine (Onstott) Day:

1051   i   Mary Day.
1052   ii   Elizabeth Ann Day, b. 20 May 1816, Lincoln County, Kentucky, d. 8 Feb. 1870, Clinton, DeWitt County, Illinois; m. 4 June 1835, Decatur, Macon County, Illinois, to Sylvanus Shurtleff, b. 16 Aug. 1811, Isle La Motte, Vermont; d. 24 March 1903, Chicago, Illinois; posthumous son of Oliver and Mary (Smith) Shurtleff. Sylvanus Shurtleff was a pensioner of the Black Hawk War.[720]
• 1053   iii Edward O. Day, b. 25 May 1818 in Kentucky; d. 15 May 1884; m. 3 Jan. 1840 Caroline Hurley.
1054   iv   Rebecca Robbins Day, m. --- Hawlins.
1055   v   Hiram Thomas Day, of Clinton, Illinois.
1056   vi   Caroline Day, m. --- Barnes.
1057   vii George A. Day.
1058   viii John W. Day, of Clinton, Illinois. Issue:
             1. Ellis Day, m. Rose Sacket.
             2. Grace Day.
             3. Ella Day.

144. Rebecca Day, b. 2 Feb. 1790, Charlotte County, Virginia;[721] married (1st) date of bond, 13 March 1806 in Lincoln County, Kentucky, to James Johnson, her brother Valentine Day being security.[722] James Johnson was drafted into the company of Capt. William Sprat in the Lincoln County militia in the War of 1812, but secured his wife's first cousin William C. Sublet (#148) as a substitute.[723] On 11 Dec. 1815 Valentine Day was granted "Letters of Administration of the

716   Benjamin Shurtleff, *Descendants of William Shurtleff of Plymouth and Marshfield, Massachusetts*, Revere, Massachusetts, 1912. p. 310.

717   Illinois State Historical Library, *Collections*, v. 26, p. 162.

718   *History of Menard and Mason Counties, Illinois*, Chicago, Baskin, 1879, p. 371.

719   *History of DeWitt County, Illinois*, Philadelphia, Brink, 1882, pp. 286-287; his death date supplied by Mrs. Gladys D. Swearingen, Pueblo, Colorado.

720   Shurtleff, *op. cit.*, p. 310, q.v. for descendants of this couple.

721   Family Bible of Archer Herndon in the possession of Mrs. Earl Bice (Grace Herndon), Springfield, Illinois, 1961.

722   Lincoln County, Kentucky, Marriage Index.

723   William C. Sublett, War of 1812, Bounty Land Files, Act of 55-80, Wt. 45680, National Archives, Washington, D.C.

Estate of James Johnston decd. The said Valentine having procured a certificate from the widow and relict of the said James resigning her right to said administration."[724] On 9 March 1817 in Green County, Kentucky, Rebecca m. (2nd) Archer Gray Herndon, a veteran of the War of 1812. Herndon was born 13 Feb. 1795 in Madison County, Virginia, son of William and Mary (Bohannon) Herndon, and died 3 Jan. 1867, Springfield, Illinois. He became an Illinois state senator and was U.S. Receiver of Public Moneys in the Land Office, 1842-1860. Rebecca died 19 Aug. 1875 at Springfield, Illinois.[725]

Telling of her Kentucky childhood, Rebecca said: "We sang songs against the Yankees then. Now all that prejudice is gone — gone long since. They are good people — good neighbors — good citizens. A Scotch lady gave me a copy of Burns as early as 1812 or 1815. We — my sisters and myself — learned Burns by heart — sang his songs — such as "Bonny Doon," "Highland Mary," "Soldiers Return" ... Sang cheerful songs — Christian ones, too. We danced. Am a Methodist — parents old school Presbyterian. I was a school mistress in Kentucky in 1812 or 15. We visited — were social, more so than now. We raised our own cotton — carded — spun it — have picked cotton many, many a day — seeded it with my own fingers."[726]

Issue of Archer G. and Rebecca (Day) Herndon:

1121   i   William Henry Herndon (1818-1891), Abraham Lincoln's law partner and controversial biographer. Herndon on one occasion wrote: "My mother prides herself on her descent — so does my father. ... I, on the other hand, claim that I have come from 'Poor White trash' ..." It is difficult to escape the conclusion that he had a singular notion of what constitutes poor white trash. At least the Hunts, Minges, Herndons, Jeffersons, etc., were not given to thinking of themselves in these terms, even though they were not F.F.V.s perhaps.

1122   ii   Elliott Bohannon Herndon (1820-1895)

1123   iii   Archer Gray Herndon (1825-1890)

1124   iv   Nathaniel F. Herndon (1827-1835)

148. William C. Sublett was born 16 August 1792 in Virginia. In the War of 1812 he served as a private in the company commanded by Capt. Armstrong Kerr (who m. William's first cousin Susanna Dudgeon) (#123) in the 13th Regiment of the Detached Kentucky Militia under the command of Lt. Col. William Dudley. He served therein as a substitute for James Johnson of Lincoln County, Kentucky, (presumably the husband of William's first cousin Rebecca Day) (#144). "Johnson (i.e., presumably his substitute Wm. C. Sublett) was drafted on or about 29 March 1813 for the term of six months and continued in actual service until 5 May 1813 at which time he was taken prisoner by the enemy and was released about 13 May on Lake Erie near the mouth of the Big Miama River." He was honorably discharged at Stanford, Lincoln County, Kentucky, 3 Aug. 1814. "His principle James Johnson was drafted at time and place aforesaid under Capt. Wm. Sprat but that he as substitute for Johnson served under Capt. Armstrong Kerr

724   *Lincoln County, Kentucky, Order Bk. 1812-1815*, folio 167.

725   John Goodwin Herndon, *The Herndon Family of Virginia, Vol. II* (*The Herndons of the Am. Rev.*), Pt. III, Lancaster, Pa., pp. 194-197.

726   Herndon-Weik Collection, *loc. cit.*

as aforesaid."[727]

William C. Sublett m. (date of bond) 6 April 1818 in Lincoln County, Kentucky, Elizabeth Barnett.[728] He is listed in the 1830 Census of Lincoln as aged 30-40, with wife 30-40, two sons 10-15, two sons 5-10, and one son and one daughter under 5.[729] By 2 March 1842 William C. Sublett and Betsy B. his wife had moved on to Lewis County, Missouri, for on that date the couple conveyed a Lincoln County tract to Allen Logan.[730] On 3 Sept. 1851 William C. Sublett aged 59 of Lewis County, Missouri, applied for bounty land as a War of 1812 veteran, but on 20 Oct. 1852 he died in that county.[731] On 22 Nov. 1852 Willis A. Sublett, Hubbard A. Sublett and Akin M. Sublett, minor heirs over the age of 14 years of Wm. C. Sublett decd. came into court in Lewis County and chose William Knox Sublett guardian of their persons. On 20 Feb. 1856 William Knox Sublett guardian of the person and curator of the estate of Akin Sublett applied for additional bounty land for Akin Sublett, "only minor heir of Wm. C. Sublett who departed this life on 20th Oct. 1852 in the County of Lewis leaving 3 children under age 21 all of whom are now over 21 except said Akin Sublett who was born 23 Feb. 1838 ... William C. Sublett had no wife living at his death, not having been married for a number of years."[732]

Issue of William C. and Elizabeth (Barnett) Sublett:

1161	i	William Knox Sublett, b. ca 1819.[733]
1162	ii	son, born ca 1820.
1163	iii	son, born ca 1822.
1164	iv	son, born ca 1824.
1165	v	son, born ca 1826.
1166	vi	daughter, born ca 1828 or 1829.[734]
1167	vii	Willis A. Sublett, b. ca 1832.
1168	viii	Hubbard A. Sublett, b. ca 1834.
1169	ix	Akin Miller Sublett, b. 23 Feb. 1838.[735]

161. George Allen Sublett, b. say 1790, m. 29 May 1821 in Rutherford County, Tennessee, to Elizabeth M. Ledbetter.[736] In the 1820 Census of Rutherford County "G.A. & A.C. Sublett" are listed as heads of an all-male household, two men being between the ages of 26-45, two between 16-26, one between 16-18, and one boy between 10-16.[737] Rather surely not all these men referred to were Subletts, for the Sublett brothers, George A. and Abner C., were printers and this

---

727   War of 1812 Bounty Land Files, Act of 55-80-Wt. 45680, William C. Sublett, National Archives, Washington, D.C.

728   Lincoln County, Kentucky, Marriage Index.

729   Fifth Census of the U.S., 1830, Lincoln County, Kentucky, p. 47.

730   *Lincoln County, Kentucky, Deed Bk. R*, p. 191.

731   War of 1812 Bounty Land Files, Act of 55-80, Wt. 45680, above.

732   *Ibid.*

733   Wm. Knox Sublett b. 6 Jul 1824, Lincoln County, Kentucky, d. 19 Aug 1866, Lewis County, Missouri, m. 26 Mar 1857, Missouri, Sarah Barclay (dau Wm.) b. 11 Jun 1939 Missouri, d. 21 Feb 1872, according to correspondence with descendant [DJS].

734   Isabelle Akin Sublett b. 10 Jun 1828 Lincoln County, d. 30 Mar 1862 Lewis County, m. Rhodam Lunsford Adams b. ca 1825, Kentucky, according to correspondence with descendant [DJS].

735   Akin Miller Sublett b. 18 Feb 1838, according to correspondence with descendant [DJS].

736   Rutherford County, Tennessee, Marriages, 1804-1837.

737   Houston, *1820 Census of Rutherford County, Tennessee*.

census entry would appear to account for all the personnel of their bachelor printing establishment. "On June 16, 1814, Murfreesboro's first newspaper, the Courier, was established by the noted publisher brothers, G. A. and A. C. Sublett. It was printed on a Franklin style press. The Courier was a weekly newspaper. ... The length of life of the Courier is uncertain. The latest original copies of this paper found today in various libraries throughout the country are dated 1827, while quotations from the Courier appear in Nashville papers as late as 1831. Whether the Subletts were editors all that time is uncertain, but there are indications that they were as long as Murfreesboro was the capital of the state. The Subletts also appear to have done considerable printing for the state while the legislature was meeting in Murfreesboro. The Courier naturally acquired great prestige among the papers of the state while Murfreesboro was the capital. As a result of this its news items were frequently copied by other newspapers. ... In 1828 the Subletts founded the short-lived National-Vidette, whose sole aim was to help elect Andrew Jackson president of the U.S. ... The Subletts did their share in introducing the opinions of the rugged west into Jeffersonian Democracy."[738] "In 1817 Murfreesboro(ugh) was formally incorporated ... The first aldermen of the town included George A. Sublett."[739] He was also among the charter members of the first Methodist (Church) class in Murfreesboro, organized in 1821.[740]

Issue of George Allen Sublett and Elizabeth (Ledbetter):

1241   i   George Allen Sublett, Jr.

1242   ii   David Sublett.

1243   iii   Capt. Joseph Sublett, of Yazoo, Mississippi.[741]

1244   iv   Isaac Sublett.

1245   v   Rebecca Sublett.

1246   vi   Adelatine Sublett, m. Duke Harrison; resided at Greenville, Texas.[742] Issue:
    1. Irvine Harrison.
    2. Allen Harrison.
    3. Robert Harrison.
    4. N. D. Harrison.

1247   vii   Mary A. Sublett, m. James W. Stewart.[743]

1248   viii   Sarah Sublett, m. James Stewart.[744] Issue:
    1. Mattie Stewart, m. --- Herrigus, Nashville, Tennessee.
    2. Mary Stewart.
    3. D. M. Stewart.
    4. James Stewart.

---

738   Carlton C. Sims, ed., *A History of Rutherford County*, (Tennessee) (1947), pp. 107-108.
739   *Ibid*. p. 40.
740   Acklen, op. cit., p. 452.
741   Joseph Sublett, b. ca 1839.
742   Addie b. ca 1844, m. 6 Oct 1856, Rutherford County, Tennessee. Duke A. b. ca 1837, according to correspondence with descendant [DJS].
743   M. James W. Stewart, 30 Nov 1847, Rutherford County, according to correspondence with descendant [DJS].
744   M. Jas. W. Stewart, 28 Nov 1850, Ruth County, Sarah b. ca 1833, according to correspondence with descendant [DJS].

5.   Joseph Stewart.
1249   ix   Jane Isabella Sublett.

164. William Sublett, b. ca 1800, m. 9 Feb. 1821 in Rutherford County, Tennessee, Ann Robinson (Robertson).[745] Migrated to Tarrant and Dallas Counties, Texas, where in Tarrant County the hamlet of Sublett, Texas, is named for his immediate family. He and his wife are buried in the Watson Cemetery, near Arlington, Texas.

Issue of William and Ann (Robinson) Sublett:[746]

1271   i   John William Sublett, of Cottonwood, Texas; m. Martha West; both are buried in the Watson Cemetery, near Arlington, Texas. Issue:
1.   Preston Sublett.
2.   Charles Sublett, m. Carrie Vaughn.
3.   Mary Sublett, m. Edward Elliot.
4.   John Sublett, m. Naomi Thomas.
5.   Sarah Sublett, m. Bob Elliot.
6.   Henry Sublett, m. Alice Matlock.
7.   Cora Sublett, m. John Elliot.
8.   Augustus Collier Sublett, m. 25 Dec. 1892 to Maggie Charity Matlock. Issue:
   i   Weaver Sublett.
   ii   Collier Matlock Sublett.
   iii Mattie Sublett.
   iv Coulter Robert Sublett, of Dallas, Texas; m. Annie Bob Rainey.
1272   ii   Preston Sublett, of Denton, Texas; m. Susan Cotton.[747]

1273   iii   Daniel Sublett; killed in the War Between the States; m. Mollie Thrasher.

1274   iv   Susan Sublett, m. (1st) R. Collins; (2nd) Sam Hook; resided at Sublette, Texas.

1275   v   Sarah Sublett, m. John Purvis; resided Brambleton, Texas.

1276   vi   Mary Sublett, m. B. Y. Sawyer.[748]

171. George Allen Lowe, b. 20 Sept. 1782, Charlotte County, Virginia, married (1st) (date of bond) 4 April 1809 in Lincoln County, Kentucky, Martha (Patsy) Wilkerson, daughter of John Wilkerson.[749] He m. (2nd) 1816 Tabitha Owen. He migrated to the vicinity of Huntsville,

---

745   *Rutherford County, Tennessee, Marriages, 1804-1837*, p. 94.

746   Family Tree drawn by Sarah (Sublett) Stewart in 1859 in Rutherford County, Tennessee, as copied by Mary (Sublett) Elliot in 1898, owned by Miss Mattie Sublett, of Arlington, Texas (1961), in photostatic copy. Information kindly furnished by Mrs. Coulter R. Sublett, of Dallas, Texas, 1961.

747   Isaiah P(reston) Sublett m. 25 Sep 1841, Wilson County, Tennessee, Susan Cawthorn, according to correspondence with descendant [DJS].

748   Mary Sublett, m. 24 Dec 1843, Wilson County, Tennessee, E. Bartlett Sawyer, according to correspondence with descendant [DJS].

749   Lincoln County, Kentucky, Index to Marriages.

Alabama, and later to Hot Springs County, Territory of Arkansas. His will there, dated 7 Sept. 1835, was filed for probate 4 Oct. 1835.[750] He died on 17 Sept. 1835, for an Alabama newspaper reported: "Died on Friday last at the residence of Mrs. Black at Big Prairie after an illness of 2 or 3 days, Mr. George A. Loe, a respectable citizen of Hot Springs County and late from Alabama aged about 50 years."[751]

Issue of George Allen Lowe and Martha (Wilkerson):[752]

- 1301   i   Mary Wilkerson Lowe, b. 1 July 1810 Huntsville, Alabama; d. 20 Aug. 1849 Sabinetown, Louisiana; m. Samuel Walker Walton.
  1302   ii   Louisa H. Lowe, m. Benjamin Key.

  1303   iii   Philip Lowe, m. Elsie Key.

Issue of George Allen Lowe and Tibitha[753] (Owen):

  1304   iv   Elizabeth P. (Betsy) Lowe, m. 28 Nov. 1833 in Madison County, Alabama, to Robert Walton of Lawrence County, Alabama, son of George and Rebecca (Isaacs) Walton, and brother of Samuel Walton who married Elizabeth's sister Mary above.[754]
  1305   v   Jesse Lowe.

  1306   vi   Thomas Lowe, died without issue.

- 1307   vii   Martha (Patsy) Lowe, b. 23 Feb. 1823 near Huntsville, Alabama; d. 10 Jan. 1886, Shreveport, Louisiana; m. Reuben White.
  1308   viii   George Lowe.

  1309   ix   Mary Lowe (*sic*). Note: George Allen Lowe names a daughter Mary Walton <u>and</u> a daughter Mary Lowe by his will, daughters by his two successive wives.

180. John Jefferson Lowe (called "Jeff"), son of Jesse and Susannah (Sublett) Lowe, born 18 July 1800 in Lincoln County, Kentucky, married his triple cousin Elizabeth Jordan Sublett (#1802), born ca 1811/12 in Warren County, Kentucky, daughter of William and Mary (Sublett) Sublett. Their children were as a consequence remarkably inbred, *e.g.*:

---

750   *Hot Springs County, Arkansas, Record Bk. A*, p. 127.

751   Huntsville, Alabama, *Democrat*, 14 Oct. 1835, copying from the *Arkansas Gazette*, 22 Sept. 1835, abstracted in Kathleen Paul Jones and Pauline Jones Gandrud, *Alabama Records*, v. 6, p. 64, typescript in National D.A.R. Library, Washington, D.C.

752   Information kindly contributed by Mrs. H. N. (Louise Walton) Barnett, Benton, Louisiana; based on memorandum found in the effects of Maj. William Martin Walton.

753   Tabitha [DJS].

754   Huntsville (Alabama) *Democrat*, 5 Dec. 1833, abstracted in Jones and Gandrud, *op. cit.*, v. 6, p. 44.

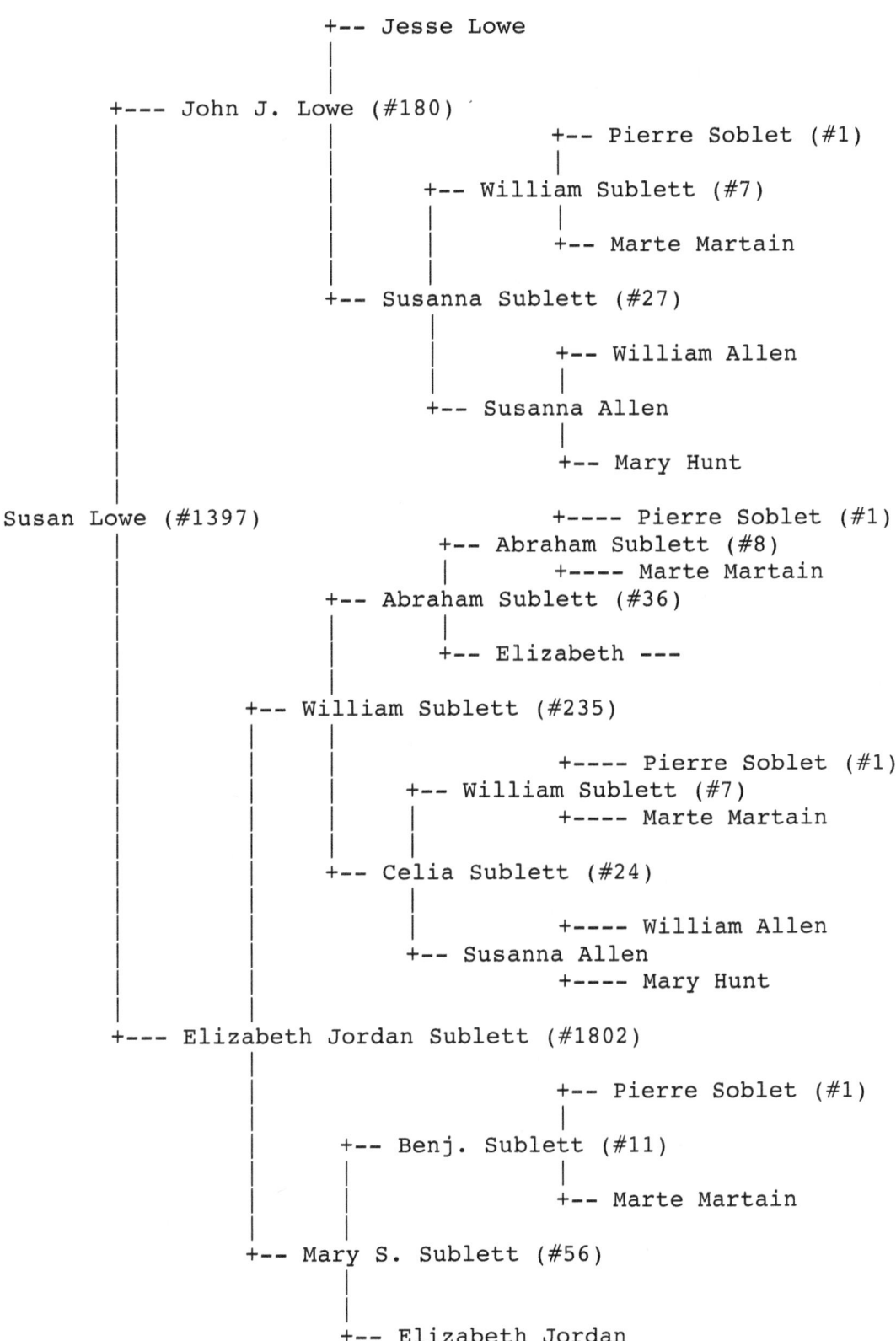

```
                              +-- Jesse Lowe
                              |
        +--- John J. Lowe (#180)
        |                     |                +-- Pierre Soblet (#1)
        |                     |                |
        |                     |      +-- William Sublett (#7)
        |                     |      |         |
        |                     |      |         +-- Marte Martain
        |                     |      |
        |                     +-- Susanna Sublett (#27)
        |                            |
        |                            |         +-- William Allen
        |                            |         |
        |                            +-- Susanna Allen
        |                                      |
        |                                      +-- Mary Hunt
        |
Susan Lowe (#1397)                            +---- Pierre Soblet (#1)
        |                       +-- Abraham Sublett (#8)
        |                       |         +---- Marte Martain
        |             +-- Abraham Sublett (#36)
        |             |         |
        |             |         +-- Elizabeth ---
        |             |
        |      +-- William Sublett (#235)
        |      |      |
        |      |      |                +---- Pierre Soblet (#1)
        |      |      |      +-- William Sublett (#7)
        |      |      |      |         +---- Marte Martain
        |      |      |      |
        |      |      +-- Celia Sublett (#24)
        |      |             |
        |      |             |         +---- William Allen
        |      |             +-- Susanna Allen
        |      |                       +---- Mary Hunt
        |      |
        +--- Elizabeth Jordan Sublett (#1802)
               |
               |                       +-- Pierre Soblet (#1)
               |                       |
               |      +-- Benj. Sublett (#11)
               |      |                |
               |      |                +-- Marte Martain
               |      |
               +-- Mary S. Sublett (#56)
                      |
                      |
                      +-- Elizabeth Jordan
```

John Jefferson Lowe and his family migrated to Arkansas in 1848 and settled near Arkadelphia. After the War Between the States, the couple and most of their children moved to Texas, where the parents died.

Issue of John Jefferson Lowe and Elizabeth (Sublett) :[755]

1391	i	Willis Lowe, eldest son.
1392	ii	Thomas Lowe.
1393	iii	Philip Lowe, a clergyman.
1394	iv	Monroe Lowe.
1395	v	Celia Lowe, eldest daughter, m. --- Huffman or Hoffman.
1396	vi	Mary Jane Lowe, m. --- McMillan.
1397	vii	Susan Dement Lowe, m. --- Robinson.
1398	viii	Martha Ann Lowe.

181. Celia Williams Lowe, born 11 March 1802, Lincoln County, Kentucky, died 30 Oct. 1852, Madison County, Alabama. On 1 Oct. 1820 she was married to John Dement, a native of Sumner County, Tennessee, b. 28 Nov. 1797 at Gallatin, Tennessee, d. 26 June 1848, son of Charles Dement.[756] Shortly after their marriage, the couple settled in Madison County, Alabama, where John was a Justice of the Peace.

Issue of John and Celia W. (Lowe) Dement:

1401	i	Alfred Thomas Dement.
1402	ii	Willis Fields Dement, died young.
1403	iii	Susan Sublett Dement, m. George B. Smith of Phillips County, Arkansas.
1404	iv	Mary Ann Dement, died young.
1405	v	John Jefferson Dement, b. 13 May 1830, Madison County, Alabama; d. 10 Aug. 1892 at Lithia Springs, Georgia, where he had gone for his health. Graduated from the Medical Department of the University of Pennsylvania, 1853; Surgeon in the Confederate Army, 1862-1865; imprisoned at Camp Chase, Ohio. Practiced at Huntsville, Alabama; President of the Medical Association of Alabama, 1876; one of the first trustees of Vanderbilt University. He married 27 Jan. 1869 Cornelia Clopton Binford, daughter of Dr. Henry A. Binford of Huntsville. Issue:

1. Henry B. Dement.
2. Robert S. Dement.
3. Sarah B. Dement, b. ca 1879.
4. John J. Dement, b. 1881, d. 1889.
5. William R. Dement.
6. Susan Dement, b. ca 1887, m. M. R. Moorman; resided 1958 in Huntsville, Alabama.

| 1406 | vi | Elverton Fields Dement. |
| 1407 | vii | Cornelia Jane Dement, b. ca 1834; m. (1st) Robert H. Hereford; m. (2nd) R. J. Searcy, Cullman, Alabama. |

---

755   This sketch is based almost entirely on a manuscript by Sarah (Wilburn) Hall, dated 1910, Stevenson, Alabama, in the possession (1960) of the author's granddaughter, Mrs. Margie (Norwood) Jackson, Dallas, Texas.

756   *Memorial Record of Alabama*, Madison, Wisconsin, 1893, v. 2, pp. 457-459.

1408   viii   Martha Eliza (Mattie) Dement, b. 1 June 1838, m. Feb. 1855 Lucian B. Burrus. Issue, 12 children, 8 of whom reached adult years, including:[757]
  1. LaFayette Burrus.
  2. Fletcher Burrus, Memphis, Tennessee.
  3. Jefferson Burrus, Memphis, Tennessee.
  4. Kathleen Burrus, m. --- Alexander, Crescent, Tennessee.
  5. Susan Burrus, m. --- Watson, Providence, Kentucky.

1409   ix   Philip Lowe Dement, died young.

1410   x   Ann Catherine (Kate) Dement, m. Benjamin Robert Thompson, of Madison County, Alabama; later in life she resided in New York City with her son John Jefferson Dement Thompson. She gathered a considerable body of notes on the Sublett history which were lost when their last possessor, her son Percy Thompson's widow Beatrix, remarried. Kate Thompson was much interested in the Sublette suit in St. Louis.

1411   xi   Lowe Adolphus Dement, a Confederate soldier, killed at Jackson, Mississippi.

185. William M^c. Greenwood (called "Mac"), b. 6 March 1791, Botetourt County, Virginia, was reared in Kentucky. As a young man, he learned the carpenter trade. He made two trips floating produce down the Mississippi to New Orleans, and made the 600 mile return trip each time on foot. He enlisted in August 1812 for the term of one year in the 1st Kentucky Rifles, commanded by Col. R. M. Johnson, and served therewith at the Battle of the Thames. "Mac" Greenwood m. ca 1814 Elizabeth Legg, b. 3 August 1796, d. in 1860 in Mercer County, Illinois. They lived for some time in Mead County, Kentucky (formerly Breckenridge), before moving on in 1830 to Illinois, and in 1836 to Mercer County, Illinois. Mac Greenwood died 7 Sept. 1873 in Mercer County.[758]

Issue of Mac and Elizabeth (Legg) Greenwood:[759]

1441   i   Sophia Greenwood, b. 3 Sept. 1815, m. George Emerick and migrated with him to Oregon; there at the Roseburg Land Office the couple ("George J. Emrick and Sophia A. his wife") entered for 322 acres in T. 19S., R. 3W, S. 4.[760]

1442   ii   John M. Greenwood, b. 29 Dec. 1817, Breckenridge County, Kentucky (that portion now Mead County). He m. 23 Nov. 1848 in Mercer County, Illinois, Catherine Flora.[761] Issue:[762]
  1. Thomas J. Greenwood, b. 23 Sept. 1849; attended Lombard Univ., Galesburg, Illinois; m. 22 Sept. 1881 Jennie Goddard.[763]

---

757   Letter, Mattie E. Burrus to Mrs. Julia White Robards, dated 16 Sept. 1898, Crescent, Tennessee.

758   Account based on memoranda left by George W. Greenwood (#1449) of Topeka, Kansas, in the possession (1961) of his grandson George W. Greenwood of Topeka.

759   Mercer County, Illinois, 1840 Census, p. 1. Mercer County, Illinois, 1860 Census, Pope Creek, p. 40, family #270. Mercer County, Illinois, 1870 Census, Norwood, Suez Twp., p. 29, family #29.

760   Genealogical Forum of Portland, Oregon, Index to Oregon Donation Land Claim Files in the National Archives, v. 4, p. 2.

761   Nelson Bateman, ed., Historical Encyclopedia of Illinois and History of Mercer County, Chicago, 1903, p. 796.

762   Mercer County, Illinois, 1850 Census, p. 361, family #228. Mercer County, Illinois, 1860 Census, Pope Creek, p. 40, family #266. Mercer County, Illinois, 1870 Census, Norwood, Suez Twp., p. 29. Mercer County, Illinois, 1880 Census, Norwood, Suez Twp., p. 18, family #141. (All census citations on #185 William Greenwood and his family kindly supplied by Lt. Col. Kenneth P. Darling, Washington, D.C.)

763   History of Mercer and Henderson Counties, Illinois, Chicago, 1882, pp. 646-647.

          2.   Robert Greenwood, b. ca 1851, m. Sena ---.
          3.   John Edward Greenwood, b. ca 1853.
          4.   Emily F. Greenwood, b. ca 1857.
          5.   Abbie Greenwood, b. ca 1863.
          6.   Frank Greenwood, b. ca 1867.
          7.   Charles Greenwood, b. January 1870.

- 1443   iii Bartlee Greenwood, b. 24 Oct. 1820, m. Dorothy (Dolly) Clifton; resided in Iowa, Missouri and Kansas.

1444   iv Joseph Greenwood, b. 16 March 1823, d. in infancy.

1445   v William Lewis Greenwood, called Lewis, b. 27 March 1824, Breckenridge County, Kentucky (now Mead County); d. 15 March 1887; migrated to Oregon in 1852; there at the Roseburg Land Office he and his wife entered 321 acres in T.18S, R. 3W, S. 33 and 34, and T. 19S, R. 3W, S. 3 and 4, which property adjoined his sister Sophia Emerick's place.[764] His son Jack Greenwood is known to have resided in Seattle.

1446   vi Elizabeth Greenwood, b. 3 June 1828, d. in infancy.

1447   vii Thomas A. Greenwood, b. 8 July 1832, Illinois; migrated to Oregon in 1852 with his brother Wm. Lewis; returned to Illinois in 1859; m. there in 1860; served in the 102nd Illinois Infantry during the Civil War; after the War, he migrated to Montana. One son and two daughters are known to have resided in Seattle.

1448   viii Caroline F. Greenwood, b. 19 Nov. 1835 in Illinois; m. 1 June 1854 in Mercer County, Illinois, to Samuel Brown, b. 13 May 1823, Breckenridge County, Kentucky, son of Alfred and Mary (Mordock) Brown.[765] Issue:[766]
          1.   Harmon G. Brown.
          2.   Maxy Brown, b. ca 1858, m. George G. Cheney.
          3.   George E. Brown, b. ca 1861.
          4.   Grant Brown, b. ca 1863.
          5.   Mary E. Brown, b. ca 1866.
          6.   Samuel Brown, Jr., resided at Rock Island, Illinois.
          7.   Katy G. Brown.

1449   ix George Washington Greenwood, b. 20 May 1838, Mercer County, Illinois; d. 30 Jan. 1927, Topeka, Kansas; m. 9 Jan. 1861 in Mercer County, Illinois, to Sarah McKinley Hardy, b. 1 June 1841, d. 13 or 23 Feb. 1925, daughter of Ashford and Sophia (Moorehead) Hardy. George W. Greenwood attended Lombard College, Galesburg, Illinois; served as a Captain in the 11th Illinois Cavalry; participated in the Battles of Shiloh and Corinth and the Siege of Vicksburg. In 1872 he settled in Wabansee County, Kansas; later he removed to Topeka. Issue:[767]
          1.   Theodore Greenwood, b. 20 Nov. 1861, Mercer County, Illinois.
          2.   Ashford William Greenwood, b. 6 Oct. 1865, Mercer County, Illinois.
          3.   Lewis Henry Greenwood, b. 15 Aug. 1867, Mercer County, Illinois; d. 5 Jan. 1911.
          4.   Trissa Ellen Greenwood, b. 10 Oct. 1870, Mercer County, Illinois;

---

764   Genealogical Forum, *op. cit.*, v. 4, p. 57.

765   History of Mercer and Henderson Counties, Illinois, p. 622.

766   Mercer County, Illinois, 1870 Census, North Henderson Twp., p. 4.

767   *Ibid.*, North Henderson Twp., p. 3, family #15.

m. R. G. Merrick.
5. Octavia Greenwood, b. 6 June 1878, m. --- O'Neil.

186. Susanna A. Greenwood (her middle name presumably Allen, as she was named for her maternal grandmother, Susanna Allen), b. 16 Feb. 1793, was married (1st) to Richard Flint (Flynt) in Lincoln County, Kentucky, 24 Feb. 1813 (date of bond).[768] Susanna married (2nd) 17 October 1823 (date of bond) in Lincoln County, Kentucky, John Cox, b. ca 1780/81, d. 4 April 1859, Mercer County, Missouri; son of James Cox. They migrated shortly after marriage to Orange County, Indiana; then to Clay County, Illinois; and finally to Mercer County, Missouri, where Susanna died in 1886. John Cox served in the War of 1812, for which service he subsequently received bounty land; his widow was later a pensioner of that conflict.[769]

Issue of Richard and Susanna A. (Greenwood) Flint:[770]

1451   i   Martha Flint, b. 26 Aug. 1813, Lincoln County, Kentucky; m. 15 Aug. 1829 in Orange County, Indiana, to Gideon Bosley, b. 24 May 1807, Lincoln County, Kentucky, d. 2 Aug. 1853, Clay County, Illinois, son of Abraham and Rebecca (Myers) Bosley. Martha d. in 1901 in Grundy County, Missouri. Issue:
1. Abraham Greenwood Bosley, b. 19 July 1830, Orange County, Indiana; d. 11 Dec. 1865, Freemont, Mahaska County, Iowa; m. 14 Oct. 1855, Mahaska County, Iowa, Priscilla McCray, b. 4 Aug. 1831, d. 15 March 1915, daughter of William and Nancy (Briant) McCray. Priscilla m. (2nd) Levy Burkey. Four Bosley children.
2. Susanna Bosley, b. 21 Sept. 1831, Clay County, Illinois.
3. John M. Bosley, b. 22 Oct. 1832, Clay County, Illinois.
4. Benjamin F. Bosley, b. 15 March 1837.
5. George B. Bosley, b. 21 Jan. 1840.
6. James Perry Bosley, b. 1 Feb. 1843.
7. Joseph Lee Bosley, b. 19 Jan. 1846.
8. Lucretia Bosley, b. 18 Oct. 1848.
9. Richard Milton Bosley, b. 10 Feb. 1850.
10. Rebecca N. Bosley, b. 5 May 1853.

Issue of John and Susanna A. (Greenwood) Cox:[771]

1455   ii   James Monroe Cox, b. 12 July 1824, Orange County, Indiana; d. 11 April 1874, Mercer County, Missouri; m. 1 Feb. 1849 Clay County, Illinois, Miranda Elizabeth Helm, b. 17 May 1830, d. 8 Oct. 1915, Greenacres, Washington,

---

768   Lucy K. McGhee, *Historical Records of Old Crab Orchard, Lincoln County, Kentucky, vol. 3*, p. 47 (Marriage bonds of Lincoln County, Kentucky).

769   John Cox, War of 1812 Pension File WC 28770, National Archives, Washington, D.C.

770   Contributed by Mrs. F. Dickinson Letts (Josephine Nell Haney), Washington, D.C., 1962, granddaughter of Abraham Greenwood Bosley (1830-1865) above, by his daughter Martha Jane Bosley who married David Nathaniel Haney.

771   All information kindly supplied by Mrs. Earl E. McDonough (Helene Florence Seeley), Bellevue, Washington, 1964, granddaughter of Launa Elizabeth (Cox) McHargue. The dates of birth were taken from a Prayer Book given by John Cox to his daughter Lucretia, and later given by Susanna (Greenwood) Cox to her granddaughter Launa (Cox) McHargue. Other information derives from the Civil War Pension File WC 440189 of James Monroe Cox, National Archives, Washington, D.C.

daughter of Joseph Helm. After James' death, Miranda m. (2nd) David Gentry, Grundy County, Missouri. Issue:

1. Isham Hester Cox, b. 1849, Clay County, Illinois; d. 1851.
2. Lucretia Caroline Cox, b. 3 Dec. 1851, Clay County, Illinois; d. 27 April 1906; m. Joseph Denny.
3. Alice Catherine Cox, b. 2 Oct. 1854, Mercer County, Missouri; d. 2 Feb. 1946; m. Riley Dixon.
4. Joseph Reid Cox, b. 29 Dec. 1856, Mercer County, Missouri; d. 22 May 1916.
5. Launa Elizabeth Cox, b. 5 April 1861, Mercer County, Missouri; d. 3 Nov. 1947; m. 31 Jan. 1875 Joseph Harrison McHargue.

1456	iii	Oliver H. D. Cox, b. 6 Jan. 1826.
1457	iv	Bartlett Cox, b. 29 August 1828.
1458	v	John Cox, b. 13 March 1831.
1459	vi	Lucretia Cox, b. 5 Feb. 1833, d. 12 Sept. 1847, unmarried.

197. Mary Sublett[772] married 22 March 1821 in Green County, Kentucky, Robert Smith,[773] quite possibly a relative through her mother, Polly (Smith) Sublett, for some of her mother's people had migrated out to Green County, Kentucky, with her parents. Robert and Mary (Sublett) Smith migrated to Texas, settling in Sabine County, in January 1855, along with their younger children.

Issue of Robert and Mary (Sublett) Smith:[774]

1540	i	Sir Sidney Smith (*sic*), b. 15 June 1821 Green County, Kentucky; served in the Mexican War in Company I, 1st Regt., Kentucky Foot Volunteers, having been mustered in 17 May 1846 at Louisville, Kentucky, for a period of one year, and having been mustered out 17 May 1847 at New Orleans Barracks.[775] He m. Rosa Vance, and in 1883 resided at Jeffersonville, Indiana.
1541	ii	Philip Smith, served in the Mexican War as a private; mustered in with his brother Sir Sidney on 17 May 1846 at Louisville, Kentucky; discharged for disability 16 Oct. 1846 at Monterey, Mexico. Family tradition says that he died on the way home from service. He also served in Company I, 1st Regt., Kentucky Foot Volunteers.[776]
1542	iii	Robert Smith, Jr.; served in the Mexican War; after his discharge he started overland for California in the '49 Gold Rush and was never heard from again.
1543	iv	Nan Smith,[777] m. (1st) John Vance, (2nd) --- Keay or Kear; (3rd) --- Meglasson; residing in Galveston, Texas, 1881; later moved to Colorado. Issue: 1. Mary Frances Vance.
1544	v	Julyann Smith, b. 12 Dec. 1829, Green County, Kentucky; m. Aug. 1846 John Richard Bell; d. 1879, Sabine County, Texas.
1545	vi	Lucinda Smith, m. as his second wife John Force, b. ca 1834; resided in San Augustine County, Texas. Issue:

---

772   Mary Sublett b. 1802, Green County, Kentucky, according to correspondence with descendant [DJS].

773   Robert Smith b. 1801, Henry County, Virginia, son of Moses, according to correspondence with descendant [DJS].

774   Based on information obtained through the courtesy of Mrs. Sam Radde, Meridian, Texas.

775   Information from the Office of the Adjutant General, Military Department, Commonwealth of Kentucky.

776   *Ibid.*

777   Nan Smith b. 1839, according to correspondence with descendant [DJS].

     1. Tom Force, m. Elvirey Jordan.
     2. Josephine Force, m. --- Easley.
     3. Charles Force.
     4. James Force.
     5. Alice Force m. Henry Birdwell.
     6. Jack Force.
     7. Sidney Force, b. 1876.
     8. Lily Force.

1546 vii Martha Smith,[778] m. as his second wife, Mose Morris. Resided and died, San Augustine County, Texas, where both are buried in Centerview Cemetery. Issue:
     1. Mary Morris, b. 1855, m. Lewis Ware.
     2. Mose Morris, m. Hattie Woods.
     3. Lee Morris.
     4. Georgiann Morris, m. --- Walker.
     5. Josephine Morris, m. Tom Jacks.
     6. Alice Morris, m. Ike Garey.

1547 viii Abram[779] Smith, named for his maternal grandfather, b. ca 1840[780] Green County, Kentucky; d. 1882 Sabine County, Texas, having been shot in the back by Pete Loggins. He is said to have served with Quantrill's Raiders during the Civil War. He and first wife are buried at Brookeland Cemetery, Sabine County. He m. (1st) Mary Ann Ware, no issue. He m. (2nd) Martha Jane Ware, sister of his first wife. Issue by her:
     1. Sidney Smith,[781] m. Etta Green.
     2. Philip Smith, m. Lily Ferguson; resided Victoria, Texas, 1955.
     3. Belle Smith, m. George Milligen; resided Dallas, 1955.
     4. Emma Smith, m. Hugh Milligen; d. Victoria, Texas.
     5. Ollie Smith, m. Bert Arnold, resided Crockett, Texas, 1955.

1548 ix Jane Smith,[782] m. Henry Robbins; resided Sabine County, Texas, where both are buried at Brookeland Cemetery. Issue:
     1. Julyann Robbins, m. --- McGound.
     2. Arminta Robbins, not married.
     3. Molly Robbins, not married.
     4. Melissa Robbins, m. --- Hargrove.
     5. George Robbins, m. Ida Maze.
     6. Bob Robbins, not married.
     7. Etta Robbins, b. 16 Aug. 1874, m. Charles Woods.

198. Philip Allen Sublett, born in Green County, Kentucky, 22 May 1802, moved in 1824 to Durango, Mexico, in response to the invitation in 1823 by the Congress of the Mexican Nation to the citizens of the United States to become inhabitants of Texas, with the added inducement of one section of land for each family for so doing. On 31 May 1828 he was granted Mexican

---

778 Martha Smith b. 1837, Green County, Kentucky, d. 1881, Sabine County, Texas, according to correspondence with descendant [DJS].

779 Abraham b. ca 1835, according to correspondence with descendant [DJS].

780 B. ca 1835, according to correspondence with descendant [DJS].

781 Sidney Smith b. 1870, d. 1940, according to correspondence with descendant [DJS].

782 Jane Smith b. 1843, Green County, Kentucky, according to correspondence with descendant [DJS].

citizenship papers by the ayuntamiento of Nacogdoches, Texas. He purchased the cabin and improvements of one Joseph Frith just east of the Ayish settlement (now San Augustine), and perfected his title by obtaining permission from the Mexican federal government, for the land was in the border leagues. He participated in the Battle of Nacogdoches 2 Aug. 1832.[783] He received title to 1,357 acres of land 8 Sept. 1835 situated in the present county of San Augustine. On 9 Oct. 1835 he received title to one league in Velein's Colony, surveyed in what are now Liberty and Polk Counties. Sublett was a delegate from the District of Ayish Bayou to the first convention of Texas, which opened at San Felipe de Austin 1 Oct. 1832, and a delegate to the second convention at San Felipe in 1833.[784] In 1835 he served as chairman of the Committee of Vigilance and Safety for San Augustine and Nacogdoches and as such he signed the resolution 6 Oct. 1835 nominating Sam Houston as commander-in-chief of the forces of the department of Nacogdoches and participated in the siege of Bexar in Dec. 1835. Lt. Col. Philip Allen Sublett was one of the two immediate commanders of the Texas army before Bexar under Gen. Stephen Austin.[785] At a mass meeting held on August 15, 1836, at San Augustine, Col. Sublett nominated Gen. Houston President of the Texas Republic. Soon after the Texas Revolution, Houston and Sublett were associated together in developing the town of Sabine, where Sabine Lake enters the Gulf of Mexico.[786]

Philip Allen Sublett m.[787] Esther J. (Easter) Roberts, daughter of his Texas neighbors Elisha and Martha (Gill) Roberts. Elisha Roberts was Alcalde of the Ayish Bayou District. Sam Houston boarded for several years with him on his arrival in Texas. Stephen F. Austin, James Bowie, David Crockett, William B. Travis also are known to have stopped with Roberts.[788] It is generally assumed that Col. Sublett d. 25 Feb. 1850. The Texas Gazette of Austin, however, in its issue of 16 March 1850 announced that he died at San Augustine on 2 Feb. 1850. His wife Esther, b. 27 Feb. 1808, d. 19 Sept. 1891, is buried with him in the family graveyard two miles east of San Augustine.

Issue of Philip Allen Sublett and Esther (Roberts) :[789]

1550	i	Franklin Bolivar Sublett, b. ca 1829.
1551	ii	Philip Allen Sublett, Jr. , b. ca 1842, of Trinity County, Texas.
1552	iii	Henry W. Sublett,[790] b. ca 1845, of San Augustine County, Texas.

201. Henry Williams Sublett,[791] b. Green County, Kentucky, 27 May 1817 came to Texas in March 1835 and settled near Philip A. Sublett. Henry's parentage has not yet been established. One source states that he was a brother of Philip; another that he was nephew. The Kentucky

---

783   John Brown, *History of Texas, vol. 1*, p. 192.

784   H. P. N. Gammel, comp., *The Laws of Texas, 1822-1897*. Austin, 1898. vol. 1, p. 480.

785   Brown, *op. cit.*, vol. 1, pp. 402-403.

786   Walter Prescott Webb, ed., *The Handbook of Texas*. Austin, 1952. vol. 2, p. 683.

787   Philip Allen Sublett m. 6 Mar 1828 [DJS].

788   Amelia W. Williams and Eugene C. Barker, ed., *Writings of Sam Houston, 1813-1863*. Austin, Univ. of Texas, 1938-1941, vol. 2, pp. 311-312.

789   San Augustine County, Texas, Census of 1850. The entire family is again named in both the 1860 Census of San Augustine County, Texas, and the Census for the same year in Trinity County, Texas.

790   Henry W. Sublett b. 27 Aug 1845, d. 27 May 1922, m. 15 Jul 1865 Mollie Garrett (dau. Wm.) d. 23 Dec 1883, according to official Texas state records [DJS].

791   This is NOT #1552 [DJS]. Possibly the youngest son of Abraham Sublett (#29) and Polly Smith [PLS].

census records would seem to indicate the latter. A lawyer by profession, Henry W. Sublett was appointed District Attorney for the Sixth Judicial District on 15 January 1842. He married Jane Belle Anderson, daughter of Kenneth L. Anderson, Vice-President of the Republic of Texas.[792] Henry Williams Sublett died 3 Oct. 1859 at Austin and is buried there in Oakwood Cemetery.[793]

208. Sophronia Fuller Sublette, born ca 1802 in Pulaski County, Kentucky, was married 31 March 1825 in Callaway County, Missouri, to Grove Cook.[794] Their marriage was an unhappy one, and Sophronia on 29 Mar. 1841 sued for and obtained a divorce 4 Oct. 1841 from Cook on grounds of habitual drunkenness, abandonment and non-support.[795] Sophronia did not long survive the termination of her marriage, expiring 20 April 1843 near St. Louis, Missouri.[796]

While the divorce proceedings were yet under way, Cook joined a band of immigrants headed for California at the Kansas River camp 18 May 1841 under the leadership of Capt. John Bartleson.[797] In October of 1841 he killed a treacherous Indian guide. He was naturalized in 1844 as a citizen of Mexican California. In 1845 he was at Sutter's Fort working on a distillery and there in July an argument over his mule with Elijah, son of Chief Yellow Serpent, led to Cook's murder of the Indian, which killing precipitated threats of revenge by the Indians.[798] In December 1845 he was married by Sutter to Mrs. Rebecca Fowler, daughter of David Kelsey, a married woman who had deserted her husband, William Fowler.[799] Cook in 1846 moved to Yerba Buena (San Francisco) and then to San Jose, where he was a member of the council and junta. There he acquired considerable wealth, subsequently lost. He died at Santa Cruz in 1852. He is described as a "man whose wit and generosity went far to counterbalance some less desirable qualities."[800] Despite his divorce from Sophronia, Grove Cook seems to have remained on good terms with his brothers-in-law, and when Andrew W. Sublette fell ill in California, Cook nursed him back to health.[801]

Issue of Grove and Sophronia (Sublette) Cook:

1581   i   Theresa Cook, d. 12 May 1849, unmarried, St. Louis, Missouri, in a cholera epidemic. During her parents' marital troubles, Theresa was provided for by her uncle William L. Sublette, who paid for her education at Sacred Heart Convent in St. Louis where she was a boarding student.[802]

229. William Sublett, born ca 1779 in Charlotte County, Virginia, resided there until he with his father's other heirs sold the father's land in 1817. Shortly thereafter he moved to Montgomery

---

792   Webb, *op. cit.*, vol. 2, p. 683; George Louis Crockett, *Two Centuries in East Texas: A History of San Augustine and Surrounding Territory.* Dallas [ca 1932], Crocket calls Henry W. Sublett a brother of Philip A. Sublett, which is erroneous.

793   Mrs. Malcolm B. Biggerstaff, *Four Thousand Inscriptions from Texas, 1745-1870.* 1952, mimeo. p. 68.

794   Adah Redden Ferguson, *Marriage Records of Callaway County, Missouri, 1821-1871.* Fulton, Missouri, 1936, mimeo.

795   St. Louis, Missouri, Court of Chancery, Chancery Record No. 2, 1838-1845, p. 97; p. 113.

796   Sunder, *op. cit.*, p. 198; *Daily Missouri Republican* (St. Louis), 21 April 1843.

797   Hubert Howe Bancroft, *History of California*, San Francisco, 1886, vol. 4, pp. 577-578.

798   *Ibid.*, vol. 4, pp. 544-545; vol. 5, pp. 300-301.

799   *Ibid.*, vol. 3, p. 746; vol. 4, p. 698.

800   *Ibid.*, vol. 4, pp. 577-578.

801   Sunder, *op. cit.*, p. 231.

802   Sister Marietta (Jennings), *op. cit.*, p. 51.

County, Virginia, where the 1850 Census lists him as aged 70 years, wifeless, and living with him was his sister Sarah Leaker, aged 66 years.[803] William had married in July 1805 in Halifax County, Virginia, Elizabeth (Betsy) Redden. William Sublett's will was probated in Montgomery County, Virginia, in 1857.

Issue of William and Elizabeth (Redden) Sublett:[804]

> 1751   i   William Sublett, Jr., m. 18 Nov. 1834 in Montgomery County, Virginia, to Matilda Mitchell. His will was probated in 1844 in Montgomery County. Issue:
> 1. John W. Sublett, m. Margaret ---.
> 2. William R. Sublett, m. 9 Dec. 1862 to Rebecca F. Sowder.
>
> 1752   ii   Samuel Sublett, m. 7 June 1838 in Montgomery County, Virginia, to Margaret Crockett. Will probated in 1868. Issue:
> 1. Emily Sublett, b. 1840, m. James W. Tinsley 4 Feb. 1858.
> 2. Samuel Sublett, b. 9 Aug. 1855.
> 3. James Sublett.
>
> 1753   iii   Abraham Sublett, b. 1815, d. 19 Jan. 1886; m. 24 Jan. 1846 to Martha Jane Franklin in Montgomery County, Virginia. She was b. 27 Feb. 1826; d. 23 Oct. 1900, daughter of James B. Franklin. Issue:
> 1. Elizabeth Sublett, b. 1847, m. the Rev. Campbell McDaniel.
> 2. William James Sublett, b. 1849, d. 18 May 1877; m. 1872 Rhoda Elizabeth Rainey (1852-1901).
> 3. Mary Franklin Sublett, b. 1850.
> 4. Henrietta Frances Sublett, b. 1855, d. 13 Feb. 1938, m. William Robert Knox.
>
> 1754   iv   Edward James Sublett, m. ca 1840, Sarah Jane Hall. Issue:
> 1. Freburn Thomas Sublett, b. 1841, m. 15 Jan. 1864 Susan C. Hall.
> 2. William Sublett, m. Margaret Smith.
> 3. Elizabeth E. Sublett, m. 1862 James W. Kirby.
> 4. Lucy Sublett, m. 1875 William F. Doyle.
> 5. Alice F. Sublett, m. 1877 Samuel T. Winfrey.
> 6. Mary Sublett, m. William F. Dooley.
> 7. John D. Sublett, m. 1873 Marcilla Pillery.
> 8. Sarah Margaret Sublett, m. William Davis.
> 9. James Edward Sublett, b. 1848, d. 1920, m. 10 Jan. 1870 to Ellen Douglas Taylor.

235. William ("Billy") Sublett, born say 1785 in Charlotte County, Virginia, migrated with his parents to Lincoln County, Kentucky, about 1798. He married 10 Jan. 1809 in Warren County, Kentucky, his cousin Mary Scott Sublett (#56), b. 12 Feb. 1788 in Charlotte County, Virginia; d. 8 April 1862, Jackson County, Alabama.[805] They migrated first to Franklin County, Tennessee, where they are listed in the 1820 Census, he aged 26-45, she the same, one son 10 or over, and

---

803   Montgomery County, Virginia, 1850 Census.

804   All information on William and his descendants through the courtesy of Miss Della Spencer, Johnson City, Tennessee, granddaughter of James E., son of #1754.

805   Family Bible of her daughter Celia Ann (Sublett) Johnson in the possession (1960) of Celia's grandson Lon Johnson, Guntersville, Alabama.

one son and two daughters under 10.[806]

A few years later, by 1826, they moved to Jackson County, Alabama, settling at Long Hollow. On 28 Sept. 1830 William Sublett of Jackson County filed for 80 acres in S.5 T.5 R.5; on 2 Oct. 1830 he filed for 79 acres in S.31 T.3 R.7.[807] The 1830 Census lists William there, aged 40-50, wife 30-40, one son 15-20, one daughter 10-15, one daughter 5-10, one son and one daughter under 5 and one slave.[808] On 25 Jan. 1832 William and Mary Sublett deeded a tract in Jackson County to Richard McDuff.[809] During the course of the year 1832 William Sublett died, for on 24 Jan. 1833 Mary Sublett, administratrix of William Sublett, decd., advertised that she had qualified as such in Jackson County, Alabama, in August 1832.[810]

Family tradition has it that he died in early 1832, and that his youngest son, John S. Sublett, born in 1832, was posthumous. William Sublett was buried on his farm at Long Hollow, Larkinsville community, six miles northwest of Scottsboro, Alabama. His widow Mary is listed in the Jackson County 1840 Census, aged 40-50, with one daughter 15-20, one daughter and one son 10-15, one son 5-10 and four slaves.[811]

The widow Mary is listed in the 1850 Census of Jackson County as aged 57, with son William A., age 24, and daughter Mary, age 21.[812] On 23 September 1850 Mary Sublett of Jackson County, Alabama, "late wife of Wm. Sublett decd. as well as administratrix of sd. decedent" appointed her son William A. Sublett agent "to collect money coming to me from the estate of Abram Sublett."[813] Mary Sublett divided her slaves among her children in 1854 and died in Jackson County, 8 April 1862.

Issue of William and Mary Scott (Sublett) Sublett:[814]

    1801   i   Benjamin Branch Sublett, b. ca 1809/10, Warren County, Kentucky; migrated to near Arkadelphia, Arkansas, in 1842; d. without issue there.

•   1802   ii   Elizabeth (Betsey) Jordan Sublett, named for her maternal grandmother; b. ca 1811/12, Warren County, Kentucky; migrated in 1848 to Arkadelphia, Arkansas, with her husband (and cousin) John Jefferson Lowe ("Jeff") (#180), b. 18 July 1800, Lincoln County, Kentucky, son of Jesse and Susanna (Sublett) Lowe. See #180 for descendants.

    1803   iii   Andrew Monroe Sublett, b. ca 1813/14, Warren County, Kentucky; d. Madison County, Alabama; m. Polly Ann Moon, daughter of John Moon of Madison

806   Martha Lou Houston, *Tennessee Census Reports, No. 5, Franklin County, 1820*. Washington, D.C., 1934, mimeo.

807   Certificates 3164 and 3375, Huntsville, Alabama, Land Office; Land Record Section, National Archives, Washington, D.C.

808   Jackson County, Alabama, 1830 Census, p. 16.

809   In one of the two deed books which survived the firing of the Jackson County, Alabama, Courthouse, Scottsboro, by Federal troops during the dying days of the War Between the States.

810   *The Democrat*, Huntsville, Alabama, 24 Jan. 1833, abstracted in Kathleen Paul Jones and Pauline Jones Gandrud, *Alabama Records*, v. 13, p. 1, typescript, National D.A.R. Library, Washington, D.C.

811   Jackson County, Alabama, 1840 Census, p. 62.

812   *Ibid.*, 1850 Census, p. 64.

813   Lincoln County, Kentucky, Circuit Court, Equity Papers, File Box 1850, suit styled "Abram Sublete's Heirs against Abram Sublete's Heirs."

814   Based on a long-hand record made about 1910 by Sarah Ellen (Wilburn) Hall, in the possession (1960) of Mrs. Margie (Norwood) Jackson, Dallas, Texas.

County, Alabama.[815]

1804   iv   Celia Ann Sublett, b. 24 August 1817, Warren County, Kentucky; d. 24 March 1891, Marshall County, Alabama; named for her paternal grandmother, Celia (Sublett) Sublett. Married 1830 to Benjamin Johnson, b. 10 April 1811, Southampton County, Virginia; d. 10 Feb. 1862, Marshall County, Alabama; both buried in the Diamond Cemetery, Marshall County. Issue:
1. William P. Johnson, b. 9 May 1833; d. 22 Nov. 1866.
2. Mary E. Johnson, b. 28 June 1835; m. Austin Alexander.
3. Rebecca Johnson, b. 1 Sept. 1838; d. 29 Sept. 1910; not married.
4. Sarah Frances Johnson, b. 12 Oct. 1841; d. 14 Feb. 1911; m. Oran Williams.
5. Lucy Ann Johnson, b. 21 Feb. 1844; d. 23 Oct. 1867; m. Wm. Cates.
6. Mathew Branch Johnson, b. 6 Nov. 1847; d. infant.
7. John Solomon Johnson, b. 25 Feb. 1849; d. 1933; m. Lizzie Renfroe.
8. Henry William Johnson, b. 9 July 1852; d. infant.
9. Benjamin P. Johnson, b. 10 May 1856; d. 23 Apr. 1945; m. 9 Jan. 1875 Nancy M. Nabours.
10. Amanda Johnson, b. 5 Dec. 1859; d. 1929; m. Gaines Blackburn.

•   1805   v   Martha Jane Sublett, b. 18 Sept. 1822, Franklin County, Tennessee; d. 28 Aug. 1868, Jackson County, Alabama; m. (1st) 6 March 1846 to Joshua Jefferson Willburn (1818-1855); m. (2nd) 11 Jan. 1857 Thomas Logan.

1806   vi   William Allen Sublett, b. ca 1826, Jackson County, Alabama; m. Sallie Harrison; migrated to Arkansas or Texas in the 1860s.

1807   vii   Mary Holman Sublett, b. ca 1829, Jackson County, Alabama; m. (1) John Walker; moved to Ripley, Mississippi. Issue:
1. John Walker.
2. Callie Walker.
3. Carral Walker.
4. Nannie Walker.
After John Walker's death, Mary H. (Sublett) Walker m. (2nd) Benjamin Moore. Issue:
5. Martha Lowe Moore.

1808   viii   John S. Sublett, b. ca 1832, Jackson County, Alabama. One account calls him John Solomon, but another gives his name as John Sally.[816] The latter seems correct, as he would appear to be named after John Sallee, the husband of his father's sister Elizabeth (#236). Never married. Served in Capt. Lindsey's Company, 4th Alabama Regiment in the War Between the States. Participated in the Battle of Manassas and was killed in action at the Battle of Gettysburg.[817;818]

237. Abraham Sublett, b. say 1789, Charlotte County, Virginia; migrated to Lincoln County,

---

815   Madison County, Alabama, Estate Bk. 11, p. 114; Bk. 12, p. 99.

816   Based on a long-hand record made about 1910 by Sarah Ellen (Wilburn) Hall, in the possession (1960) of Mrs. Margie (Norwood) Jackson, Dallas, Texas.

817   Based on a long-hand record made about 1910 by Sarah Ellen (Wilburn) Hall, in the possession (1960) of Mrs. Margie (Norwood) Jackson, Dallas, Texas.

818   Information on William and his descendants was kindly contributed by Charles C. and Icle (Johnson) Smith, Guntersville, Alabama, who have made an intensive study of the northern Alabama Subletts.

Kentucky, with his parents about 1798 and there married Temperance V---.[819] By 1822 or earlier the couple had migrated to Jackson County, Alabama. On 1 June 1831 Abraham Sublett received a patent from the U.S. for a 79.87 acre tract in S.13 T.4 R.6 East, Jackson County, Alabama, near the Tennessee line, having filed for it 22 Sept. 1830.[820] Two years later he and Temperance sold this to a Wood (probably a cousin) and moved further south in Jackson County, Alabama, on the Tennessee River, where he established a ferry at a spot known as Sublett's Ferry up until recent times when a T.V.A. project destroyed the location. He is listed as Abram Sublett in Jackson County in the 1830 Census, aged 40-50, wife 30-40, one daughter 15-20, one son and two daughters 10-15, one son and one daughter 5-10, and one son and one daughter under 5.[821] He was deceased by 1840 when his widow T. V. Sublett is listed in the census, aged 40-50 with two daughters 20-30, one son and one daughter 15-20, one son and two daughters 10-15, one daughter 5-10, and one son under 5.[822]

On 25 August 1842 G. A. Sublett swore in DeKalp County, Alabama, that he was acquainted with "Temperance Sublet the widow and relic of Abraham Sublet deceased and also with fractional S.17 in T.4 R.7 in the Coosa Land District and that the said Abraham Sublet decd. settled on the south part of said tract of land prior to the first of Jan. 1838, he had a dwelling house upon it in which he lived and made his home from that time until his decease in January 1840, that from the 22nd of February to the 22nd of June 1838 he cultivated about three acres on said tract of land ... and that the said A. Sublet was the head of a family having wife and children."[823] Another certificate was issued 1 June 1845 to Temperance Sublett, assignee of George A. Sublett for part of fractional section 20 in fractional T.4 of R.7 East in the District of Lands Subject to Sale at Lebanon, Alabama. When George A. Sublett had filed for this tract on 8 Sept. 1842, the printed form shows that he was "head of a family having a wife" but the words "and children" were significantly crossed out.[824]

Issue of Abraham and Temperance (V---)[825] Sublett:[826]

| 1814 | i | Elizabeth Sublett, b. say 1814, m. George W. Matthews; resided in Talladega County, Alabama, in 1850. |
| 1815 | ii | George A. Sublett, b. ca 1816, Lincoln County, Kentucky; m. ca 1840 Rebecca ---.[827] Listed in the 1850 Census of Jackson County, Alabama, with issue: David, b. ca 1842; John B. , b. ca 1844/5; Mary, b. ca 1847.[828] Another son was Abraham C. Sublett of Jackson County, b. ca 1852.[829] On 23 Dec. 1878 George A. Sublett of Lampassas County, Texas, sold a tract in Jackson to Allen Ellis, |

819   Abraham Sublett, m. 28 Oct 1810, Pulaski County, Kentucky, Temperance Vaughan. [DJS].

820   Certificate 3019, Huntsville, Alabama, Land Office; Land Record Section, National Archives, Washington, D.C.

821   Jackson County, Alabama, 1830 Census, p. 30.

822   *Ibid.*, 1840 Census, p. 2.

823   Certificate 7174, Lebanon, Alabama, Land Office; Land Record Section, National Archives.

824   Pre-emption Certificate 6749, Lebanon, Alabama, Land Office; Land Record Section, National Archives.

825   Temperance (Vaughan) Sublett [DJS].

826   First six children named in Lincoln County, Kentucky, Circuit Court, Equity Papers, 1850 File Box, suit styled "Abram Sublete's Heirs against Abram Sublete's Heirs."

827   Rebecca Ambrester [DJS].

828   Seventh Census of the U.S., 1850, Jackson County, Alabama, v. 6, p. 49.

829   Homestead Certificate No. 1146, Application No. 5438 by John B. Sublett, for tract in S.15 T.4 S. R.7 E. of Huntsville Meridian, 17 Sept. 1879, Land Record Section, National Archives.

who had paid "my son John B. Sublett" for it.[830]

1816   iii   Lucinda Sublett, b. ca 1819, m. ca 1842 her cousin Joseph Jordan Sublett (#385). Lucinda died shortly; one child.

1817   iv   Samuel V. Sublett, b. ca 1821, Jackson County, Alabama. On 25 Aug. 1842 Samuel D. Sublett of Jackson County, Alabama, (signing by mark) filed for 42 acres in fractional S.20 in fractional T.4 of R.7, "being a single man over the age of 21."[831]

1818   v   Frances Jane Sublett, b. ca 1826, Jackson County, Alabama.

1819   vi   Sarah M. Sublett, b. ca 1831, Jackson County, Alabama.

1820   vii   Abraham Sublett, c. ca 1837; apparently died between the taking of the 1850 Census and Nov. 1850.

238. John S. Sublett,[832] b. say 1792 in Charlotte County, Virginia, was drafted in March 1813 in Lincoln County, Kentucky, into the militia company of Capt. Armstrong Kerr, 13th Regiment of Kentucky Infantry commanded by Lt. Col. William Dudley. On 21 March 1836 in Green County, Kentucky, Sublett deposed that the company "marched to Lexington, rendesvoused there — about 1 April [1813] marched against the British and Indians from Lexington on to the Miami River [in Ohio] near Fort Meggs and that on 5th of May 1813 a battle was fought between the British and Indians and the troops under Coln. Dudley, that the battle took place on the bank of the Miami River opposite to Fort Meggs ... that Col. Dudley was defeated by the enemy and his troops retreated in confusion and disorder and disorder and this applicant together with his Capt. and the greater part of his captain's company were made prisoners by the enemy and that this applicant immediately after he was made prisoner was struck by an Indian with a Tomahawk on the right side of his head about one inch above the right ear, that the blade of the tomahawk fractured his skull and produced a most painful and distressing wound that appeared to threaten his life for a number of months thereafter ... that during the first twelve months after he received his wound he was entirely unable to do any kind of work, that all the hare came off of his head..."[833] Two comrades, Isaac Newcomb and Capt. Armstrong Kerr (his cousin's husband) deposed in his behalf, relating how they nursed him, how they "passed through Lake Erie on board a British ship with said Sublett and landed with him at the mouth of the Huron River; that the prisoners had all been parolled while on the lake;" how Newcomb travelled with Sublett and waited on him on the long road home through the wilds of Ohio to his home in Lincoln County, Kentucky; how Sublett frequently was unable to travel at all and that "his life was despaired of."

"A few years after" returning to Lincoln County, John S. Sublett moved to Green County, Kentucky, where his uncle Abraham lived, and resided there for the greater part of the remainder of his life.[834] He died, however, it is said, in Lincoln County, Kentucky, 25 August 1844.[835] He married (date of bond) 5 August 1821 in Green County Nancy Walker, the Rev. John Harding performing the ceremony.[836] Chances are that she was the Nancy Hubbard who previously, in

830   Jackson County, Alabama, Deed Bk.

831   Pre-emption Certificate 6134, Lebanon, Alabama, Land Office; Land Record Section, National Archives.

832   John Sallée Sublett [DJS].

833   John S. Sublett, War of 1812, O. W. Inv. File 25864, National Archives.

834   *Ibid.*

835   John S. Sublett, B. L. Wt. 29777-80-55, National Archives.

836   Green County, Kentucky, Marriage Bk. 3, p. 24.

March 1815, had married Thomas Walker in Green County, the officiant being the Rev. John Harding.

Issue of John S. and Nancy (Hubbard) Sublett:

1841   i   James A. Sublett ("Jr."), b. ca 1822; married (date of bond) 28 Nov. 1844 in Green County, Kentucky, to Nancy Dodegeon (Dudgeon).[837] Listed in the 1850 Census of Taylor County, Kentucky, aged 28, with wife Nancy, aged 28, and three children: William H., aged 4; Nancy S., aged 2, and Elizabeth, aged 4 months.[838] James A. Sublett died in Taylor County, Kentucky, 27 March 1875.

1842   ii   Caroline A. C. C. Sublett, b. say 1825, m.[839] George R. Watson; resided in Adair County, Kentucky, in 1850.

1843   iii   Elijah C. Sublett, b. say 1828, m. (date of bond) 17 Oct. 1848 in Taylor County, Kentucky, Sophia Dudgeon, a Justice of Peace in Adair County, Kentucky, 1855.[840]

1844   iv   Mary F. Sublett, b. 16 June 1830.[841]

1845   v   Nancy C. Sublett, b. 31 July 1832.[842]

1846   vi   John G. Sublett,[843] b. 2 or 31 Oct. 1841.[844]

239. Valentine Sublett, b. say 1794, married (date of bond) 12 December 1820 in Lincoln County, Kentucky, Maria O'Bannon, daughter of Benjamin O'Bannon.[845] O'Bannon was a Revolutionary pensioner, born 23 Nov. 1759 in Fauquier County, Virginia.[846] Valentine Sublett appears to have lived for a time in Franklin County, Tennessee, where his brother William also settled briefly. His wife Maria was deceased by 20 June 1834 when O'Bannon made his will, mentioning "my grandson Abraham Sublett, son of my deceased daughter Mariah."[847] Valentine was also deceased by September 1848 when Abram is listed as "son, heir, and only representative of Valintine Sublett."[848]

Issue of Valentine and Maria (O'Bannon) Sublett:

1861   i   Abraham Sublett, born 23 November 1822, Lincoln County, Kentucky; died 12 May 1884, Boone County, Missouri; buried in the churchyard of Olivet

---

837   *Ibid.*, Marriage Bk. 3.

838   Taylor County, Kentucky, Census of 1850, p. 306.

839   Caroline A. C. C. Sublett m. 10 Aug 1848, Green County, Kentucky according to Kentucky official records [DJS].

840   Adair County, Kentucky, Order Bk. H, p. 538.

841   Mary F. Sublett m. Elijah White [DJS].

842   Nancy C. Sublett m. --- Holdeman [DJS].

843   John G. Sublett m. (1st) Mary Howard, (2nd) Laura Bell Burress [DJS].

844   Issue listed in B. L. Wt., note 3, and Lincoln County, Kentucky, Circuit Ct., Equity Papers, 1850 File Box, "Abram Sublete's Heirs v. Abram Sublete's Heirs."

845   Lincoln County, Kentucky, Index to Marriage Bonds, unpaged.

846   Benjamin O'Bannon, Revolutionary Pension Application S 4629, National Archives, Washington, D.C.; abstracted in Lucy Kate McGhee, *Historical Records of Old Crab Orchard, Lincoln County, Kentucky*, p. 103.

847   Lincoln County, Kentucky, Will Bk. M, p. 152.

848   *Ibid.*, Circuit Court, Equity Papers, 1850 File Box, suit styled "Abram Sublete's Heirs against Abram Sublete's Heirs."

Christian Church, Boone County, Missouri.[849] He married in Lincoln County, Kentucky, 26 Sept. 1844 Elizabeth Hogan (Logan?), b. 10 April 1827 in Lincoln County; died 15 May 1884 in Boone County, Missouri. They are listed in the 1850 census of Boone County.[850] Issue: (*inter alia*)

1. William H. Sublett, b. 5 Aug. 1845; d. 5 April 1914.
2. John Green Sublett, b. ca 1847; m. Sally Barnes.
3. Thomas B. Sublett, b. ca 1849.
4. James A. Sublett, b. 17 April 1851; d. 18 March 1915.[851]
5. Maria Sublett, b. ca 1856.
6. Martha Sublett, b. ca 1858.
7. Abraham Sublett, b. ca 1860.
8. Eliza Sublett, b. ca 1862.
9. Lee Sublett, b. ca 1865.
10. Samuel Sublett, b. ca 1868.
11. Alice Sublett, b. ca 1871.[852]

276. Hill Sublett (named for his paternal grandmother's family) was probably born about November, 1786, for on 20 Jan. 1801 "Hilly Sublet son of Littlebury Sublet ... by the consent of Sarah Sublet his mother puts himself an apprentice to William Sutton of Green County Joiner and Carpenter to learn his art trade or mistery, to serve him for the term of 6 years and 10 months next ensuing."[853] In all probability this term of apprenticeship coincided with the remainder of his minority. "Hilly" agreed not to "haunt ale houses play houses or taverns" during this period, while Sutton agreed "to teach the said apprentice Reading writing and cyphering including the Rule of 3 and give him a set of bench Planes." On 11 Dec. 1809 (date of bond) in Adair County, Kentucky, Hilly Sublett was married to Delphy Ginnett (Delphine Jennet).[854] In 1822 he removed to Montgomery County, Missouri. with his children, who ultimately totalled ten.[855] He died in 1846, while his wife died in 1876.[856]

Issue of Hill and Delphine (Ginnett) Sublett:[857]

2303   i   Joseph Sublett, b. ca 1811, d. 1863/64; m. Sally --- ; six children, including Elizabeth, Flementine, 'Berry, Nancy, and Martha.[858]

2304   ii   Littleberry Sublett, named for his paternal grandfather; d. 1 Nov 1883; m. 10 Dec. 1845 in Boone County, Missouri, to Catherine Jones,[859] daughter of Tyre

---

849   Rella Bright Evans and Mrs. J. Frank Thompson, *Tombstone Records of Boone County, Missouri*, Columbia, Missouri, 1934, mimeographed, p. 100.

850   Gerald McKinney Petty, Index of the 1830, 1840 and 1850 Censuses of Boone County, Missouri, 1950, p. 827.

851   Evans and Thompson, *op. cit.*, p. 100.

852   Boone County, Missouri, Census of 1880.

853   Green County, Kentucky, Deed Bk. 2, p. 226.

854   Adair County, Kentucky, Marriage Register.

855   William S. Bryan and Robert Rose, *A History of the Pioneer Families of Missouri*, St. Louis, 1876, p. 294.

856   *Data on the Sublette Family*, copied by Council Grove Chapter, D.A.R., Putnam City, Oklahoma. 1953-1954; typescript in the National D.A.R. Library, Washington, based on records in St. Louis filed by hopeful heirs of the realty of William L. and Solomon P. Sublette.

857   *Ibid.*

858   Montgomery County, Missouri, Census of 1850, p. 179.

859   Rella Bright Evans and Mrs. J. Frank Thompson, comp., *Marriage Records of Boone County, Missouri 1821-1870*.

H. Jones.[860] Four children.

2305 iii   James B. Sublett, b. ca 1822; of Audrain County, Missouri.

2306 iv   Christiana Sublett, m. --- Sanders.

2307 v   Eliza Sublett, m. John Calhoun; she was b. ca 1829.

2308 vi   Patsy Sublett, d. 6 July 1882; m. Marion Thurman.

2309 vii   Thomas H. Sublett, d. 29 July 1880, m. Mary ---;[861] five children.

2310 viii Sallie Sublett, d. 25 Dec. 1857, m. Smith Griggs; seven children.

2311 ix   Emily Sublett, d. 1849, m. Urign Zumwalt. Two children:
            1. Susan Zumwalt m. --- Idler.
            2. Artemisia Elizabeth Zumwalt, m. 13 March 1870 Asa Bolivar Chapman.[862]

2312 x   Betsey[863] Sublett, m. Urign[864] Zumwalt, her sister's widower. Children:
            1. Eliza Ann Zumwalt, m. Frank Dean.
            2. Jane Zumwalt, m. James M. Brown.
            3. W. M. Zumwalt,[865] m. Jane Young.

277. Samuel Sublett was probably born about 1788; on 20 January 1801 "Samuel Sublet son of Littlebury Sublet ... by the consent of Sarah Sublet his mother" apprenticed himself to William Sutton to learn joining and carpentry.[866] By 30 Dec. 1809 he was probably of age; on that date "Jonathan Smith and Sarah his wife (late Sarah Sublett and widow of Little Berry Sublett decd.) of Green County deeded over her right of dower in Littlebury Sublett's 150 acre tract to Samuel Sublett.[867] On 27 Oct. 1813 (date of bond) in Adair County, Kentucky, Samuel Sublett married Polly (Mary) Trabue, daughter of Daniel Trabue,[868] (1760-1840) and Mary (Haskins). Their children are said to have been: Sallie, Mary, Judith, Robert, William, and Daniel Sublett.[869] Samuel Sublett died 14 April 1865.[870]

Issue of Samuel and Mary (Trabue) Sublett:[871]

2316 i   Sallie Sublett, named for her paternal grandmother, d. 19 Sept. 1895, m. --- Gill. Three children.

Columbia, Missouri, 1933, mimeo. p. 28.

860   Rella Bright Evans and Mrs. J. Frank Thompson, comp., *Wills and Administrations of Boone County Missouri, 1821-1870.* Columbia, Missouri, 1932, mimeo., p. 31. (Will of Tyre H. Jones) Littleberry Sublett resided in Boone County, Missouri, where he is listed in the 1850 Census. See Petty, *Index of the 1830, 1840, and 1850 U.S. Censuses of Boone County, Missouri,* 1950. 1850 Census, p. 850.

861   Mary Mimmo, according to correspondence with descendant [DJS].

862   *Data on the Sublette Family*, previously cited, states that A. Elizabeth Zumwalt died without issue. Her grandson, Frank Chapman Roe, Colts Neck, New Jersey, 1964, furnished information, however, that A. Elizabeth (Zumwalt) Chapman died in October, 1935, having had ten children, including his mother Amanda Bethsheba Chapman (1876-1912) who m. 1900 Frank Charles Roe.

863   Elizabeth, according to correspondence with descendant [DJS].

864   Urijah Zumwalt, according to correspondence with descendant [DJS].

865   Wm. Martin Zumwalt b. 24 Dec 1849, d. 24 Aug 1914, according to correspondence with descendant [DJS].

866   Green County, Kentucky, Deed Bk. 2, p. 228.

867   *Ibid.*, Deed Bk. 6, p. 136.

868   Adair County, Kentucky, Marriage Register.

869   Lillie DuPuy V.C. Harper, *Colonial Men and Times.* Philadelphia, 1916, pp. 225-226.

870   Data on the Sublette Family, cited above.

871   Information as to death dates and marriages is from *Data on the Sublette Family.*

2317   ii   Mary Sublett, named for her maternal grandmother, d. 11 April 1876, m. ---
               Hill. Four children.
2318   iii   Judith Sublett.
2319   iv   Martha Sublett, m. --- Penick.[872]
2320   v   Robert J. Sublett, d. 15 July 1913, m. Green County, Kentucky, Fidelia Wilson.
               Four children: Mollie, Robert W., Samuel Bolling, Ada.[873]
2321   vi   William Sublett; died in boyhood.[874]
2322   vii   Daniel Sublett, named for his maternal grandfather; died in boyhood.[875]

278. Littlebury Sublett, Jr., was born 14 July 1790, for on 10 Sept. 1806 "Jonathan Smith of Green County Guardian of Little Berry Sublet infant orphan of little Berry Sublet deceased hath placed the said Little Berry Sublet of the age of 16 years the 14th day of July last with him the said Thomas C. Pile during the term of 4 yrs. and 10 months or until he shall arrive to age of 21 years ... to instruct the said Apprentice the art and mistery of saddling."[876] Earlier on 5 Dec. 1803 Littleberry Sublett "with the consent of his mother Sarah Smith" had been apprenticed to Jacob Smith, saddler and saddletree maker.[877] On 16 Jan. 1814 (date of bond) Littleberry Sublet was married in Green County, Kentucky, to Mary (Polly) Crouch.[878] She was the daughter of John Crouch who names her in his will, dated 5 July 1825, probated 19 Dec. 1825.[879] Littleberry Sublett, Jr., and his bride shortly after their marriage removed to Woodford County, Kentucky, and then in 1826 to Clay County, Missouri, near Liberty.[880] There Littlebury Sublett died in 1863.[881] His will was probated 4 Aug. 1863.[882]

Issue of Littlebury and Mary (Crouch) Sublett:[883]

2328   i   William Alburtus Sublett,[884] residing in Arbuckle, California, in 1893.
2329   ii   Linneus (Linaeus) Bowlin Sublett, named for a paternal uncle, b. 3 Feb. 1820,
               Versailles, Kentucky, Judge of the County Court of Clay County, Missouri.
               Judge Sublett served as a Lieutenant in the First Regiment of Missouri Cavalry
               in the Mexican War, was at the taking of Chihuahua, and was a pensioner of
               that war.[885]

---

872   Martha Sublett m. Littleberry Penick. [DJS].

873   Statement of Robert J. Sublett, given about 1896 to George Loe Walton, in possession of Mrs. H. N. Barnett.

874   *Ibid.*

875   *Ibid.*

876   *Adair County, Kentucky, Deed Bk. A*, p. 423.

877   *Green County, Kentucky, Deed Bk. 4*, p. 91.

878   *Green County, Kentucky, Marriage Bk. 2*, p. 109.

879   *Ibid.*, Will Bk. 2, p. 123.

880   *Portrait and Biographical Record of Clay, Ray, Carroll, Chariton and Linn Counties, Missouri.* Chicago, Chapman, Bros.,
        1893. p. 442.

881   Data on the Sublette Family, cited previously.

882   Will of Littleberry Sublett, Clay County, Missouri, abstracted in Genealogy and History, vol. 8, no. 1 (whole number 80),
        p. 4, 15 Feb. 1947.

883   *Ibid.*

884   William Alburtus Sublett m. 15 Sep 1867, Carrie Hardwick, according to correspondence with descendant [DJS].
        However, Caroline Hardwick married L. B. Sublette on 15 Sep 1867 in Clay County, according to *Missouri Marriages,
        1851-1900* [PLS].

885   *Portrait and Biographical Record of Clay ...*, p. 442.

2330   iii   Zerelda Sublett, m. 17 Feb. 1831, Clay County, Missouri, to Henderson Dougherty; two children.[886]

2331   iv   Elizabeth Sublett, m. 29 Oct. 1840, Clay County, Missouri, to Norris Hillman Lingenfelter (Lincolnfelter) by John Edwards of the Old School Baptist Church.[887] She d. 8 Jan. 1880. Nine children.

2332   v   John H. Sublett, not married.

2333   vi   Ephraim Sublett, not married.

2334   vii   Margaret A. Sublett, m. George Anderson Chanslor, 25 Nov. 1852, Clay County, Missouri, by William H. Price, Baptist minister.[888]

279. Joseph Burton Sublett was born about 1792 for on 5 Dec. 1803 "Joseph Burton Sublett, son of Littleberry Sublett decd. with the consent of his mother Sarah Smith" was apprenticed to John Campbell, tanner and currier.[889] It was stipulated that "at cards or dice he shall not play, taverns or alehouses he shall not frequent, fornecation he shall not commit, Matrimony he shall not contract." (Shades of *Fra Lippo Lippi*!) Eventually he did contract matrimony, 5 Dec. 1816 (date of bond) in Green County, Kentucky, to Edith Radford.[890],[891] He died in June, 1865.[892]

Issue of Joseph Burton Sublett and Edith (Radford):[893]

2338   i   Amanda Sublett, d. February 1880; m. --- Blaydes;[894] two children: J. W. Blaydes; Stephen Blaydes.

2339   ii   Lafayette (Lafe) Sublett,[895] d. 1864. Four children: Mary E., John F., Mattie, and William Sublett.

2340   iii   Mary Sublett,[896] m. --- Bagley. Eight children: R. S., Joseph, J. D., G. W., W. H., D. M., J. T., and Martha.

2341   iv   John S. Sublett,[897] b. ca 1824.[898]

2342   v   Marcus Sublett, b. ca 1828; it seems possible that this Marcus and #2339 are one and the same person, for an exceptionally popular name of the 1820s, the decade of birth, was Marquis Lafayette, which as often as not was corrupted into Marcus Lafayette.

2343   vi   Reubin Sublett, b. ca 1834.[899]

2344   vii   Martha Sublett, c. ca 1837.[900]

---

886   Nanon Lucile Carr, *Marriage Records of Clay County, Missouri, 1822-1852*, mimeo., 1957., p. 15.

887   *Ibid.*, p. 33.

888   *Ibid.*, p. 10.

889   *Green County, Kentucky, Deed Bk. 4*, p. 75.

890   *Ibid.*, Marriage Bk. 2, p. 112.

891   Edith Radford b. 25 Dec 1816, dau. of Reuben, according to correspondence with descendant [DJS].

892   Data on the Sublette Family, cited previously.

893   *Ibid.*

894   Amanda Sublett m. Dabney Blades, according to correspondence with descendant [DJS].

895   Marquis Lafayette Sublett m. 22 Jan 1852, Phebe B. Gupton, according to correspondence with descendant [DJS].

896   Mary Sublett m. (1st) John A. Carr, m. (2nd) Thos. Bagley, 26 Mar 1849, according to correspondence with descendant [DJS].

897   John T. Sublett, d. bef 1862, m. 15 Mar 1849, Margaret Dorinda Craig, according to correspondence with descendant [DJS].

898   Seventh Census of the U.S., 1850, Green County, Kentucky, p. 114, Household #487.

899   Reubin Sublett m. Mary F. Radford who m. (2nd) 1861 Calvin Cayce, according to correspondence with descendant [DJS].

280. Lineus (Lenius) Bowlin Sublett was born probably in Green County, Kentucky, ca 1797, for on 5 Oct. 1814 Sarah Smith "hath placed and bound Lenious Bolin Sublett her son under the age of 21 years ... for four years to learn the art and mistory of hous joining" to William Miller.[901] On 10 Jun 1818 Lineus Bowlin Sublett joined his brother Littlebury in deeding away their interests in the paternal property to their brother Samuel, so presumably on that date or before he had reached his majority.[902] In Nov. 1819 Lenious was in St. Clair County, Illinois, but in 1820 settled in Randal Township, Cape Girardeau County, Missouri, where he operated a ferry at Cape Girardeau. He died there in 1849, leaving a widow Harriet and five children.[903] Harriet appears to have been the daughter of John Abernethie of Wake County, N.C. (Town of Washington?)

Issue of Lineus B. and Harriet (---) Sublett:

2348   i   James G. Sublett, b. ca 1828, Missouri.[904]
2349   ii   John A. Sublett, b. ca 1831, Illinois.
2350   iii   Robert L. B. Sublett.[905]
2351   iv   Mary Anne Sublett, b. ca 1833, Illinois.
2352   v   H. Clara Sublett, b. ca 1836, Illinois,[906] d. 6 March 1851.[907]

285. James Sublett, b. 15 July 1785, Woodford County, Kentucky (then Fayette County, Virginia); served as a private in the War of 1812, in a company designated at various times as Capt. James Alexander's Company and Capt. Samuel Lapsley's Company, 2nd Regiment (Jenning's), Kentucky Volunteers. His service extended from 1 Sept. 1812 to 15 Oct. 1812.[908] He was m. 3 Sept. 1807 in Virginia to Susan Edzard, b. 17 May 1789, Culpepper County, Virginia; d. 12 June 1860, Hickman County, Kentucky, daughter of William and Martha (Lightfoot) Edzard. Her husband d. the same day as she did in Hickman County; the couple is buried in the Sublett Cemetery near Clinton, Kentucky.

Issue of James and Susan (Edzard) Sublett:[909]

2381   i   Lewis H. Sublett, b. 5 June 1808, d. 7 Jan. 1826.
2382   ii   Martha Ann Sublett, b. 10 May 1810, d. 20 Nov. 1885; m. (1st) Bob Walker; (2nd) Dr. Tomlinson.

---

900   Martha Sublett m. 31 Oct 1858, Jas. Wesley Davis, according to correspondence with descendant [DJS].

901   *Green County, Kentucky, Deed Bk. 7*, p. 35.

902   *Ibid.*, Deed Bk. 8, p. 327.

903   Cape Girardeau County, Missouri, wills; abstracted in Sunder, *op. cit.*, p. 242-243.

904   James G. Sublett m. Susanah L. ; 5 Children, according to correspondence with descendant [DJS].

905   Robert L. B. Sublett m. 16 Sep 1847, Cape Girardeau, Missouri, Mary F. Thompson, according to correspondence with descendant [DJS].

906   Estimated dates of birth for the children were taken from the U.S. Census, 1850, Cape Girardeau County, Missouri, Family #648.

907   The Rev. William J. Gannon, *A Belated Census of the Earliest Settlers of Cape Girardeau, Missouri*; reprinted from the National Genealogical Society Quarterly; Special Publication No. 18 of the N.G.S., Washington, 1958, p. 61.

908   Records in the Adjutant General's Office, War Dept., Washington, D.C.

909   All information on the descendants of James and Susan contributed by Mrs. Thaddeus Ed Dodge, Albany, Texas, whose husband is the grandson of Thaddeus Lewis Dodge above (1835-1901), by his son William Edzard Dodge.

2383   iii   William Edzard Sublett, b. 4 July 1812, d. Dec. 1892; m. 13 June 1837 to Mary Cook.

2384   iv   Mary Frances Sublett, b. 12 Dec. 1814, Westport, Oldham County, Kentucky; d. 6 July 1867, Hickman County, Kentucky; m. 11 Sept. 1832 at Westport, Oldham County, Kentucky, to Israel Rowley Dodge, b. 1 Jan. 1810, Montgomery County, N.Y.; d. 11 May 1865, Hickman County, Kentucky, son of Daniel R. C. Dodge and Nancy (Blyndenburg). Israel and Mary Frances are buried in the Sublett Cemetery, Near Clinton, Kentucky. Issue:

    1.   Thaddeus Lewis Dodge, b. 26 March 1835, d. 8 Oct. 1901, m. 25 Oct. 1860, Anderson County, Kentucky, to Octavia Jane Jordan, b. 10 Feb. 1839, Anderson County, Kentucky; d. 22 July 1903, Clinton, Kentucky. Three children.

    2.   Edwin Walker Dodge, b. 4 June 1839, d. 25 Sept. 1840.

    3.   Marion Dodge, b. 24 June 1841; d. 13 Dec. 1847.

    4.   James Edwin Dodge, b. 16 June 1844, d. 16 Dec. 1860.

    5.   Irena G. Dodge, b. 8 Feb. 1847, d. 16 Feb. 1908, m. 1866 Joseph Gayle.

    6.   Thomas Edzard Dodge, b. 1 Oct. 1849, d. 26 Oct. 1896, m. 19 Feb. 1894 Ida Belle Franklin.

    7.   William Taylor Dodge, b. 10 Jan. 1852, d. 28 May 1928, m. 1870 Ella Holliday.

    8.   Susan Mary Dodge, b. 10 Jan. 1855, d. 28 Oct. 1887, m. 18 June 1880 Dr. E. O. Reid.

    9.   Robert Walker Dodge, b. 8 Jan. 1859, d. 12 Dec. 1859.

2385   v   Margarite Sublett, b. 24 April 1817, d. 13 March 1841, m. 27 July 1836, I. G. Ramsey.

2386   vi   Eliza T. Sublett, b. 3 Sept. 1819, m. 19 Oct. 1841 David W. Holeman.[910]

2387   vii   Aphiah W. Sublett, b. 29 Oct. 1822, d. 15 Oct. 1845; not married.

2388   viii   James T. Sublett, b. 20 June 1825, d. 31 Oct. 1897; m. Mrs. Austin.

2389   ix   George Sublett, b. 14 May 1828, d. 16 Aug. 1828.

2390   x   John C. Sublett,[911] b. 5 Nov. 1830, d. 28 Feb. 1896, m. Ann Martha Ringo.

289. Thomas S. (Samuel?) Sublett was born 20 August 1795 in Woodford County, Kentucky, and apparently named for his maternal grandfather, Thomas Samuel. He migrated to Springfield, Arkansas. He married Mary Moorehead on 11 February 1821. She was born 26 August 1797.[912] The Logan MS. says that Thomas married Mary Neil.

Issue of Thomas S. and Mary (Moorehead) Sublett:[913]

2411   i   James Dudley Sublett, b. 12 September 1823; m. Sarah Durnal. Issue:

    1.   Frances Sublett, m. --- Hill.

    2.   Isabelle Sublett, m. --- Smith.

    3.   Sarah Sublett, m. (1st) --- Small; (2nd) --- Brown.

    4.   Angeline Sublett, m. Monroe Spradlin.

---

910   David W. Coleman, according to correspondence with descendant [DJS].

911   John Calhoun Sublett b. Adair County, Kentucky, m. 15 Nov 1855, Ann Martha Ringo, b. 5 Feb 1838, d. 24 Nov 1914, Clinton County, Kentucky, according to correspondence with descendant [DJS].

912   Charles E. Oates, *History of Oates-Sublett Family* (North Little Rock, Arkansas), 1953, 94 pp. 6, 9, 10.

913   *Ibid.*

        5.   Samuel Sublett, b. 9 April 1864, d. 31 Dec. 1940; m. 1890 Annie Price.

2412   ii   Adeline Sublett, b. 11 February 1825; m. William Durnal. Six children listed in Oates.

2413   iii   Rowena Emoline Sublett, b. 5 February 1827, m. Robert Scroggins. Two children.

2414   iv   Samuel Sublett, b. 13 January 1829. He is said to have died in an accident in 1847, although another source says that he died while with the Confederate Army in Mississippi.

2415   v   Mary Neil Sublett, b. 31 March 1831, d. 1908, married James Durnal; nine children.

2416   vi   Elizabeth Caroline Sublett, b. 10 August 1835, died about 1868, married Robert Scroggins, the widower of her sister Rowena. After Elizabeth's death, Robert married a third time to Martha Hill. Robert and Elizabeth had five children.

2417   vii   Margaret Angeline Sublett, b. 16 April 1838; died soon after her marriage to R. M. Clibourn. He married, 2nd, Erzula Jane Oates.

2418   viii   Harriet Malissa Sublett, b. 27 April 1842, d. 25 March 1890; married 14 February 1862 William Wallace Oates, b. 13 April 1837, d. 22 Feb. 1927, son of Louis Thomas Oates and Margaret (Martin). Eleven children.

302. Polly Malinda Sublett was married 30 Sept. 1830 in Chesterfield County, Virginia, to Alexander Sims, b. 21 Nov. 18--, d. 25 Sept. 1841.[914] Polly died about 1834 or 1835, and on 11 Jan. 1836 (date of bond) in Chesterfield County Alexander Sims married (2nd) Phebe F. Cheatham, b. ca 1806, daughter of Francis Cheatham.[915] Alexander Sims was the son of John and Tabitha (Rudd) Sims.

Issue of Alexander and Polly M. (Sublett) Sims:

2511   i   Eugenia Ann Sims, b. 28 Dec. 1831, Chesterfield County, Virginia; d. 10 Nov. 1911;[916] married (1st) 29 Nov. 1851 John F. Porter. Issue of John F. and Eugenia (Sims) Porter:[917]
    1.   Glendora C. Porter, b. ca 1853.
    2.   Bettie T. Porter, b. ca 1855.
    3.   John Porter, b. ca 1856.
    4.   Mollie F. Porter, b. ca 1858, m. 25 Jan. 1880 in Chesterfield County to Egbert T. Bailey, son of Thomas and Mary E. Bailey.
    5.   Charles D. Porter, b. ca 1862.
    6.   Morton E. Porter, b. ca 1863.
    Eugenia (Sims) Porter m. (2nd) 10 Jan. 1367 James K. Polk Goode, b. 10 Sept. 1846, d. 20 April 1920, son of John Goode, Jr., and Lucy A. (Bass).[918] Issue of James K. P. and Eugenia (Sims) Goode:[919]
    7.   Thornton Goode, b. ca 1868.

---

914   All data on her descendants through the courtesy of Mr. John Stuart Sims, Washington, D.C., grandson of #2512, by his 1st son.

915   Chesterfield County, Virginia, Marriage Register.

916   Tombstone inscription, Mt. Hermon Baptist Church, Chesterfield County, Virginia.

917   Chesterfield County, Virginia, Census of 1860, v. 6, p. 7; Census of 1880, p. 15.

918   *Ibid.*, Marriage Register.

919   *Ibid.*, Virginia, Census of 1880, p. 15.

8. Berkley Goode, b. ca 1870.
9. Victor S. Goode, b. ca 1871.
10. Maude O. Goode, b. ca 1873.

2512 ii John William Sims, b. 28 Aug. 1833, Chesterfield County, Virginia; d. 15 Dec. 1901;[920] m. 1 Feb. 1859 Martha Ann Goode, daughter of John. and Lucy (Bass) Goode; b. 26 July 1836, d. 22 May 1862 or 1863. They had issue a son Marion, b. 1860, and another child. The mother and the two children are said to have died of typhoid fever while the father was serving in the Confederate Army, 6th Virginia Infantry. John W. Sims m. (2nd) 5 Jan. 1867 in Chesterfield County his first wife's sister, Lucy Jane Goode, b. 30 Jan. 1843, d. 15 Dec. 1886, Chesterfield County.[921] Issue of John Wm. and Lucy Jane (Goode) Sims:

1. Mitford Sims, b. 8 Jan. 1868, d. 8 Sept. 1939;[922] m. 19 April 1898 Emma Michum Blunt, b. 13 Oct. 1874; d. 20 March 1953.
2. May Sims, b. 20 May 1870; d. 30 Sept. 1937; m. Egbert Bailey.
3. David Winfree Sims, b. 2 Nov. 1872; d. 14 Dec. 1941; m. 14 Nov. 1895 Virginia Washington Morecock.
4. John Goode Sims, b. 22 Oct. 1875; d. 26 June 1951; m. 5 Dec. 1898 Carrie Knox Blunt.

345. Elizabeth Sublett, b. 27 Nov. 1800, married Mark[923] Kuykendall,[924] born 12 March 1796, son of Matthew and Margaret (Hardin) Kuykendall.

Issue of Mark and Elizabeth (Sublett) Kuykendall:[925]

2821 i Andrew Kuykendall, b. 7 June 1819; d. 20 Oct. 1840.
2822 ii William S. Kuykendall, b. 22 March 1821; d. in Texas 1888; m. Mahala Jane Wilson.
2823 iii John Kuykendall, b. 9 Feb. 1823; d. 14 Jan. 1852 at Grand Gulf, by the explosion of the steamer *George Washington*.
2824 iv Polly Davis Kuykendall, b. 24 May 1825; d. 25 April 1901; m. James M. Cook.
2825 v Mark Hardin Kuykendall, b. 29 June 1828; d. in Mississippi; m. Martha McDowell.
2826 vi Moses Warren Kuykendall, b. 2 Jan. 1831; m. his cousin Eliza Kuykendall.
2827 vii Temple Davis Kuykendall, b. 27 June 1833; d. in Denver, Colorado, date unknown; m. Vitula A. Hines.
2828 viii Hezekiah James Kuykendall, b. 13 Nov. 1835; m. 19 Nov. 1856 Emily E. Clark. Sheriff of Butler County, Kentucky.
2829 ix Thomas P. Kuykendall, b. 25 Feb. 1840; d. 19 Sept. 1845.

380. William B. Sublett was born in Charlotte County, Virginia, in 1800, and migrated with his

---

920   Tombstone inscription, Mt. Hermon Baptist Church, Chesterfield County.

921   *Ibid.*; see also G. Brown Goode, *Virginia Cousins*, Richmond, 1887, p. 199.

922   Tombstone inscription, Riverview Cemetery, Richmond, Virginia.

923   Mark Kuykendall, brother of Matthew (see #3181), according to correspondence with descendant [DJS].

924   Elizabeth Sublett m. 1 Dec 1817, Warren County, Kentucky, according to correspondence with descendant [DJS].

925   George Benson Kuykendall, *History of the Kuykendall Family Since Its Settlement in Dutch New York in 1646*. Portland, Oregon, 1919. pp. 220-221.

father and grandfather to Warren County, Kentucky, in 1806 or 1807. When his father migrated down to Jackson County, Alabama, in the 1820s, William was old enough to make the decision to remain in Kentucky. He married about 1826 Mary, daughter of John and Margaret (Mitchell) Tyler of Butler County, Kentucky. She was born in 1810 and died in 1864. William ultimately moved to Logan County, Kentucky, where he died in 1862.[926] That William B. Sublett of Logan County, Kentucky, was the son of Benjamin Branch Sublett of Jackson County, Alabama, is known from two sources: A local history says of William: "He was the son of Benjamin, who died in 1842 and whose father was a Revolutionary soldier."[927] An Alabama cousin wrote of the situation: "Benjamin Sublett my Grandmothers Bro came to Alabama with her & settled on the Tennessee River not far from Romans Landing, died there ... they raised a large family Six Sons & Six daughters, of the sons William (Buck) stopped in Logan County, Kentucky near Richlieu."[928]

Issue of William B. and Mary (Tyler) Sublett:

3181   i   James H. Sublett, b. 22 Oct. 1827, Butler County, Kentucky, migrated to Christian County, Kentucky, in 1849 and to Ballard County, Kentucky, in 1856. He married 15 Nov. 1852 Margaret E. Kuykendall, daughter of Matthew[929] and Martha B. (Tolbert) Kuykendall, of Butler County, born 1830. Issue:
  1. Lou C. Sublett,[930] m. --- Ransdell.
  2. Mary E. Sublett, m. --- Snook.
  3. James K. Sublett.
  4. Robert W. Sublett.
  5. Margaret E. Sublett.
  6. Addie D. Sublett.[931]
  7. Maud J. Sublett.[932]

3182   ii   Pauline Jane Sublett, b. 29 July 1829, Butler County, Kentucky; died near Springfield, Missouri, about 1866. On 14 December 1847 she married John Adams Williams, b. 18 Nov. 1821, Robertson County, Tennessee; died about 1902 at Ozark, Christian County, Missouri; son of John Robertson Williams and Sally Ann (Crain) . Issue:
  1. Thomas Jefferson Williams, b. 25 Aug. 1848, at Bowling Green, Warren County, Kentucky; m. (1st) Minnie Strickler; m. (2nd) Virginia Rosella Forbis, 1887. T. J. d. 18 Aug. 1930, Hagerman Gooding, Idaho.
  2. Leonidas Roger Williams, b. 18 May 1860, at Ozark, Christian County, Missouri; d. 23 May 1938; Ontario, California; m. Kate Forester.
  3. Walter Williams, b. ca 1864, Ozark, Christian County, Missouri.

3183   iii   Mary Sublett, m. --- Robinson.[933]
3184   iv   Angeline Sublett, m. --- Farmer.
3185   v   Brinkley C. Sublett.

---

926   Informant: Mrs. Paul Williams, Moses Lake, Wash., 1961, daughter-in-law of Thos. J. Williams.
927   James Battle, et al., *History of Kentucky*, 1885, p. 160.
928   MS. of Sarah Ellen (Wilburn) Hall, cited previously.
929   Matthew Kuykendall, brother of Mark (see #345), according to correspondence with descendant [DJS].
930   Lou C. Sublett b. 29 Nov 1853, Christian County, Kentucky, according to correspondence with descendant [DJS].
931   Addie D. Sublett m. --- Barnes, according to correspondence with descendant [DJS].
932   Maud J. Sublett m. --- Pease, according to correspondence with descendant [DJS].
933   Mary Sublett m. Wm. Robinson, 10 Oct 1880, Ballard County, Kentucky according to correspondence with descendant [DJS].

3186   vi   Joseph J. Sublett.[934]
3187   vii   Curran T. Sublett; served in Company F, 12th Kentucky Cavalry, Federal
              Troops, War Between the States.
3188   viii Amanda Sublett, m. --- Hobbs.
3189   ix   Tabitha Sublett, m. --- Hurt.
3190   x   Adeline Sublett, m. --- Morris

385. James Jefferson Sublett, b. ca 1811 in Warren County, Kentucky; migrated with his parents via Rutherford County, Tennessee, to Alabama. On 8 Sept. 1835 James Sublett of Jackson County, Alabama, filed for 40 acres in S.5 T.5 R.5 East.[935] On 4 May 1844 James J. Sublett filed for 62 acres in fractional S.5, fractional T.6 R.5 East which he had settled on "about 5 June 1843, commenced the erection of a dwelling house on that day ... and has continued to reside thereon from that period to the present and has cleared about four acres of said land and has also built a meat house ... and is head of a family, having a wife and children."[936] James Jefferson Sublett is said to have been "killed" in Jackson County, Alabama.[937] He married Tabitha Wilborn of Jackson County, Alabama, and the couple are listed in the 1850 and 1860 Censuses with the following children.[938] Tabitha was the daughter of Elias Wilbourn, (C. 1790-1865), a native of North Carolina.

Issue of James Jefferson and Tabitha (Wilborn) Sublett: (He is said to have had 14 in all).

3231   i   William Sublett, b. ca 1836.[939]
3232   ii   Sarah Sublett, b. ca 1837, m. John Mathews. No issue.
3233   iii   Mary Sublett, b. ca 1840, d. 1914, m. (1st) --- Rains; m. (2nd) Mike Galbreath.
3234   iv   Elias W. Sublett, b. ca 1844.[940]
3235   v   Tabitha Sublett, b. ca 1847, m. John C. Logan.[941]
3236   vi   Benjamin Sublett, b. ca 1849.
3237   vii   Amanda Sublett, b. ca 1850.
3238   viii Caroline Sublett, b. ca 1852.
3239   ix   Eliza Sublett, b. ca 1855.
3240   x   Lucinda Sublett, b. ca 1858.
3241   xi   Rebecca Sublett.
3242   xii   George Sublett.

386. Joseph Jordan Sublett (called Jordan or Jud), b. ca 1812 in Warren County, Kentucky, migrated with his parents via Rutherford County, Tennessee, to Alabama. On 10 April 1843

---

934   Joseph Jordan Sublett, b. 10 Mar 1837, Kentucky, d. 31 Jul 1909, Adair County, Missouri, m. 14 Nov 1861, Mary Davidson (1840-1887), according to correspondence with descendant [DJS].

935   Certificate 8453, Huntsville, Alabama, Land Office; Land Records Section, National Archives, Washington, D.C.

936   Certificate 8006, Lebanon, Alabama, Land Office; Land Records Section, National Archives.

937   Recollection of his nephew William M. Sublett (#3246) as published in Samuel Sublett, *A Partial History* ..., p. 6.

938   Jackson County, Alabama, Census of 1850, p. 73; Census of 1860.

939   William Starnes Sublett, b. Jan 1836, Jackson County, Alabama, m. ca 1856, Martha Ann Floyd, according to correspondence with descendant [DJS].

940   Elias W. Sublett, b. 13 Jul 1844, m. 1871 Rebecca Adaline Gilbreath.

941   Tabitha Sublett, b. 24 Jun 1848, Jackson County, Alabama, d. 3 Feb 1881, Texas, m. 1886, John Calhoun Logan, 1847-1912, according to correspondence with descendant [DJS].

Joseph J. Sublett of Jackson County, Alabama, filed in DeKalb County, Alabama, for 134 acres in fractional S.5 and parts of S.8, T.6 R.5 in the Coosa land district, swearing that he had entered it 1 June 1840. It was stated that on the latter date he was "residing ... in a dwelling in which he lived and made his house and at that time he cultivated about 15 or 20 acres," being "the head of a family, having relatives living with him and dependent upon him for support."[942] He married (1st) his cousin Lucinda Sublett (#1816), daughter of Abraham and Temperance (V---)[943] Sublett of Jackson County, Alabama.[944] Following her early death, Jordan m. (2nd) Mary Sarah Wood, d. 1856, said to have been a cousin of his first wife.[945] Jordan Sublet m. (3rd) ca 1858 Mrs. Eliza Hauck Woodall, said to have been a cousin of his second wife, also.[946] If the second wife was a cousin to the first wife, she probably was a descendant of Caldwell and Nancy (Sublett) Wood (#40). Abraham Sublett (#237) is known to have sold a tract in Jackson County, Alabama, to a Wood. Joseph Jordan Sublett died in 1867.

Issue of Jordan and Lucinda (Sublett) Sublett:[947]

    3245   i   Margaret Sublett.

Issue of Jordan and Sarah Mary (Wood) Sublett:

    3246   ii   William Madison Sublett. Issue:
               1. Carl Sublett.
               2. Orion Sublett.
               3. Kate Sublett, m. --- Hodges.
               4. Lillian Sublett, m. --- Armbrester.
    3247   iii   Richard Anderson Sublett, b. 23 Jan. 1850 in Jackson County, Alabama; d. 24 May 1924 in Little Rock, Arkansas; a Baptist minister in Texas, South Carolina, Georgia and Florida.[948] M. 16 Oct. 1879 at Summerton, S.C., to Laura Alice Tindal.
    3248   iv   John Benjamin Sublett, resided in 1910 at San Marcos, Texas.
    3249   v   Mary Ann Sublett, b. 1854, d. 20 June 1932 Mina, Arkansas; m. William Worth Harris Harrison.

390. Sophronia Elizabeth Sublett, b. 1819,[949] died 21 April 1846 at San Marcos, Texas. She was married 12 May 1834 at Bellefonte, Alabama, to William Washington Moon, b. 25 March 1814, Madison County, Alabama, son of Joseph and Martha (Moore) Moon. His father Joseph was killed two days after his birth at the Battle of Horseshoe Bend, 27 March 1814, in the War of

---

942   Certificate 7196, Lebanon, Alabama, Land Office; Land Records Section, National Archives, Washington, D.C.

943   Temperance (Vaughn) Sublett. [DJS].

944   Lincoln County, Kentucky, Circuit Court, Equity Papers, 1850 File Box, suit styled "Abram Sublete's Heirs against Abram Sublete's Heirs."

945   Kathleen Paul Jones and Pauline Jones Gandrud, *Alabama Records*, v. 19, p. 89. ("Miscellaneous Notes on Jackson County, Alabama, Families," contributed by Howard S. Woodall, Dallas, Tex., 1933). Typescript, National D.A.R. Library, Washington, D.C.

946   *Ibid.*

947   Lincoln County, Kentucky, suit in Note 233 above.

948   His life is sketched at some length in a pamphlet: Walter M. Lee, *Historical Sketch of the First Baptist Church*, Moore Haven, Florida.

949   Sophronia Elizabeth Sublett, b. 1819, Jackson County, Alabama, according to correspondence with descendant [DJS].

1812.[950]

William Washington Moon himself had, for a civilian soldier, an amazingly diverse military record, having served in three of our nation's conflicts. First of all, he served in the Florida War of 1837, as a private in Captain Coffey's Company, Snodgrass' Regt., North Alabama Mounted Volunteers. He was enrolled Oct. 26, 1837, at Bellefonte, Alabama, for a six-month term, and was mustered out with his company 9 April 1838.[951] Shortly after his discharge, Moon migrated to Texas, and by 30 Dec. 1839 had applied for land, which was granted 2 May 1842, by the Board of Land Commissioners of Milam District, now Bell County.[952] Moon next served in Capt. H. E. McColloch's Company, Texas Mounted Volunteers, during the Mexican War. He enlisted at San Marcos, Texas, 22 October 1846 and served until 21 Oct. 1847. For this service he received a pension.[953] Finally, William W. Moon served as a private in Company "A," 36th Regt., Texas Cavalry, Confederate States Army, during the War Between the States. He enlisted 7 March 1862 at San Marcos and was mustered into service 22 March 1862 at Camp Salado, Texas, aged 48 years. He was discharged 5 Aug. 1862 by reason of surgeon's certificate of disability.[954]

Issue of William W. and Sophronia E. (Sublett) Moon:

3271	i	Mary Moon, b. 29 April 1836, Madison County, Alabama; m. Isaac Wootten.
3272	ii	Sarah Moon, b. 8 Oct. 1839, Madison County, Alabama; m. Alfred Dockery.
3273	iii	Susan Elvira Moon, b. 31 July 1842 Bastrop County, Texas; m. (1st) 21 Feb. 1859 William Rufus Driskill; m. (2nd) 23 May 1872 Willis Haden Ferguson. Issue of the 2nd marriage:

       1. Lilia Lillie Ferguson, b. 11 March 1873; d. 24 May 1943 Hays County, Texas; m. 5 Oct. 1892 in Hays County, Texas, to Light Sumner Townsend, b. 15 April 1869 San Antonio, Tex.; d. 17 March 1928 Hays County, Texas. One of their four children was Tula Townsend, who married William A. Wyatt, and whose intensive study of the Sublett family is mentioned elsewhere.

3274	iv	Lavinia Moon, b. 15 July 1845 Bastrop County, Texas; m. Louis Dockery. Issue:

       1. Fannie Dockery.
       2. Arthur Dockery.
       3. Mary Dockery.
       4. Ellis Dockery.

415. Thomas Sublett,[955] b. ca 1804, Campbell County, Virginia, married (date of bond) 2 Oct. 1826 a cousin, Elizabeth Jordan, daughter of Matthew Jordan.[956] He was listed in the Campbell County, Virginia, Census of 1840 as between 30-40.[957]

---

950   William Washington Moon d. 1897, San Marcos, Texas, according to correspondence with descendant [DJS].

951   Service Record, Florida War, 1837, Adjutant General's Office, Washington, D.C.

952   Certificate No. 399, Board of Land Commissioners, Milam Dist.

953   Pension Application, Mexican War, 1 C 13030, National Archives.

954   Old Records Division, Adjutant General's Office, Washington, D.C.

955   Thomas Sublett b. 13 Jan 1804; d. 6 Jun 1872; m. Eliz. b, Sep 1802, d. 7 Oct 1874, according to correspondence with descendant [DJS].

956   Hinshaw, op. cit., p. 857 (Campbell County, Virginia, Marriage Bonds).

957   Campbell County, Virginia, Census of 1840, p. 4.

Issue of Thomas and Elizabeth (Jordan) Sublett:[958]

3381   i   Martha Sublett, not married.[959]
3382   ii   Mary Sublett, m. a Mr. Driskill.[960]
3383   iii   Nancy Sublett, m. William Lane.[961]
3384   iv   Thomas Sublett, Jr., m. a Miss --- Joy. Issue:
                1. Wesley Sublett.
                2. Sallie Bet Sublett.
                3. Maggie Sublett.
                4. Otha Sublett (a boy).
                5. Lillian Sublett.
                6. Mattie Belle Sublett.
3385   v   Samuel Sublett,[962] m. Mary Jane Foster. Issue:
                1. Mattie Sublett, m. (1st) a Mr. LeBrie; (2nd) Charles Gyllenflyck.
                2. William Thomas Sublett, b. 6 Aug. 1870, d. 10 Feb. 1921; m. (1st) Mary
                    Morris; (2nd) 1 June 1898 Sallie Ann Clark; (3rd) Mary Elizabeth
                    Marshall. Six children.
                3. Norman Samuel Sublett, m. Miss Woody Twitty; no issue.
                4. Sarah Sublett, m. Ike Moyer. Issue: one dtr., Fayetta.
                5. Annie M. Sublett, b. 6 June 1879; d. 27 Feb. 1920; m. 24 Sept. 1899
                    Bernice Walker Johnson, b. 10 April 1878. Ten children.
                6. Lillie Sublett, m. Hudson Joy.
                7. Lola Sublett, m. Mack C. Madren.
                8. Charlie Bob Sublett, b. 5 April 1889, m. 9 March 1912 to Ola Nash. b. 29
                    Oct 1888. Three children.
                9. Flossie Sublett, m. --- Martin.

416. Benjamin Branch Sublett, b. 29 March 1805, d. 5 Feb. 1897; m. (date of bond) 20 Nov.
1826, the marriage took place 23 Nov. 1826 in Campbell County, Virginia, Nancy Johnston
Cunningham, b. 1805, daughter of Richard and Elizabeth (Johnston) Cunningham.[963] Nancy died
6 August 1861, and Benjamin m. (2nd) 12 Sept. 1865 in Charlotte County, Virginia, Martha Witt
Reams, daughter of William and Nancy Ziller (Pugh) Reams. They resided in Charlotte County,
Virginia. Martha died in Charlotte County 9 Oct. 1922.[964]

Issue of Benjamin Branch Sublett and Nancy (Cunningham) :[965]

3391   i   James Allen Sublett, b. 9 Nov. 1827, m. 22 Feb. 1851[966] to Mary Elizabeth

958   Information on all these issue from Mrs. Andrew Lee Roberts, Williamsburg, Virginia.

959   Clarissa M. b. 9 Mar 1828, according to correspondence with descendant [DJS].

960   Mary Eliz., 1830-1890, according to correspondence with descendant [DJS].

961   Nancy M. b. 23 Apr 1833, according to correspondence with descendant [DJS].

962   Matthew Samuel Sublett, according to correspondence with descendant [DJS].

963   Hinshaw, *op. cit.*, 6:857.

964   Information on all the descendants of #416 Benjamin B. Sublett has been gathered and made available very graciously by
        Mrs. Andrew Lee Roberts (Semple Fourqurean Davidson), Williamsburg, Virginia, granddaughter of #3393 Amanda F.
        (Sublett) Davidson by her son Luther J.

965   Charlotte County, Virginia, 1850 Census, p. 51, Household #763.

Garret;[967] died without issue.

3392   ii   Richard Thomas Sublett, b. 23 Nov. 1829; m. Jane Bigger; died without issue.

3393   iii   Amanda F. Sublett, b. 26 March 1837, d. 26 June 1930; m. 1 Dec. 1859 as his second wife, Archer Vaughan Davidson, b. 13 Dec. 1822, d. 28 April 1903, son of Allen and Lucy (Walker) Davidson. Issue:

1. Nancy Richard Davidson, b. 8 Aug. 1862, Charlotte County, Virginia; m. Charles Edward Harris; nine children.
2. Luther Judson Davidson, b. 27 Oct. 1865, Bedford County, Virginia; d. 4 Jan. 1951; m. 23 Feb. 1889 Alice Willis Vernon Sweeney, b. 9 June 1867; d. 29 Oct. 1948, daughter of Martin and Martha Ann Dunnavant (Willis) Sweeney; seven children.
3. Mary James Davidson, b. 23 Nov. 1867, Bedford County, Virginia; m. Joseph Brown; five children.
4. Lowry Davidson.
5. Tyree Vaughan Davidson.
6. Jesse Lee Davidson.

3394   iv   Martha Watkins Sublett, b. 27 April 1838, d. 22 May 1927, Charlotte County, Virginia; m. 23 Nov. 1870 in Charlotte County to (William) Richard Hamersly, b. Campbell County, Virginia, 12 Oct. 1838; d. 1 Sept. 1917, Charlotte County, Virginia, son of James and Anne (Holt) Hamersly. Issue:

1. Ennis Hamlet Hamersly, b. 1872, Bedford County, Virginia; m. 12 April 1899 at Norfolk to Anne L. Harden, b. 27 Jan. 1882, Windsor, N.C., daughter of Levy W. and Harriet C. (McGlaughon) Harden.
2. Annie Fleetwood Hamersly, b. 10 July 1877, Charlotte County, Virginia; m. 20 Dec. 1899, Charlotte County to John Richard Carter, b. 3 July 1872, Appomattox County, Virginia, son of Richard and Joanna Wilmoth (Lewis) Carter; five children.
3. Wilfred Leslie Hamersly, b. 31 March 1882, Charlotte County, Virginia; m. 5 June 1912, Charlotte County, to Mary Williams Paris, b. 15 Nov. 1882, Charlotte County, daughter of Charles Craddock Paris and Lily (Middleton); two children.
4. Venable (Vennie) Hamersly.
5. James Sublett Hamersly, m. Annie Maud Chitty.

3395   v   Benjamin Venable Sublett, b. 1841, d. 2 July 1915, Lynchburg, Virginia; m. Charlotte County, Virginia, 29 Jan. 1869 to Willie Ann Harvey, b. 31 May 1849, Charlotte County, Virginia, daughter of John Chapel Harvey and his wife Susan Ann (---). Issue:

1. Nannie Florence Sublett, b. 12 Nov. 1869; d. 28 June 1882.
2. [John] Cabell Sublett, b. 16 Dec. 1871; died without issue.
3. James Walter Sublett, b. 5 March 1873; d. 15 Feb. 1932.
4. Benjamin Flournoy Sublett, b. 8 Jan. 1875, m. 25 Sept. 1901, Lynchburg, Virginia, to Mary Elizabeth Thompson, b. 31 March 1872, Amherst County, Virginia. Eight children.
5. William Winthrop Sublett, b. 4 April 1877; d. 12 Jan. 1901.
6. Annie Laura (Lottie) Sublett, b. 31 July 1879; m. 1st, Willie Austin Wright, 23 Dec. 1902; he d. 7 March 1903; m. 2nd, Richard Frederick Durrum, 6 Sept. 1909. One child.

---

966   *Ibid.*, according to correspondence with descendant [DJS].

967   Mary Elizabeth Garret, dau of William, according to correspondence with descendant [DJS].

       7.   Bessie Watkins Sublett, b. 22 March 1881; m. 25 Nov. 1903, Thomas Matthew Viar, b. 16 April 1880, d. 30 Dec. 1931.

       8.   Daniel Witt Sublett, b. 14 March 1885.

       9.   Susie Marion Sublett, b. 18 Nov. 1886; d. October 1910.

       10. Thomas Isham Sublett, b. 9 July 1888.

       11. Charles Harvey Sublett, b. 28 Sept. 1890.

       12. Robert Edward Sublett, b. 24 Jan. 1893.

3396   vi   Robert W. Sublett, d. young.

Issue of Benjamin Branch Sublett and Martha W. (Reams):

3397   vii   William Joseph Sublett, b. 11 July 1866, m. 15 July 1888 Sarah Idell Ramsey, b. 11 June 1867, Charlotte County, Virginia, daughter of John Richard Ramsey and Mary Susan (Layne). Issue:

       1.   Luther Hudnell Sublett, b. 3 Aug. 1889; d. 21 March 1891.

       2.   Jesse Branch Sublett, b. 3 Sept. 1891; d. 15 April 1960.

       3.   Richard Thomas Sublett, b. 16 Feb. 1893; m. 1st, Ruby Videll Lawrence, one child; m. 2nd, 11 May 1922 Gillie Leah Wilson, daughter of Richard David and Alice Leigh (Witt) Wilson.

       4.   Mary Grace Sublett, b. 12 Nov. 1894, m. 26 Jan. 1913 Charles Henry Pillow, son of Martin Beauregard and Frances Elizabeth (Carwile) Pillow; six children.

       5.   Charles Spurgeon Sublett, b. 13 Sept. 1896, m. 2 Jan. 1919 Lucy Webster Pillow, dtr. of Martin Beauregard and Frances Elizabeth (Carwile) Pillow.

       6.   Ruth Vernon Sublett, b. 6 Feb. 1898; d. 11 June 1898.

       7.   Joseph Warren Sublett, b. 8 Feb. 1901, m. Dec. 1931 Ollie Harper.

       8.   Pearl Irene Sublett, b. 6 March 1903, m. 23 Jan. 1920 Roy Rastus Pillow, son of Martin B. and Frances E. (Carwile) Pillow.

       9.   Annie Louise Sublett, b. 18 Aug. 1904; m. 2 March 1921 Morell Thomas Mason, son of John Albert and Drucilla Thomas (Hamlet) Mason.

       10. Helen Barnhardt Sublett, b. 17 May 1907.

3398   viii   Nancy Branch Sublett, b. 7 Feb. 1871, d. 14 April 1916, m. Walter Thomas Jordan, b. 14 Sept. 1860 Red House, Virginia, d. 6 June 1932, son of William Thomas and Martha Ann (Maloney) Jordan. Issue:

       1.   Walter Thomas Jordan, b. and d. 25 Nov. 1891.

       2.   William Benjamin Jordan, b. 15 Feb. 1893, m. 21 Dec. 1913 to Grace McClellean Jones, b. 30 Aug. 1893. Four children.

       3.   Ira Franklin Jordan, b. 16 July 1895, m. 1916 Elsie May Sublett, b. 3 Oct. 1896; eight children.

       4.   Walter Thomas Jordan, Jr., b. 29 April 1898, m. 8 May 1921 Ebeth Howard Ford b. 23 March 1900; two children.

       5.   Mattie Lorine Jordan, b. 28 Jan. 1900, m. 6 Jan. 1923 Nathan Clifford Pillow, b. 26 May 1899.

       6.   Evadne Newton Jordan, b. 25 July 1903, m. 24 Nov. 1920 Jim Frank Trent, b. 8 March 1894.

       7.   Baby boy, b. and d. 15 Nov. 1906.

       8.   Archer Paul Jordan, b. 18 March 1908, m. Mary Louise Elliott.

       9.   Baby boy, b. and d. 8 June 1910.

       10. Baby girl, b. and d. 9 Feb. 1916.

3399   ix   Albert E. Sublett, b. March 1873, d. April 1873.

424. Samuel D. Sublett, b. ca 1822, m. Petro (Peterora?) ---, b. ca 1821/22. In 1850 and 1860 they

resided in Giles County, Virginia; and in 1870 and 1880 they resided in Bland County, Virginia.

Issue of Samuel D. and Petro (---) Sublett:[968]

3441	i	James Sublett, b. ca 1843/45.
3442	ii	Martha Sublett, b. ca 1848.
3443	iii	Elizabeth Sublett, b. ca 1850, m. --- Alley.
3444	iv	Joseph I. Sublett, b. ca 1853, m. 22 Nov. 1883 Minnie Jones.
3445	v	Margaret Sublett, b. ca 1854.
3446	vi	John Sublett, b. ca 1856.
3447	vii	Susan Adella (Della) Sublett, b. 11 Oct. 1858, Giles County, Virginia.
3448	viii	Jacob H. Sublett, b. 1 October 1860, Giles County, Virginia.
3449	ix	Matilda Sublett, b. ca 1863.

502. James Sublett,[969] b. 4 Feb. 1786, Henry County, Virginia, married Sally Ford. She was born 31 Jan. 1793, and died 9 Sept. 1845. They migrated in the Fall of 1833 from Kentucky to Coles County, Illinois, with his brothers. Here James died 6 August 1844. Presumably Sally Ford was related to her husband, whose mother was Ruth Ford.

Issue of James and Sally (Ford) Sublett:[970] (their descendants came to spell the name Sublette)[971]

3551	i	Lucinda Sublette, b. 15 Feb. 1812; d. April 1879; n.m.
3552	ii	William Sublette, b. 16 Jan. 1814; d. 4 Oct. 1880; married Miriam R. Warfield.[972] Issue:

    1. Sarah Elizabeth Sublette, b. 18 March 1850;[973] d. 1 Oct. 1929 at Ashmore, Illinois; n.m.

    2. Eliza Jane Sublette, b. Feb. 1857; m. (1st) Charles Sullivan; m. (2nd) 1 Jan. 1888 Thomas Jefferson Stites; one child by each marriage.

    3. William Sublette, b. 20 Feb. 1858, d. 1 August 1859.

    4. James Warfield Sublette, b. Feb. 1861; d. 23 Nov. 1918; m. 1884 Mary Elizabeth Smith. 4 children.

    5. Thomas Sublette, b. 7 Nov. 1863; d. 19 Aug. 1864.

3553	iii	Mary (Polly) Sublette, b. 1 Dec. 1815; d. 8 Sept. 1895; n.m.
3554	iv	Peter Jackson Sublette, b. 11 March 1818, Madison County, Kentucky; he served in the Mexican War, following which he settled in St. Louis County,

---

968   Giles County, Virginia, 1850 Census, Household #670; Giles County, Virginia, 1860 Census, #838; Bland County, Virginia, 1870 Census, #85; Bland County, Virginia, 1880 Census, #97; all census information and birth dates contributed by Robert D. Nance, Radford, Virginia.

969   For complete list of descendants see Sublette, 1981, *James Sublett & Sally Ford.*

970   Notes gathered by George W. Sublette, son of Peter Jackson Sublette (#3554), and by Miss Mary Frances Sublette, daughter of Colvit Sublette (#3556) in the 1920s, now in the possession of Mrs. W. Arthur Mitchell, Boulder, Colorado, previously cited.

971   All children born Madison County, Kentucky, except Thomas Christopher Sublette (#3560), according to correspondence with descendant [DJS].

972   Miriam R. Warfield b. 13 Dec 1803, Md., d. 4 Dec 1905, Coles County, Illinois, according to correspondence with descendant [DJS].

973   Sarah Elizabeth Sublette b. St. Louis, Missouri, according to correspondence with descendant [DJS].

Missouri, where he was m. 2 Nov. 1848 to Sarah R. Warfield. She was b. at Warfieldsburg, Md., 16 April 1828, daughter of George and Sarah Warfield. She died 10 March 1904 at Sublette, Missouri. About 1854 Peter J. Sublette settled in Adair County, Missouri, where in 1869 he platted the village of Sublette. Peter died at Sublette 24 0ct. 1899. Issue:

1. George Washington Sublette, b. 24 Dec. 1849; d. 6 Nov. 1926; m. Miss Annabell Baldwin.[974] 2 children.
2. James M. Sublette, b. 28 Sept. 1851; d. 28 Nov. 1857.
3. Thomas Eli Sublette, b. 9 Dec. 1853, St. Louis County, Missouri; d. 7 Sept. 1931; m. 26 April 1893 to Kate Florence Funk. 4 children.
4. Miriam Roberts Sublette, b. 19 March 1856, d. 17 March 1942; m. William Mitchell. One child.
5. Sarah Sublette, b. 19 March 1856 (twin); d. Nov. 1856.
6. William Henry Sublette, b. 29 April 1857; d. 18 Jan. 1901; m. Clara Russell. 5 children.
7. Reuben Harvey Sublette, b. 27 June 1860; d. 7 Aug. 1925; m. 20 Feb. 1912 at St. Paul, Minn., to Josephine Marie Philion.
8. Daniel Webster Sublette, b. 16 June 1862.
9. Mary Ellen Sublette, b. 3 May 1864; d. 5 March 1923.
10. Willard Jackson Sublette, b. 21 March 1866; d. 28 Feb. 1950; m. 15 Oct. 1902 to Zoe L. Baldwin. 4 children.
11. Warren Francis Sublette, b. 27 Jan. 1870, m. 3 Oct. 1894 to Edith Eleanor Wallis. 5 children.

3555   v   James Harrison Sublette, b. 4 June 1820; d. 7 Nov. 1872; m. 8 Oct. 1845 Letitia Wiley,[975] b. 21 Feb. 1822; d. 21 Feb. 1896. Issue:
1. Sarah Belle Sublette, b. 14 Jan. 1850; d. 26 Feb. 1912; m. 29 Oct. 1872 to Walter F. Heath; 5 children.
2. Elizabeth Seal Sublette, b. 29 April 1852; d. 18 Jan. 1878; m. 18 March 1874 to James Wilson; 2 children, both d. infancy.
3. Georgianna Sublette, b. 16 Nov. 1855; d. 13 Nov. 1926; m. 30 July 1885 to Benjamin Mathewman. Two children.

3556   vi   Colvit Sublette, b. 13 Aug. 1823; d. 13 June 1883; m. 21 Jan. 1862 to Rosannah E. Oliver. One child:
1. Mary Frances Sublette, b. 22 Jan. 1863.[976]

3557   vii   Nathaniel F. Sublett, b. 11 Feb. 1826; d. Nov. 1893; n.m.

3558   viii   Elisa (Elizor?) Colwell Sublett; b. 15 March 1828; d. 1 Jan. 1873; n.m.

3559   ix   Lucretia Elizabeth Sublette, b. 6 June 1832; d. Oct. 1872; n.m.

3560   x   Thomas Christopher Sublette, b. 26 March 1834;[977] d. 8 Jan. 1916; m. 4 June 1862 to Sarah Frances Lafferty, b. 6 June 1843; d. 17 Sept. 1870. Issue:
1. Sarah Lucinda Sublette, b. 22 April 1863; d. 2 Oct. 1881.
2. James McClelland Sublette, b. 21 July 1865; d. 11 Oct. 1928; m. 1886 Catherine Heath. 3 children, including the writer, Clifford Sublette, b. 16 Aug. 1887, d. 12 Nov. 1939, author of *The Scarlet Cockrel*, etc.
3. John William Sublette, b. 6 Nov. 1869; d. 17 Jan. 1922; m. 5 June 1895 to

974   George Washington Sublette d. 6 Nov 1925; m. Miss Anabel Baldwin [DJS].

975   Coles County, Illinois, Marriage Register, 2, p. 36, as published in *Detroit Society for Genealogical Research Magazine*, 24:162.

976   Mary Frances Sublette d. 17 Feb 1938, Az., according to *James Sublett & Sally Ford* [DJS].

977   Thomas Christopher Sublette b. Coles County, Illinois, according to *James Sublett & Sally Ford* [DJS].

Flavia Pinnell. 3 children.

505. William Sublett, b. 1 July 1791, was married 27 Oct. 1813 in Garrard County, Kentucky, to Liney Wearin (*i.e.*, Regina Warren), daughter of Jacob Wearin.[978] She was born 7 July 1787 and died 2 July 1843. William migrated with his brothers to Coles County, Illinois, in 1833. There on 22 Oct. 1850 and again on 10 March 1855, as a resident variously of Edgar County, Illinois, and Coles County, Illinois, he applied for bounty land for his service in the War of 1812. He had served in that conflict as a private, volunteering 1 August 1812 at Lancaster, Kentucky, in the company of Capt. James Anderson in the First Regiment of Kentucky Volunteers, commanded by Col. Jennings. He was honorably discharged 25 March 1813 at Cincinnati, Ohio.[979] He died in Coles County, Illinois, 5 November 185(7)?, and is buried in the Shields Cemetery, about four miles from Kansas, Illinois.

Issue of William and Regina (Warren) Sublett:

3571   i   Drewry (Drury) Sublett, b. 29 Oct. 1814;[980] m. (1st) Thelda Irvin (Thelday Ervin) 7 Dec. 1836, Coles County, Illinois;[981] m. (2nd) Sarah Irvin, d. 23 May 1864, aged 44 years, 9 mos., 22 days; buried Shields Cemetery. Issue, the first child by Thelda, the remainder by Sarah:
   1. William Sublett, settled in Missouri.[982]
   2. James Sublett.[983]
   3. John Sublett, m. Martha Vance.[984]
   4. Eliza Jane Sublett, m. William Buckler.[985]
   5. Amanda Sublett, m. her sister's widower, William Buckler.
   6. Thelda Sublett, settled in Missouri.[986]

3572   ii   Sarah Sublett,[987] b. 28 July 1819, m. 28 Sept. 1835 in Coles County, Illinois, to the Rev. John Shields, a Baptist clergyman.[988] Sarah (Sublett) Shields d. 11 Dec. 1898; John Shields was b. 1 Nov. 1814, d. 13 May 1873; both are buried in the Shields Cemetery.[989] Issue:
   1. John Shields.
   2. Susannah Shields.
   3. Rebecca Shields,[990] m. John Patton.
   4. William Shields,[991] m. (1) Mary Buckler; (2) Anna Spry.

---

978   Annie Walker Burns, *Record of Marriages. Garrard County, Kentucky, 1796-1851*, typescript, 1932.

979   William Sublett, Bounty Land Files, Act of 55-80-W^t 21411, National Archives, Washington, D.C.

980   Drewry (Drury) Sublett b. Girard County, Kentucky, according to *James Sublett & Sally Ford* [DJS].

981   *Coles County, Illinois, Marriage Register 1*, p. 35, as published in *Detroit Society for Genealogical Research Magazine*, 24:27.

982   William Sublett 1837-1922, m. 1860 Missouri, Nancy Wall, according to *James Sublett & Sally Ford* [DJS].

983   James Lawson Sublett b. 4 Jul 1847, Illinois, d. 6 Jan 1939, Edgar County, Illinois, according to *James Sublett & Sally Ford* [DJS].

984   Martha Vanener b. 28 Feb 1840, d. 3 Aug 1929, according to *James Sublett & Sally Ford* [DJS].

985   Eliza Jane Sublett m. 8 Feb 1867, Coles County, Illinois, according to *James Sublett & Sally Ford* [DJS].

986   Thelda Sublett b. 1842 Illinois, m. Hiram Erwin, according to *James Sublett & Sally Ford* [DJS].

987   Sarah Elizabeth Sublett, according to *James Sublett & Sally Ford* [DJS].

988   *Ibid.*, 1:28 in *Ibid.*, 24:26.

989   Tombstone information from Shields Cemetery furnished by Donald J. Sublette of Detroit, Michigan.

990   Rebecca Shields b. 11 Apr 1841, Edgar County, Illinois, according to *James Sublett & Sally Ford* [DJS].

5. Lucinda Shields, m. Justin H. Hanley.
6. Jesse Shields.[992]
7. Daniel Shields,[993] m. Martha Comstock.
8. Nancy (Mary?) Shields,[994] m. Joseph Comstock.
9. Sarah Ellen Shields, m. --- Dean.[995]

506. Daniel Sublett, b. 25 April 1794, settled in 1820 in Bath County, Kentucky, where he married Julia Oakley, daughter of Edmund and Elizabeth (McGuire) Oakley of Bath County, Kentucky. He died in Bath County in 1836, though he is buried in Montgomery County, Kentucky.

Issue of Daniel and Julia (Oakley) Sublett:[996]

3573	i	Elizabeth Sublett, b. 1823.
3574	ii	George O. Sublett, b. 1825.
3575	iii	James Sublett, b. 1828.[997]
3576	iv	Ruth Sublett, b. 1830, named for her paternal grandmother.
3577	v	David Dudley Sublett, b. 9 March 1833, Bath County, Kentucky; d. 27 Dec. 1916 at Salyersville, Kentucky; m. Virginia Carolina Gardner, b. 25 Aug. 1838, Greenup County, Kentucky; d. 31 Oct. 1925. Issue.[998]

1. Joseph M. Sublett, b. 19 Aug. 1862; d. 8 Jan. 1914.[999]
2. Ben Oakley Sublett, b. 15 Dec. 1865.[1000]
3. Lizzie Sublett, b. 29 Aug. 1869; m. H. Atkison; Harrodsburg, Kentucky.
4. May Rose Sublett, b. 23 May 1872; m. Wiley Rice, Salyersville, Kentucky.
5. Julia Sublett, b. 22 Jan. 1875; d. 7 July 1907; m. E. B. Arnett, Salyersville, Kentucky.
6. Rufus Dale Sublett, b. 28 June 1878.
7. David Glenn Sublett, b. 22 Apr. 1881; McGoffin County, Kentucky.
8. Charles D. Sublett, b. 22 Feb. 1862; d. 4 March 1923.[1001]

3578	vi	Mary Sublett, b. 1836.

---

991   Wm. Jackson Shields, according to *James Sublett & Sally Ford* [DJS].

992   Jesse Shields, 1852-1930, m. 15 Dec 1869, Edgar County, Illinois, Jane Hita, according to *James Sublett & Sally Ford* [DJS].

993   Daniel Shields, 1854-1929, according to *James Sublett & Sally Ford* [DJS].

994   Nancy (Buchanan) Shields, 1856-1935, m. 25 Dec 1873, according to *James Sublett & Sally Ford* [DJS].

995   Sarah Ellen Shields b. 17 Nov 1858, m. Willard Dean, according to *James Sublett & Sally Ford* [DJS].

996   Notes gathered by George W. Sublette, son of Peter Jackson Sublette (#3554), and by Mary Frances Sublette, daughter of Colvit Sublette (#3556), cited previously.

997   James Sublett m. Morgan County, Kentucky, Parthenia ---, according to *James Sublett & Sally Ford* [DJS].

998   Indian Mounds Chapter, D.A.R., Kentucky, *Wills and Bible Records, 1948*, p. 5, typescript at the National D.A.R. Library, Washington, D.C. Notice the closeness in age of Joseph and Charles. Mrs. Helen (Arnett) Donaldson, daughter of their sister Julia, states that Charles was an illegitimate son of David D., raised willingly by his wife Virginia.

999   Joseph M. Sublett m. Mary Armenia Kerns, according to *James Sublett & Sally Ford* [DJS].

1000   Benjamin Oakley Sublett b. Magoffin County, Kentucky, d. 1946, m. Katherine Elam, according to *James Sublett & Sally Ford'* [DJS].

1001   Indian Mounds Chapter, D.A.R., Kentucky, *Wills and Bible Records, 1948*, p. 5, typescript at the National D.A.R. Library, Washington, D.C. Notice the closeness in age of Joseph and Charles. Mrs. Helen (Arnett) Donaldson, daughter of their sister Julia, states that Charles was an illegitimate son of David D., raised willingly by his wife Virginia.

3579   vii   Miriam (Minerva?) Sublett, b. 1838.(?)

510. Peter Sublett, b. 13 June 1802, Patrick County, Virginia, was married 17 Dec. 1828 in Madison County, Kentucky, to Tully Timberlake, b. 1 Feb. 1805, and d. 22 April 1875.[1002] He removed to Coles County, Illinois, where he died 7 May 1875.

Issue of Peter and Tully (Timberlake) Sublett:[1003]

    3587   i   Mary Anne Sublett, d. in infancy.
    3588   ii   Ruth Jane Sublett, d. in infancy.
    3589   iii   Elizabeth Frances Sublett, b. 28 Oct. 1832; d. 23 Nov. 1893; m. 1st, Anderson Walton; m. 2nd, William Kierzer.[1004] Issue:
        1.   Peter Walton,[1005] m. Geneva Phelps.
        2.   Mary Elizabeth Walton, m. 1st, Thomas Grant, m. 2nd, Aden Wiley.
        3.   John Walton.[1006]
        4.   Emily Jane Walton m. Franklin Cutter.[1007]
        5.   Joseph Walton, m. 1st, Delilah Johns, m. 2nd, Jennie Cooper, m. 3rd, Annie Smith; he died 11 April 1916.
        6.   Annie Walton.
        7.   Thomas E. Walton, m. Lizzie Burke.
        8.   Leona Walton, m. Carson Cutter.[1008]
        9.   Viola Walton, m. John Gosset; she d. 12 Feb. 1931, Sayre, Oklahoma.
        10. Elizabeth Walton.[1009]
        11. Geoffrey Walton, died in infancy.[1010]
        12. Sophia Walton, d. in infancy.[1011]
        13. George Walton, d. in infancy.[1012]
    3590   iv   Eliza Sublett, d. in infancy.[1013]
    3591   v   Matilda Sublett, b. 28 Aug. 1836; d. 7 March 1926.[1014]
    3592   vi   Emily Miriam Sublett, b. 20 Feb. 1838, m. William Land.[1015] Issue:
        1.   Tully Land.[1016]

1002   Annie Walker Burns, Record of Marriages in Madison County, Kentucky, 1785-1851 Inclusive, mimeo. 1936, p. 166.

1003   Notes gathered by George W. Sublette, son of Peter Jackson Sublette (#3554) and by Mary Frances Sublette, daughter of Colvit Sublette (#3556), previously cited; corrected by family Bible data in possession of Mrs. Robert H. Coffey (Susan Catherine Coyle), of Charleston, Illinois, granddaughter of Thomas Turner Sublett (#3597); furnished by Donald J. Sublette of Detroit.

1004   Elizabeth Frances Sublett m. (only once) 26 Jun 1851, Anderson Walton, according to *James Sublett & Sally Ford* [DJS].

1005   Peter Walton 1852-1877.

1006   John Walton, 1855-1877, Coles County, Illinois. Not married. According to *James Sublett & Sally Ford* [DJS].

1007   Emily Jane Walton m. Benj. Franklin Cutter, Jr., according to *James Sublett & Sally Ford* [DJS].

1008   Leona Walton m. Kit Carson Cutler, according to *James Sublett & Sally Ford* [DJS].

1009   Elizabeth Walton b. 1869, m. Wm. Kierzer, according to *James Sublett & Sally Ford* [DJS].

1010   Geoffrey Walton b. ca 1876, according to *James Sublett & Sally Ford* [DJS].

1011   Sophia Walton b. ca 1871, according to *James Sublett & Sally Ford* [DJS].

1012   George Walton b. 1872, according to *James Sublett & Sally Ford* [DJS].

1013   Eliza Sublett b. ca 1834, according to *James Sublett & Sally Ford* [DJS].

1014   Matilda Sublett, not married, according to *James Sublett & Sally Ford* [DJS].

1015   Emily Miriam Sublett d. Dec 1865, m. 17 Oct 1857, according to *James Sublett & Sally Ford* [DJS].

1016   Tully Land, 1861-1903, m. Ora Nay, according to *James Sublett & Sally Ford* [DJS].

          2.   Lula Land, d. Feb. 11, 1923, m. Roland O. Zimmerman.

          3.   Peter Land,[1017] m. Katherine Ashmore.[1018]

3593   vii   Sarah Caroline Sublett, b. 11 April 1840, m. 1863 David Morris. Issue:

          1.   Emily Morris; not married.

          2.   Thomas Morris, m. Rose Thornton; without issue.

          3.   Sarah Morris, m. George McCivitt; without issue.

          4.   Desoto Morris, m. Laura Shaver; one daughter, Elsie.

          5.   Timmie Morris, m. Heza Carnes; two sons, Cecil C., and Thomas.

          6.   Albert Morris, not married.

          7.   North Morris, m. a Miss Rich, without issue.

          8.   Nellie Morris, m. Harvey Reigle, 1908; without issue.

3594   viii   Nancy Ann Sublett, b. 15 Aug. 1841; d. 31 July 1900; m. Newton Young. Issue:

          1.   William Young.

          2.   Zona Ellen Young, m. Pleasant Brown.

          3.   Albert Young.

          4.   Peter Fane Young.

          5.   Maude Almeda Young.

          6.   Susan Young.

          7.   Charles Young.

          8.   Georgia Young.

3595   ix   Lucinda Ellen Sublett, b. 26 March 1843; d. 23 March 1926.

3596   x   William Henry Sublett, b. 10 Nov. 1844; d. 12 Oct. 1905; m. (1st) Sarah Laws. Issue:

          1.   Pearl Sublett, m. 1907 Clarence Comstock.

          2.   John Thomas Sublett, m. a Miss Fields.

         William Henry Sublett m. 2nd, Mrs. Malinda Coppic. Issue:

          3.   Nellie Sublett.

3597   xi   Thomas Turner Sublett, b. 8 Nov. 1846; d. 19 Oct 1929; m. Susan Brown. Issue:

          1.   Matilda Sublett, d. in infancy.

          2.   Bessie Allen Sublett, m. 1900 Charles Coyle.

3598   xii   James Peter Sublett, b. 28 Apr. 1849; d. 17 Nov. 1926; m. 1st, Amanda Lumfic.[1019] Issue, one child:

          1.   Cephas Sublett, d. in infancy.

         James Peter Sublett m. 2nd, L. Walker. Issue, one child:

         2.   Lindsey Sublett.

         James Peter Sublett m. 3rd, Candace Walker, who d. 1914. He then m. 4th, Mrs. Alice Emerick; resided at Creighton, Missouri.

511. David Sublett, b. ca 1806/7, m. 13 Oct. 1831 in Garrard County, Kentucky, to Mary Ann Marshall; migrated from Kentucky to Illinois, but from Illinois moved to Putnam County, Indiana, where the Census of 1850 lists: David aged 44, Mary A., aged 37, and issue.

1017   Peter Land b. Apr 1860, according to *James Sublett & Sally Ford* [DJS].

1018   Katherine Ashmore b. Dec 1861, according to *James Sublett & Sally Ford* [DJS].

1019   James Peter Sublett m. Amanda M. Lumbrick, according to *James Sublett & Sally Ford* [DJS].

Issue of David and Mary Ann (Marshall) Sublett:[1020]

3601	i	Elisha Sublett, b. ca 1832, Kentucky.[1021]
3602	ii	William Sublett, b. ca 1833 in Kentucky.[1022]
3603	iii	George W. Sublett, b. ca 1835 in Kentucky.[1023]
3604	iv	Nancy J. Sublett, b. ca 1838 in Kentucky.
3605	v	Martha A. Sublett, b. ca 1840 in Kentucky.
3606	vi	Sarah Sublett, b. ca 1842 in Indiana.
3607	vii	Minerva Sublett, b. ca 1844 in Indiana.
3608	viii	James Sublett, b. ca 1848 in Indiana.[1024]

885. Caldwell Sublett, b. ca 1810 in Green County, Kentucky, reared in Franklin County, Tennessee, moved to Benton County, Alabama (renamed Calhoun County in 1858), prior to the 1840 Census, where he is listed, aged 30-40, wife 20-30, one male 15-20 (too old to be his son), one female 10-15 (possibly a daughter), two sons 5-10, and a daughter and a son under 5.[1025] In the 1850 Census of the County, he is listed as age 40, b. in Kentucky, Sheriff of Benton County, a resident of the town of Jacksonville, with wife Nancy, aged 35, born in Tennessee.[1026] Issue shown therein.

Issue of Caldwell and Nancy (---) Sublett:

| 4001 | i | Henry T. G. Sublett, b. ca 1831 in Tennessee. |
| 4002 | ii | William C. Sublett, b. ca 1834 in Tennessee. This is said to be the William Colum [Caldwell] Sublett, known as "Old Ben," who was quite a colorful prospector for gold in the Guadalupe Mountains of southwest Texas and New Mexico, who lived at Odessa, Texas. He died in 1892 and is buried at Odessa.[1027] Issue: |

     1. Ross [Rolth] Sublett,[1028] res. at Carlsbad, N.M.
     2. A daughter[1029] who married Sid Pitts of Roswell, N.M.[1030]

| 4003 | iii | Joseph F. Sublett, b. ca 1836 in Tennessee. Among issue: |

     1. William G. Sublett, b. ca 1872 in Alabama; d. 2 Jan. 1942, Beaumont,

---

1020   U.S. Census, 1850, Warren Twp., Putnam County, Indiana, p. 532.

1021   Elisha Sublett m. 1874, Adeline Young Sublett, according to *James Sublett & Sally Ford* [DJS].

1022   William Sublett d. ca 1872, m. 1856 Ays Supra, according to *James Sublett & Sally Ford* [DJS].

1023   George W. Sublett m. 1856, Indiana, Mary Eliz Roberts, according to *James Sublett & Sally Ford* [DJS].

1024   James Sublett b. 6 Oct 1847, Putnam County, Indiana, d. 10 Oct 1919, m. 3 Jul 1879, Indiana, Mary Wheeler, according to *James Sublett & Sally Ford* [DJS].

1025   Sixth Census of the U.S., 1840, Benton County, Alabama, furnished by Miss Maud McLure Kelly, Huntsville, Alabama, to Mrs. W. A. Wyatt, San Marcos, Texas.

1026   Seventh Census of the U.S., Benton County, Alabama.

1027   William C. Sublett m. Laura L. Denny, according to correspondence with descendant [DJS].

1028   Rolth Sublett, according to correspondence with descendant [DJS]. A sworn affidavit by Rolth Sublett (witnessed by D.S. Libbey, Carlsbad Caverns superintendent, on Oct. 2, 1947) states: "This is to certify that I, Rolth Sublett, of Artesia, New Mexico, Rt. No. 1, first visited what is now known as Carlsbad Caverns in 1883 when I was 12 years of age. ... My father, William Caldwell Sublett, was with me." ("Who Discovered Carlsbad Caverns?" edited by Park naturalist Neal R. Bullington, National Park Service, May 1968) [PLS]

1029   Jessie Cornelia Sublett, according to correspondence with descendant [DJS].

1030   J. Frank Dobie, *Coronado's Children: Tales of Lost Mines and Buried Treasures of the Southwest*, N.Y., 1931, pp. 256-268. This account is, of course, to be taken with a grain of salt.

Texas.

2. J. C. Sublett,[1031] d. 24 March 1948, Muskogee, Oklahoma.

4004   iv   Mary Ellen Sublett, b. ca 1841 in Benton County, Alabama.

4005   v   Alfred A. Sublett, b. ca 1843, Benton County, Alabama.

4006   vi   James D. Sublett, b. 1849, Benton County, Alabama.

Caldwell Sublett is placed as a son of Field Sublett (#119) for these reasons: with the name of Caldwell, he presumably was a descendant (grandson) of Margaret (Caldwell) Sublett (wife of Valentine Sublett [#21]). He was not a son of Valentine's son Branch (#118) whose children are known; he was too old to be son to William (#121); Allen (#117) is not known to have settled in Tennessee, while Field (#119) did move to Tennessee, and the 1810 and 1820 Censuses show Field had an otherwise unknown son the age of Caldwell. Further, Caldwell named a daughter Mary Ellen, possibly for his mother, who was variously known as Eleanor and Ellen. Caldwell Sublett moved from Tennessee to Alabama between 1836 and 1838, for on 3 Nov. 1838 in Talladega County, Alabama, Caldwell Sublett of Benton County, Alabama, filed for 80 acres, the West half of the N.E. 1/4 of S.12 in T.14 R.7 East in the Coosa land district, which he swore he had entered prior to 22 Feb. 1838.[1032]

1041.   Franceway Day was b. 5 July 1814 in Lincoln County, Kentucky; anglophobia was at its height from the War of 1812; his parents, it seems, were conscious of their French heritage, and attempted to give their eldest as Gallic a name as possible, of which Francois represented to them the acme. Unfortunately, as frontiersmen, the niceties of French spelling were lost upon them, and the spelling "Franceway" seems to have represented their most strenuous effort at reproducing or approximating the French pronunciation of Francois.

As a young man, Franceway studied medicine with Dr. Rainier of Petersburg, Illinois, which profession he subsequently practiced. During the Mexican War, he and his brother Philip served together in the 4th Illinois Regiment. Following the termination of the war, he located a homestead in Keokuk County, Iowa. There he m. 1st, Mary Ann Noble, daughter of Samuel Spencer Noble and Grace Caldwell (McGinnis). She died in 1863 in Sullivan County, Missouri, and he m. 2nd, a widow, Mrs. Elizabeth Jane Robinson. Franceway Day moved his family in 1856 to Sullivan County, Missouri. There he died 10 Feb. 1896, and is buried in Wintersville Cemetery.[1033]

Issue of Franceway and Mary Ann (Noble) Day:[1034]

4151   i   William Noble Day, d. at age 14.

4152   ii   Dorothy Day, m. Andrew Jackson Busick.

4153   iii   Sonora Day, m. James R. McDonald; died without issue.

4154   iv   Sarah Day (twin to Samuel), b. 29 July 1854, Keokuk County, Iowa; m. George Strawser.

4155   v   Samuel Sublette Day, b. 29 July 1854, Keokuk County, Iowa; m. Olive Penick,

---

1031   Jas. Caldwell Sublett b. ca 1865, according to correspondence with descendant [DJS].

1032   Certificate 5093, Land Records Section, National Archives.

1033   All information above derived from MS. written by Samuel S. Day (#4155), deposited in S.A.R. Library, Los Angeles, California and copied and sent to the compiler by Mr. Max McKee, Redondo Beach, California.

1034   Information as to descendants of Franceway from the above MS., supplemented by information contributed by Miss Jean Richardson, Trenton, Missouri.

daughter of James and Lucy (Wells) Penick. Issue:

1. Mary Day, b. ca 1876; d. March 1941; m. Robert G. Sheets.
2. Elsie Day, b. 27 Dec. 1878, Sullivan County, Missouri; d. 29 Dec. 1955, LaCanada, California; m. Winfred Rucker.
3. Minnie Day, b. 1879, d. 1896.
4. Arthur Day, b. 3 Aug. 1884, Sullivan County, Missouri; d. 15 July 1953, Los Angeles, California; m. Nelle Eileen Kenefick, Kansas City, Missouri.
5. Vane Day, b. 19 Dec. 1896, Harris, Sullivan County, Missouri; m. 1st, 1917 Ella Sue Fisher; m. 2nd, Marguerite White.

4156   vi   James Edward Day, b. 13 Aug. 1859, Sullivan County, Missouri; m. Willa Jackson.

1046.   Philip S. Day, b. 25 Feb. 1824, Madison County, Illinois; reared in Menard County, Illinois (formerly Sangamon County), and resided there until May 1846, when he enlisted in the 4th Illinois Regiment with his brother Franceway during the Mexican War. In that conflict he served for one year, and participated in the Battles of Vera Cruz and Cerro Gordo, in the latter of which he received a leg wound, which partially disabled him. He was married in Nov. 1847 to Miss Grace Taylor, and settled in 1848 on 160 acres in Keokuk County, Iowa, from a land warrant for services in the Mexican War.[1035]

Issue of Philip S. and Grace (Taylor) Day:[1036]

4201	i	Solomon Day, m. Belle Craft.
4202	ii	Clarissa E. Day, m. Eli Oakes.
4203	iii	William N. Day, m. Jane Rooks.
4204	iv	Robert B. Day, m. Sophia ---.
4205	v	Franklin Day, m. Fannie E. Shultz.
4206	vi	James Day, m. Rose ---.
4207	vii	Philip S. Day, m. Susan ---.
4208	viii	George Day, m. Della Hawkes.
4209	ix	Rebecca Day, d. in infancy.

1047.   Joseph Peyton Day, b. 25 January 1826, Sangamon County, Illinois (that portion now Menard County); m. 1st, Eliza Ann Smith in Menard County, Illinois, where she died; m. 2nd, Susan Elizabeth Noble, b. 6 July 1831, Westmoreland County, Pennsylvania; d. 22 Aug. 1859, Keokuk County, Iowa; daughter of Samuel Spencer Noble and Grace Caldwell (McGinnis), and sister of his brother Franceway Day's first wife. Following Susan's death, Joseph P. Day m. 3rd, her sister Francina Jane Noble, b. 8 Oct. 1829, Westmoreland County, Pennsylvania; d. 8 Feb. 1914, Sullivan County, Missouri. Joseph died 3 May 1896 in Sullivan County, Missouri.[1037]

Issue of Joseph P. and Eliza Ann (Smith) Day:

1035   Gravestones in Rayburn Cemetery, Keokuk, Ia., R. S. Day, 1824-1908; Grace 1829-1911 according to correspondence with descendant [DJS].

1036   *History of Keokuk County, Iowa.* DesMoines, Union Historical Co., 1880. p. 665, supplemented by information provided by Miss Jean Richardson, Trenton, Missouri.

1037   All information kindly supplied by Mr. Max McKee, Redondo Beach, California, grandson of #4219, and by Miss Jean Richardson, Trenton, Missouri, daughter of #4217.

4211 i   Margaret Jane Day, b. 1 May 1849, Menard County, Illinois; d. 25 June 1849, Menard County, Illinois.

4212 ii   William Benjamin Day, b. 2 July 1850, Menard County, Illinois; d. 29 April 1925, Centerville, Iowa; m. Sarah Pierson.[1038]

4213 iii Charles Allen Day,[1039] d. young.

Issue of Joseph P. and Susan Elizabeth (Noble) Day:

4214 iv   Eliza Ann Day, b. 15 Feb. 1857, Keokuk County, Iowa; d. 22 Aug. 1927 Sullivan County, Missouri; not married.

4215 v   Elizabeth Day, b. 1859; d. at about 6 months, Keokuk County, Iowa.

Issue of Joseph P. and Francina Jane (Noble) Day:

4216 vi   Edward Baker Day, b. 11 June 1861, Sullivan County, Missouri; d. 6 Dec. 1879, Sullivan County, Missouri.

4217 vii Rosetta May Day, b. 21 July 1863, Keokuk County, Iowa; d. 6 June 1942, Sullivan County, Missouri; m. 17 Feb. 1887, Sullivan County, Missouri, to George Prentiss Richardson, b. 3 Nov. 1862, Sullivan County, Missouri; d. 24 Nov. 1951, Sullivan County, Missouri.

4218 viii Mattie Emma Day, b. 11 April 1866, Keokuk County, Iowa; d. 11 May 1943; at South Bend, Indiana; m. John Elihu Keller.

4219 ix   Effa Grace Day, b. 3 April 1869, Keokuk County, Iowa; d. 2 Feb. 1958, Sioux Falls, S. Dak.; m. 11 Feb. 1902 to William Edward Beale, b. 9 Sept. 1875, Sullivan County, Missouri; d. 9 Oct. 1916, Putnam County, Missouri.

4220 x   Alma Jane Day, b. 5 June 1872, Keokuk County, Iowa; d. 25 May 1893, Sullivan County, Missouri.

1050.   Dorothy Day, b. ca 1833 in Sangamon County, Illinois (that portion now Menard County); m. 28 Feb. 1851, Menard County, Illinois, to George Washington Taylor, called "Washington." Dorothy (Day) Taylor died 15 July 1863 in Menard County, Illinois.

Washington Taylor was b. 22 Sept. 1824 in Bath County, Kentucky, but was brought as a child to Menard County, Illinois, where he was reared. Following his first wife's death, he enlisted in Company B, 8th Illinois Infantry, in which he served from 1 Oct. 1864 until 26 Sept. 1865, and participated in the siege of Mobile and the charge on Ft. Blakely. In 1867 he moved to Keokuk County, Iowa, having married 2nd, 8 May 1867 to Mrs. Mary A. Miner.[1040]

Issue of G. Washington and Dorothy (Day) Taylor:

4241 i   Mary Melissa Taylor, m. Jacob Messersmith.

4242 ii   Sarah A. Taylor, m. Theodore Porter.

1038   Sarah Pierson, 1865-1902, according to correspondence with descendant [DJS].

1039   Charles Allen Day b. ca 1852, according to correspondence with descendant [DJS].

1040   *History of Keokuk County. Iowa.* Des Moines, Union Historical Co., 1880, p. 665, supplemented by information provided by Miss Jean Richardson, Trenton, Missouri, who corrected a statement in the history that Louisa Taylor (#4244) d. in childhood.

4243 iii James Z. Taylor, m. 1st, Belle Knight, m. 2nd, Mattie Robbins.
4244 iv Louisa Taylor, m. Elijah Craft.
4245 v Dollie A. Taylor, d. in childhood.

1053. Edward O. Day, b. 26 May 1818 in Kentucky; d. 15 May 1884 at DeWitt, Illinois; m. 30 Jan. 1840 to Caroline Hurley, b. 28 Oct. 1821; d. 1 June 1888, DeWitt, Illinois.

Issue of Edward O. and Caroline (Hurley) Day:[1041]

4271 i Benjamin F. Day, b. 16 Nov. 1840; d. 28 March 1841.
4272 ii Margaret Ann Day, b. 5 Jan. 1842; d. 24 August 1903; m. 31 Oct. 1858 Joseph Marsh. Issue:
    1. Mary Kate Marsh, b. 9 March 1861, d. 4 May 1882; m. 29 Apr. 1879 James William Brown.
    2. Alzina Marsh, b. 27 Jan. 1863, d. 27 Jan. 1940; m. 25 Oct. 1887 Robert Bryden Dillin.
    3. George Marsh, m. Cora ---.
4273 iii Catherine C. Day, b. 11 Sept. 1843, a twin; d. 25 Sept. 1915, Champaign, Illinois; m. 13 Aug. 1860 Jacob R. Dillavou, b. 12 July 1837, d. 23 Nov. 1918. Issue:
    1. Edward O. Dillavou, b. 30 May 1861, DeWitt; d. 3 Oct. 1947, Champaign, Illinois; m. Minnie Stephenson.
    2. Samuel Elmer Dillavou, b. 20 April 1865, DeWitt; d. 28 Sept. 1947, Champaign; m. Mary McDaniel.
    3. Idella Dillavou, b. 20 Jan. 1867; d. 4 Aug. 1950; m. 24 April 1885, Champaign, to Joseph H. Sackett.
    4. Naomi Dillavou, b. 24 Sept. 1872; d. infancy.
    5. Olive Ann Dillavou, b. 2 Sept. 1876, DeLand, Illinois; d. 22 Aug. 1958, Champaign; m. 27 Dec. 1905, Champaign, Arthur Frederick Hamersmith.
    6. Nellie Blanche Dillavou, b. 17 Nov. 1878, DeLand: d. 12 Feb. 1925, Chicago; m. Wm. S. Kuhl.
4274 iv Mary M. Day, b. 11 Sept. 1843, a twin; d. March 1916; m. 9 Dec. 1862 to James H. Cobb. Issue:
    1. Charles Cobb.
    2. William Cobb.
    3. Stella Cobb.
    4. Lurah Cobb, m. --- Siemer.
4275 v Eliza J. Day, b. 20 Nov. 1845, m. Isaiah Wilson, 14 Nov. 1871. Issue:
    1. Harry Wilson.
    2. Frank Wilson.
    3. Charles Wilson.
    4. Maude Wilson.
    5. Otto Wilson.
4276 vi Dennis H. Day, b. 11 Sept. 1847; m. 16 June 1870 to Elizabeth Trego.
4277 vii Caroline Day, b. 12 Nov. 1849, m. 20 Dec. 1870 to William Stone. Issue:
    1. Jesse Stone.

1041   All information herein kindly furnished by Mr. Arthur Paul Hamersmith, Dixon, Illinois, 1961, son of Olive (Dillavou) Hamersmith.

               2.   William Stone, res. Sacramento, California.

               3.   Charles Stone.

               4.   Cecil Stone, m. --- Wilson.

4278   viii   America Day, b. 6 Dec. 1851; d. 25 May 1913; m. 1 Nov. 1883 to Charles Braymiller. Issue:

               1.   Earl Braumiller.

               2.   Edna Braumiller, not married.

4279   ix   Martha Day, b. 23 March 1854, d. 7 Oct. 1857.

4280   x   Elizabeth Day, b. 31 Aug. 1856; d. 31 Aug. 1915; m. 25 May 1880 to Henry Fristoe. No issue.

4281   xi   John S. Day, b. 6 Jan. 1860, d. 16 Feb. 1882.

4282   xii   Edward M. Day, b. 11 May 1864, d. 19 Sept. 1869.

1301.   Mary Wilkerson Lowe, b. 1 July 1810 near Huntsville, Alabama, d. 20 Aug. 1849, at Sabinetown, Louisiana, on a trip to Texas. She married 1st, 22 Jan. 1829 in Madison County, Alabama, Samuel Walker Walton.[1042] He was born in Georgia in 1800 and died 27 Jan. 1839 at Vaiden, Carroll County, Mississippi, son of George and Rebecca (Isaacs) Walton.

Issue of Samuel W. and Mary W. (Lowe) Walton:[1043]

5801   i   George Lowe Walton, b. 27 Jan. 1830; d. 21 Feb. 1909 Concordia Parish, Louisiana; m. 5 April 1855 near Vidalia, Concordia Parish, Louisiana, Amanda Moore, b. 12 Oct. 1833 Concordia Parish, Louisiana; d. 10 Jan. 1922 Natchez, Mississippi, daughter of Charles Hamilton Moore and Matilda (Graham). Issue:

               1.   George Sublett Walton, b. 16 Jan. 1856 Austin, Texas;[1044] m. 4 Jan. 1888 in Austin, Texas, Emilie Palm, b. 14 Aug. 1865, Austin; d. 15 Feb. 1942, Austin, daughter of Carl Gustaf and Susanna (Palm) Palm. Their daughter Louise Walton m. 1st, Edwin Warnken, and 2nd, Herbert N. Barnett, M.D.; res. Benton, Louisiana.

               2.   William Graham Walton, not married; planter, Concordia Parish, Louisiana.

               3.   Matilda (Mattie) Walton, m. 1888 at Natchez. Mississippi, William L. Jackson.

5802   ii   William Martin Walton, b. 17 Jan. 1832, Canton, Mississippi; d. 1915 Austin, Texas; m. 1854 Letitia A. Watkins (1835-1914). Attorney General of Texas, 1866. Issue:

               1.   Newton Walton

               2.   Sarah Walton, m. J. J. Parmelee.

5803   iii   Philip Walton, d. at age 18 without issue.

5804   iv   Jesse Newton Walton, d. at age 14.

5805   v   Mary Louise Walton, d. at age 4.

After Samuel W. Walton's death in 1839, Mary m. 2nd, in Carroll County, Mississippi, Benjamin C. Strange, who died ca 1848 in Carroll County.

1042   Huntsville (Alabama) *Democrat*, 30 Jan. 1829: "Married on 22d inst. Samuel W. Walton of Lawrence County to Mary, daughter of George A. Loe, of Madison"; abstracted by Jones and Gandrud, *Alabama Records, v. 6*, p. 6.

1043   All information contributed by their great-granddaughter, Mrs. H. N. (Louise Walton) Barnett, Benton, Louisiana.

1044   George Sublett Walton d. Mar 11 1922, according to correspondence with descendant [DJS].

Issue of Benjamin C. and Mary W. (Lowe) Strange:

5806   vi   Susan Virginia Strange, b. 12 Feb. 1844 Carroll County, Mississippi; d. 27
              Nov. 1896 New Orleans, Louisiana. Married in 1860 at New Orleans Newell
              Tilton, b. 24 Nov. 1836 at Merideth, New Hampshire, son of Newell and Alice
              (Clough) Tilton. Mr. Tilton was a mechanical engineer; the couple resided in
              New Orleans; 9 children.[1045]
5807   vii   Emily Strange, b. 1846, d. 1880, m. Arthur St. Clair.
5808   viii Robert Strange, died in infancy.

1307.   Martha Lowe, b. 23 February 1823 near Huntsville, Alabama; d. 10 January 1886,
Shreveport, Louisiana; m. 1st, --- Mandeville, who was tragically killed in being thrown from a
horse only three months after his marriage; m. 2nd, 22 November 1841 Reuben White.

Issue of Reuben and Martha (Lowe) White, ten children, of whom only three lived to
maturity.[1046]

5851   i   Julia Tabitha White, b. 6 Jan. 1845, m. 6 May 1868, to Charles Lewis Robards,
              who died 22 Nov. 1870. Issue:
              1. Mattie Robards, m. August Mayer, Shreveport, Louisiana. Issue:
                  i. Julia Robards Mayer.
                  ii. Randolph H. Mayer.
                  iii.Katherine Mayer.
                  iv.Vernon Robards Mayer.
                  v. Lowe Reade Mayer.
                  vi.Charles Lewis Mayer.
5852   ii   Annie White,[1047] m. J. H. VanHoose, Shreveport, Louisiana. Issue:
              1. Julia M. VanHoose, m. Harvy N. Cornell.
              2. Hugh VanHoose.
              3. Gordon VanHoose.
5853   iii   Lillian White, m. Dr. W. L. Egan, Shreveport, Louisiana. Issue:
              1. Ardis Loe Egan.
              2. Cronan Egan.
              3. Lillian Egan.

1443. G. Bartlee Greenwood, b. 24 Oct. 1820 in Breckenridge County (now Mead County),
Kentucky, moved as a child with his parents to Illinois. He m. Dorothy (Dartha or Dolly) Clifton
and settled in Jefferson County, Iowa. After some years there, he moved to Daviess County,
Missouri, then back to Illinois, residing there until 1865 when he resettled in Daviess County,
Missouri, only to return to Illinois in 1870, and then move on to Clay County, Kansas, and finally
to Norton County, Kansas. He was a member of the Christian Church.[1048]

1045   John Bennett Boddie, *Historical Southern Families, vol. 4*, Redwood City, California, 1960. pp. 74-76, sub "Allin."
1046   Information from Mrs. H. N. Barnett, Benton, Louisiana.
1047   Annie White b. ca 1847, according to correspondence with descendant [DJS].
1048   *Portrait and Biographical Album of Washington, Clay and Riley Counties, Kansas*. Chicago, Chapman Bros.

Issue of Bartlee and Dolly (Clifton) Greenwood.[1049]

7431   i   William L. Greenwood, b. 14 July 1844, Jefferson County, Iowa; served in the 11th Illinois Cavalry during the Civil War, 1862-65. Settled in Sherman Twp., Clay County, Kansas, where in 1876 he m. Martha J. Patch, b. 25 Feb. 1852 in Indiana, daughter of Thomas and Caroline (Seegar) Patch. Issue:
1. Zuda Greenwood, died at age 3.
2. Bryant Greenwood.
3. Lucretia Greenwood.
4. Floyd Greenwood.

7432   ii   John Ira Greenwood, b. 25 Apr. 1845/7, d. 15 Nov. 1933, Smith County, Kansas, m. Mary E. Belden, b. 11 Aug. 1855, Mercer County, Kansas; d. 18 Feb. 1939, Smith County, Kans., daughter of Orlando and Melissa (Engle) Belden. Issue:
1. Emma Bell Greenwood, b. 14 Aug. 1872, Clay County,Kans.; m. 1887 George Darling, b. 23 Jan. 1867, d. 4 Jan. 1937, Norton County, Kans., son of Joseph and Mary J. (Swearingen) Darling.[1050]
2. Lewis B. Greenwood, b. 28 Mar. 1875, Republic County, Kans.; d. 11 Jan. 1960, Omaha, Nebr.; m. Annie Woods.
3. Edward C. Greenwood, b. 17 July 1880, Mitchell County, Kans.; m. 3 Sept. 1902 Myrtle Laura Carter, b. 19 Sept. 1883, Taylor County, Iowa, d. 23 Jan. 1924, Norton County, Kans., daughter of Joseph and Delilah (Markle) Carter.

7433   iii   Joseph W. Greenwood; m. Elizabeth --- .[1051]
7434   iv   Lee Greenwood, b. ca 1850.
7435   v   Sarah Greenwood, b. ca 1856.
7436   vi   James J. Greenwood, b. ca 1857.
7437   vii   Dinah E. Greenwood, b. ca 1860.
7438   viii   Stephen A. Greenwood, b. ca 1861.
7439   ix   Samuel B. Greenwood, b. ca 1863.
7440   x   Addie B. Greenwood, b. ca 1865.
7441   xi   Laura A. Greenwood, b. ca 1867.
7442   xii   Cantha Greenwood, b. ca 1868.

1544.   Julyann Smith, b. 12 Dec. 1829, Green County, Kentucky; d. 4 March 1879, Sabine County, Texas; buried Brookeland Cemetery, Sabine County, Texas; m. August 1846 in Green County, Kentucky, to John Richard ("Jack") Bell, b. 12 Jan. 1821, Green County, Kentucky, son of William S. Bell; d. 4 August 1904, Sabine County, Texas.

Issue of John Richard and Julyann (Smith) Bell:[1052]

8311   i   George Alford Bell, b. 20 Aug. 1847, Green County, Kentucky; d. 7 Oct. 1933;

1049   Mercer County, Illinois, 1870 Census, Norwood, Suez Twp., p. 27, #183 Daviess County, Missouri, 1860 Census, Grand River Twp., pp. 52-53, #204 Cloud County, Kans., 1880 Census, Grant Twp., p. 10.

1050   All information on the descendants of #1443 kindly furnished by Lt. Col. Kenneth P. Darling, Washington, D.C., her grandson.

1051   Clay County, Kans., 1880 Census, Sherman Twp., p. 13, #140.

1052   All information kindly furnished by Mrs. Sam Radde, Meridian, Texas.

m. 16 Oct. 1872 Mary Louisa Polley.

8312 ii Martha M. Bell, b. 11 Dec. 1850, Green County, Kentucky; d. 18 Dec. 1929; m. Romantie G. Hamilton.

8313 iii William Thomas Bell, b. 23 Sept. 1852, Green County, Kentucky; d. 11 May 1923; m. Ellen Tucker, Celeste Tucker, Mattie Warner.

8314 iv John Henry Bell, b. 5 March 1855, Sabine County, Texas; d. 15 July 1921; m. 9 July 1874 Frances Bener Essley.

8315 v Franklin Fither Bell, b. 17 July 1857, Sabine County, Texas; d. 20 Sept. 1882; m. Patsy Powell.

8316 vi Luther Sidney Bell, b. 29 Jan. 1860, Sabine County, Texas; d. 12 April 1943; m. Rebecca Magee.

8317 vii Robert L. Bell, b. 3 July 1861, Sabine County, Texas; d. 3 July 1903; m. Julia Angeline Beardshaw.

8318 viii Philip A. Bell, b. 8 April 1864, Sabine County, Texas; d. 16 July 1932; m. Laura Ramey.

8319 ix James Walter Bell, b. 11 Dec. 1868, Sabine County, Texas; d. 22 March 1950; m. 7 April 1885 Nellie Catherine Dickerson.

1805. Martha Jane Sublett, b. 18 Sept. 1822, Franklin County, Tennessee, married 1st, 6 March 1846 to Joshua Jefferson Willburn, b. 2 Nov. 1818, d. 13 April 1855. The couple resided at Romans Landing on the Tennessee River, near Coffeytown, Alabama.

Issue of Joshua Jefferson and Martha Jane (Sublett) Willburn:[1053]

9901 i Sarah Ellen Willburn, b. 23 March 1848, m. 22 July 1863 George J. Hall, b. 17 July 1842, a Confederate soldier. Issue:
1. Charles A. Hall, b. 6 March 1865, m. 29 Aug. 1888 Mary Wyeth May.
2. Mary Hugh Hall, b. 8 Feb. 1867, m. 27 Apr. 1883 Willie Smith.
3. Ann Eliza Hall, b. 5 Oct. 1869; d. 19 Sept. 1871.
4. George Lafayette Hall, b. 7 Jan. 1872, m. 17 Jan. 1893 Jessie Pankey.
5. Tempie E. Hall, b. 16 Oct. 1873, m. 19 Jan. 1892 San [Samuel] W. Norwood.
6. Samuel Jerome Hall, b. 17 Apr. 1876, d. 25 June 1878.
7. Conrad B. Hall, b. 15 July 1878.
8. Joseph Marvin Hall, b. 10 Feb. 1881; m. 1st, 23 Aug. 1899 Bulah Wilson; m. 2nd, 6 Sept. 1909 Dora Smith.
9. William Olin Hall, b. 14 Jan. 1884; d. 11 Oct. 1897.
10. Clara Mason Hall, b. 17 June 1886; m. 1st, 1 June 1908 Charles Steward; m. 2nd, 26 Dec. 1912 Pryor Plumlee.

9902 ii Mary Willburn, b. 22 Aug. 1849, m. Jim Brock. Resided at Erick, Oklahoma. Issue:
1. Jessie Brock, m. Olen Clayton.
2. Orah Brock, m. Claud Reid.
3. Delbert Brock, twin.
4. Elbert Brock, twin.

9903 iii Eliza Willburn, b. 4 Sept. 1851, m. Robert Carter. Resided at Ennis, Texas.

1053 Ms. by Mrs. Sarah (Willburn) Hall, 1910, Stevenson, Alabama, in possession of her granddaughter Mrs. Margie (Norwood) Jackson, Dallas, Texas (1960).

Issue:
1. Alice Carter, m. --- Bush.
2. Julia Carter.
3. Joseph Carter.
4. Orin Carter.

9904   iv Elvira Sublette Willburn, b. 1 April 1853, m. W. P. Pool. Issue:
1. Ann Eliza Pool, m. George Johnson.
2. Robert Pool, m. Willie Rainey.

After her first husband's death, Martha (Sublett) Willburn m. 2nd, 11 Jan. 1857 Thomas Logan, "who made a good step-father and we all loved him." He d. July 1865 shortly after returning from service in the War Between the States. Martha (Sublett) (Willburn) Logan died 28 Aug. 1868.

Issue of Thomas and Martha Jane (Sublett) Logan:

9905   v   Hugh Lawrence Logan, d. 17 March 1866.
9906   vi John Robert Logan (a girl); resided in Wyoming.
9907   vii Jessie Logan, d. infancy.

PLEASANT[5] SUBLETT AND VALENTINE DAY[6], DESCENDANTS OF ABRAHAM SOBLET OF MANAKINTOWN, KING WILLIAM PARISH, VIRGINIA

Contributed by Mrs. Garner Ray Searl of Patterson, California

"The (Soblet-Sobley) Sublett Family of Manakintown, King William Parish, Virginia," compiled by Cameron Allen of East Orange, New Jersey, was published in *The Detroit Society for Genealogical Research Magazine* in twelve parts, begining Fall 1963, Volume 27, p. 3 and ending Summer 1966, Volume 29, p. 161. Additional records of two descendants, Pleasant[5] Sublett [#513] and Valentine[6] Day [#133] have been contributed by Mrs. Searl., who found them while researching the John[1] and Abigail (Wright) Hester family.

Pleasant[5] Sublett[1054] (*William*[4], *James*[3], *Jacques*[2], *Abraham*[1] *Soblet*) was born either in Madison or Garrard County, Kentucky, son of William Sublett and his second wife, Mrs. Nancy (---) Harris (Allen, *Ibid*, 28:155). He died ca 1893 near Mondamin, Harrison County, Iowa, "at the home of my folks when I was a small child." [Mrs. Dora Belle (Marshall) Alexander of Modale, Iowa, granddaughter, to Mrs. Garner Roy Searl., 1 December 1970] Pleasant Sublett married first, in Kentucky, Patsy Floyd; he moved to Indiana and there married second, Susan Sales.

"Pleasant Sublett lived in Missouri until just after the Civil War when he moved to Iowa. He was a wealthy land owner in Missouri but the carpet baggers ran out." [Mrs. Gale Albert (Mary Charles) Sublett of Morristown, Tennessee, a great granddaughter-in-law, to Mrs. Garner Roy Searl., 9 November 1970.]

Children of Pleasant [5] and Patsy (Floyd) Sublett:[1055] (Allen, *op. cit.*, 28:155).

- i   James[6] [?John] Sublett.
- ii William Sublett.
- iii David Sublett.
- iv Jane Sublett. "I met my mother's half-sister in 1915. She lived in Kansas City, Missouri, at that time and was about 75 years old." (Alexander, *op. cit.*, 1 December 1970).

Children of Pleasant [5] and Susan (Sales) Sublett: (Family records)

- v   Enos Sublett, d. in 1904, m. Amelia Schwertley, d. in 1939. One son, surname *Sublett*: Albert William, b. 22 September 1891; d. 10 November 1933; m. 12 December 1912, Ruth Esther Hester, b. 3 January 1891. Enos and Amelia are buried in Magnolia Cemetery, Magnolia, Harrison County, Iowa.
- vi Jack Sublett,[1056] m. --- Foreman. Three daughters, surname *Sublett*: 1) Nette; 2) Clara; 3) a daughter, name unknown.

1054   Pleasant Sublet CA #513; all these additions by DJS are based on correspondence with the author and other descendents.

1055   1850 Census: Sarah 22, John 19, Wm. 17, Mary 14, Nancy 13, Rebecca 11, David 9, Julia 7, Marion 2, Geo. 5/12 [DJS].

1056   Marion Jack Sublett m. Mary F. Foreman [DJS].

vii   George Sublett,[1057] b. Gentry County, Missouri. Five children, surname *Sublett*: 1) Emory; 2) Thomas; 3) Ora; 4) Jennie; and 5) Mollie.

viii Thomas Sublett,[1058] b. Clinton County, Missouri, m. Sarah Puckett. Five children, surname *Sublett*: 1) Thomas; 2) Arthur; 3) Cora; 4) Matilda; and 5) Ina

ix   Joseph Sublett,[1059] m. Lena Barger. Seven children.

x   Peter F. Sublett, m. Sophia Schwertley. Seven children, surname *Sublett*: 1) William; 2) Ray; 3) John; 4) Gladys; 5) Florence; 6) Blanche; and 7) Helen.

xi   Armazinda Sublett,[1060] m. William Foreman. Seven children, surname *Foreman*: 1) Dick; 2) William; 3) Lee; 4) Sadia; 5) Rose; 6) Kate; and 7) Nora.

xii   Sarah Susan Sublett,[1061] b. near Savannah, Andrew County, Missouri, m. Joseph Marshall. Eight children, surname *Marshall*: 1) Harvey; 2) Clarence; 3) Clyde; 4) John Pleasant; 5) Jesse; 6) Dora Belle, m. Jack Alexander; 7) Rosa Angela; and 8) Bessie Laura.

xiii Caroline Sublett,[1062] m. 1st, William Aldrich. Four children, surname *Aldrich*: 1) William; 2) Fannie; 3) Hattie; and 4) Nellie Caroline. She m. 2nd, John Calan. One daughter: Katie Calan.

xiv   Ollie Sublett,[1063] m. Charlie Hale. Eight children, surname *Hale*: 1) Cleve; 2) Ora; 3) Fred; 4) Abbie; 5) Dottie; 6) Anna; 7) Cuba; and 8) Ollie.

xv   Mary Sublett,[1064] m. Hank Hammond. One son: Joseph Hammond.

Valentine[1065] Day [6] (*Ursula*[5], *William*[4], *Peter*[3], *Pierre*[2], *Abraham*[1] *Soblet*) was born ca 1780 in Charlotte County, Virginia; died perhaps in Missouri, son of Edward and Ursula (Sublett) Day. He married in Mercer County, Kentucky, 31 July 1809, Elizabeth "Betsy" Adams. (Allen, *op. cit.*, 28:155)

Valentine Day was enumerated in the 1810 census of Lincoln County, Kentucky with 1m (26-45); 1m (-10); and 1f (16-26). His name is not listed there in the 1820 returns, but in 1830 his household included: 1m (-15); 2m (10-15); 2m (15-20); 1f (-5); 2f (5-10); and 1f (10-15). (1810, 1830 U.S. Censuses, Lincoln County, Kentucky).

An indenture dated 25 July 1831, recorded same day, wherein "Alfred Hocker, Deputy Sheriff for Gabriel Lackey, Sheriff of Lincoln County, of the first part and Nicholas Martin of the other part on 6 June 1831 served a writ of *fieri facias* [a writ for recovering judgment in debt] in favor of Benjamin Duncan and Thomas Vaughn, executors of Thomas Vaughn deceased, against the estate of Nicholas Martin and Valentine Day for the sum of $106 ... On 4 July 1831, Valentine Day gave up to said Hocker a tract of land upon which Day then resided, about 135 acres. On 25

1057   George Sublett b. 15 Jul 1850, m. Cynthia A. Mullenix [DJS].

1058   Thomas W. Sublett, b. 13 Mar 1855 [DJS].

1059   Joseph Sublett, b. 1863, Iowa; d. Nebraska; m. 26 Jun 1896, Iowa [DJS].

1060   Armazinda Sublett, b. 1851; m. 4 Jul 1861, Harrison County, Iowa [DJS].

1061   Sarah Susan Sublett, b. 8 Feb 1853 [DJS].

1062   Caroline Sublett, b. ca 1859 [DJS].

1063   Olive Ann Sublett, b. 1865; d. 1932 [DJS].

1064   Mary Sublett, b. ca 1869 [DJS].

1065   Valentine Day CA #133 [DJS].

July 1831, said land was sold at public outcry at Stanford and Nicholas Martin became the purchaser and said Hocker does sell and convey to Nicholas Martin the 135 acres on Logan's Creek adjoining lands of Joseph Hall, Mrs. Chapman, and Thomas Stevenson, free from claim by Valentine Day." (Lincoln County, Kentucky Deed N:262).

On 16 September 1839, acknowledged and recorded 21 September 1839, "Valentine Day and Elizabeth Day his wife and Elijah Hiatt of Lincoln County conveyed to John Lynn of same county for $460, 40 acre in Lincoln County on Logan's Creek adjoining land where Elijah Hiatt now lives." On the same day, 16 September 1839, acknowledged and recorded 30 September 1839, Valentine Day deeded to Henry Ousley of same county 112 1/2 acres on Logan's Creek in Lincoln County, bounded by Joseph Hall, --- Baughman, and John Lynn. Witnesses: A. Perrin, J.P., B. Shanks, J.P. Elizabeth Day relinquished her dower before the justices above named, 19 September 1839. (Lincoln County, Kentucky Deeds Q:89, 90)

In Allen, *op. cit.*, Vol. 28, p. 158, only two children of Valentine and Elizabeth (Adams) Day were recorded: 1) Clarinda A., m. 24 June 1835, Nudgett Owsley; and 2) Polly, m. 20 June 1837, Benjamin Cornett. A third daughter, Elizabeth Day has been identified in *History of California with a Record of Coast Counties* (J. M. Guinn, comp., 1904, p. 1387): "Valentine Day and Elizabeth Day with part of their family migrated to Buchanan County, Missouri in 1839." They were enumerated there in 1840 with a family of eight: 1m (5-10); 2m (10-15); 1m (15-20); 1m (40-50); 1f (10-15); 1f (15-20); and 1f (40-50). "Elizabeth Day, born 14 October 1825, married in Missouri Byram Linville,[1066] born in Lafayette County, Missouri, 17 March 1821; died near Cloverdale, Sonoma County, California, 7 November 1901, son of Zachariah and Nancy (Cash) Linville. Byram and Elizabeth (Day) Linville are both buried in the Cloverdale Cemetery there.

"Zachariah Linville was born and reared in North Carolina but moved to Tennesse after his marriage. About 1817 he took up land in Missouri and resided there until 1849 when he followed the tide of emigration to the gold fields of the Pacific Coast. Leaving his wife and family, he crossed the plains with an ox team and began mining operations at Hangtown [now Placerville], El Dorado County, California, on Weaver [?Webber] Creek. He died a few months after his arrival at age 65. Byram Linville, his family, and widowed mother remained in Missouri until 1853 when they moved to Glenwood, Mills County, Iowa, where Nancy (Cash) Linville died at age 65. In 1857, Byram and Elizabeth (Day) Linville crossed the plains and mountains with their family to Sonoma County, California, and Byram headed a caravan of covered wagons."

Children of Byram and Elizabath (Day)[7] Linville: (Family records)

   i   Jasper[8] Linville, b. in Missouri ca 1845, m. Sarah J. Heald, daughter of Jacob G. Heald who came to Sonoma County, California, in 1852.

   ii   Pleasant Day Linville.

   iii   Valentine Linville, never married.

   iv   Pamela Hazeltine Linville, m. M. E. C. Munda, an attorney.

   v   Ida Linville, d. age 10; buried in family plot in Cloverdale Cemetery.

1066   Elizabeth Day Linville, m. 26 Aug 1841, Missouri [DJS].

vi   Elizabeth "Lizzie" L. Linville, m. Joseph L. Wisecarver.[1067]

vii Ada Mary Linville b. Sonoma County, California, 11 December 1865; d. in Modesto, Stanislaus County, California, in May 1952; m. 16 December 1883, Thomas Jefferson Wisecarver. He was b. in Albany, Oregon, 5 September 1863; d. in Modesto in March 1938, son of Joseph R. and Jane (Black) Wisecarver — both buried in Modesto Cemetery. Two children, surname Wisecarver: 1) Arthur Pleasant, and 2) Floyd Linville.

viii Clement R. Linville.

1067   Joseph L. Wisecarver, bro. Thos. J. [DJS].

FRENCH ORIGINS OF THE (SOBLET-SUBLEY) SUBLETT FAMILY OF MANAKINTOWN, KING WILLIAM PARISH, VIRGINIA

Transcribed by Donald J. Sublette of Detroit, Michigan

In 1972, the compiler visited places of Huguenot interest in England, Germany, the Netherlands, Switzerland, and France as a member of the "Admiral Gaspard de Coligny Memorial Pilgrimage." The tour culminated at Fontainebleau, France, where the World Huguenot Congress commemorated the historic events of St. Bartholomew's Day, 24 August 1572.

Although time was limited, Mr. Sublette inspected *Soblet* records in the library of the Huguenot Society of London [67 Victoria Road, Kensington, London W 8] and the Société de l'Histoire du Protestantisme Française in Paris [54 Rue des Saint-Pères, Paris 75], and found data to supplement the definitive genealogy compiled by Cameron Allen of New Jersey. ("The (Soblet-Subley) Sublett Family of Manakintown, King William Parish, Virginia," *DSGR Magazine*, beginning Fall 1963, Vol. 27, p. 3, and ending Summer 1966, Vol. 29, p. 161; The American Society of Genealogists, *Genealogical Research, Vol. II*, 1971, p. 259).

Mr. Allen has shown that the American progenitor, Abraham Soblet, was a native of "Sedan, Ardennes, France, and that his wife was Susanne Brian, not Dupuy or Chastain as set forth in previous genealogical accounts." (Allen's *Soblet*, Vol. 27, p. 3). In addition, "Abraham Soblet, b. 1648, Sedan, France, son of Jean Soblet, the latter born at Beaumont; Abraham resided at nearby Saint-Menges; fled France by 1681 for Mannheim, Germany; by 1693 residing at Wesel; migrated thence to London; from there to Virginia, 1700." (Allen's account in *Research*, p. 259).

There are six volumes of transcribed — how and when not ascertained — baptismal records of the Reformed Church of Sedan in the Société de l'Histoire du Protestantisme Française, but only four volumes, covering the years 1647 to 1684, were examined by the contributor, with the following new facts uncovered:

1   Children of Jean[1] Soblet and wife Judith Lombard (order of birth uncertain), three previously reported by Cameron Allen:
  i   Elisabeth, b. 16 July 1647; godparents, Jeremie Brandone and wife Elisabeth Jannon.
  ii   Abraham, b. 4 December 1648, bap. 6 December 1648, a son of Jean Soblet and Judith Lombard; godparents, Abraham Duclous and wife Rachel Brandin. (Additional data to follow).
  iii Catherine, b. 21 June 1652; godparents, Jean Bruyerères and wife Catherine Descamps.
  iv   Judith, b. 7 May 1656.
  v   Marie, b. 26 October 1663.
  vi   Simon, d. [?buried], 28 September 1677 aged 7. The record states, "of Jean Soblet *notaire et de* Judith Lombard, *ses frères*, Jean Soblet *écrivain et* Abraham Soblet." [Witnesses brothers, Jean Soblet, writer, and Abraham Soblet].
  vii Jean. No birth record found, but named in above record. (Additional data to follow)

2   Children of Philbert Soblet and wife Ann Godin, eight previously reported by Cameron Allen. [Relationship of Philbert to Jean Soblet unknown, but reasonable to assume they may have been brothers]:

i   Henry, b. 5 March 1648; godparents, Henry Duchene and wife Elisabeth Loriac.

ii   Anne, b. 11 August 1650; godparents, Jacques Godin and wife Anne ?Salomare.

iii   Jean, b. 7 September 1651; godfather, Jean Godin. (One of three children born to this family who was named "Jean").

iv   Marie, b. 16 November 1652; godparents, Paul Sacrelaire and wife Marie ?Genoteau.

v   Jean, b. 19 October 1654, died in childhood.

vi   Jeanne, b. 17 January 1656.

vii   Jacque, b. 4 March 1657.

viii Elisabeth, b. 28 July 1658, d. in childhood.

ix   Judith, b. 25 August 1660.

x   Rachel, b. 8 January 1662.

xi   Jean, b. 30 August 1664.

xii   Elisabeth, b. 10 December 1665.

3   The only entry for Jacques Soblet, son of Philbert, is in the baptismal record of Guillaume Soblet on 9 March 1681, son of Jacques Soblet and Marie Boulande. Jacques and Guillaume could be the father and son who were "lecteur-chantre" ("reader-chanter") in Emmerich, and who died, respectively, in 1705 snd 1752. (Allen's *Soblet*, Vol. 27, p. 4).

4   An entry for Anne Soblet, either daughter of Jean[1] or Philbert, appears as wife of Jacob or Jacques de Villette. They are listed as godparents of Jacques de Villette baptized, 16 August 1682. They had children:
i   Marie, bap., 30 January 1670; godfather, Jacques Soblet. She d. [buried], 20 December ?1680 aged 10 years. [cf. Marie #iv].
ii   Elisabeth, bap., 3 June 1676.
iii   Daniel, bap., 24 September 1679.
iv   Marie, bap., 8 December 1680; godparents, Jacques Soblet and wife Marie Boulande.

5   Three children were found for Jean[2] Soblet and wife Marie:
i   Jean b. 6 September 1677.
ii   Abraham, bap., 24 August 1679.
iii   Ann, bap., 20 August 1681, daughter Jean Soblet, "*écrivain à Sedan.*"

6   An entry for the birth of Susanne Brian, wife of Abraham Soblet, appears in the Sedan Reformed Church records, 23 January 1660, baptized, 29 January 1660, daughter of Daniel Brian, serrurier [locksmith] à Sedan and wife Racel Beguin; godparents, Daniel Cellia, potier [potter] à Sedan and wife Rachel Vulion. In 1679, Daniel Brian and wife transferred their membership from Sedan to the Threadneedle Huguenot Church in London.

7   The four children of Abraham and Susanne (Brian) Soblet, shown in the Sedan records:
i   Anne, bap., Sedan, 27 October 1675, daughter of Abraham Soblet, *ouvrier* [craftsman] *en tobac* and wife Susanne Brian; godparents, Philbert Soblet and wife Anne Godin. Susanne (Brian) Soblet was age 15 years when daughter Anne was baptized. There may have been a second or older Susanne, although none was found in the records inspected. Ann Soblet, b.

ca 1684, d. in Virginia, 1723; m. ca 1701, as his second wife, Pierre Chastain, b. 1660, d. 1723. (Allen's *Soblet*, Vol. 27, p. 6).

ii   Jean, bap., 29 April 1677, d. 26 April 1678.

iii   Jacob, bap., 14 September 1678; godparent, Jacob Lambert. This may be the Jacques, estimated by Cameron Allen to have been born ca 1689, who accompanied his parents to Virginia.

iv   Jean, b. 10 March 1680, son of Abraham Soblet of Saint-Menges and wife Susanne Brian; godparents, Jean Soblet of Sedan and wife Marie Martinet. Jean died, 17 October 1680 aged 8 months, "son of Abr. Soblet, *bourgeois de Saint-Menges* and Susanne Brian." Witness, Jean Soblet, "*écrivain à Sedan*, uncle and godfather of deceased."

8   Marte Martain, bap., Sedan, 21 January 1682, daughter of Jeremie Martain *de Sedan* and wife Marie Archambeau. In Allen's *Soblet*, Vol. 27, p. 6, this is the name given for perhaps the second wife of Pierre-Louis, b. ca 1686, son of Abraham and Susanne (Brian) Sublet. It is from Pierre-Louis and Marte (Martain) Soblet that over 90 percent of the American Subletts are descended.

FRENCH ORIGINS OF THE (SOBLET-SUBLEY) SUBLETT FAMILY OF MANAKINTOWN, KING WILLIAM PARISH, VIRGINIA: ADDITIONS AND CORRECTIONS

Transcibed by Donald J. Sublette of Detroit, Michigan

In April, 1976, Don and Elizabeth Sublette made a return visit to the Société de l'Histoire de Protestantisme Française in Paris [54 Rue des Saint-Pères, Paris, 75] determined, this time, to inspect all records available there of the Reformed Church of Sedan, the oldest known residence of his ancestor, Abraham Soblet, who had immigrated to the Colony or Virginia in 1700.[1068] Limitation of time in 1972 had prevented Don from examining all the Sedan registers, which are transcriptions, in French. It is not known whether these transcriptions were made directly from original records, which, so far as we know, are no longer in existence, or are copies of older copies. Further, there are gaps in the records, which may leave the searcher without pertinent data. An analysis of his findings and correction of earlier interpretations follows the presentation of the translated records.

After completing their Paris research, the Sublettes toured Sedan and vicinity (now the Department of Ardennes), an area where many major military engagements have taken place — the Franco-Prussian War of 1870-1871, and two World Wars in the 1900s. Until the 1630s, Sedan, known as the Geneva of the North, had been an independent principality and an important center for the French Reformed Church (Huguenot). One of the four principal Protestant Universities was situated there, as well as also the seat for the manufacture of woolens, arms, farming equipment, and a variety of steel and iron articles. Genealogical research for the ancestry of adherents of the Protestant cause is complicated because communicants flocked to the flourishing centers of Sedan and La Rochelle not only from a wide area of France, but also from other countries. Many changed the spelling of their names to avoid real or fancied persecution.

Due to changing political alignments, Sedan was ceded in 1642 to the French King, Louis XIII, and the rights and privileges of the members of this religious group began to diminish until, at the revocation of the Edict of Nantes in 1685, many thousands went into exile, mostly Holland and England, to escape persecution and death. Because Sedan was its population had easy access to escape routes. Today, the area is a modern industrial complex so that the effort to locate graves, dwellings, or even the smaller towns of the 16th and 17th centuries is an impossible task.

The compiler found seven volumes of baptismal transcriptions labelled: "*Sedan, Eglise*

[1068]   *DSGR Magazine* has served as the major, if not sole vehicle, for recording data on the *Soblet* (*Sublett*) family which has been determined and/or verified by research as contrasted with traditional approaches. The twelve-part history by Cameron Allen, F.A.S.G., is the "Bible" of the Sublette genealogy and his monumental work in assembling and publishing the American data included the discovery of the true last name of Abraham Soblet's wife Suzanne, thus ending generations of speculation, as well as the French site of the 17th-century home of this family (Cameron Allen, "The (Sobley-Subley) Sublette Family of Manakintown, King William Parish, Virginia," *DSGR Magazine*, beginning Fall 1963, Vol. 27, p. 3 and ending Summer 1966, Vol. 29, p. 161). Additional pertinent *Soblet* data was published by Mr. Allen in The American Society of Genealogists, *Genealogical Research*, 1971, Vol. II, p. 259. Other published accounts in regard to this family are: Nancy Louise Sublette, *Generations Remembered, the Sublette Family, 1700-1850*; Donald J. Sublette, "French Origins of the (Sobley-Subley) Sublett Family of Manakintown, King William Parish, Virginia," *DSGR Magazine*, Fall 1974, Vol. 38, No. 1, p. 1; Mrs. Garner Roy Searl, "Pleasant[5] Sublett and Valentine Day[6], Descendants of Abraham Soblet of Manakintown, King William Parish, Virginia," *DSGR Magazine*, Winter 1973, No. 2, p. 55.

Reformé, Registres de Baptismes": Mss #6634, 1631-1638; #6635, 1630-1646; #6636, 1647-1665; #6637, 1656-1664; #6638, 1665-1672; #6639, 1673-1682; and #666, 1667-1683 and 1670-1784. One book of Marriages, mss #6642, 1631-1682. There were some deaths included, and the baptisms were not as duplicative as indicated.

MARRIAGES

11 Aug 1601   PIERRE BRIAN, son of William Brian of Sedan, and MARIE POUPART, daughter of Mathias Poupart from Brie.

6 Jul 1631   PIERRE SAUBLET, son of Jean Saublet of Jametz and Susanne Vallet, and MARIE LESPINE, daughter of Jean Lespine and Judith Briset of Jametz.

16 Ja/Ag 1643   PHILBERT SOUBLET, son of Elie Soublet, deceased, and Susanne Renaudin, resident of Beaumont, and ANNE GODIN(?), daughter of Antoine Godin(?), deceased, and Bastienne de l'Escot [Note the German language feminine ending in Renaudin].

11 Feb 1670   ANNE SOBLET, aged 20, daughter of Filbert Soblet and Anne Godin and JACQUES DE VILLETT, aged 24, son of Jacques de Villett and Elisabeth Robinet.

31 Mar 1679   ABRAHAM SOBLET, son of Jean Soblet and Judith Lombart of Boscy(?), aged 26, and SUSANNE BRIANT, aged 22, of Sedan, daughter of Jacques Brian of Sedan and Susanne Gerard, deceased. Witnesses: Jean Soblet, school teacher, Philbert Soblet; Jacques Briant; Daniel Briant, tobacco merchant [Could the date 1679 be an error in transcription? Abraham Soblet was born in 1648, so, if married at age 26, the marriage date would be 1674. His first child, Susanne (Anne), was baptised 27 October 1675].

7 Aug 1678   JACQUES SOBLET, aged 22, son of Philbert Soblet, merchant of Sedan, and Anne Godin, and MARIE BOULANDE, aged 19, daughter of Guillaume Boulande, draper, and Elisabeth Cherillon. Witnesses: Jacques de Villett and others.

12 May 1680   RACHEL SOBLET, aged 18, daughter of Philbert Soblet and Anne Godin and JACQUES BENOIT, aged 22, son of Pierre Benoit, merchant of Vitry le François, and Suzanne Colin(?). Witnesses: Jacques Soblet, brother, and others.

3 Aug 1681   ELISABETH SOBLET, aged 25 daughter of Jean Soblet, notary of Corsey(Curcy) and Judith Lombart and DANIEL RENAUD, aged 35 [no parents stated]. Witnesses: Daniel Renaud, uncle, of St. Menges; Jean Soblet, scribe, brother, and Dan'l Peron, friend [The last entry in this register was 22 November 1682].

DEATHS

31 Aug 1636	JEAN SOLLET(?), aged 14, son of Jean Sollet(?) and Margaret Cossou(?) [This may not be a *Soblet* entry].
15 Oct 1651	JEAN SOBLET, son of Philbert Soblet [No age given].
7 Feb 1653	SUSANNE RENAUDIN, widow of Elie Soblet, aged 63.
17 Apr 1656	JEANNE SOBLET, aged 3 months, daughter of Philbert Soblet.
10 Apr 1659	SUSANNE GERARD, aged 47, wife of Jacques Bryan.
5 May 1659	ELISABETH SAUBLET, aged 9 months, daughter of Philbert Saublet and Anne Godin.
18 Feb 1661	HENRI SOBLET, aged 13, son of Phillipps [*sic*] Soblet and Anne Godin.
16 Apr 1666	ELISABETH SAUBLET, aged 4 months, daughter of Philbert Saublet and Marie [no surname given].

BAPTISMS

11 Oct 1601	MARIE GAILLE, daughter of Jean Gaille, workman of Sedan, and Melotin Bell; godparents, Pierre Brian and Marie Poupporton.
2 Jun 1631	PAUL SAUBERT, child of Robert Saubert, papermaker, and Madelaine La Riviere.
9 Jan 1633	ABRAHAM SAUBERT.
24 Jan 1635	JEANNE SAUBERT.
6 Jul 1637	JEAN SAUBERT.
11 Oct 1640	CHARLES SOUBLET, son of Pierre Soublet of Jametz and Marie ?Fierra, ?Pierra, or ?Sierra (See marriage, 6 Jul 1631, Pierre Saublet and Marie Lespine).
11 Dec 1644	JEAN SOBLET, son of Jean Soblet, notary, and Judith Lombart.
30 Mar 1645	?BHIERY SOBLET, child or Robert Soblet and Madelaine La Riviere; godparents, Gerrard and Jeanne La Riviere, his wife [Note spelling of *Saubert* in first four baptismal entries].
29 Aug 1645	HENRY SOBLET, son of Philbert Soblet and Anne Gaudin; godparents, Jean [*sic*] Soblet and his wife, Susanne Renaudin.

CONCLUSIONS

1. In *DSGR Magazine*, Vol. 38, Fall 1974, No 1, p. 2, it was stated that "Susanne Brian, b. 23 January 1660, was a daughter of Daniel Brian and Rachel Beguin," and was [thought by the transcriber to be] the wife of Abraham Soblet. The marriage record of Susanne Briant, aged 22, to Abraham Soblet (see marriages, hereinbefore) definitely establishes the fact that she was a child of Jacques Briant and Susanne Gerard, deceased. No baptismal record for this Susanne Briant was found.

2. The foregoing records indicate that Philbert Soblet and Abraham Soblet were not brothers. Philbert's parents were Elie Soblet and Susanne Renaudin who lived in Beaumont, and Abraham's parents were Jean Soblet and Judith Lombart.

3. Pierre Saublet, married 6 July 1631, has not been identified. He may have some relationship to the Peter Soblet found in London records in 1690. He is definitely the same Pierre of Jametz, father of Charles, baptized 11 October 1640. All other *Soblet* entries in the Sedan records can he ascribed to either Jean or Philbert.

4. Although coincidental, Abraham Soblet and Susanne Briant named a son *Robert* who was baptized in London in 1698. Could there be a relationship to Robert Saubert, and later spelled Soblet? (see baptismals of *Saubert*, hereinbefore).

5. In *DSGR Magazine*, Vol. 38, *ibid.*, p. 2, the compiler was unsure as to the correct parentage of Anne Soblet, wife of Jacques de Villette. The marriage record of 11 February 16<u>70</u> proves that Anne Soblet who married Jacques de Villette was a daugther of Philbert Soblet and Anne Godin. Either the baptism of Marie, 30 January 16<u>70</u>, daughter of Jacques de Villette and Anne Soblet, or their marriage date may be an error in transcription.

6. Assuming that the *Saubert* entries, beginning 1631 are actually *Soblets*, this would be the earliest known record of any of that surname, while the *Brians* are recorded as early as 1601 (see baptisms, hereinbefore). Some reasons for this name to appear first in the year 1631 may be: 1) The family was converted to Protestantism at this date. 2) They may have come to the Sedan area from "some distance" about 1630. 3) Under increasing disciplinary action from French authorities, smaller Protestant registration of sacramental records.

7. It would appear that the Soblet family left the Sedan area between 1685 and 1698. Pasteur Denis Vatinel, *bibliothéscaire* [librarian], showed the compiler two such entries in the German Registers (Protestant):

> <u>31 Dec 1698</u> *At Emmerich, Jacques Soldet de Sedan, lecteur et faseur de Gaze, sa femme et 4 enfants (Same entry in 1700).*

> -- --- *1698 At Königsburg (Wesel), Jacque Briant, 8 persons, professor "en la langue Française."*

At the library of the Huguegot Society of London [67 Victoria Road, Kensington, London W 8], this additional record was found:

> -- <u>May 1698</u> *Abraham Soblet, his wife and 4 children were on the Royal Bounty Rolls, receiving £1.15.0. Some Soblets (Sobelet) continued in the London area at least until the end of the 18th century. There is a record of a Jacques Sobelet (also known as James Soblet) who was born about 1709 in England and died 6 February 1753.*

APPENDIX 1

Huguenot Migrations

by Cameron H. Allen, FASG
Edited by Kenn Stryker-Rodda, FASG
Originally published in *Genealogical Research, Volume 2*
Part 2, Chapter II, pages 256-290

HUGUENOT MIGRATIONS
Originally published in *Genealogical Research, Volume 2* (1971)

By Cameron Allen, FASG

Not long ago an observer wrote pessimistically: "The (Huguenot) historian's task is not easy because there are no records, no source materials, no fundamental documents to record this migration." Nothing could be much further from the truth. There is a great mass of Huguenot source material extant, far greater than we have a right to expect, and the difficulty comes only from picking one's way judiciously through this rich mass of material, whether published or archival. There is not a single national or religious group where a careful study and consideration of migratory patterns will pay greater dividends than in the case of the French Huguenots.

This is the more important because difficulty arises from the fact that Huguenot migration to America was almost invariably a complex, multi-stage process. Never does a searcher find the typical English one-remove migration from Saffron Walden, Essex, let us say, to Hartford, Connecticut. Obviously, anyone fleeing a French town in dead of night hadn't the ability or the resources to execute a trans-Atlantic voyage immediately. He got out of France in haste in any manner he could, by any route he could, to any destination he could that he believed would be hospitable. Then, and only then, could he ponder the question of whither he desired to go on a permanent basis. This pondering ordinarily was a long process in his new temporary abode. Where could he make the best new life for himself, economically, religiously, and as a social animal?

For many, the ultimate answer seemed to be America, where land was abundant, where the prevailing religion was, if not eagerly hospitable to him, at least comparatively neutral and forebearing. Here, too, as a social animal, he perhaps entertained the hope that he had the best chance of preserving the French tongue and way-of-llfe, among French relatives and friends, untrammelled by the crowding in on him of an alien culture.

But the eventual answer of America was slow in being obvious, and, meanwhile, he may have made two or three moves within Europe outside France in order to find more congenial surroundings and associates from his old home town. He may have fled from France to Switzerland, where officials tended to hurry him on toward more hospitable Germany. After some period there, he may have discovered by correspondence that there was a larger concentration of relatives and home-town friends in London, and migrated there. After some period there, perhaps a group decision was made to cast fortunes in some favored part of America where other friends had preceded him.

In the whole migration process, it cannot be emphasized too strongly that the French were very clannish. They clung together, and sought each other out. They were then, as now, chauvinistic, and decidedly conscious of the superiority of their culture to that of the alien cultures among which they found themselves. Once in America, the clannishness continued. If he found himself unhappy with South Carolina, he migrated to some other French settlement, Boston or New Rochelle. Instances can readily be cited of migration from Massachusetts to South Carolina and also the reverse; from New York to Virginia, from South Carolina to New York.

Consequently, if a student desires to track down his Huguenot ancestor step by step of the way as near as may be, the chances are that he is going to have to familiarize himself not alone with the records of the American colony where the ancestor ultimately settled, but perhaps with the records of another American colony, then with the records of one or two non-French countries of Europe, and ultimately, he may hope, with the records of France itself. In the process he will keep his eyes open for clues as to the reason for a particular migration, in the hope that that will shed further light on other stages of the migration.

The Huguenot hunter has frequently an advantage over the descendant of another nationality: The Huguenot took great care in a variety of records to record his place of origin. Frequently his will will say "formerly of town of X in the Province of Y." Often the pastor of his new congregation or the clerk recorded in his marriage record his place of nativity and his parentage. Sometimes he brought with him his *témoignage* (certificate of communicant status) from his former congregation in France.

What about those Huguenots whose origin is not set out in their records in this country? The most obvious thing to do is to search the records of the Huguenot congregations of Europe beyond the borders of France itself. The chances of success vary considerably. If one is working with an unusual surname, the problem may be fairly simple of solution. If, on the other hand, the name is a very common French surname, the problem may prove insoluble. Take one Manakin Town name: that of Jean Martin. In Switzerland alone one may identify perhaps twenty refugees bearing that name from as many different places in France.

Actually the migratory process may have begun long before his exit from France. He may have come from a town where Protestantism was weak, and have sought out one of the Protestant strongholds, LaRochelle, Sedan, or Montbéliard, so that he could feel more secure. Even after the Revocation he might seek the anonymity of the big city, Paris. These then, are the possible migratory stages, through some combination of which a particular ancestor may have gone:

1. *Within France, either prior to or following the Revocation.*
2. *From France to the most convenient Protestant country.*
3. *From one country of refuge to another European country, seeking relatives.*
4. *From the final European refuge to America.*
5. *From one American colony to another.*
6. *From America, discontented, back to Europe.*
7. *Occasionally, even, back to France itself.*

To be practical, let us examine some well-authenticated instances of multi-stage migration:

- Pierre Villepontoux, born 1643 at Berzerac, near Guyenne; fled to England; from there he migrated to New York City; after residence there he settled in New Rochelle; later he migrated to St. James Parish, Goose Creek, South Carolina, where he died. (I. Heyward Peck, "The Villepontoux Family of South Carolina," *S. C. Hist. & Gen. Magazine*, 50:29-45.)

- Abraham Soblet, born 1648, Sedan, France, son of Jean Soblet, the latter born at Beaumont; Abraham resided at nearby Saint-Menges; fled France by 1681 for Manheim, Germany; by 1693 residing at Wesel; migrated thence to London; from there to Virginia, 1700.

- An excellent example of multiple migrations concerns Pierre David the younger, born in Bolbec in Normandy, son of Abraham David and Henrietta (Hue). His uncle, Pierre David the Elder, had moved from London to Virginia in 1712; Pierre the younger joined his uncle at Manakin Town in Virginia in 1717, and there married Rachel Morel. Not finding Virginia to his liking, apparently, he returned to London about 1728 and there the remainder of his family were born and reared. However, one of his sons, Abraham David, felt the call of the New World, and in the 1740s settled among the French of St. Helena Parish, S. C. Abraham returned to Virginia briefly to dispose of his mother's interest in Morel land in Virginia to his uncle by marriage, David LeSueur, also a Londoner transplanted to Virginia. One of the witnesses to this Virginia deed, Charles Amonnet, presumably spellbound by Abraham David's description of South Carolina, very shortly moved down to South Carolina and settled among the French neighbors of Abraham David. And so another migration between Huguenot settlements had begun. But notice the sequence of migrations involving the Davids: Normandy to London to Virginia, back to London, then to South Carolina; and in every instance a Huguenot settlement was involved. One also derives some hints of the factors at work which produced particular instances of migration from one to another of the settlements.

Because not all stages of a migration can always be predictable, there is value in searching for traces of the name in various European sources and in various American colonies. Even if references thus located do not concern the particular line sought, one may thus find information on other branches of the family. The genealogical world has barely begun to tap the rich veins of information available on a literally world-wide basis to those interested in a given Huguenot family.

Before going into sources available to the student on a country-by-country, colony-by-colony basis, it may be well to set forth the general time limits of the Huguenot migrations. There is a regrettable tendency to feel that all Huguenot migration occurred dramatically almost overnight in 1685 with the Revocation of the Edict of Nantes. Such is certainly not the case. Huguenot migration had begun well over a century in advance of this, as a matter of fact very shortly on the heels of the Reformation in France, with the first of the Wars of Religion. Much of the early international migration of Huguenots was the result of Spanish persecution of Protestants along the constantly-shifting Hispano-French border (present-day Belgium). Many of these persecuted Walloons fled to Germany and England. Much of the Huguenot migration caused by French conditions was an internal one within France, with Protestants in weak areas seeking out the fortified Protestant strongholds. But some Huguenot emigration occurred all the while, and as restrictive measures were applied with greater intensity, there was an increasing rate of exit from France. By 1680 Huguenots seeing the handwriting on the wall were fleeing in great numbers, and the Revocation of the Edict of Nantes in 1685 only proved to be the last straw for those who remained. The exodus from France continued for decades afterward and in a sense may be said to have terminated for religious reasons only with the French Revolution. The period of Huguenot migration may then be placed roughly as between the Reformation in France and the French Revolution (1550-1789).

Estimates of the numbers involved in the migration have varied wildly. Perhaps the sanest most conservative estimate is that of Scoville that only 200,000 (10% of the Huguenots in France) fled France in the period 1681-1720. He estimates that they were scattered as follows:

United Provinces (Netherlands)	75,000
England	50,000
Ireland	10,000
Germany	30,000
Switzerland	25,000

plus small groups to America, South Africa, Denmark, etc.

France

The materials available for the study of the origins of Huguenot families are rich and varied. Of first utility, unless the place of origin is already known, are the following:

Société de l'histoire du Protestantisme français. BULLETIN. 1852 —
>   There exists a three-volume index (pub. 1928-1931) to the first 50 volumes; unfortunately, from that point forward it is necessary to consult the index to each volume. The Bulletin has printed many valuable documents concerned not alone with Huguenots within France, but with Huguenots of the dispersion as well.

Haag, Eugene; et Emile Haag. *La France protestante.* Paris, 1847-1859. 10 v.; 2d edition, Paris, 1877-1887, 6 v. only, which carry the alphabet to G (Gasparin).
>   The ms. materials for its projected continuation were deposited in the library of the Société de l'histoire du Protestantisme français. Haag contains many clues that can be valuable if selected judiciously and followed up.

In addition to the above works of national and international coverage, many monographs and periodical articles exist which limit their coverage of Huguenot history to a province, a department, or a community. It is surprising how many special local historical journals and *annuaires* exist for even very small towns. These works, if they can first be ascertained and then a set located, can be even more valuable than the works of broader scope. References to a portion of these may be located through good bibliographies included in such works as:

Mours, Samuel. *Les églises réformées en France.* Paris, Llbrarie-Protestante, 1958.

Scovell, Warren C. *The Persecution of Huguenots and French Economic Development, 1680-1720.* Berkeley, Univ. of California Press, 1960.

When printed sources available in this country have been exhausted, it may be desirable to visit Paris and make use of the library and archives of the Société de l'histoire du Protestentisme français, 54, Rue des Saints-Peres, Paris, VIIe. This venerable society, founded in 1852, possessed as of 1932 some 70,900 volumes of printed works, and some 12,000 manuscripts, including some originals and some copies of Huguenot parochial registers, both in France and abroad. The manuscript holdings as of 1930 are cataloged in:

France. Ministère de l'instruction publique. *Catalogue général des manuscrits des Bibliothèques Publiques de France.* Tome 48. Paris, 1930.

The library is open Monday, Tuesday, Wednesday and Thursday afternoons from 1:00 to 5:00, except that' it is entirely closed from July 14 to the end of September.

The Archives Nationales, Paris, may also be Visited with profit if one knows what he is after. A letter of introduction is required in order to gain access to its facilities. The archival *Serie TT* contains such contemporary documents as listings of possessions abandoned by religious fugitives who had fled France, abjurations of "heresy," banishments, certificates of conversion to the Roman faith, requests to re-enter France, imprisonments, and *procès-verbaux* of the trials of fugitives. Some of these have, of course, been printed in the *Bulletin*, but many have not. They are described by Edith Thomas, "Les sources de l'histoire du Protestantisme aux Archives Nationales," in the *Bulletin*, 1949, p. 107. Several other archives in Paris contain significant Huguenot material:

Archives (Administratives du Ministère) de la Guerre

Archives de la Bastille (at the Bibliothèque de l'Arsenal)
   (individual dossiers on religious prisoners)

La Bibliothèque de l'Institut (some parish registers)

Archives (Le Ministère) des Affaires Étrangères

Outside Paris, the most important of the archives are the departmental archives, some eighty-eight in number. They are of uneven importance. Some have felt the heavy hand of war; others are archives not alone for the department, but also for the mother province from which the department was carved. The archives of the ancient province of Dauphiné, for example, are to be found at the Archives Départementales de l'Isère at Grenoble. The archives of Burgundy are in the Archives Départementales de la Côte d'Or at Dijon.

While it is far more pleasant and profitable to visit the Archives Départementales, one may frequently obtain *some* vital information by correspondence, if one states his problem clearly in French, makes a request for a moderate bit of information and encloses an International Reply Coupon.

Assuming the place of origin of a Huguenot ancestor is known, obviously the most valuable information obtainable is probably going to come from the Protestant registers of the locality. Many of these registers have perished, but many more still exist than we have a right to hope for. Very few of these Protestant registers have been published:

deHallu, Johannes. "Lille, Bethune, and Mons,"
   Huguenot Society of London Proceedings, 16:98.

Jallobert, Paul-Paris. *Registres de Vitre* (Brittany).

Jallobert, Paul-Paris. *Registres de Dinan* (Brittany).

Lart, C. E. "LaRoche-Beaucourt in the Angoumois," 1579-1612,
   Huguenot Society of London Proceedings, 12:408-416.

Lart, C. E. *Loudun*, 1566-1582. 1905.

Lart, C. E. *Caen*. 1907.

Though unpublished, handmade copies of a number of others exist: those of Montauban, LaRochelle, St. Quentin, and Sedan are preserved in the Card Index of the Bibliothèque Wallonne, for example. Others are at the Société de l'Histoire du Protestantisme Français, Paris; in the Archives de l'Église Réformée in Nîmes ; and fragments of others are in the Lart Collection at the Huguenot Society of London.

Where copies are not available, one of the most difficult tasks is to determine (1) whether the originals survive, and, if so, (2) where they are preserved. Unfortunately no master list has ever been prepared. (The current Mormon work in France to which we shall presently allude will in due time probably fill this hiatus.) In the face of this situation, there are procedures which may be followed, nonetheless. A first step is to consult:

> Mours, Samuel. *Les églises réformées en France.* Paris, 1958. Originally published in part in the *Société de l'histoire du Protestantisme français. Bulletin.*

M. Mours attempts to list every hamlet in France (alphabetically by department) which is known from any source to have possessed a Huguenot congregation. If it is thus determined that a locality had a Huguenot congregation, the next step may be to consult the *Société de l'histoire du Protestantisme français. Bulletin*, Table Alphabétique, Tome III, pp. 461-64, sub "Registres." This will lead the searcher to any information on the location and availability of parish registers for any given locality which appeared in the first fifty volumes of the Bulletin. Of course, some of this information is outdated, for some places of deposit have changed in the meantime.

Failing to find information on registers by the method above outlined, the searcher might try writing (in French) to the Archives of the municipality or of the department. Parish registers in France *may* (rarely) date as far back as 1539, when they were first required by law to be kept by the parish. In 1666/67 congregational vital records were required to be kept in duplicate, the duplicate to be turned over by the parish to the Greffe du Tribunal Civil (Office of the Clerk of the Court). At the time of the French Revolution, the task of recording vital statistics was transferred to the Mairie (Town Hall) where the parish priests and ministers were required to deposit all the old registers in their possession. From that time the new registers are known as the *Registres de l'État Civil*, the older deposited registers as the *Registres de l'État Civil Catholique* or the *Registres de l'État Civil Protestant* (or *Non-Catholique*).

One should first inquire of the Mairie as to the availability of given registers. They are kept either in the Bureau de l'État Civil (Registry Office) of the Mairie, in the Archives Municipales (or Communales), or in the library of the Mairie. The duplicates from 1666/67 on either remain with the Greffe du Tribunal Civil or have been turned over to the Archives Départementales. Occasionally also the Mairie copy has been lodged with the Archives Départementales, apparently as a result of an abortive attempt in the 1920s to centralize the registers in the Archives Départementales. Many of the old registers have alphabetical indices for each volume, but each "volume" typically covers a very short span of time.

If the registers are not to be found either at the Mairie or at the Archives Départementales, it is possible that they may still be located at the Archives Nationales, occasionally at the Bibliothèque de l'Arsenal, at the Société de l'Histoire du Protestantisme Français, or at the Archives de l'Église Réformée in Nîmes. One register has strayed as far away as Charleston, South Carolina!

The mention of the deposit of the Roman Catholic parish registers in the Mairie along with Huguenot registers should serve as a reminder that the careful genealogist *must* search the Roman Catholic registers of the area for information on the family even though he may start with the assumption that the particular family under investigation was thoroughly, loyally, and irradicably Huguenot. In the first place, this assumption should not be made. Some families were divided in their religious allegiance; other families, while Huguenot, occasionally found it essential to record ecclesiastical acts in the Roman Catholic registers. Particularly is this so after 1685, when the French stopped recognizing a Huguenot marriage ceremony as having any legal efficacy, the partners simply being regarded as "living in sin" unless the union had been blessed by a priest. Rather than bear this stigma in the eyes of the community, some Huguenot couples did resort to the Roman Catholic Church for this purpose alone.

The Genealogical Society of the Church of Jesus Christ of Latter-Day Saints in Salt Lake City has since 1959 been engaged in microfilming the registers deposited in various French archives, and out of eighty-eight départements, the Roman Catholic registers from earliest extant date down to approximately 1860 have been copied almost completely for the following five départements (as of 1967):

Ardennes	approximately 400 parishes
Drôme	approximately 300 parishes
Eure	approximately 500 parishes
Indre et Loire	approximately 350 parishes
Oise	approximately 225 parishes

Microfilming is currently being conducted in Calvados, Loir-et-Cher, Nièvre, and Ardèche. The invitations of the departmental archivists are an important factor in determining the sequence of the microfilming operations. The microfilmers sent by the Society to France are further attempting to locate and copy the parish registers yet in the possession of the municipal archives and town halls. This is being done at the same time that the largest part of the filming is progressing at the départemental archives. By such a thorough operation, the Mormons will ultimately make available to the genealogical world a complete set of the older extant vital records from France. In due course a genealogist will be able to determine very quickly exactly what records still exist for a given locality in France, whether Huguenot or Roman Catholic. Records already copied are now available in Salt Lake City, having been entered in the magnificent card catalogue of the Society alphabetically by community *within* the département.

Having first utilized specific Huguenot sources and all religious vital registers available, the searcher will next wish to consult more general primary and secondary sources. These are described in two succinct articles which should be consulted:

Rubicam, Milton. "Pre-American Ancestry: France," pp. 391-395, in American Society of Genealogists, *Genealogical Research: Methods and Sources.* 1960.

Rabino di Borgomale, H. L. "Genealogical Research in France," *The Genealogists' Magazine*, vol. 9, pp. 565-571 (Sept. 1946), erroneously printed as vol. 10, pp. 1-7.

Particular attention is called therein to the Minutes of the Notaries Public (wills, deeds of division, marriage contracts, deeds of purchase and of sale), kept in various depositories, and the Registers of "Insinuations," ordinarily consisting of abstracts of notarial documents subject to taxation.

The Netherlands (The United Provinces)

Of all the receiving countries for Huguenot emigrants, the United Provinces played perhaps the most prominent role. A larger number of Huguenots probably settled in the Protestant portion of the Low Countries than in any other nation. A good number of strong refugee congregations sprang up, some of which are still flourishing. Nearly a century ago, in 1877, a historical society was founded, the Commission pour l'Histoire des Églises Wallonnes, which, in the quarter century which followed, produced a remarkable genealogical monument: a card index to all entries 1566-1812 (variously estimated at from 1½ million to three million) contained in all extant Huguenot and Walloon registers in the Netherlands and Belgium, a great many extant Huguenot registers in Germany, and in four of the largest Huguenot congregations in France: Montauban, LaRochelle, St. Quentin, and Sedan.

This card index ("Collection des fiches") is housed in the Bibliotheque Wallonne, Leyden, The Netherlands. [Currently (1970) and possibly temporarily housed at the Centraal Bureau voor Genealogie, 18 Nassaulaan, The Hague. (Ed.)] The cards are arranged alphabetically by family name, lexicographically by given names, and at the same time chronologically for each family. Each card is headed with the original and correctly-spelled family name. The variants in spelling and subsequently corrupted forms of the names are given between brackets, and the most deviating corruptions are entered on cross-reference cards. Approximately two-thirds of the cards deal with the eighteenth century Netherlands, and are consequently of less interest to Americans than the earlier ones. Most of the cards are in French, but a few later cards are in Dutch.

Around 1900 it was planned to issue a printed catalogue of all the cards, but this plan was abandoned after the deaths of several of the more energetic originators of the index. Just prior to the 1929 crash, the Commission Wallonne agreed to assist the Huguenot Societies of America in making two card-index copies of the older cards in the index at relatively modest cost, but a "modest" cost in 1928 had become out of the question with the economic debacle of 1929.

It is a pleasure to report that the omnipresent L.D.S. microfilmers succeeded in making a copy of the entire index and bringing it back to Salt Lake City, where it is available for consultation on microfilm in 199 rolls (Call Number: 26809, Pts. 1-199). Those who find it as much a trip to Salt Lake City as to Leyden will be pleased to learn that for a modest fee (half a guilder per entry, about 14 cents) the staff of the Bibliotheque Wallonne is prepared to provide all entries on a given family of interest. This is a simple and inexpensive matter when the family name is an uncommon one; it may be both more tedious for the staff and more costly for the inquirer if the name is a common one. Letters to the Bibliotheque Wallonne should be written in French, giving all available information pertinent to the inquiry, should inquire as to the number of cards relating to the given family, and should enclose an International Reply Coupon. Address: Secretaire de la Commission de l'Histoire des Églises Wallonnes, Pieterskerkhof 40, Leyden, The Netherlands.

In addition to its monumental card index, the Commission has also issued since 1885 a *Bulletin*, only partially available in this country: 1st series, 1885-1892; 2nd series, 1893-1895; 3rd series, 1896-1927; 4th series, 1928-1938; 5th series, 1942 to date.

It would be well to check to see whether a history of any branch of the family in the Netherlands has been written; these are indexed in:

Beresteyn, Dr. E. A. van. *Genealogisch Reportorium*. The Hague, Centraal Bureau voor Genealogie. 1948.

Two survey articles on general genealogical sources and techniques in The Netherlands should be consulted by those whose Huguenot connections in The Netherlands were other than very transitory:

Fahy, T. C. "Genealogical Research in The Netherlands," *The Genealogists' Magazine* (London), vol. 13, pp. 366-71 (Dec. 1961).

Hoffman, William. "Pre-American Ancestry: The Netherlands," pp. 382-90, in American Society of Genealogists, *Genealogical Research: Methods and Sources*. 1960.

The observation should be made that the Genealogical Society in Salt Lake City has an extremely large collection of microfilm copies of many of the primary sources referred to in these articles, including very large numbers of parish registers.

A small Belgian society has also published material on Protestantism in the Catholic portion of the Low Countries, including some information on French refugees: The *Société d'histoire du Protestantisme belge Bulletin* has been published in four series (in either French or Flemish): 1st series, 1904-1913; 2nd series, 1914-1935; 3rd series, 1936-1951; 4th series, 1952 to date.

Switzerland

The Swiss cantons were, because of their geographical location, one of the most important exits from France. However, the French remained in Switzerland in much smaller numbers than they entered it. The Swiss cantons could ill afford to sustain additional population, and Swiss authorities busied themselves with arrangements for resettlement of the French in the underpopulated German states. Other French left Switzerland for the Netherlands, England, or America.

Suggestions for research in Switzerland are contained in:

> Lacoste, Auguste. "Le Grand Refuge (1685-1700) Particulièrement en Suisse: Sources et Bibliographie." (*Publications de la Société Suisse d'Études Généalogiques*, Series 1, Fasc. 19). Bern, 1951, or *Schweizerische Gesellschaft für Familienforschung, Veröffentlichungen*.

The state archives in the Protestant cantons (especially Geneva and Zurich) contain much, as does the Bibliothèque Publique de Geneva. The most important single documents are the censuses of the French refugees made in 1693, 1696, and 1698, since one may find many references to places of origin of a given refugee, he may be able to trace into another country. These censuses were published in the *Bulletin*, tomes 82-88 (1933-1939). (*Société de l'histoire du Protestantisme français*.)

Germany

Many of the refugees who initially sought refuge in Switzerland moved on to the various German states, which were still underpopulated from the decimations of the Thirty Years' War, and eager to receive additional co-religionists. Of course, there was direct migration into the German states from France as well. The largest number of the French settled in Brandenburg-Prussia, but there were also important settlements in Hessen-Kassel, Mittelfranken, Wurtemberg, der Kurpfalz, Niedersachsen, and Baden-Durlach. The French who settled in the Hansesatic cities carried the blood through the Baltic area, just as the French who settled among the Dutch found themselves settling wherever the Dutch themselves settled, in South Africa, in South America, and in St. Petersburg in Russia.

Several of the German rulers vied with each other within weeks of the Revocation to encourage Huguenot immigration, by granting concessions and privileges to the refugees who settled within their territories: housing, tax exemption for a period, as well as all the rights of natural-born citizens. The most famous of these grants was the Potsdam Decree of the Great Elector Friedrich Wilhelm, which helped account for the heavy migration into his territories.

Much information on the Huguenots in Germany has been published by the Huguenot organization in that country, the Deutscher Hugenotten Verein (founded 1890), in two series: *Geschichtsblätter*, 1890-1937, 1963 —; *Der Deutsche Hugenott*, 1929 —.

These have published numerous original documents, as well as studies of given groups and congregations. Each volume has an index to all names of persons. Numerous individual volumes and sets have also dealt with narrower geographical areas. One of the fullest works is:

> Erman et Reclam. *Mémoires pour servir à l'histoire des réfugiés français dans les états du Roi*. Berlin, 1782-1799. 9 v.

Another good illustration of this class of work is:

> Tollin, H. *Geschichte der französischen Kolonie von Magdeberg*. Halle, 1886-1894. 6 v.

An overall view of Huguenot settlements in the German states is given in:

> Erbe, Hellmuth. *Die Hugenotten in Deutschland*. Essen, 1937.

England

It is well to remember that there were two principal waves of Huguenot immigration into England, the first occurring circa 1560, and the second circa 1680-1695. The first wave, which produced considerable American Huguenot ancestry, was the result of Spanish persecution of Protestants both in the Low Countries and along the constantly-shifting Hispano-French border (modern Belgium), the home of the Walloons.

The Walloons and French who came to England settled in Norwich, London, Canterbury, Southampton, Thorney (Cambs.), Bristol, Plymouth, Stonehouse, Thorpe-le-Soken, Dover, Faversham, Exeter, Dartmouth, Barnstaple, Bideford, Greenwich, and the Channel Islands.

To the Huguenot Society of London, founded in 1885, the genealogical world owes perhaps its most significant series of published Huguenot material:

> Huguenot Society of London. *Publications*. v. 1 (1887-88)
> This series has made available virtually all the extant Huguenot Parish Registers to be found in England and Ireland, as well as those of Guisnes and Cadzand. In addition, its volumes print the important Letters of Denization and Acts of Naturalization for Aliens in England; and the Returns of Aliens Dwelling in the City and Suburbs of London. All the volumes are indexed with great care.

> Huguenot Society of London. *Proceedings*. v. 1 (1885-86).
> This periodical contains many significant articles on specific congregations and families, as well as important finding lists.

The Huguenot Society of London maintains a library at University College, Gower Street, London, W.C. 1. The library is open upon advance application by members as follows: Monday-Friday, 9:30-5:00, and Saturday, 9:30-12:30, except during summer vacation. Library searches involving a fee can be arranged.

The library is important for several manuscript collections it possesses: the Royal Bounty

Papers (charities for the benefit of the Refugees) ; the Henry Wagner Huguenot pedigrees — some 900 in number, many of them unpublished; the Charles Edmund Lart Manuscript Collection, which includes notes and extracts from a number of Huguenot Registers in French archives; and the Henry Wagner Collection of Abstracts of Wills of Huguenots at Somerset House, as well as some in other depositories ; arranged alphabetically and with a full index.

The latter collection, while extremely valuable and a great time-saver, is certainly not exhaustive. It is fuller and more reliable for Prerogative Court of Canterbury wills at Somerset House than those for the Archdeaconry Court of London and the Commissary Court of London (both at the Guildhall); the Episcopal Consistory Court of London (at the London County Council Record Office) ; and the Archdeaconry Court of Middlesex (at the Middlesex County Record Office). These latter wills should be searched independently by those with London Huguenot problems.

It is a mistake to confine the search for Huguenot vital statistics to Huguenot registers alone. Many ordinary Church of England parish registers contain a few or many Huguenot references. Particularly popular with Huguenots in London were St. Giles in the Fields, Christ Church, Spitalfields, and St, Leonards, Shoreditch. Any of the London parish registers conceivably could turn up items of interest, of course, and those that are readily available in print, such as those in the British Record Society's *Index Library* and the Harleian Society series, should be methodically searched via their indices.

Occasionally the student of an American Huguenot family will find that a closely related British Huguenot family has been written up (the Lucadou family, for example) if he consults the indices to printed British pedigrees:

Marshall, George W. *The Genealogist's Guide* (3rd ed., 1903).

Whitmore, W. B. *Genealogical Guide.* 4 vols., 1947-53.

Ireland

The extant Irish Huguenot registers have all been published, as mentioned, by the Huguenot Society of London. As in the case of England, the parish registers of the then-established Church of Ireland should also be searched for Huguenot entries outside their ethnic congregations. The person whose Huguenot tracking takes him to Ireland may wish to read for background material, despite certain deficiencies:

Lee, Grace Lawless. *The Huguenot Settlements in Ireland.* London, 1936.

For a wealth of research suggestions, one should consult:

Falley, Margaret Dickson. *Irish and Scotch-Irish Ancestral Research: A Guide to the Genealogical Records, Methods and Sources in Ireland.* Evanston, 1962. Especially (but of course not limited to) Chapter 4: "Records of the French Huguenot Churches and Settlements in Ireland," pp. 309-334.

South Africa

A group of Huguenots was landed at the Cape of Good Hope by seven Dutch East Indiamen in 1688-89. They settled primarily at Drakenstein and French Hoek and formed an important part of early South African white ancestry. Information on the settlement may be found in:

Botha, Graham. *The French Refugees at the Cape*. Capetown, 1919.

Hérisson, Charles D. "Les Réfugiés Huguenots du XVIIe Siècle, et la Survivance Francaise en Afrique du Sud." *Bulletin de la Société du Protestantisme Français* (Avril-Juin, 1953).

A copy of the Drakenstein register is at Leyden, as are those for Paramaribo in Pernambuco.

MIGRATION TO AMERICA

The second stage of Huguenot migration, from one of the Protestant receiving nations of Europe to America, had factors working both in its favor and opposing it. In favor of the second migration was the availability of large tracts of undeveloped land and greater economic opportunity. Growing out of this factor was the possibility of developing self-consciously French, ethnically monolithic communities, where the French could continue their own tongue to some extent and where French Calvinism hopefully would not be polluted by contact with the more conservative Protestantism of Germany (Lutheranism) or with the even more conservative Anglicanism of England or its alternative there, the over-liberal elements of nonconformity.

Opposing the second migration were at least two other factors. The first was a temporary one which arose out of the almost-mystical thought of one of the leading Huguenot writers of the day, Jurieu. This revered man predicted that in 1689 the anti-Huguenot measures of France would be reversed and that the Protestants would be welcomed back to their beloved motherland. As long as this hope burned in any French heart, there was a great reluctance to venture any farther geographically than would permit a hurried return to France. When the year 1689 came and went without fulfillment of Jurieu's prediction, and further years passed making a change-of-heart unlikely in France, there was a gradual relinquishment of this bright hope. As a matter of fact, it was exactly a century later that, with the French Revolution, a law was passed welcoming the descendants of the religious expatriates back, and permitting any descendant in any degree of any man or woman exiled for the sake of religion to claim his birthright, French citizenship.

The other opposing factor was the reluctance of the English colonists to permit settlement of the French in their own communities. The wild fear was entertained that the French Huguenots, if permitted to settle separately, would somehow join forces eventually with the hated French Catholics of Canada to upset the yet precarious English hold on North America; that somehow ties of French blood and civilization would prove to be stronger than religious differences. Consequently the English tended to discourage unduly large concentrations of the Huguenots which would have been the French preference and tendency.

The single work that covers the Huguenot migration to this country most fully is:

Baird, Charles W. *History of the Huguenot Emigration to America*. New York, Dodd, Mead, 1885. 2 V.

Because this work is to be found widely throughout this country in libraries which have virtually nothing else on the subject, a few words are in order. It is an extremely interesting and potentially useful work. There are many clues on the origin of particular families, which should be followed up by those interested. However, the author recorded certain traditions of various descendants, many of which are more than doubtful. He was also given to some real leaps of faith in identifying a settler with a common French name in this country with a person of a similar name in France, when there was no documentary evidence to connect the two. In sum: to be used, but to be used intelligently and with caution.

New York

From the days of Dutch control, New York was an early favorite with the Huguenots and Walloons. In fact, the generalization can be made that wherever the Dutch settled, the Huguenots were quick to follow. The well-known Joris Rapelje and wife Cathalyntje Trico arrived with a party of fellow Walloons in 1624. Some Walloon and Huguenot baptisms may be located in New York Reformed Dutch Church Records (*Baptisms, 1639-1800*, and *Marriages, 1639-1801*), New York Genealogical and Biographical Society *Collections*, volumes I-III.

The influx of Post-Revocation Huguenots into New York City is recorded in:

Wittmeyer, the Rev. Alfred V., ed. *Registers of the Births, Marriages and Deaths of the 'Église Françoise a la Nouvelle York,' from 1688 to 1804*. New York, 1886. (Huguenot Society of America. *Collections*. v. 1) (Reprint 1968, Genealogical Publishing Co., Baltimore.)

In the meantime many Huguenots and Walloons had arrived in the 1650s-1660s and proceeded to spread from New Amsterdam proper into nearby communities. Harlem was laid out in 1658, nearly half the early inhabitants being French. For these consult:

Riker, James. *Harlem (City of New York): its origin and early annals* ... New York, 1881.

Riker, James. *Revised History of Harlem (City of New York): its origin and early annals* ... New York, 1904.

A sizable number of French took up residence on Staten Island, where they formed a French congregation. Their parish register has been lost; eventually the congregation was absorbed into the local Dutch Reformed Church or into the Anglican congregation. Some French entries occur in:

Port Richmond Dutch Reformed Church. Baptisms, 1696-1790. *N.Y.G.B. Record*, v. 36-37.

Still other French settled at Bushwick, Long Island, or at Flatbush:

Flatbush Dutch Reformed Church Records. Holland Society of New York. Yearbook, 1898.

New Paltz (*le "nouveau Palatinat"*) was founded by a group of French refugees who had come from Frankenthal and Mutterstadt in the Palatinate (*die Pfalz*) and the settlement was named from that fact. A French congregation was formed there in 1683. Prior to that time, some entries relating to the group occur in:

Hoes, Roswell R., ed. Baptismal and Marriage Registers of the Old Dutch Church of Kingston, Ulster County, New York, N.Y., 1891.

Vital records from 1683-1702, 1730-1799, are contained in:

Records of the Reformed Dutch Church of New Paltz, New York. New York, 1896. (Holland Society of New York. *Collections.* v. 3 p. 60 ff) and also in

LeFevre, Ralph. *History of New Paltz, New York, and Its Old Families.* 2nd ed. Albany, 1909. (pp. 37-43)

Neither version is satisfactorily edited, however. Individual genealogies have been issued for a larger percentage of the New Paltz families than is perhaps the case with any other Huguenot settlement in America. Some further information is contained in the *Publications* of The Huguenot Historical Society of New Paltz (1953-).

Somewhat later in its establishment was New Rochelle. This Huguenot community received many of its settlers from the French islands of the West Indies, from New York City, from Oxford, Mass., and from the Narragansett settlement in Rhode Island. Sources to be consulted for its families include:

Forbes, Jeanne A. *Records of the Town of New Rochelle, 1699-1828.* New Rochelle, 1916.

Old Wills of New Rochelle: Copies of Wills by Citizens of New Rochelle, New York, 1784-1830. New Rochelle, New Rochelle Chapter, DAR, 1951.

Seacord, Morgan H. *Biographical Sketches and Index of the Huguenot Settlers of New Rochelle, 1687-1776.* New Rochelle, The Huguenot and Historical Association of New Rochelle, 1941.

In addition to the specific Huguenot works cited above, the researcher will be sure to look at the standard general works which contain basic source material on families of whatever nationality, including such items as:

Abstracts of Wills on File in the Surrogate's Office, City of New York, 1665-1800. (N.Y. Historical Society *Collections*) 17 v.

Fernow, Berthold, ed. Calendar of Wills on File and Recorded at Albany.

New England

The most enduring of the Huguenot settlements in New England was that which organized the French congregation in Boston. This organization existed from 1685 to 1748 when it ceased, because of the decline of numbers through migration elsewhere, such as to South Carolina and New York; and through absorption of the French into the general populace.

Another Massachusetts settlement about which much has been written, Oxford, came to naught because of Indian attacks. The surviving inhabitants dispersed to Boston, to Milford and Hartford, Connecticut, and to New Rochelle and New York City.

The interesting settlement of the French at Narragansett, Rhode Island, was also short-lived, its inhabitants going largely to New Rochelle and New York City. The congregation's vital records exist from 1686-1691, and are published in the *New York Genealogical and Biographical Record* (v. 70, pp. 236-241, 359-365; and v. 71, pp. 51-61.)

Pennsylvania

While numerous French settled in Pennsylvania, research for their origins is probably more difficult than anywhere else in the American colonies. The reason for this is that they were very decidedly diffused among the vastly more numerous Germans with whom they came from the Rhineland to the New World. They belonged entirely to German-speaking congregations, and French names are retrieved only with great difficulty and discerning imagination from under the German encrustations which conceal their origin. Several French names can be recognized in the record of St. Joseph's (Hill) Church, Oley, Berks County, for example. (Transcription in Franklin and Marshall College, Lancaster, Pa.) Others settled in Lancaster County.

Virginia

Huguenot settlement in Virginia began very early. Dating from 1621 is a petition of some Walloons to the Virginia Company. They were welcomed haltingly by the Company who "conceive that for the prosperity and principally the securing of the plantation in his Majesty's obedience, it is not expedient that the said families should set down in one gross and entire body, but that they should rather be placed by convenient numbers in the principal cities, boroughs and corporations in Virginia."

In the 1620s several French "vignorones" out from London settled in Elizabeth City: Elias laGuard, James Bonall, and David Poole. Their assignment was to introduce the culture of the grape to Virginia.

In the 1630s, Charles River County [now York] became the home of such men as Nicholas Jarnew, John Broche, William Savary, Nicholas Sabrell, Nicholas Martian, Giles Tavernor, John Vallett, and John Galliott. In the same decade, the Upper County of New Norfolk attracted settlers bearing such names as John Bodin, William Durand, Jasper Laflyn, Jon. Helier, Wal. Manet, Esay Delaware, Abraham Peltree, Robert Brasseur, Marin Delamundayes, Emblence Prouse, Reene Besairdier, Francis Mauldin, Thomas Serridon, John Carre. Isle of Wight County at the same time contained James Pointeau, Anthony Lufurrier, and Peter Rey.

Additional French names appear in these and other counties in the 1640s, 1650s and 1660s. The southeastern portion of Virginia in this era seems to have held particular attraction for French settlers in the counties of Lower Norfolk, Princess Anne, and Isle of Wight.

In the Post-Revocation period, there were two principal French settlements effected in Virginia; Manakin Town and the freshes of Mattapony, as well as smaller scattered groups at such places as Williamsburg and in Hanover County. An excellent history of Manakin Town gives the background of the entire French migration of 1700-01 to Virginia:

Bugg, James L., Jr., "The French Huguenot Frontier Settlement of Manakin Town," *Virginia Magazine of History and Biography*, 61:359-394.

The migration utilized four ships, which arrived within a few months of each other: the *Mary and Ann*, the *Peter and Anthony*, the *Nassau*, and a fourth unidentified one. The passengers on disembarking headed in various directions, but the two largest groups settled at Manakin Town and on the Mattapony.

The following works enable many Manakin Town families to construct reliable genealogies, despite the destruction of many records:

Published primary sources:

Brock, Robert A. "Documents, Chiefly Unpublished Relating to the Huguenot Emigration to Virginia and to the Settlement at Manakin-Town." *Virginia Historical Collections*, new series, v. 5 (Richmond, Virginia Historical Society, 1886; reprinted 1966). This basic work contains the following material: the passenger list of the *Peter and Anthony* (pp. 14-16); the Dec. 1700 list of the same (pp. 22-25); the passenger list of the *Nassau* (pp. 29-34) ; the Falling Creek Miller's list of Feb. 1701 (pp. 26-28); the Wm. Bird list of 10 Nov. 1701 (pp. 45-48); and the Parish Register of King William Parish.

Virginia Historical Collections, n.s., v. 6, contains the passenger list of the *Mary and Ann*.

Calendar of State Papers, Colonial Series, 18:456-457, contains a variant passenger list.

Virginia Magazine of History and Biography, v. 11-13, contains the Vestry Book of King William Parish (with tithe lists).

Jones, W. Mac, ed. *The Douglas Register*.

Unpublished primary sources (all available on microfilm at Richmond): (Resort must be had to all these as the Manakin Town area fell within the various starred counties at the different periods indicated.)

Virginia Patent Books, especially Books 10 and 11, which contain many of the French grants; * Henrico County Records (Wins, Deeds, Order Books, etc.) (1700-1727/8); * Goochland County Records (1727/8-1748/9); * Chesterfield County Records (1749-); * Cumberland County Records (1748/9-1777); * Powhatan County Records (1777-).

Western migration took their descendants in numbers to such counties as Amelia, Albemarle, Buckingham (the records of this county are very largely destroyed, which has created many puzzles), and Charlotte.

Much material has been published on the Manakin Town families in:

The Huguenot Society Founders of Manakin in the Colony of Virginia. *Publications* (1924-). (This material is of uneven merit, but does include such things as Bible records unavailable elsewhere and wills from the unpublished county records above.)

The student of a family settled on the Mattapony faces a much more difficult problem. Most of Brock's work above applies to Manakin Town rather than Mattapony. Most of the Mattapony settlers seem to have come on the fourth ship, the passenger list of which did not survive. The Mattapony group settled in what was then King William County, perhaps attracted there by the tact that a Huguenot clergyman, James Boisseau, had settled there a decade or so earlier.

Later the Mattapony area of King William County was cut off as Caroline County. Here we know that another Huguenot clergyman, the Rev. Francis Fontaine, served in St. Margaret's Parish, Caroline County, 1721-1722. Unfortunately the county records of both King William and Caroline (save the Order Books of the latter) have been destroyed, as have the Church of England Parish Records. Among the Huguenots resident in this settlement were the families of Seay, Peay, Derieux, Desmaizeau, Dismukes [originally DesMeaux, it is said], Jeter, Mallin, LaFoe, Chenault, DeJarnette, Micou, Flippo, Duval, Vigon, Micalle, Debusie, and DeShazo [DeChazeau]. The Mattapony settlement seems never to have been as strong as Manakin Town, and there was some tendency to gravitate from the first to the latter. Charles Perrault and Joseph Asselin both early removed from the one area to the other. Contact between the two settlements must certainly have been maintained for decades. Families from both participated and were closely associated in the development of Amelia County.

Several French families of 1700 settled at Williamsburg, including the Contesses, the Marots and the LaPrades. Bruton Parish records contain a number of Huguenot entries. The LaPrades later became identified with the Manakin Town area, another example of the magnetism that Manakin continued to have for the French.

North Carolina

Very little has been written on Huguenot settlements in North Carolina. The migration there tended to be a sub-migration or offshoot of the South Carolina or Virginia Huguenot settlements.

The most significant migration involved a fairly substantial group of the Manakin Town settlers who, after some religious squabbles, left Virginia under the leadership of the Rev. Claude Phillippe de Richebourg about 1707 and established themselves on the Trent River in (what is now) Craven County. As a result of the Indian massacre of 1711, this infant settlement ceased for a time to exist, the few survivors apparently moving on to the Santee in South Carolina. A generation later, about 1736, a few other of the Manakin families resettled the area, most notably Calvet, Caillau, Cantepie, Debroul, Depp, Dupree, Fonvielle, and Morrissett. Other French names found here include Provow, Rieusset, Legardere, LaPierre, and Autrey.

Early French names occur in other parts of North Carolina, as in Chowan and Perquimans Counties. These latter French were quite probably overflow from the French population of adjacent southeastern Virginia. One of the most prominent French families in North Carolina was the later arriving DeRosset family of New Hanover County. Other French New Hanoverians included the Poitevints [Portevints], the Befrits, the DuBoses, and the Burdeaus [Bourdeaus]. Most of the New Hanoverians probably came from South Carolina, adjacent.

South Carolina

In no American colony did the Huguenots play a more conspicuous role than in South Carolina, even though their settlement here was later than in New York and Virginia. They came in several discernible waves, the first being in 1680 and the last properly Huguenot wave arriving in 1764. The first group to arrive was brought in the ship *Richmond*. The most valuable single document concerning these early South Carolina Huguenots is:

"Liste des Francois et Suisses Refugiez en Caroline qui souhaittent d'etre naturalizes Anglais." Published in Huguenot Society of South Carolina *Transactions*, no. 5 (1897), pp. 26-42, and as a separate pamphlet, 1888, by Thomas Gaillard Thomas, New York City. This list was prepared about 1696 concerning 154 heads of family who desired naturalization. The information set out includes the place of origin of both husband and wife, the names of their parents, and the names and birthplaces of their children.

Much other valuable material on the South Carolina Huguenots, including translations of French wills, is contained in the Huguenot Society of South Carolina *Transactions*, (1889-).

The most convenient source for the Huguenot will now, however, is:

Moore, Caroline T., and Agatha Aimar Simmons, comp. *Abstracts of the Wills of the State of South Carolina, 1670-1740*. Columbia, S. C., Bryan, 1960.

Moore, Caroline T., comp. Abstracts of the Wills of the State of South Carolina, 1740-1760. Columbia, S.C., 1964.

The compiler based her French wills on the translations done for the *Transactions*.

There were five principal Huguenot settlements in South Carolina:

• *Charleston*:
French Protestant Church — early records destroyed, but see entries in:

Balley, A. S. *Registers of St. Philip's Parish, Charles Town, S.C., 1720-1758*. Charleston, 1904. 355 pp.

Smith, D. E. Huger and A. S. Salley, *Register of St. Philip's Parish, Charles Town, S.C., 1754-1810*. Charleston, 1927. 505 pp.

Howe, Mrs. C. G.; and Mrs. Charles F. Middleton, *The Minutes of St. Michael's Church of Charleston, S.C., from 1758-1797*. (Charleston), n.d. 214 pp. St. Michael's Parish Registers were lost in the War Between the States.

• *St. John's Parish, Berkeley* (western branch of the Cooper River):
"The parish register of St. Andrew's Parish, 1719-1774," is published in the *South Carolina Historical Magazine*, v. 12-15 (1911-1914).

• *St. Dennis Parrish, Orange Quarter or French Quarter* (eastern branch of the Cooper River):
Clute, Robert F. *The Annals and Parish Register of St. Thomas and St. Dennis Parish in South Carolina from 1680 to 1884*. Charleston, 1884. 111 p.

• *French Santee*:
"Parish Register of St. James Santee," *South Carolina Historical Magazine*, v. 15, 17 (1914-1916).

• *New Bordeaux* (1764):
List of names taken while the group was at Plymouth, England. Huguenot Society of South Carolina Transactions, No. 5, pp. 77-78.

Numerous other registers contain Huguenot entries. These are referred to in the following excellent bibliography:

Easterby, J. H. *Guide to the Study and Reading of South Carolina History: A General Classified Bibliography.* Columbia, 1950.

South Carolina continued to be a favored destination for the French, so much so that there were instances of Acadian dispersal there, and very large numbers of the Santo Domingo refugees late in the eighteenth century. Care is required to separate these later Catholic groups from the initial Huguenot settlers.

Nova Scotia

It is known that some of the earliest inhabitants of Acadia and Quebec were Huguenots. By 1627 Huguenots were prohibited from settling in the French King's possessions in the New World. Nevertheless, even as late as the Revocation (1685) there were Huguenots yet resident in Quebec, for ten cases of abjuration of Calvinism are cited in Tanguay's *Dictionnaire Généalogique des Familles Canadiennes, depuis la fondatiooi dela colonie jusqu' a nos jours.* Several other Protestants are known to have fled Quebec to join co-religionists in New York and New England.

The only real group Huguenot settlement in Canada did not occur until much later, and then under English auspices and protection. The English were long interested in a Huguenot peopling of Nova Scotia. The Huguenot pastor at Boston, the Rev. Andrew LeMercier, petitioned the Governor of Nova Scotia on 28 September 1729 on behalf of a group of one hundred families of Huguenots, then in England, to be permitted to establish a settlement in Nova Scotia. In the winter of 1730/31, Major Cope, a member of the Council of Nova Scotia, was sent to Boston to interest "several hundred" French Protestant families *in Boston* in settling in Nova Scotia. Nothing came of this project, however. Nearly two decades later, in 1749/50, the Rev. Jean Baptiste Moreau was appointed "Missionary to the French" by the Society for the Propagation of the Gospel and held services in French at St. Paul's Anglican Church, Halifax, Nova Scotia.

In 1752 a group of some hundreds from Montbéliard landed at Halifax and wintered there. Numerous references to them can be gleaned from the parish registers of St. Paul's, Halifax. In succeeding years they settled at Lunenburg and along the Northwest Ranges and St. Margaret's Bay southwest of Halifax. In 1771 many of these people migrated up to Tatamagouche and later yet to River John in northern Nova Scotia. Some of the prominent and widespread Nova Scotian names of the Protestant French which owe their origin to the Montbéliardian settlement include Boutillier, Dauphinee, Coulon, Jolimois [Jollimore], Grosrenaud [Grono], Tetteray, Langille, Joudry, and Petrequin. The best account of the Nova Scotian settlements is:

Bell, Winthrop Pickard, *The "Foreign Protestants" and the Settlement of Nova Scotia.* Toronto, Univ. of Toronto Press, 1961.

West Indies

In the period from 1625 to 1685 many Huguenots settled in the Antilles, especially on St. Christopher, Guadeloupe and Martinique, where they were tolerated and where many achieved prosperity. With the Revocation this situation changed abruptly, and many sought refuge in South

Carolina, Boston, New Rochelle, and New York. Useful censuses prior to the Revocation have been published, enabling many continental American Huguenots to be traced to the Indies:

> Dessalles, Adrien. *Histoire générale des Antilles*. Paris, 1847. 5 v; "Role Général des Habitants de Martinique," Tome 1, pp. 562-572 (1671); "Role Général des Habitants de Saint Christoph," Tome II, pp. 417-437; "Role Général des Habitants de Guadeloupe," Tome II, pp. 438-453.

Despite the flight of many Huguenots, others remained in the West Indies through the period of religious persecution.

A much later migration to continental North America occurred in the 1790s and 1800s, principally from Santo Domingo, but also from other of the French West Indies, as a result of the racial war conducted by Toussaint L'Ouverture. The first wave of these terrified refugees (predominantly Catholic, but containing undoubtedly a number of Huguenots) broke on American shores in 1793, large groups settling in the cities of the Eastern Seaboard: New York, Philadelphia, Baltimore, Charleston, Augusta, and Savannah, as well as in small centers. Many of these refugees returned to Santo Domingo to claim their property once it appeared that the revolution had run its course, only to be victims of a more terrible massacre in 1803. Those who were able to escape the second massacre scattered to the United States, to France, and to Cuba, whose Eastern Provinces contain large numbers of French. An informative account of these French Indies refugees is contained in:

> Houdaille, Jacques A. "French Refugees in the United States, 1790-1810," *National Genealogical Society Quarterly*, 51:209-213 (1963).

Care must be taken when tracing French families in South Carolina and Georgia particularly not to form a premature conclusion that a given family was Huguenot, in view of this later, largely Catholic, element.

AN EXAMPLE OF HUGUENOT RESEARCH

Having taken an altogether too brief look at the sources available for tracing steps of a multi-stage migration, first by country, and then by North American settlement, we may find some value in synthesizing this information in the approach to the construction of a history of one large American family of Huguenot origin, the Sallé (Sallee) family.

We start with the fact that Abraham Sallé appeared at Manakin Town in Virginia in the infancy of the settlement, with a wife and family. His name does not appear on the ship lists of the settlement, so that his arrival there must be accounted for otherwise. His will is silent as to his place of birth.

In scanning extant records of other Huguenot settlements in the country, we discover in the printed records of the New York City Huguenot Congregation the baptism of two of his children there before his residence in Virginia. Still there is no clue as to his point of origin.

We next examine the publications of the Huguenot Society of London. Here we find two documents which indicate that he came from the Ile de Ré: his "reconnaissance" at the French Church of the Savoy in London in 1698, aged 25 years, and his Petition for Naturalization in

1700, which states that he was "born at St. Martin in France, son of John Salle by Mary his wife."

Armed with this clue, we seek information from that part of France, and locate a book by Pierre Dez, *Histoire des Protestants et de L'Église Réformée de l'Ile de Ré*. This work sets forth the abjurations of heresy in 1685 and 1686 of Jean Sallé, aged 62, Marie Martin his wife, aged 51, and three of their children, Theophile, 16, Abraham, 12, and François, 14. This work also refers to the extant Huguenot registers of St. Martin, and to a 1677 document in the Archives Nationales in which Jean Sallé explains his arrival in St. Martin and gives information on his family background.

On writing for the Huguenot Church Register entries at St. Martin, we find the various baptism and marriage records give Abraham's parentage, and the names of his grandparents on both sides of his family, including both grandmothers' maiden names. The registers also indicate that Abraham's grandfather, Jean Sallé, *père*, resided at Courteil in the Paroisse de Mougon en Poictou.

To recapitulate, we have had resort to:

1. Archival records in the Archives Nationales, Paris;
2. Archival records in the Archives Départementales;
3. A printed local history on Protestantism on the Ile de Ré;
4. The publications of the Huguenot Society of London;
5. The printed registers of the New York City Huguenot congregation;
6. The microfilmed records of Henrico County, Virginia;
7. Published journals of Virginia history.

By combining these successful searches (out of many more that were negative, of course) we have established these migratory stages for the Sallé family:

1. Within France, Courteil, Poitou, to St. Martin, Ile de Ré;
2. St. Martin to London;
3. London to New York City;
4. Within the American colonies, from New York to Manakin Town, Virginia.

This is an extremely typical example of the rather complex migratory patterns of the Huguenots. But that is not all: just before his life closed, Abraham Sallé was growing very unhappy in Virginia, so that he drew up a petition to the King, asking for assistance in joining the French colony in Ireland, where he was certain things would be much better.

But note: to the close of his life, he sought always to settle among other French. That, too, is typical, and if the researcher in this field will act on that assumption, that the Frenchman ordinarily sought out his compatriots, he will know that the entire body of Huguenot material on a global basis will yield grist for his mill.

APPENDIX 2

The Soblets of the European Refuge

by Cameron Allen, FASG
edited by David L. Greene, FASG
Originally published in *The American Genealogist*
Volume 75, No. 2 (April 2000): pages 99-108

The American Genealogist
P.O. Box 398
Demorest, GA 30535-0398
(www.AmericanGenealogist.com)
$40.00 a year (four issues).

THE SOBLETS OF THE EUROPEAN REFUGE
Ancestral to the Soblet-Sublett Family
of Manakin Town, Virginia

By Cameron Allen, FASG

The Soblet-Sublett family of Manakin Town, Virginia, originating at Sedan, has been extensively chronicled over the past thirty years.[1069] However, certain key references relating to the family's part in the Huguenot dispersion have yet to be published.

Sedan, the geographical focus of the migrating family, was always on the frontier of France, being today only a few kilometers from the Belgian border. Its ownership was contested for centuries. It was in the fourteenth century a dependency of the Abbey of Mouzon, the possession of which was disputed by the bishops of Liège and Rheims.

United briefly to the crown of France by Charles V, it was ceded by Charles VI to Guillaume de Bracquemont, whose son sold it to his brother-in-law, Evrard de la Marck. For two centuries, this family continued to control it, and Robert IV de la Marck (d. 1556), Marshal of France, erected Sedan on his own authority into an independent principality. In the sixteenth century, the town became an asylum for many Protestant refugees, who laid the foundation for its industrial prosperity, and it became the seat of a Protestant seminary; it was sometimes referred to as the "Geneva of the North." Sedan became permanently a part of the French royal domain in 1642.

The uncertainties that were a part of the everyday existence of the residents of Sedan for many decades before the Revocation of 1685 resulted in some gaps in the Protestant temple's record of sacraments for its adherents.[1070]

[1069]　Cameron Allen, "The (Soblet, Subley) Sublett Family of Manakintown, King William Parish, Virginia," *The Detroit Society for Genealogical Research Magazine* 27 (1963-64):3-10, 49-54, 97103, 141-48; 28 (1964-65):3-8, 49-57, 103-10, 151-59; (1965-66): 14-22, 62-70, 105-14, 15161 [12 parts]; Cameron Allen, *The Sublett (Soblet) Family of Manakintown, Virginia* (Detroit: Detroit Society for Genealogical Research, 1982) [a reprint of articles in *The Detroit Society for Genealogical Research Magazine]*; Cameron Allen, comp., *The Soblett (Sublet) Family of Manakintown, King Parish, Virginia*, ed. James N. Jackson (Detroit: Detroit Society for Genealogical Research, 1994) (hereafter cited as Jackson, *Soblet Family*) [this new edition incorporates material contributed by others which lacks authority]; original articles largely republished without acknowledgment in Nancy Louise Sublett, *Generations Remembered: Sublette Family, 1700-1850* (1974); also incorporated without acknowledgment in Hester Geraldine Lester Searl, *Genealogy of John Hester* (Patterson, Calif., 1972); incorporated with permission and acknowledgment in Donald J. Sublette, *James Sublett and Sally Ford: Genealogy and Family History* (Detroit, 1981).

[1070]　"Sedan," *Encyclopædia Britannica*, 11th ed. (New York, 1911), 24:574-76.

1. JEAN^A SOBLET was buried at Sedan on 10 *février* 1674, native of Beaumont, aged 56 years, *notaire royal*; [present to] assist at the burial were Abraham Soblet, his son, and Pierre Soblet, his brother. Jean Soblet and his wife, JUDITH LOMBARD of Sedan, had the following known children:[1071]

				Parents	*Godparents*
2	i	JEAN SOBLET	bp. 11 *décembre* 1644	Jean Soblet, *notaire*	Jean L'Oreaux
				Judit Lombard	Jeane Brandon
	ii	ELISABETH SOBLET	bp.16 *juillet* 1647 [inferentially d. young]	Jean Soblet Judit Lombard	Jeremie Brandon Elisabeth Jannon, *sa femme*
3	iii	ABRAHAM^1 SOBLET	b.4 *décembre* 1648 bp. 6 *décembre* 1648	Jean Soblet Judit Lombard	Abraham Duclous Rachel Brandon
	iv	CATHERINE SOBLET	b. 21 *juin* 1652 bp. 23 *juin* 1652 [inferentially d. young]	Jean Soblet Judit Lombard	Jean Bruyeres Caterine Descamps, *sa femme*
	v	JUDIT SOBLET	bp. 9 *mai* 1655	Jean Soblet Judit Lombart	Bartelemy Bondet Judit Bassange, *sa femme*
	vi	ELISABETH SOBLET	bp. 2 *janvier* 1658	Jean Soblet Judith Lombard	Daniel Peron Elisabeth Pilton, *sa femme*
	vii	CATHERINE SOBLET	bp. 19 *août* 1662	Jean Soblet, *notaire à Torcy*[1072] Judith Lombard	Jean Rosanstol *m. de la poste* Catherine Loens, *sa femme*
	viii	MARIE SOBLET	bp. 30 *octobre* 1663	Jean Soblet Judit Lombart	Simon Chenin Marie Colis, *sa femme*
	ix	SIMON SOBLET	bp. not recorded bur. Sedan, 28 *septembre* 1677, aged 7 years, son of the deceased Jean Soblet, *notaire* [notary], and Judith Lombart; [present] at the burial were his brothers Jean Soblet and Abraham Soblet.		

The marriages of two of the daughters of Jean Soblet and Judith (Lombard) are known:

JUDITH SOBLET (no. v above), daughter of the deceased Jean^A Soblet, notary at Torcy, and Judith Lombart, aged 24 years, m. Sedan, 4 *juin* 1679, HUBERT TOUSSAINT,

---

[1071]   All Sedan records cited in this article are taken from one of the two modem transcriptions of the Sedan Huguenot registers that have survived, this transcription incorporated into the stupendous Card Index, *Bibliothèque Wallonne*, Leiden, gathered over many decades by the *Commission pour f'histoire des églises wallonnes* and now available in microfilm copy at the Family History Library [FHL], Salt Lake City. The portion of the alphabet covering *Soblet* is contained in FHL film #199,932.

[1072]   Torcy is a nearby community with a separate identity, but essentially part of Sedan.

son of Jean Toussaint and Suzanne LeRoy, aged 24 years.[1073] Hubert was bp.
Sedan, 17 *janvier* 1655, son of Jean Toussaint and Susane LeRoy.[1074]
Two known children:

1. Jean Toussaint, bp. 29 *septembre* 1680, bur. Sedan, 12 *octobre* 1682.
2. David Toussaint, bp. 8 *février* 1682, bur. Sedan, 8 *novembre* 1682.

ELISABETH SOBLET (no. vi above), aged 25 years, daughter of the deceased Jean[A] Soblet,
notary at Torcy, and Judith Lombart, m. Sedan, 3 *août* 1681, DANIEL RENARD,
bourgeois, aged 35 years, living at Sedan.[1075]

Both of the known surviving sons of Jean[A] Soblet (d. 1674) ultimately sought refuge abroad,
both initially at the same place, Mannheim, in the modem state of Baden-Württemberg. Abraham
arrived at Mannheim by 1681, *before* the Revocation of 1685; Louis XIV's increasingly stringent
policies directed at his Huguenot subjects enabled perceptive Protestants to see the handwriting
on the wall, and the exodus from France had reached flood tide before the Revocation finally
sealed their fate. The dispersion of Huguenots occurred to any nearby Protestant country they
could conveniently reach. The Netherlands (whose prevailing religion was Dutch Reformed),
Switzerland (whose prevailing religion was Swiss Reformed), and the Calvinist principalities of
Germany (which confessed the German Reformed faith, as opposed to the numerically more
significant Lutheran faith of the other non-Catholic principalities) were particularly attractive to
the Huguenots (who were, of course, French Reformed). There they felt assured of a warm and
sympathetic welcome from their co-religionists.

Mannheim had some very substantial advantages: It was under Calvinist control and had been
for nearly a century. The man who established modern Mannheim, the Elector Palatine of the
Rhine, Frederick IV (1574-1610), though baptized a Lutheran, was reared and educated as a
Calvinist. He peopled Mannheim largely with refugee Dutch and Walloon Calvinists who were
fleeing Catholic portions of the Low Countries. Frederick IV's early death brought to power his
son, Frederick V (1596-1632), as Elector Palatine of the Rhine. During this time, the Thirty Years
War (1618-1648) was wreaking havoc in Mannheim, which was taken and retaken five times
during the course of that protracted conflict. The depopulation of much of Germany as a result of
the Thirty Years War made the surviving Germans even more hospitable to religious refugees,
and the Elector Palatine Charles Louis (1617-1680) welcomed Huguenots to Mannheim.[1076]

While Louis XIV was pursuing his policy of internal repression against his Huguenot subjects
at home, he was simultaneously instituting an unlimited aggrandizement against his neighbors,
and his armies invaded the Rhineland and the Palatinate. In response, a number of the threatened
powers formed the League of Augsburg on 9 July 1686. Undeterred, Louis's armies occupied the
major fortified cities of the Palatinate — Mannheim and Heidelberg — by 1688. In Mannheim
the French armies announced that they had uncovered a "plot" to overthrow Louis among the
French refugee congregation. Thereupon the French army seized a major portion of the
congregation and packed them back to France to be imprisoned at Vincennes. Following that, the
French army burned Mannheim to the ground in early 1689. The seizure of the Huguenot

---

[1073]   Card Index, *Bibliothèque Wallonne*, Leiden [Toussaint] [FHL #199,941].

[1074]   Card Index, *Bibliothèque Wallonne*, Leiden [Toussaint] [FHL #199,940].

[1075]   Card Index, *Bibliothèque Wallonne*, Leiden [Renard] [FHL #199,917].

[1076]   "Mannheim," *Encyclopaedia Britannica*, 11th ed., 17:588-89.

refugees at Mannheim is one of a half dozen precipitating causes for the enlargement of the League of Augsburg into the Grand Alliance to counter the military designs of Louis XIV; the Alliance was formed by the Treaty of Vienna (12 July 1689). There then ensued the war variously denominated the War of the League of Augsburg, the War of the Grand Alliance, and the Nine Years' War (1688-1697).[1077]

Although a major portion of the Huguenot congregation at Mannheim was imprisoned at Vincennes, a remnant fled with their congregational records to Magdebourg, where they were granted asylum. Abraham[1] Soblet somehow avoided imprisonment at Vincennes but did not join the flight to Magdebourg. Instead he went to Wesel in Westphalia. His brother Jean's ultimate fate is unknown; he simply disappeared from the records. Perhaps he was one of the unfortunates who were thrown into prison at Vincennes.

2. JEAN SOBLET (bp. 1644 above), son of the deceased Jean[A] Soblet and Judith Lombart, *mr. écrivain* [master scrivener], aged 31 years, living at Sedan; married at Sedan on 24 *novembre* 1675, MARIE MARTINET, aged 25 years, daughter of Nicolas Martinet and Jeanne Buisset, living at Sedan. Their known issue:

			Parents	*Godparents*
i	JEAN SOBLET	bp. 29 *avril* 1677 Sedan	Jean Soblet, *mr. écrivain* Marie Martinet	Jean L'Orcan Marthe Martin, *sa femme*
ii	ABRAHAM SOBLET	bp. 24 *août* 1679 Sedan	Jean Soblet, *mr. écrivain* Marie Martinet	Nicolas Martinet Ester, *sa soeur*
iii	ANNE SOBLET	bp. 30 *août* 1681 Sedan	Jean Soblet, *mr. écrivain* Marie Martinet	Jean Toussaint Anne Dufray, *sa femme*
iv	ANTOINE SOBLET	b. 24 *octobre* 1683 bp. 28 *octobre* 1683 Mannheim[1078]	Jean Soblet Marie Martinet	Sr. Antoine de la Place Amande Drapier, *sa femme*
v	ISAAC SOBLET	b. 15 *septembre* 1685 bp. 20 *septembre* 1685 Mannheim[1079]	Jean Soblet Marie Martinet	Abraham Bonenfant Rachel Scobel, *sa femme*
vi	LOUISE CHRISTINE SOBLET	b. 4 *novembre* 1687 bp. 12 *novembre* 1687, Mannheim[1080]	Jean Soblet Marie Martinet	[*blank*] [*blank*]

1077   Paul Wiriath, "France (History of)," *Encyclopaedia Britannica*, 11th ed., 10:844.
1078   *Troisième Registre des baptêmes dans l'église française Mannheim*, bp. #81, p. 58 links [FHL film #1,418,023].
1079   *Troisième Registre des baptêmes dans l'église française Mannheim*, bp. #76, p. 77 *rechts*.
1080   *Troisième Registre des baptêmes dans l'église française Mannheim*, bp. #77, p. 104 *links*.

3. ABRAHAM[1] SOBLET (bp. 1648 above), son of Jean[A] Soblet and Judith Lombart his wife, aged 26 years, living at Sedan Torcy; married at Sedan on 31 *mars* 1675, SUZANNE BRIANT, daughter of Jacques Briant and the deceased Suzanne Gerard of Sedan. Their known issue:

			Parents	*Godparents*
i	ANNE[2] SOBLET	bp. 22 *octobre* 1675 Sedan	Abraham Soblet, *ouvrier en tabac* [tobacco worker] Susanne Briant	Philbert Soblet Anne Godin, *sa femme*
ii	JEAN SOBLET	bp. 29 *avril* 1677 Sedan	Abraham Soblet Suzanne Brient	Jean Lorrean Esther Lorrean, *sa fille*

bur. Sedan, 7 *août* 1678, Jean Soblet, son of Abraham Soblet, *monteur* [setter or mounter of jewels], and Suzanna Briant; at the burial [were present to] assist: his father and Jean Lorcan [i.e., Lorrean]

iii	JACOB SOBLET	bp. 14 *septembre* 1678 Sedan	Abraham Soblet Suzanne Brian	Jacob Lombart Jeanne LeChenny
iv	JEAN SOBLET	bp. 10 *mars* 1680 Sedan	Abraham Saublet *md.*[1081] *à St. Menges* Susanne Briant	Jean Sobley Marie Martinet, *sa femme*

bur. Sedan, 17 *octobre* 1680, Jean Soblet, native of Sedan, aged 8 months, son of Abraham Soblet, *bourgeois* of St. Menges, and Susanne Briant; at the burial [were present] to assist: his father and Jean Soblet his uncle and godfather.

v	AGNES SOBLET	bp. 17 *août* 1681 Mannheim[1082]	Abraham Saublet Susanne Brian	Walter de Houst, *bourgmaistre* Agnes Conquart, *sa femme*
vi	MARIE SOBLET	b. 30 *septembre* 1688 bp. 2 *octobre* 1688 Mannheim[1083]	Abraham Soblet Susanne Brian	Jean Soblet Marie Martinet, *sa femme*
vii	FRANÇOIS SOBLET	b. 15 *janvier* 1694 bp. 19 *janvier* 1694 Wesel[1084]	Abraham Soblet Susanne Brian	Mr. de Bresson, *Capt. de Cavallerie* Madel. Vernicourt
viii	PIERRE SOBLET	b. 15 *août* 1695 bp. 19 *août* 1695 Wesel[1085]	Abraham Soblet Susanne Brian	Pierre Leroy Demlle Bosser, *sa femme*

1081   Probably *marchand* [merchant].

1082   *Troisième Registre des baptêmes dans l'église française Mannheim*, bp. #53, p. 36 *links*.

1083   *Troisième Registre des baptêmes dans l'église française Mannheim*, bp. #101, p. 118 *links*.

1084   *Registre des baptêmes, mariages et sepultures administris dans l'eglise française ou wallonne de la Ville de Wesel de 1694-1755*, bp. #6 [FHL film #106,810].

1085   *Registre des baptêmes, mariages et sepultures administris dans l'eglise française ou wallonne de la Ville de Wesel de 1694-1755*, bp. #87.

				Parents	Godparents
ix	ROBERT SOBLET	b. 20 *avril* 1698 bp. 1 *mai* 1698, London[1086]		Abraham Soblet *de* *Sedan en France* Susanne Brian	Robert de Camp Dlle. Judith deLogue

Following the periods of refuge in Mannheim, Wesel, and London, Abraham Soblet and his wife Susanne Brian took their family to Manakin Town in Virginia in 1700. There Abraham died about 1717-19.[1087] Of the nine children shown above, Anne, born 1675, is probably the Anne who married as his second wife Pierre Chastain.[1088] It seems likely that Abraham Soblet's documented son Pierre-Louis Soblet is the Pierre who was baptized in 1695. While it has been suggested that Abraham's known son Jacques was probably the same as Jacob (b. 1678),[1089] this does not seem likely: The French made a clear distinction between the two names, although in German James and Jacob can be interchangeable. Consequently, he would have to be postulated for placement in one of the available time gaps, 1682-87, 1689-93, as would his brother Abraham, who is found in none of the records abstracted above.

PHILIBERT SOBLET OF THE REFUGE

1   One other family group of Soblets needs to be considered in the Refuge, the descendants of PHILIBERT SOBLET; baptismal sponsorships indicate that he was related to Jean Soblet père (b. ca. 1617-18, d. 1674), both of whom came to Sedan from Beaumont, though the exact nature of the relationship is still not settled. "Married at Sedan 16 *avril* 1643, Philibert Saublet, son of the deceased Elie Saublet and Susanna Renaudin, living at Beaumont, and ANNE GODIN, daughter of Antoine Godin and Bastienne L'Escot." Their known issue:

			Parents	*Godparents*
i	HENRY SOBLET	bp. 29 *avril* 1645 [inferentially d. young]	Philbert Soblet Anne Godin	Jean Soblet Susanne Renaudin, *sa femme*
ii	HENRY SOBLET	bp. 8 *mars* 1648	Philbert Soblet Anne Godin	Henry duChene Elisabet Loriot
		bur. Sedan, 18 *février* 1661, Henri Soblet, aged 13 years, son of Philippe [*sic*] Soblet and Anne Godin.		
2 iii	ANNE SOBLET	bp. 14 *avril* 1649	Philbert Soblet, *md.* Anne Godin	Jean Godin Anne Salomon, *Vve* [widow] Denyens

1086   Susan Minet, ed., *Registers of the Churches of La Patente de Soho, Wheeler Street, Swanfields, and Hoxton; Also the Repertoire general*, Pubs. Huguenot Soc. of London, 45 (London, 1956):xiii.

1087   For discussion of date, see Jackson, *Soblett Family*, 6.

1088   Cameron Allen, "The Chastain Families of Manakin Town in Virginia and Their Origin Abroad," *TAG* 39 (1963):149-56; 40 (1964): 1-12, 135-47, at 40:5-6.

1089   This suggestion was made by Donald J. Sublette in Jackson, *Soblett Family*, 142.

	iv	JEAN SOBLET	bp. 10 *septembre* 1651	Philbert Soblet Anne Godin	Jean Gollin Claude Piette, *sa femme*

bur. Sedan, 15 *octobre* 1651, Jean Soblet, aged 5 months, son of Philbert Soblet.

	v	MARIE SOBLET	bp. 16 *novembre* 1652	Philbert Soblet Anne Godin	Paul Sacrelaire Marie Genoteau, *sa femme*

bur. Sedan, 11 *novembre* 1653, Marie Soble, aged 1 year, daughter of Philbert.

	vi	JEAN SOBLET	bp. 20 *octobre* 1654	Philbert Soblet Anne Godin	Antoine Catel Judit Tellier, *sa femme*
	vii	JEANNE SOBLET	bp. 23 *janvier* 1656	Philbert Soblet Anne Godin	Pierre Guerin Jeane Flamin, *sa femme*

bur. Sedan, 17 *avril* 1656, Jeanne Soblet, aged 3 months, daughter of Philbert Soblet.

3	viii	JACQUES SOBLET	bp. 7 *mars* 1657	Philbert Soblet Anne Godin	Jacques Sacrelaire Marte Genoteau
	ix	ELIZABETH SOBLET	bp. 28 *juillet* 1658	Philbert Soblet Anne Godin	Pierre Sperlette Elisabeth Bernard

bur. Sedan, 5 *mai* 1659, Elisabeth Saublet, aged 9 months, daughter of Philbert Saublet and Anne Godin.

	x	JUDIT SOBLET	bp. 26 *août* 1660	Philbert Saublet, *md.* Anne Godin	Elie Saublet Judit Godin
4	xi	RACHEL SOBLET	bp. 8 *janvier* 1662	Philibert Soblet Anne Godin	[*blank*]
	xii	JEAN SOBLET	bp. 30 *août* 1664	Philibert Soblet Anne Godin	Jean Soblet Judith Lombard
	xiii	ELIZABET SOBLET	bp. 20 *decembre* 1665	Philbert Soblet, *md.* Anne Godin	Thomas Godet Elisabet Michau, *sa femme*

bur. Sedan, 16 *avril* 1666, Elisabet Saublet, aged 4 months, daughter of Philbert Saublet, *md.*, and Marie Bonal [*sic*].

2. ANNE SOBLET (bp. 1649), aged 20 years, daughter of Filbert Soblet and Anne Godin; married at Sedan on 11 *février* 1670, JACQUES DE VILLETT, *mr. orfèvre* [master goldsmith], aged 24 years, living at Sedan, son of Jacques de Villett, *mr. orfèvre*, and Elisabeth Robinet.

Among their children were:

			Parents	*Godparents*
i	JACQUES DE VILLETT	bp. not recorded bur. 20 *février* 1672, aged 4 months, son of Jacques de Villette, *mr. orfèvre*, and Anne Saublet.		
ii	PHILBERT DE VILLETT	bp. 2 *janvier* 1674	Jacques de Villette, *mr. orfèvre* Anne Soblet	Philbert Soblet Anne Godin, *sa femme*
		Married LaHaye, 28 *décembre* 1710, Philibert de Vilette of Sedan to ANNA ADRIENNE LUCRESE de Goege.		
iii	ELIZABETH DE VILLETT	bp. 3 *juin* 1676	Jacques de Villette, *mr. orfèvre* Anne Soblet	Claude Lormier Elizabeth deVilette, *Vv.* [widow] Lormier
		bur. Sedan, 25 *août* 1678, Elisabeth Villette, aged 3 months, daughter of Jacques Villette, *orphèvre*, and Anne Soblet; at the burial [were present] to assist: her father and Claude Lormier.		
iv	MARIE DE VILLETT	bp. 30 *janvier* 1678 [inferentially d. young]	Jacques Villette, *orphèvre* Anne Soblet	Leonard Vander Marie deVillett
v	DANIEL DE VILLETT	bp. 24 *septembre* 1679	Jacques de Vilette, *orfèvre* Anne Soblet	Daniel Genoteau Jeane Signe, *sa femme*
vi	MARIE DE VILLETT	bp. 8 *décembre* 1680	Jacques deVillette, *mr. orfèvre* Anne Soblet	Jaques Soblet Marie Boulande, *sa femme*
		bur. Sedan, 20 *décembre* 1680, Marie deVillette, aged 10 days, daughter of Jacques deVillette, *mr. orfèvre*, and Anne Soblet.		
vii	ABRAHAM DE VILLETT	bp. 15 *février* 1682	Jacques de Villette, *mr. orfèvre* Anne Soblet	Abraham Poupart Marie Poupart, *sa femme*
		bur. Sedan, 25 *février* 1682, Abraham deVillette, aged 12 days, son of Jacques deVillette, *mr. orfèvre*, and Anne Soblet.		
viii	ELISABETH DE VILLETT	bp. 13 *décembre* 1691 LaHaye	Jacques deVilette Anne Soblet	[blank] [blank]

3. JACQUES SOBLET (bp. 1657), son of Philbert Soblet and Anne Godin, aged 22 years, living at Sedan; married at Sedan in *août* 1678, MARIE BOULANDE, daughter of Guillaume Boulande, *mr. drapier* [master clothier], and Elisabeth Chevillet [*i.e.*, Chevillon] of Sedan, aged 19 years.

On 7 *février* 1705, there died at Emmerich *le sieur* Jacques Soblet of Sedan, aged 50 years, *chant-lecteur de l'église*[1090] [*i.e.*, precentor: one who leads the singing in a church].

Children of Jacques Soblet and Marie (Boulande):

			Parents	Godparents
i	PHILIBERT SOBLET[1091]	bp. 25 *juin* 1679, Maastricht	Jacques Soblet Marie Bouland	Jean Savary *en la place de* Philbert Soblet Catherine Lanoye *en la place de* Anne Godin
ii	GUILLAUME SOUBLET[1092]	bp. 9 *mars* 1681, Sedan	Jacques Soblet, *md.* Marie Boulande	Guillaume Bouland Rachel Procureur, *sa femme*

On 27 *janvier* 1752 died at Emmeric *le Sieur* Guillaume Soblet formerly *lecteur et chanteur* of our church, but during the last years of his life, *valet de ville* [civil servant] of his profession *tapissier et graissier* [tapestry-maker], aged 72 years. He was buried in the German Reformed cemetery.[1093]

			Parents	Godparents
iii	DANIEL SOBLET[1094]	bp. 9 *août* 1687, Amsterdam	Jaque Soblet Marie Bolande	Daniel Piette Elisabeth Masnet
iv	JEAN SOBLET[1095]	bp. 19 *juin* 1689, Amsterdam	Jaque Soblet Marie Boulande	Jean Rambonnet Marie Chevillet
v	RACHEL MARIE SOBLET[1096]	b. 10 *décembre* 1695 bp. 11 *décembre* 1695, Emmerich	Jacques Soblet, *lecteur et chantre de cette église* Marie Boulande	Sr. Jaques Benoit, *horlogeur* [clock-maker] *de Cleves* Rachel Soblet
vi	JUDITH SOBLET[1097]	b. 12 *mars* 1697 bp. 17 *mars* 1697, Emmerich	Jacques Soblet Marie Boulande	Sr. Bosviel, *perruquer* [wig-maker] Judith Pousse

1090   Emmerich, *Église française, décès* #382 [FHL film #106,808].

1091   Maastricht, *Église française*, v. 129, p. 2, Dopen, Trouwen, 1679-1701 [FHL film #110,287].

1092   Sedan, *Église réformée* [FHL film #199,932].

1093   Emmerich, *Église française, livre des bp., m. & d.*, #270 [FHL film #199,979].

1094   Amsterdam, *Église réformée*, v. 132 unpaged, *baptêmes*, 1667-1694 [FHL film #113,398].

1095   Amsterdam, *Église réformée*, v. 132 unpaged, *baptêmes*, 1667-1694.

1096   Emmerich, *Église française*, bp. #7 [FHL film #106,808].

1097   Emmerich, *Église française*, bp. #11.

4. RACHEL SOBLET (bp. 1662), aged 18, daughter of Philbert Soblet and Anne Godin; married at Sedan on 12 *mai* 1680, JACQUES BENOIT, aged 22 years, son of Pierre Benoit, *marchand de Vitry-le-François*, and Suzanna Colin. On 11 *janvier* 1702, died Rachel Souble, aged 40 years, native of Sedan, wife of Jaque Benoy *de Vitre en Champagne* and *maître horlogeur* [master clockmaker] in this city. She was buried the 14th at 8 hours in the evening in the Reformed cemetery.[1098] On 11 *juillet* 1703, died Jaques Benoit, aged [*blank*] years, native of Vitry en Champagne and master clockmaker in this city, and was buried the 13th at 8 hours of the evening in the Reformed cemetery.[1099]

Among the couple's children were:

			Parents	*Godparents*
i	ANNA BENOIT[1100]	b. 15 *août* 1687, Emmerich	Jacques Benoit Rachel Soblet	Philibert Soblet Anne Godin
ii	JACQUES BENOIT[1101]	b. 19 *septembre* 1696 bp. 22 *septembre* 1696	Jacques Benoy *de Vitry en Champagne maître horlogeur de Sedan* Rachel Soublé	Jacque Soublé Marie Boulant, *sa femme*
iii	DANIEL BENOIT[1102]	b. 30 *juin* 1700 bp. 8 *juillet* 1700	Jaque Benoy *de Vitry en Champagne* Rachel Soublé *de Sedan*	Daniel Couturier Jeanne Tassier, *femme* Josserant

Cameron Allen (90 Tarryton Court West, Columbus OH 43228) is retired Law Librarian at Rutgers University School of Law, Newark, N.J.

1098   Cleves, *Église française, Registre des sépultures*, p. 89 [FHL film #106,812, item 6].

1099   Cleves, *Église française, Registre des sepultures*, p. 90.

1100   Emmerich, *Église française, livre des bp., m. & d.*, #351 [FHL #199,979].

1101   Cleves, *Église française*, 1696-1798, p. 3 [FHL # I 06,812, item 6].

1102   Cleves, *Église française*, 1696-1798, p. 3.

APPENDIX 3

Ancestral Table of Susanne Brian, Wife of Abraham Soblet

by Cameron Allen, FASG
edited by David L. Greene, FASG
Originally published in *The American Genealogist*
Volume 78, No. 4 (October 2003): pages 245-252.

The American Genealogist
P.O. Box 398
Demorest, GA 30535-0398
(www.AmericanGenealogist.com)
$40.00 a year (four issues).

ANCESTRAL TABLE OF SUSANNE BRIAN, WIFE OF ABRAHAM[1] SOBLET, THE 1700 IMMIGRANT TO MANAKIN TOWN, VIRGINIA

Four Generations of Her Ancestry
Within a Single Huguenot Congregation: Sedan, France

By Cameron Allen, FASG

Abraham[1] Soblet and his wife, Susanne Brian, came to the Huguenot settlement in Manakin Town, Virginia, in 1700. The following marriage record is given here, to begin an outline of the bride's ancestry:

Abraham Soblet, *fils de Jean Soblet et Judith Lombart sa femme, âgé de 26 ans, demeurant à* [living at] *Sedan Torcy*, was married at Sedan, 31 March 1675, to Suzanne Briant, *fille de Jacques Briant et feue* [deceased] *Suzanne Gerard de Sedan*.[1103]

ANCESTRAL TABLE OF SUSANNE BRIAN

1. SUSANNE BRIAN, b. probably at Utrecht in The Netherlands, where her refugee parents were residing, say 1653.

2. JACQUES BRIAN, b. Sedan, say 1609; m. Sedan, 1637:
3. SUSANNE GERARD, b. Sedan, ca. 1611-12, bur. Sedan, 1659.

4. PIERRE BRIAN, b. say 1580, bur. Sedan, 1641; m. Sedan, 1602:
5. MARIE POUPART, bp. 1575, bur. Sedan, 1634.
6. JEAN GERARD, b. say 1580-90, d. Sedan, prior to 1637; m. Sedan:
7. JEANNE D'ORLÉANS, bp. Sedan, 1591.

8. GUILLAUME BRIAN.
10. MATHIAS POUPART.
11. JEANNE DE CORBY.
14. JACQUES D'ORLÉANS, m. Sedan, 1591:
15. ELIZABETH PERIN/PERRIN, b. ca. 1567, bur. Sedan, 1637.

28. JEAN D'ORLÉANS.
29. perhaps ANTOINETTE DE HOLE.

[1103] Registers of the Reformed Church at Sedan [as copied into the *Bibliothèque Wallonne* (Family History Library [FHL], Salt Lake City, fiche #199,932)]. For recently published information on the Soblet family, see Cameron Allen, "The Soblets of the European Refuge: Ancestral to the Soblet-Sublett Family of Manakin Town, Virginia," *TAG* 75(2000):99-108.

RATIONALE FOR THE CONSTRUCTION OF THIS ANCESTRAL TABLE

2. JACQUES BRIAN was born say 1609 and is believed to have been the son of Pierre Brian and Marie Poupart for reasons set out under #4. Jacques Brian, *tisserand, demeurant à Sedan* [weaver, living in Sedan], was married at Sedan on 8 December 1637 to SUSANE GERARD, *fille de feu Jean Gerard m[archan]d* [merchant] *à Sedan, et Jeanne d'Orléans.*[1104]

Children of Jacques and Susanne (Gerard) Brian:

	i	DANIEL BRIAN, bp. Sedan, 19 Sept. 1638, son of Jacques Brian, *tisserand* [weaver], and Susanne Gerard; sponsors: Daniel Brian, *serrurier* [locksmith], and Rachel Bruneau.[1105] Daniel Brian, *tisserand, demeurant à Sedan*, m. (1) 3 July 1660, Givonne MARIE FERET, *V[eu]ve* [widow] *du Truchot, drapier* [draper] *à Sedan*,[1106] m. (2) at the French Church of Mannheim, 8 May 1686, as Daniel Brian, *Veuf* [widower] *de Marie Fere, à* MARIE ROLAND, *veuve de Jean Froumi.*[1107]
	ii	YSAAC BRIANT, bp. Utrecht, 27 Dec. 1640, son of Jacques Briant and Susanne Gerard; sponsors: Ysaac Colin, Marie Dart.[1108]
	iii	JACQUES BRIANT, bp. Utrecht, bp. I Jan. 1643, son of Jacques Briant and Susanne *sa femme*; sponsors: Jacques Wibal and Marie Anwiel.[1109] Jacques Brian, *fils de Jacques Brian, tisserand à Sedan, et feue* [deceased] *Susanne Gerardin*, m. Sedan, 20 Nov. 1661, ESTER DESPRE, *fille de Jacques Despre, d[emeuran]t a Sedan et Marie Roger.*[1110]
	iv	CORNELIA BRIAN, bp. Utrecht, 20 April 1651, daughter of Jacques Brian and Susanne *sa femme*; sponsors: Marius Muller and Nailitjen Dierna.[1111] Lea Briant m. Sedan, 10 March 1676, NICOLAS CHUNO.[1112]
1	v	SUZANNE[1] BRIANT, *fllle de Jacques Briant et feue Suzanne Gerard de Sedan*, m. Sedan, 31 March 1675, ABRAHAM[1] SOBLET. They were the immigrants to Virginia.

It is obvious that Jacques Brian and his wife Susanne Gerard lived in Utrecht for a dozen or so years after the birth of their first child in Sedan, and it seems likely that daughter Susanne was one of the children born there, though her baptism has not been located. Following their return to Sedan, *Susanne Gerard, âgée de 47 ans, femme de Jacques Bryan, tisserand à Torcy-Sedan*, was buried at Sedan on 10 April 1659.[1113]

1104   *Bibliothèque Wallonne* [FHL fiche #199,780].

1105   *Bibliothèque Wallonne* [FHL fiche #199,780].

1106   *Bibliothèque Wallonne* [FHL fiche #199,780].

1107   *Bibliothèque Wallonne* [FHL fiche #199,780].

1108   Utrecht, *Klapper op dopen Waalsche Gemeente* [unpaged, but in precise chronological order of baptism] [FHL #121,831].

1109   Utrecht, *Klapper op dopen Waalsche Gemeente* [FHL film #121,831].

1110   *Bibliothèque Wallonne* [FHL fiche #199,780].

1111   Utrecht, *Klapper op dopen Waalsche Gemeente* [FHL film #121,831].

1112   *Bibliothèque Wallonne* [FHL fiche #199,780].

1113   *Bibliothèque Wallonne* [FHL fiche #199,834].

4. PIERRE BRIAN, born say 1580, *fils de feu Guillaume Brian; demeurant à Sedan, mariés à Sedan le 8 octobre 1602*, MARIE POUPART, *fille de Mathias Poupart, demeurant en Bru*.[1114] Marie was baptized at Sedan on 7 August 1575, daughter of Mathias Poupart, *m[archan]d à Montreuil*, and Jeanne Decorby.[1115] Marie was buried at Sedan on 22 August 1634, *âgée de 53* [sic] *ans, native d'Etang-Gourt, proche de* [near] *Conderlin, femme de Pierre Brian, m[ait]r[e]* [master] *tisserant en toile* [linen] *à Sedan*.[1116] Observe that her age given at death does not match her baptism by about six years. Following Marie's death, Pierre Brian, *m[ait]r[e] tisserant, demeurant à Sedan* married secondly, ELISABET OURLET, *V[eu]ve de Jerome Vasset* on 30 September 1635.[1117] Pierre was buried at Sedan on 7 February 1641.[1118]

Children of Pierre Brian and Marie (Poupart), bp. Sedan:

  i ELIZABETH BRIAN, bp. 10 Aug. 1603, daughter of Pierre Brian, *tisserant*, and Marie Poupart; sponsors: Jacques Cappel, *ministre*, and Elizabeth de Cenerne.[1119]

  ii SUSANNE BRIAN, bp. 12 Dec. 1604, daughter of Pierre Brian, *tisserand*, and Marie Poupart; sponsors: Adam Dardenon and Susanne Michelet.[1120]

  iii JEANNE BRIAN, bp. 28 Feb. 1606, daughter of Pierre Brian, *tisserand*, and Marie Poupart; sponsors: Regnault Guiry and Marie Largent.[1121]

At this point, there is a sizable gap in the Sedan Reformed records, which interrupts the recorded Brian baptisms.

  iv DANIEL BRIAN, b. ca. 1607, *fils de Pierre Brian et Marie Poupart, demeurant à Sedan*, bur. Sedan, 23 Aug. 1657, aged 50 years;[1122] m. Sedan, 19 Oct. 1631, RACHEL BRUNEAU, *fille de Claude Bruneau et feue Anne Pierre*.[1123] After bearing five recorded children (1632-40), Rachel died. Thereupon Daniel m. (2) Francheval, 8 March 1644, MARIE DE MAROLLES, *V[eu]ve de Jacques Gernes*.[1124] They had at least three children.

 2 v JACQUES BRIAN, b. say 1609. His baptism has not been found; and his marriage entry does not give his parentage. At the baptism of Jacques's eldest son Daniel on 19 Sept. 1638 (see #2 i), however, Daniel Brian, *serrurier*, and Rachel Bruneau *sa femme* served as sponsors. By then, Jacques's mother had died and his father had remarried. Under these circumstances, sponsorship of little Daniel at baptism by the elder Daniel Brian, for whom the infant was named, seems persuasive of the relationship.

1114 *Bibliothèque Wallonne* [FHL fiche #199,780].

1115 *Bibliothèque Wallonne* [FHL fiche #199,912].

1116 *Bibliothèque Wallonne* [FHL fiche #199,912].

1117 *Bibliothèque Wallonne* [FHL fiche #199,780].

1118 *Bibliothèque Wallonne* [FHL fiche #199,780].

1119 *Bibliothèque Wallonne* [FHL fiche #199,780].

1120 *Bibliothèque Wallonne* [FHL fiche #199,780].

1121 *Bibliothèque Wallonne* [FHL fiche #199,780].

1122 *Bibliothèque Wallonne* [FHL fiche #199,780].

1123 *Bibliothèque Wallonne* [FHL fiche #199,780].

1124 *Bibliothèque Wallonne* [FHL fiche #199,780].

6. JEAN GERARD was probably born about 1580-90, but thus far it has not proved possible to establish his parentage. He was deceased prior to the 1637 marriage of his daughter Susanne to Jacques Brian. Unfortunately there were too many contemporary Jean Gerards at and near Sedan of his approximate age. The following Jean Gerards, any of whom could have been this man, were marrying at Sedan:

I   JEAN GERARD, *tailleur, demeurant à Sedan*, m. Sedan, 20 Oct. 1602,
        CATHERINE BESCHAT, *fille de feu Simon Beschat, receveur* [collector] *de
        Douchery*.[1125] Jean Gerard, *âgé de 51 ans, natif d'Ombray, serger* [serge-
        weaver] *à Sedan*, was bur. Sedan, 20 March 1629.[1126]
        Among their children:
        i   MARIE GERARD, bp. 9 Nov. 1603, daughter of Jean Gerard, *serger*,
                and Catherine Beschet; sponsors: Daniel Goffin and Marie Marchant.[1127]
        ii   PIERRE GERARD, bp. 29 Sept. 1605, son of Jean Gerard and Catherine
                Beschet; sponsors: Pierre Grolet and Rachel Gaffin.[1128]
        iii   SUSANNE GERARD, bp. 20 July 1608, daughter of Jean Gerard, *serger*,
                and Catherine Bischet; sponsors: Henry Gerard and Susanne Perin.[1129]
        Jean Gerard m. 12 Jan. 1597, RACHEL GROLET [GROULE].[1130] It seems
        probable, in view of their occupational description (see baptism immediately
        following), that the above two Jean Gerards were one and the same man, twice
        married.
        Only child recorded:
        i   JEAN GERARD, bp. 22 Oct. 1600, son of Jean Gerard, *serger*, and Rachel
                Groule; sponsors: François Millet and Marie Lalmand.[1131]

II   JEAN GERARD, m. ALIX SIMON.
        Children:
        i   PIERRE GERARD, bp. 28 Feb. 1588, son of Jean Gerard and Alix Simon;
                sponsors: Guillaume Briant and Jeanne Vaule.[1132]
        ii   THOMAS GERARD, bp. 18 July 1593, son of Jean Gerard and Alix
                Simon; sponsor: Thomas Millet.[1133]

III   JEAN GERARD, *soldat, demeurant à Givonne*, m. 28 June 1598, MARIE
        VUALTRANGE, *V[eu]ve de Jacob de Libanchamp*.
        Children:
        i   JEAN GERARD, bp. 4 March 1599, son of Jean Gerard, *soldat à Givonne*,
                and Marie Valtrange; sponsors: Jean Thevenin and Jeanne Henry.[1134]

1125   *Bibliothèque Wallonne* [FHL fiche #199,834].
1126   *Bibliothèque Wallonne* [FHL fiche #199,834].
1127   *Bibliothèque Wallonne* [FHL fiche #199,834].
1128   *Bibliothèque Wallonne* [FHL fiche #199,834].
1129   *Bibliothèque Wallonne* [FHL fiche #199,834].
1130   *Bibliothèque Wallonne* [FHL fiche #199,834].
1131   *Bibliothèque Wallonne* [FHL fiche #199,834].
1132   *Bibliothèque Wallonne* [FHL fiche #199,834].
1133   *Bibliothèque Wallonne* [FHL fiche #199,834].
1134   *Bibliothèque Wallonne* [FHL fiche #199,834].

ii   PIERRE GERARD, bp. 4 March 1599, son of Jean Gerard, *soldat à Givonne*, and Marie Valtrange; sponsors: Pierre Berchet and Charlotte Neaume.[1135]

iii   MARGUERITE GERARD, bp. 4 March 1601, daughter of Jean Gerard, *charbonnier* [coal merchant] *à Givonne*, and Marie Vualtrange; sponsors: Gille Jasper and Marguerite Sergent[1136]

iv   JEANNE GERARD, bp. 1 April 1603, daughter of Jean Gerard, *charbonnier à Givonne*, and Marie Vualtrange; sponsors: Jean Gerard and Poncette ___ .[1137]

v   PIERRE GERARD, bp. 6 Nov. 1605, son of Jean Gerard and Marie Woltrange; sponsors: Pierre Ponsart and Suzanne Herbelot.[1138]

IV   JEAN GERARD, *d[emeuran]t à Givonne*, and MARIE BOCQUET.
Child:

i   MARIE GERARD, bp. 3 Jan. 1585, daughter of Jean Gerard, *d[emeuran]t à Givonne*, and Marie Bocquet; sponsors: Guiot Fabre and Julienne Hosquin.[1139]

V   JEAN GERARD, *demeurant à Givonne*, m. 28 Sept. 1597, PONCETTE PARIZOT, *d[emeuran]t à Illy*.
Children:

i   JEANNE GERARD, bp. 3 Oct. 1599, daughter of Jean Gerard, *m[archan]d à Illy*, and Poncette; sponsors: Jean l'Hommedieu and Jeanne de Romerville.[1140]

ii   MARIE GERARD, bp. 14 March 1604, daughter of Jean Gerard, *palonier* [wagon driver?] *à Illy*, and Poncette Parisot; sponsors: Gilbert Trouchet and Marie Cambray.[1141]

VI   JEAN GERARD, *fils de René Gerard, laboureur, à Baricourt*, m. 4 Jan. 1605, ELIZABETH COLLAS, *fille defeu Jean, d[emeuran]t à Jametz*.[1142]
Child:

i   ANNE GERARD, bp. 6 April 1608, daughter of Jean Gerard, *laboreur à Jametz*, and Elizabeth Collas; sponsors: Elie Saublet and Marie Saublet.[1143]

All that can be stated at this point is that Jean Gerard (who conceivably could be one of the above Jean Gerards remarrying as a widower) married Jeanne d'Orléans and had at least one daughter, Susanne, born about 1611-12, who married in 1637, Jacques Brian, and was buried at

1135   *Bibliothèque Wallonne* [FHL fiche #199,834].
1136   *Bibliothèque Wallonne* [FHL fiche #199,834].
1137   *Bibliothèque Wallonne* [FHL fiche #199,834].
1138   *Bibliothèque Wallonne* [FHL fiche #199,834].
1139   *Bibliothèque Wallonne* [FHL fiche #199,834].
1140   *Bibliothèque Wallonne* [FHL fiche #199,834].
1141   *Bibliothèque Wallonne* [FHL fiche #199,834].
1142   *Bibliothèque Wallonne* [FHL fiche #199,834].
1143   *Bibliothèque Wallonne* [FHL fiche #199,834].

Sedan on 10 April 1659, aged 47. Unfortunately, she was born within the period when the Reformed records of Sedan are not extant.

14. JACQUES D'ORLÉANS was born say 1570, son of Jean d'Orléans. Described as *chirurgien* [surgeon] *à soldat, demeurant à Sedan*, Jacques was married at Sedan on 17 March 1591 to ELIZABETH PERIN.[1144] He died about 1595-96. His widow, Elizabeth Perin, *V[eu]ve de Jacques d'Orléans, d[emeuran]t à Sedan*, remarried at Sedan on 18 January 1604, Gerard Bouchet, *fils de feu Antoine Bouchet, soldat, demeurant à Valenciennes*.[1145] Elizabeth Perrin, *âgée de 70 ans, V[eu]ve de Gerard Bouchet, soldat à Sedan*, was buried at Sedan on 23 March 1637.[1146]

    Children of Jacques d'Orléans and Elizabeth (Perin/Perrin):[1147]
i JANNE [i.e., JEANNE] D'ORLÉANS, bp. 26 Dec. 1591, daughter of Jacques d'Orléans, *chirurgien* [surgeon], sponsors: Jean d'Orléans and Janne Sonnet.
ii SUZANNE D'ORLÉANS, bp. 1 Aug. 1593, daughter of Jacques d'Orléans and Elizabeth Perrin, sponsors: Jacques Malicquer and Suzanne Perrin; m. (1) DENIS BONVIVER, m. (2) Givonne, 2 Feb. 1631, PIERRE BAUDA, *m[archan]d hostelier, demeurant à Sedan*. Susanne d'Orléans, *V[eu]ve in derniers noces de Denis Bonviver*.[1148]
iii JACQUES D'ORLÉANS, bp. 23 June 1596, son of *feu Jacques d'Orléans, chirurgien*, and Elizabet Perin; sponsors: Guillaume Conart and Mariele Helier.

Jacques d'Orléans *le jeune* married MARIE SAUVAGE, for whom the following children may be deduced, despite the significant hiatus in the Reformed baptismal records for Sedan:[1149]

i JACQUES D'ORLÉANS, b. ca. 1620, bur. 22 Oct. 1622, *âgé de 2 ans, fils de Jacques d'Orléans, arquebusier* [gunmaker], *et Marie Sauvage*.
ii JEAN D'ORLÉANS, b. ca. Aug. 1621, bur. 4 Nov. 1622, *âgé de 15 mois, fils de Jacques d'Orléans, arquebusier, et Marie Sauvage*.
iii SUZANNE D'ORLÉANS, b. ca. Nov. 1623, bur. 8 Dec. 1624, *âgée de 13 mois, fille de Jacques d'Orléans, arquebusier, et Marie Sauvage*.
iv JEANNE D'ORLÉANS, b. ca. 1626, bur. 23 May 1628, *âgée de 2 ans, fille de Jacques d'Orléans, arquebusier, et Marie Sauvage*.
v OBED D'ORLÉANS, b. ca. Sept. 1628, bur. 11 Nov. 1628, *âgé de 6 sem[ains]* [weeks], *fils de Jacques d'Orléans, arquebusier, et Marie Sauvage*.
vi MARIE D'ORLÉANS, b. ca. July 1630, bur. 10 Nov. 1630, *âgée de 4 mois, fille de Jacques d'Orléans, arquebusier, et Marie Sauvage*.
vii SUSANNE D'ORLÉANS (again), bp. 14 Sept. 1631, daughter of Jacques d'Orléans and Marie Sauvage, sponsors: Jacques de Larbre and Suzanne Gerard [the godmother here was probably the infant's much older 1st cousin, Suzanne Gerard, ultimately wife of Jacques Brian].
viii CHARLES D'ORLÉANS, bp. 4 Sept. 1633, son of Jacques d'Orléans, *arquebusier*, and Marie Sauvage; sponsors: Charles Dufray, *brasseur* [brewer], and Marie Morener, *sa f[em]m[e]*.

1144   *Bibliothèque Wallonne* [FHL fiche #199,901].
1145   *Bibliothèque Wallonne* [FHL fiche #199,776].
1146   *Bibliothèque Wallonne* [FHL fiche #199,905].
1147   *Bibliothèque Wallonne* [FHL fiche #199,901].
1148   *Bibliothèque Wallonne* [FHL fiche #199,901].
1149   *Bibliothèque Wallonne* [FHL fiche #199,901].

28. JEAN D'ORLÉANS. A record exists for the baptism of only one of his children, the record of which indicates that by 1589 he had married ANTOINETTE DE HOLE:[1150]

> JUDIT D'ORLÉANS, bp. 3 Jan. 1580, daughter of Jean d'Orléans, *manouvrier* [unskilled worker?] *à Fleigneux*, and Antoinette de Hole; sponsors: Jean Laurent and Jeanne Besset.

Marriages of three of his daughters name him as father:

> ESTER D'ORLÉANS, *fille de Jean*, m. Sedan, 5 May 1591, COLLIGNION DE THELIN, *soldat, demeurant à Sedan.*[1151]
>
> MARIE D'ORLÉANS, *fille de Jean, d[emeuran]t au dit lieu* [of the same place], m. Oct. 1600, ADOUIN DE STONNE, *fils de feu Robert, d[emeuran]t à St. Menges.*[1152]
>
> JUDITH D'ORLÉANS, *fille de feu Jean*, m. St. Menges, Sedan, 29 May 1605, THEVENIN ROBINET, *fils de feu Jean, d[emeuran]t à Villers.*[1153]

The marriages of persons, believed to have been other children of Jean, omit a statement about his being their father:

> JACQUES D'ORLÉANS, chirurgien à soldat, demeurant à Sedan, m. Sedan, 17 March 1591, ELIZABETH PERIN.[1154]
>
> ANNE D'ORLÉANS, m. Sedan, 28 Feb. 1593, ELOI VIGREUX, demeurant à St. Menges.

By studying the baptisms of the children of these couples, it is possible to construct a listing of the family of Jean d'Orléans:

> i   JACQUES D'ORLÉANS, b. say 1570, d. ca. 1595-96; m. 1591, ELIZABETH PERIN. See #14.
>
> ii   ANNE D'ORLÉANS, b. say 1572; m. as above, 1593, ELOI [ELIE, HELIE, HELYE, ELY] VIGREUX. Children:[1155]
> 1 *Matieu Vigreux*, bp. 5 June 1594, son of Helie Vigreux and Anne d'Orléans, *d[emeuran]t à St. Menges*; sponsors: Marie Beraut and Anne d'Orléans.
> 2 *Helye Vigreuz*, bp. 28 Sept. 1597, son of Helye Vigreux, *passementier* [trimmer], and Anne d'Orléans; sponsors: Guillaume Connart and Elisabet Perin.
> 3 *Judith Vigreux*, bp. 16 April 1600, daughter of Helie Vigreux, *passementier*, and Anne d'Orléans; sponsors: Jean Savari and Judith de

---

1150   *Bibliothèque Wallonne* [FHL fiche #199,901].
1151   *Bibliothèque Wallonne* [FHL fiche #199,938].
1152   *Bibliothèque Wallonne* [FHL fiche #199,935].
1153   *Bibliothèque Wallonne* [FHL fiche #199,920].
1154   *Bibliothèque Wallonne* [FHL fiche #199,901].
1155   *Bibliothèque Wallonne* [FHL fiche #199,946].

Lion.

    4 *Mathieu Vigreux*, bp. 9 April 1602, son of Hely Vigreux, *passementier*, and Anne d'Orléans; sponsors: [Ardouin] de Stonne and Marie d'Orléans.

    5 *Elizabeth Vigreux*, bp. 9 Sept. 1604, daughter of Elie Vigreux, *passementier*, and Anne d'Orléans; sponsors: Gerard Boucher and Elizabeth Perin.

    6 *Rachel Vigreux*, bp. 17 June 1607, daughter of Ely Vigreux, *passementier*, and Anne d'Orléans; sponsors: Thevenin Robinet and Judith d'Orléans.

    NOTES: Observe that Elizabeth Perin twice served as godmother, the first time as the recent widow of Jacques d'Orléans (though the record does not advert to that fact) and the second time, as the newly remarried wife of Gerard Boucher, joined by him as godfather [here called *Jeanne*]. Observe also the similar roles of ---- de Stonne and his wife Marie d'Orléans, and of Thevenin Robinet and his wife Judith d'Orléans. While the parentage statements in favor of Jean d'Orléans apply to both Marie and to Judith, they were not found in the case of Jacques d'Orléans and Anne d'Orléans. The presence of all three as sponsors of children of Anne (Judith, Marie and the widow of Jacques) argues for their close relationship.

    The mother of the above family, Anne d'Orléans, *âgée de 50 ans, femme d'Elie Vigreux, passementier*, was bur. 2 Nov. 1622.[1156]

iii   ESTHER D'ORLÉANS, b. ca. 1573-74; m. (1) 1591, COLLIGNION DE THELIN, as above, m. (2) JEAN DE BLAINE. Esther d'Orléans, *âgée de 86 ans, V[eu]ve de Jean de Blaine, marchand à Sedan, enterre à Sedan le 26 juillet 1660.*[1157]

iv   MARIE D'ORLÉANS, b. say 1578, m. 1599, ADOUIN DE STONNE. Children:[1158]

    1 *Hely de Stonne*, bp. 7 Jan. 1603, son of Adenin de Stonne, *d[emeuran]t à St. Menges*, and Marie d'Orléans; sponsors: Hely Vigreux and Anne d'Orléans.

    2 *Mathieu de Stonne*, bp. 5 Dec. 1604, son of Adenin de Stonne, *d[emeuran]t à St. Menges*, and Marie d'Orléans; sponsors: Nicaise Petit and Elizabeth Hannier.

    3 *Abraham de Stonne*, bp. 18 Feb. 1607, son of Adinah de Stonne, *d[emeuran]t à St. Menges*, and Marie d'Orléans; sponsors: Thevenin Robinet and Judith d'Orléans.

v   JUDITH D'ORLÉANS, bp. 3 Jan. 1580, m. (1) 29 May 1605, THEVENIN ROBINET. He was bur. 9 June 1632, *âgé de 48 ans, natif de Sedan, march[an]d crépin* [apparently: shopkeeper of leathers and/or textiles].[1159] Thereupon, *[m]ariés à Sedan le 16 janvier 1633*, JÉRÉMIE BAUJOT, *m[archan]d demeurant à Sedan; Judit d'Orléans, V[eu]ve de Tevenin Robinet.*[1160] Six years later, *[e]nterré à Sedan le 21 dec[emb]re 1639 Judith d'Orléans, âgée de 57 ans, femme de*

1156   *Bibliothèque Wallonne* [FHL fiche #199,901].

1157   *Bibliothèque Wallonne* [FHL fiche #199,901].

1158   *Bibliothèque Wallonne* [FHL fiche #199,935].

1159   *Bibliothèque Wallonne* [FHL fiche #199,920].

1160   *Bibliothèque Wallonne* [FHL fiche #199,764].

Jeremie Baujot, m[archan]d à Sedan.[1161] In the succeeding year, her widower, Jérémie Bauiot, *m[archan]d demeurant à Sedan, m[ariés] à Sedan 30 décembre 1640, Barbe Antoine, V[eu]ve de Jean Guillardit, d[emeuran]t à Sedan.*[1162] Children of Thevenin Robinet and Judith d'Orléans:[1163]

1   *Anne Robinet*, bp. 14 March 1606, daughter of Thevenin Robinet and Judith d'Orléans; sponsors: Hely Vigreux and Anne d'Orléans.

2   *Abraham Robinet*, bp. 20 May 1607, son of Thevenin Robinet, *passementier*, and Judith d'Orléans; sponsors: Jean Chaudrelin and Judit Nepveu.

3   *Isaac Robinet*, bp. 30 Dec. 1608, son of Thevenin Robinet and Judith d'Orléans; sponsors: Gerard Boucher and Jeanne d'Orléans.

The major gap in Sedan Reformed baptismal records that occurs hereafter prevents a further listing of Robinet baptisms. However, there was buried at Sedan, 23 May 1632, Elisabeth Robinet, *âgée de 15 ans, fille de Thevenin Robine march[an]d et Judith d'Orléans.*[1164]

Cameron Allen (90 Tarryton Court West, Columbus, OH 43228) is retired law librarian at Rutgers University School of Law, Newark, N.J.

1161   *Bibliothèque Wallonne* [FHL fiche #199,901].

1162   *Bibliothèque Wallonne* [FHL fiche #199,764].

1163   *Bibliothèque Wallonne* [FHL fiche #199,920].

1164   *Bibliothèque Wallonne* [FHL fiche #199,920].

INDEX